The Battle for Birth Control

The Battle for Birth Control

Exploring the Lasting Consequences of the Movement's Early Rhetoric

Jessica L. Furgerson

LEXINGTON BOOKS
Lanham • Boulder • New York • London

Published by Lexington Books
An imprint of The Rowman & Littlefield Publishing Group, Inc.
4501 Forbes Boulevard, Suite 200, Lanham, Maryland 20706
www.rowman.com

86–90 Paul Street, London EC2A 4NE

British Library Cataloguing in Publication Information Available

Library of Congress Cataloging-in-Publication Data

Names: Furgerson, Jessica, 1988- author.
Title: The battle for birth control : exploring the lasting consequences of the movement's early rhetoric / by Jessica L. Furgerson.
Description: Lanham : Lexington Books, [2022] | Includes bibliographical references and index.
Identifiers: LCCN 2022003948 (print) | LCCN 2022003949 (ebook) | ISBN 9781793643247 (cloth) | ISBN 9781793643261 (paperback) | ISBN 9781793643254 (ebook)
Subjects: LCSH: Pro-choice movement--United States. | Birth control--United States. | Reproductive rights--United States. | Birth control--Law and legislation--United States.
Classification: LCC HQ766.5.U5 F87 2022 (print) | LCC HQ766.5.U5 (ebook) | DDC 363.9/60973--dc23/eng/20220202
LC record available at https://lccn.loc.gov/2022003948
LC ebook record available at https://lccn.loc.gov/2022003949

To all those who have championed my cause.

Contents

Acknowledgments

As this project has consumed the better part of a decade, I have amassed a great personal and professional debt of gratitude for which the words in this acknowledgment can surely never reconcile. To those who have invested their time and energy into me, and by extension this project, I am forever grateful.

I came to this area of research in a Historiographic Methods class during my graduate education at Ohio University. What began as a simple term paper, quickly became my dissertation topic, and is now the subject of my first book. This trajectory would not have been possible without the support of my amazing mentors and advisers—chief among them Dr. Raymie McKerrow and Dr. Judith Lee. As a first-year graduate student I was beyond lucky to have Dr. McKerrow assigned as my adviser. While most people in the field of communication know him as an influential rhetorical scholar, I know him as a kind mentor and fierce advocate for his students. The existence of this book is a testament to his willingness to advocate on behalf of his students for it was on his insistence that I was given license to abandon many of the traditional confines of the dissertation and write what was essentially the first draft of this book. Dr. Lee was the professor in that fated Historiographic Methods class and the passion with which she talked about her own experiences in the archives was infectious—inspiring me to pursue historical research. As a member of my dissertation committee, Dr. Lee made me a better writer and scholar. I think of her fondly every time I consult the *Chicago Manual of Style* and I am grateful to have been on the receiving end of her fastidious editorial eye. Many thanks also to Dr. Katherine Jellison whose Women in American History courses taught me the power of listening to women and telling their stories. Finally, thank you to Dr. jw Smith whose friendship and mentoring sustained me through some of the most challenging times in my life both then and now. I am also immensely thankful for the comradery of my fellow graduate students at Ohio University, in particular Jenn Seifert, Justin Rudnick, Anna Wiederhold Wolfe, Rebecca Mercado Jones, and Tennley Vik who made the doctoral experience bearable and continue to inspire me to be a better scholar and teacher even as our paths diverged.

While many people abandon their dissertations and move on to new projects, I was determined to bring this one to fruition. I am thankful that it took the better part of ten years because in that time I have grown immensely as a scholar and writer. This book bears little resemblance to the original dissertation and I have several people to thank for that. First and foremost, I owe a unique debt of gratitude to Victoria Ledford who serendipitously became my most trusted confidant when writing this book. From the initial proposal to the final draft Victoria served as a sounding board, a cheerleader, and an editor; she helped me work through my ideas and thoughtfully reviewed my work providing candid feedback which immensely improved the final product. She gave freely of her time and mental energy even when they were in short supply but, perhaps most importantly, she unflinchingly believed in me and the value of this project. Working through my thoughts on long walks was an integral part of my process, and Candice Rios-Wenmoth and Scotti Branton were often on the receiving end of my ramblings. They helped me process, encouraged me through bouts of writer's block, posed interesting questions, and simply listened. Thank you for your friendship and for letting me dominate the conversation. My deepest appreciation also extends to Jeremy Frazer and Benjamin Pyle whose careful readings and insightful comments on previous iterations of this work challenged me to be a better writer and more attentive scholar.

The well-worn adage "it takes a village" aptly describes how I feel about my journey to publish this book—there likely isn't a person in my life over the last ten years that hasn't heard me talk about this project. Having moved over 1,000 miles away from home at eighteen, I have been profoundly shaped by the many villages who welcomed me with open arms. To my Western Kentucky University (WKU) family, thank you for teaching me how to be a functioning adult, fostering my passion for rhetoric, and surrounding me with profound examples of how to be an advocate. To my fellow Bobcats, thank you for teaching me the power of community and how to find the sweet spot between work and play. Athens will always be one of my favorite places on Earth because of the memories we created there and the lasting bonds it fostered. The Hilltoppers and Bowling Green get a second mention as it was the place I called home from 2013 to 2018 and the people who supported me in finishing my dissertation and starting this book. Without the steadfast support of my colleagues, friends, and students I am not sure I would have made it to the finish line. Although my return to WKU was in many ways a detour from my previously established path, I am immensely grateful for this time in my life; it gave me some of my proudest moments, my closest friends, and the love of my life. To my CrossFit Old School and CrossFit Conjugate crews thank you for giving me an outlet, a place largely free of work talk, and a daily reminder that I can do hard things.

My village is filled with friends who have become family. For their faithful companionship and unwavering support I thank Tony Sylvester, Chris Joffrion, Sherri Marsh, Jennifer Pyle, Angelo Sylvester, Danielle York, Drew Wenmoth, Chad Meadows, Eliza Jackson, Mark Allseits, Lauren Nelson, Jeanie Adams-Smith, Melissa and Jordan Propst, Jeremiah and Andrea Sharpensteen, and Drew Shade. I am most grateful for the women who have become my surrogate sisters. For Meghan Luna who has believed in me for more than two decades and who was unquestionably my first soul mate. For Liz Courtney whose measured advice and uncanny ability to make me laugh has helped me weather many storms. And for Lindsey Isaac whose friendship was perfectly timed and who always seems to know exactly what I need even when I don't. These three women will never truly understand the impact they have had on my life.

I am not convinced my wonderful husband, Damon, really knew what he was signing up for when I told him I was writing a book. Thank you for your patience and understanding as I shifted priorities to complete this project. You graciously retreated to the attic when I needed to focus, brought me snacks when I needed sustenance, and listened dutifully when I needed to vent. In our first two years of marriage, you sacrificed what should have been quality time together in service of my dream and instead of complaints or frustration you optimistically told me to get back to work on our "retirement plan." Thank you—for everything my love.

To my family, the first people to believe in me and support my ambitions even when they took us away from each other, there is no way to sufficiently express my gratitude. My grandmothers, Lou Furgerson and Sandra Simpson, have always been a shining example of the kind of hardworking woman I strive to be. I felt a special kinship with them while researching the reproductive experiences of women throughout twentieth-century America and am thankful for the many conversations we had about their own experiences. My grandfathers, Charles Edward, Sam Furgerson, and Buddy Simpson always encouraged me to ruthlessly pursue my own goals. In moments of self-doubt, I often looked at their pictures and reminded myself, as I know they would have, to give it hell. To my sister Nikki, thank you for always being my biggest fan. I really wish you could be here to read this book, but I know how proud you would have been to display it on your shelves. I miss you and I always will. My parents, Tom and Carla Furgerson, deserve a whole other book detailing the countless ways they have supported, encouraged, and empowered me to be the person I am today. Never once have they doubted my ability to achieve what I set my mind to, and never once have they judged me when things didn't go according to plan. The regular conversations with my mom about this project were instrumental. She didn't talk to me like an academic colleague would but instead like a woman who's made her own complicated choices, and my work is better for having that perspective. My dad's excitement when I told him the book was getting published is one of my favorite things I have ever heard. He never stopped asking when he could get his pre-order in and that enthusiasm and pride truly sustained me. I decided to keep the last name Furgerson in marriage not just because it was the efficient choice or the feminist choice but because I am proud to be your daughter and to bear that name.

Finally, I must acknowledge the women represented in these pages. The women who lost their lives desperately trying to give their children a better lot in life. The women denied a say in their own reproductive destiny—both those forced into motherhood and those robbed of the chance. The women who suffered in the development of modern contraception and those who continue to suffer because we as women uniquely bear the biological burden of childbearing. To the brave pioneers of the movement thank you for your fervent defense, albeit imperfect, of voluntary motherhood and reproductive autonomy. And lastly, to those who are *still* fighting for reproductive justice may we have the audacity to keep going.

Introduction

Today we are engaged in a great struggle for woman's liberty, for the freedom of her own body, for the release from the domination of church and state. Birth control is the first step toward the goal of [woman's] freedom. She can never gain political, social, or spiritual freedom so long as her body remains the slave of ignorance.

—Margaret Sanger, 1916

Best of all in 1964, planned parenthood is no longer a "cause." It is a human right, and now recognized as such. Women no longer think about it, they take it for granted as they do the vote, and their right to work at jobs, and to wear slacks instead of skirts.

—Margaret Sanger, 1944

We don't need another political fight about ending a woman's right to choose or getting rid of Planned Parenthood or taking away affordable birth control. We're not turning back the clock. We're not going backwards.

—Barack Obama, 2012

Margaret Sanger sadly never lived to see the day when birth control and planned parenthood were no longer a cause, as that day has yet to come. It has been over 100 years since Sanger formally began the battle for birth control, but it was the unexpected controversy over the Affordable Care Act's Contraceptive Mandate in 2012 that sparked this project. Like many women in my generation, I was shocked to discover most insurance companies didn't routinely provide contraceptive coverage and that a requirement to do so was such a contentious issue. Shock turned to disbelief when I uncovered nearly identical headlines from 1914 and 2012 heralding the urgency of birth control—how had we been debating this for over a century? Though much has changed in the time span between these two headlines, for starters contraception is now legal and widely available, much in the way of how we discuss birth control as evidenced in the quotations above has remained the same.

As I grappled with the absurdity of the fact that women have been fighting for basic contraceptive access for over a century, things only got worse as the fervor surrounding the contraceptive mandate reignited efforts to restrict women's reproductive rights resulting in what the Center for Reproductive Rights called a "decade-long coordinated campaign to eliminate access to abortion and shutter clinics across the country."[1] While much of the attention and outrage has focused on the staggering number of state laws passed restricting abortion access—more than 500 since 2011 and 83 in the year 2021 alone—contraceptive access remains increasingly vulnerable.[2] Renee Bracey Sherman, executive director of the abortion advocacy group We Testify, issues a dire reminder in July 2021:

> The moment abortion advocates have always warned about is here. It's always been here. Politicians who are anti-abortion are also anti–birth control and anti-queer and anti-Black because at the end of the day, they only support a way of life in which they—wealthy white people—are in charge and they are the sole dictators of when, how, and with whom we have sex, procreate, and build our families. It's about maintaining white patriarchal power and control. It always has been. And anything that allows people to determine their own futures—such as birth control and abortion—is a threat to that.[3]

Even more important than Sherman's urgent warning is her intentional reminder of the context in which the fight for reproductive rights exists in relation to the white patriarchy. As will be explored extensively in this project, discussions of reproductive autonomy cannot be divorced from issues of race, class, and gender as the normative assumptions surrounding each of these categories uniquely inform both the historical and contemporary demand for contraception.

I cannot, nor do I wish to, deny my vested interest in this particular topic. As a woman with obligations and aspirations other than motherhood, my life quite literally depends on the ability to freely make decisions regarding my reproduction and consistent access to contraception. These were privileges I took for granted at the start of this project because as a middle-class white woman, they had become expectations of my lived experience. Today, I am equal parts grateful, frustrated, and fearful. Grateful for the fact that I am privileged to have unfettered contraceptive access and the full support of family, friends, and society to make whatever decisions regarding my reproduction I see fit. Frustrated that women without my level of privilege rarely have these options. And fearful for future generations who may soon find themselves rehashing the battles detailed in this book, because despite a century of struggle, birth control remains a privilege rather than a basic human right.

As the adage goes, "Every system is perfectly designed to get the results it gets."[4] The tumultuous reproductive rights landscape we currently navigate is not incidental but is rather the lasting consequence of a system designed with the experiences of white, heterosexual, able-bodied women at its center, and early birth control advocates were its most prolific architects. Primarily under the direction of Margaret Sanger, advocates and allies navigated a political climate often hostile to the aims of the movement; in fact, when Sanger coined the term "birth control" in 1914, it was actually illegal to even use the phrase in writing or public discussion. Undeterred, Sanger worked tirelessly to give women control over their reproductive lives and was willing to do whatever it took to advance the movement's agenda even if that meant eschewing the movement's radical vision for social change. Ellen Chesler, Sanger's primary biographer, explained to the *New York Times* in 1992 that Sanger "pursued a strategy of political accommodating to make [birth control] widely available" because she "had to deal with a society that was often conservative and always deeply divided about women's rights and reproductive freedom."[5] Sanger's tenacity is admirable but, given the current state of affairs, it is incumbent upon us to look upon her actions incredulously to determine the unforeseeable consequences of the strategic decisions made by the movement with Sanger at the helm.

Sanger's accommodationist strategy produced a discourse steeped in maternalism, whiteness, and heteronormativity. By and large, the early birth control movement was created by and for white women. Two white women, Margaret Sanger and Mary Ware Dennett, were its main protagonists. Given the consonant movements for woman's suffrage and later child welfare, white female reformers and white male authority figures represented their most potent audience. Even as the movement diversified its political outreach, it remained heavily whitewashed and, perhaps more importantly, beholden to the conservative norms and values propagated by white elites and dominated by respectability politics. While the external audience for the movement was almost exclusively white, its ideal recipient was often not or at least not treated as such. Poor immigrants, often treated as racial pariahs, initially inspired Sanger to take up the cause in 1914, and later, Black communities became a site of concerted effort for advocates for many of the same reasons. The twin forces of class prejudice and abject poverty belied the movement's interest in these groups and created much of the framework still utilized today to discuss responsible parentage and contraceptive access.

Potential allies were courted through a strategic emphasis on the mechanistic benefits of birth control. Advocates pitched contraception as a solution to a vast array of social, political, and economic problems including abortion, child labor, marital discord, rising public expenditures. They vied for the support of policy makers, doctors, eugenicists, and reformers by showing them how contraceptive access could solve the problems these respective groups wrestled with. While sold on the mechanistic benefits of birth control, namely improved health outcomes and greater social stability, allies remained wary of the potential cultural transformations accompanying the ideological uptake of contraception. Afterall, each of these groups had a vested interest in maintaining the status quo requiring birth controllers dutifully reassure allies that they weren't actually seeking a revolution. The result was a focus on securing negative rights over positive rights assuring women merely the ability to make their own reproductive choices without considering the conditions influencing how those choices are made or if they are even genuinely possible. These efforts essentially gave women permission to make reproductive decisions without supporting their ability to so in any meaningful way—a move that would shroud the once radical demands of the movement in a devious veil of liberal ideology. *The Battle for Birth Control* dissects the rhetorical tactics utilized by the movement to execute its accommodationist strategy and traces the reverberations of these tactics in contemporary American discourses surrounding contraception specifically and reproductive politics more generally.

The workings of the birth control movement in America are well worn territory benefiting from a wealth of excellent historical, sociological, political, and even economic scholarship. In writing this book, I benefited greatly from this wealth of research which equipped me with a road map for navigating the complex history of reproductive politics in the United States. Among the many works cited throughout this project, Linda Gordon's *The Moral Property of Women* stands out as a guiding influence—my copy of the book is bursting with sticky notes, and I return to it often. Gordon's immaculate treatment of the subject foregrounds the search for meaning and the importance of language in creating that meaning; she writes, "in different historical periods there are specific hegemonic and resistant meanings and purposes to reproductive control" which are "socially and politically, not individually constituted" reflecting the deeply "(unstable) balances of political power between different social groups."[6] But as a communication scholar, I wanted more from the historical account provided by Gordon and others; I needed to know precisely how these meanings were discursively produced. Gordon masterfully dissected the complex decisions made by movement leaders, but I wanted to be in the room with those leaders to know how they reached these decisions and, perhaps more importantly, how they convinced reticent bystanders to cosign on these decisions. Historian Trent MacNamara describes the birth control movement in the United States as a "radically *social* social movement," but it was precisely this social element that seemed to be missing from existing accounts of the movement's trajectory.[7]

Communication scholar Celeste Condit succinctly describes my frustration explaining, "Histories usually focus on the people and events that 'cause' social changes, relegating public discourse to a supporting role in the story."[8] Much like Condit, I am not concerned with the stagnant interpretation of texts or events; rather it is the role of rhetoric in shifting the meaning of birth control over time that interests me. It is the description of "the interplay of relations within and outside" our cultural understanding of birth control that interests me.[9] For instance, prior to immersing myself in the Margaret Sanger Papers, which constitute the largest single repository of documents relating to the early birth control movement, I read ad nauseum about the monumental choice to change the name of the Birth Control Federation of America to the Planned Parenthood Federation of America in 1942. Historical accounts identified this moment as a crucial turning point but did little more than pontificate about the movement's decision to strip the phrase birth control from the name of its only national organization. So, when I found the actual meeting minutes from October 1938 where this decision was hotly debated among top organizers in the movement, I was floored. I was finally in the room with the leaders of the movement, and their internal dialogue was illuminating. Sanger explained, "A great many of us have the limitation of the birth control clinic. You can sell the idea in small ways. But more is needed. Many are familiar with the great prospects ahead of us—more prestige in utilizing those larger forces than any of us would."[10] In removing "birth control" from their name, organizers were hoping to perform a rhetorical sleight of hand capable of distancing the movement from its history of agitation and controversial reputation. This choice, like so many others, reflects the centrality of rhetoric to managing public perceptions and propelling the movement forward. Communication researchers Charles Stewart, Craig Smith, and Robert Denton argue of social movements that "persuasion is the primary agency through which social movements attempt to perform critical functions that enable them to come into existence, satisfy requirements, grow in size and influence, meet opposition from within and without, and effectively bring about or resist change."[11] For as much as we know about the historical trajectory of the birth control movement, far less is known regarding the nuanced rhetorical strategies and persuasive efforts which facilitated this trajectory. This book seeks to fill this gap.

This book is informed by a strong adherence to the reproductive justice framework developed by Black activists and women of color in the 1990s merging the conceptual underpinnings of reproductive health, reproductive rights, human rights, and social justice to facilitate an intersectional analysis of reproductive politics. In 1994, activist Loretta Ross coauthored a statement alongside members of a group known as the Women of African Descent for Reproductive Justice outlining the fundamental premise of this intersectional framework. Ross accompanied by Rickie Solinger, a scholar activist who has devoted her academic career to exploring reproductive politics, succinctly define reproductive justice in their 2017 primer explaining, "Reproductive justice is not difficult to define or remember. It has three primary values: (1) the right *not* to have a child; (2) the right to *have* a child; (3) the right to *parent* children in safe and healthy environments. In addition, reproductive justice demands sexual autonomy and gender freedom for every human being. The problem is not defining reproductive justice but achieving it."[12] My commitment to reproductive justice informs this project by attenuating me to the ways in which the discourses of early birth controllers failed to advocate for and create conditions conducive to the enactment of reproductive justice.

Previous frameworks for addressing reproductive issues broached the subject from relatively singular perspectives, reproductive health or reproductive rights, and in doing so reduced the complexity of reproductive politics to fit neatly within the liberal ideologies of personal choice and social order. Reproductive justice was and continues to be a direct response to these ideologies and the way they obscure the lived experiences of women struggling to manage their reproductive lives in a world not suited for them to do so. Reflecting on the initial demands made by reproductive justice advocates, Ross argues: "We challenged how liberal ideology misused the concepts of rights and justice to situate responsibility for health and wellness in individual choices, while ignoring the institutionalized barriers that constrict individual choices such as racism, homophobia, sexism, classism, ableism, or xenophobia, or more simply, lack of access to appropriate healthcare."[13] Early birth control advocates actively ignored these institutional barriers in part because acknowledging them undercut their strategy of essentialism and in part because as predominantly white middle-class women, these barriers rarely featured into their own lived experiences. This project unearths these transgressions and historicizes their role in creating the contemporary landscape of reproductive politics.

Such an investigation stands in stark contrast to the prevailing mode of thought surrounding reproductive politics in the United States. Communication scholars Tasha Dubriwny and Kate Siegfried argue that despite the vocal critique of liberalism advanced by reproductive justice advocates, "the liberal logic of 'constrained choice,' a mode of supervised reproductive consumerism in which the government regulates reproduction through control of information and services, has widespread public currency."[14] As the first major movement for reproductive health and autonomy in the United States, the strategic decisions of early birth control advocates continue to animate the reproductive rights landscape of contemporary America. The perpetual treatment of the Hyde Amendment and Title X funding as potent political footballs indicates the ease at which programs supporting women's reproductive autonomy are used as both a talking point and a bargaining chip with zero regard to the women whose lives are impacted by this constant jostling of their basic freedoms and the services that facilitate their fulfillment. Contemporary battles such as this are rooted in the neoliberal state that privileges personal responsibility over state accountability and clears the way for reproductive control in the language of choice. Beyond complicit, early birth controllers were the original purveyors of this neoliberal framing of reproductive rights. *The Battle for Birth Control* traces the duplicity of the movement's early rhetoric and argues that their accommodationist strategy only yielded increased contraceptive access because of their willingness to endorse the neoliberal regime of reproductive control largely responsible for the current threats to reproductive autonomy in the twenty-first century.

Ross and Solinger note the importance of historicizing reproductive politics from within the reproductive justice framework:

> We understand that the past explains a great deal about the present and also shapes the future. When politicians, judges, and policy makers make decisions that affect our lives . . . they are building on the past. . . . Reproductive justice presents a real and present engagement with the world of reproductive politics that produces new forms of knowledge and different understandings of history.[15]

This project returns to the first major reproductive rights movement in the United States, the birth control movement, as a site of inquiry into the rhetoric that produced the very norms and assumptions undergirding the systems of knowing, being, and doing which are rightfully challenged by reproductive justice scholars and activists today.

At its core, *The Battle for Birth Control* seeks to answer the question of how we got here. Here being a time where access to reproductive options such as abortion and birth control are under constant threat. Here being a framework of reproductive health that rarely centers the actual needs of women. Here being a framework of reproductive rights that offers choices to women shrouded in caveats. Here being a time where reproductive justice exists as the only tenable way forward. Subsequently, this book also functions as a cautionary tale to contemporary advocates against the use of accommodationist strategies to advance the movement and concludes with a plea to fully adopt the framework of reproductive justice in the fight to finally and fully secure reproductive autonomy, health, and rights for all women.

The complexity and tension of engaging historical discourses from a reproductive justice framework is not lost on me. While working on this project,

Planned Parenthood of Greater New York decided to remove Margaret Sanger's name from its Manhattan clinic given her "harmful connections to the eugenics movement."[16] And there I was scouring over her handwritten notes—intimately aware of both the nuance of Sanger's relationship with eugenicists and the devastating consequences of that relationship on the lived experiences of countless women. My skin crawled as I read words like feeble-minded and dysgenic used with such a cavalier disregard for the people given those labels. These words, among others, have been rightfully relegated to the ash heaps of history, but their rhetorical legacy lingers infiltrating contemporary discourses in a litany of ways. Historicizing their importance is neither an act of apologia nor an attempt to justify their use; rather, it is a moment of reckoning necessary to make sense of their insidiousness in the modern landscape of reproductive politics. Ross makes the charge to white allies like myself abundantly clear: "For white allies (and people of color, too) to successfully engage RJT with integrity, they must question neoliberal discourses about individual rights and the marketplace of choices denied to the vulnerable members of our society."[17] The sentiment evoked by Merle McGee when announcing the removal of Sanger's name is fitting for this project as well: "We're not going to obliterate her. If we obliterate her, we cannot reckon with her."[18] *The Battle for Birth Control* is most certainly a reckoning—not just for Sanger but for the movement as a whole.

The achievements of the birth control movement in the United States have been truly life changing for the generations of women who have come of age with the option to engage in intimacy without the fear of pregnancy, with the ability to plan for their futures as people not just parents, and with a plethora of choices afforded to them by the right to make autonomous decisions about their reproduction. However, these same women still face very real struggles with equitable access to contraceptive services, stigma surrounding their reproductive choices, and a lack of true agency to make the best decisions for themselves. So, while we should be grateful for the work our foremothers did to bring us to this moment, we must not ignore the shortfalls of their advocacy that created fertile ground for the problems we now face. This project is simultaneously a thank you note to the advocates who fought tirelessly to secure the reproductive rights of women and an admonishment for their shortsightedness—I believe both are necessary to traverse the current political climate threatening to undo their hard work and, more importantly, to correct their grave missteps.

NOTES

1. Center for Reproductive Rights, "Protect, Defend," para. 1.

2. Nash and Cross, "2021 is," para. 3–5.
3. Jong-Fast, "The Anti-Birth Control," para. 6.
4. "Quotes," para. 1. Although this quotation is often attributed to W. Edwards Deming its true origin remains contested. The W. Edwards Deming Institute explains: "An early source exploring the origin suggested 1 of 2 people Dr. Deming worked with, Dr. Paul Batalden or Donald Berwick originated the quote. Given that the newer article from IHI lists Paul Batalden as a co-author and he remembers slightly altering Arthur Jones' quote it seems likely Arter was the original source."
5. Kelves, "Sex Without Fear," BR1.
6. Gordon, *The Moral Property*, xi.
7. MacNamara, *Birth Control*, 20–21.
8. Condit, *Decoding Abortion*, 1.
9. Foucault, *Archaeology of Knowledge*, 29.
10. Margaret Sanger Papers, 222762.
11. Stewart et al., *Persuasion*, 84.
12. Ross and Solinger, *Reproductive Justice*, 65.
13. Ross, in Ross et al., *Radical Reproductive*, 19.
14. Dubriwny and Siegfried, "Justifying Abortion," 3.
15. Ibid., 5.
16. Stewart, "Planned Parenthood," para. 4.
17. Ross, "Conceptualizing Reproductive," 223.
18. Stewart, "Planned Parenthood," para. 4.

Chapter One

The Battle for Leadership

The summer of 1912 was one of the hottest on record in New York City when Margaret Sanger, a young nurse, was called to the house of Jake and Sadie Sachs. Having made frequent house calls to the Lower East Side neighborhood where the Sachses lived, Sanger expected nothing out of the ordinary. This visit, however, and her subsequent return in October 1912 left an indelible mark on this once meek nurse. Since their marriage seven years prior, Jake and Sadie had lived a far from comfortable life; with three small children in the house, Sadie's days were consumed with chores and childcare and Jake's meager wages as an unskilled laborer left the family with just enough to cover the necessities.

The financial strain of taking his wife to the hospital prompted Jake to call Sanger after finding Sadie huddled on the floor, surrounded by his crying children, when he returned home from work on a sweltering day in July of 1912. Sadie, desperate to avoid having another child, had ingested various drugs and purgatives hoping to induce a miscarriage. Undeterred by their ineffectiveness, Sadie attempted to abort the pregnancy using an instrument she had procured from a friend. When Sanger and the doctor arrived, Sadie, suffering from blood poisoning, lay helpless. As if by miracle, the doctor and Sanger stabilized Sadie's condition, and Sanger would remain in the Sachs's residence for three weeks, closely shepherding the feeble 28-year-old mother of three back to health.

While neighbors, family members, and friends swarmed the Sachses' residence with words of sympathy and relief, Sadie remained wary. During her final checkup with the doctor, an exasperated Sadie pleaded, "Another baby will finish me, I suppose. But how can I prevent it?" For Sanger the question stung, but not as much as the doctor's response. Chuckling a bit to himself, he replied, "You want to have your cake and eat it too, do you? Well, it can't be done. I'll tell you the only sure thing to do. Tell Jake to sleep on the roof!"[1] *Sanger had nothing more to offer Sadie and she left the Sachs's home wracked with guilt.*

When Jake called again just three months later in October 1912, Sanger knew instantly "it was almost useless to go."[2] *Having become pregnant yet again, this time seeking out the assistance of a "five-dollar professional abortionist,"*[3] *Sadie died within minutes of Sanger's arrival. When Sanger left the Sachses' home this time, it wasn't guilt that overcame her but outrage. Reflecting on the night almost twenty years later, Sanger proclaimed: "I resolved that women should have knowledge of contraception. They have every right to know about their bodies. . . . I would tell the world what was going on in the lives of these poor women. I would be heard."*[4]*And heard she was.*

Broken by her experience with the Sachs family, Sanger knew she could no longer pay witness to such callous treatment of women. She recounts in *My Fight for Birth Control*, "I came to a sudden realization that my work as a nurse and my activities in social services were entirely palliative and consequently futile and useless to relieve the misery I saw about me."[5] Convinced women could and would regulate their reproduction if simply provided the tools to do so, Sanger spent the summer of 1913 traveling to Boston and Washington, DC, speaking with doctors and digging through medical libraries. At every turn, Sanger was rebuked—in equal measure—by those who were ignorant themselves and those unwilling to speak of the subject for fear of impropriety. Sanger explains that she was warned to "keep off that subject or Anthony Comstock would get me. . . . This was the reply from every medical man and woman I approached."[6] This experience would become a familiar one for Sanger and the advocates that later joined the movement and undoubtedly informed their eventual adoption of an accommodationist posture toward entities whose assistance was vital to secure contraceptive access.

The stilted replies of the medical profession illuminated the path forward for Sanger—challenging the restrictions placed on contraceptive information by the Comstock Act of 1873. The rudimentary nature of contraceptive technology in the early twentieth century heightened the need for a public discussion of birth control; however, because of its classification as an obscene topic under Comstock, these conversations existed purely underground. Historian Andrea Tone laments, various entrepreneurs such as Antonette Hon and Charles Goodyear distributed products aimed at preventing conception such as vaginal suppositories and rubber condoms, but obscenity laws "made contraceptives illicit goods to be confiscated not merchandise to be regulated and inspected."[7] Relegated to the pages of subscription based magazines and often deceptively sold under the label of feminine hygiene products, contraceptives remained a luxury available only to those whose wealth and education granted them access to what Tone refers to as the birth control black market. Euphemisms such as "female regulators" and the use of "French" or “Portuguese” as descriptors served as a code of sorts, facilitating covert conversations and black-market advertisements of early abortifacients and contraceptives.[8] Tucked behind paywalls in costly catalogs and newspapers such as *The New York Sun*, this conversation remained largely out of reach for the women, such as Sadie Sachs, who Sanger believed needed it most.[9]

The majority of women hoping to stave off pregnancy relied on advice and home remedies passed from one generation to the next through word of mouth. Yet, primitive knowledge of the reproductive process left even those with access to relatively sophisticated pessary devices only marginally better off than those who douched with Lysol® as their main preventative measure.[10] Despite mounting concern over the safety of these black-market contraceptives and the oft-labeled quacks who promulgated them, the Comstock Act of 1873 silenced public discussion of contraception and left thousands of sexually active couples with a choice between remaining celibate or risking pregnancy. Sanger’s preeminent mission was to pull the discussion of birth control out from the shadows—to make it both acceptable and accessible for *all* women.[11] Certain conjecture alone wouldn’t be enough to effectively challenge the Comstock Laws and “convinced there was no practical medical information available in America,” Sanger traveled to Europe in search of Havelock Ellis whose *Psychology of Sex* was the only meaningful takeaway from her years spent researching.

In 1914, Sanger returned from Europe brimming with new discoveries from Ellis and others whom she met on her trip. Eager to get started, Sanger called together a group of radical friends to discuss her new idea for a magazine and subsequently a movement. The heated discussion of the movement’s would-be name referenced preexisting ideas on the issue of reproduction, such as “Neo-Malthusianism, Family Limitation, and Conscious Generation”; however, Sanger refused to repackage a preexisting term as the moniker for her budding movement leery of being misconstrued as a one-child or two-child system or lumped together with the economically driven ideas of English Malthusians concerned with population growth outpacing available resources.[12] She reflects in *My Fight for Birth Control*: “that was the first time the words [birth control] were used together” to signify “the conscious control of the birth rate by means that prevent the conception of human life.”[13] For Sanger, creating a new phrase to define the movement functioned “to separate the issue of fertility restriction from some of its nineteenth-century political and economic associations.”[14] In doing so, Sanger gave birth to a concept and a movement that would soon garner attention on a national and international level.

CHARTING A COURSE FOR THE MOVEMENT: BIRTH CONTROL AS A FREE SPEECH ISSUE

Entering the political discourse at the height of American radicalism and the push for woman suffrage, Sanger initially sought to add birth control to the agenda of existing reform groups. Despite their similar inclinations toward progressive social policy, these groups refused to give birth control the priority Sanger thought it deserved. She laments, "from everyone I approached I met the same answer: 'Wait!' 'Wait until women get the vote' 'Wait until the Socialists are in power.' Only the boys of the IWW (International Workers of the World) seemed to grasp the economic significance of this great social question."[15] An undeterred Sanger capitalized on these tentative relationships publishing articles in the Socialist organ the *New York Call* concerning issues of sex and reproduction and later utilizing members of the IWW to circulate her educational materials.[16] Despite the Socialist Party's (SP) refusal to formally endorse birth control, Sanger found a sympathetic audience among socialists, such as Emma Goldman, and the labor activists in the IWW who saw the denial of contraception as an oppressive tool of the ruling elites and a threat to the prosperity of the worker.[17] As will come to light in this work, Sanger's search for a sympathetic audience quickly became the modus operandi for the movement resulting in an array of rhetorical strategies aimed at courting allies rather than preserving the integrity of the movement's initial ambitions.

With the support of the IWW and the Free Speech League (FSL), two radical organizations Sanger associated with during a brief stint as a Labor activist, she started *The Woman Rebel* in 1914 with the express purpose of exciting a fight over the classification of contraception as obscene under the Comstock Act. This was not the first time Sanger's work had been threatened by the ever-looming Comstock Act. A 1913 column in *The Call,* entitled "What Every Girl Should Know," faced temporary censorship for its use of the words "syphilis and gonorrhea," but was later published after readers and key officials objected on free speech grounds. Historian Peter Engelman suggests Sanger's early experience with censorship was "fortuitous, [giving] her some instant notoriety among the free speech crowd" and creating a template for her future struggles with Comstock.[18] In its first issue, Sanger vehemently questioned, "Is it not time to defy this law?" and announced, in clear violation of the law, *The Woman Rebel* would "advocate the prevention of conception [and] impart such knowledge in the columns of this paper." Sanger's rhetoric in the inaugural issue of *The Woman Rebel* was clearly an enticement of censorship; however, because the paper contained no substantive articles on contraception, it remained mailable—a calculated move drawing the government's attention but avoiding full suppression after just one issue.[19] As planned, *The Woman Rebel* eventually caught Comstock's eye culminating in five of its seven total issues deemed unmailable by the Postmaster.

In August 1914, shortly after the June release of the first edition of *The Woman Rebel*, Sanger received an indictment for nine counts of violating the Comstock Laws. News of the paper's suppression garnered national attention with both major outlets such as the *New York Times* and local papers like the *Xenia Daily Gazette* of Ohio carrying the story.[20] Fearful coverage of World War I might overshadow her newfound publicity and hoping to refocus her eventual trial on a soon-to-be-released publication on sex and contraception, *Family Limitation*, Sanger fled the country in 1915. Far from a cowardly move, Sanger's exile galvanized supporters and gave them a platform to launch their attack on the Comstock Laws as a violation of free speech. A 1930 report prepared by the John Price Jones Corporation, an influential fund-raising consultant firm, reflected: the "small feminist paper [published] to challenge the freedom of speech with regard to the Federal Postal Law . . . accomplished its purpose of gathering together men and women who would assist in organizing the birth control movement."[21] Pulling from a radical playbook built during her time with the Socialist Party, Sanger catalyzed support for her fledging movement through agitation and antagonism.

While exiled in Europe, Sanger's husband William kept birth control on the public's radar thanks to his own legal battles. Unlike Margaret, who had intentionally violated the obscenity laws to drum up support for their repeal, William was arrested by Anthony Comstock himself for unknowingly providing an undercover agent a copy of *Family Limitation*—making him, according to Peter Engelman, the perfect "free speech martyr."[22] William, advised in part by the FSL, chose to forgo official counsel instead defending himself in court—a masterful move that essentially converted the courtroom into a pulpit. The *New York Times* on September 5, 1915, printed his remarks almost in their entirety. He proclaimed:

> I deny the right of the State to compel the poor and disinherited to rear large families, driving their offspring into child labor when they should be at school and at play. I most certainly deny the right of the State to arm a prudish censorship with the right of search and confiscation to pass judgment on our art and literature. I deny as well, the right to hold laws of this obscenity statute, to heckle, to hinder, and deprive those best fitted by years of training and experience, from aiding those ignorant of the methods of birth control. For nearly half a century the entire nation has been under this self-appointed censorship of our morality, and it has been instrumental in keeping America woefully behind the nations of Europe.[23]

With a captive audience in the courtroom and the press William's testimony advanced several key arguments in support of birth control. First, his testimony pinpointed censorship as the main barrier to effective contraceptive instruction. On the issue of contraception, America fell woefully behind its European counterparts not because of a lack of information, but because censorship prohibited doctors from dispensing contraceptive instruction. Second, by labeling them as prudish and equating their enforcement with mere heckling, William's testimony effectively questioned the very necessity of the Comstock laws. Margaret may have initiated the claim for birth control on free speech grounds, but William's testimony solidified the viability of this rhetorical strategy within public discourse. Shortly after his trial, birth control received a full endorsement from the liberal magazine the *New Republic* and took center stage in a series of articles appearing in *Harper's Weekly*.[24]

Arguments premised on free speech resonated widely. Fola La Follette, an influential labor activist, suffragist, and daughter of prominent politician Robert La Follette, defended Sanger in the *Washington Post* on January 25, 1916. She ardently proclaimed: "The right to freedom of speech and freedom of pen is questioned in the indictment of Mrs. Sanger . . . that is why so many persons are rallying to her support. Whether one agrees with her methods of agitation or not, her cause ought to arouse public opinion and initiate a movement to change our archaic Federal and State legislation to accord with modern ideas."[25] La Follette's statement demonstrates the salience of the movement's early appeals to freedom of speech. Although an outspoken activist like La Follette could be expected to support the cause on such grounds, even those opposed to the movement's aims voiced their support on the basis of free expression. *Outlook*, a more conservative magazine of the times, boldly stated on November 30, 1921, that although they did not sympathize with Sanger and questioned the "wisdom of discussing the subject of birth control . . . in a public hall meeting before a popular audience," attempts to halt such a discussion were "clearly a dangerous [and] illegal violation . . . of the fundamental right of free speech guaranteed by the United States Constitution."[26] Though occasionally successful, the tactics of opponents often backfired—generating more publicity for the movement and forcing papers to side with birth controllers in the name of free expression. Sanger explained in a 1944 speech entitled "Birth Control Then and Now," "the most conservative papers were placed in the trying situation of defending birth control advocates or endorsing a violation of the principle of free speech."[27] Set against a backdrop of government-sponsored censorship in the name of national security during WWI, the movement's appeals to the sanctity of free speech secured them an audience concerned with civil liberties but with no immediate interest in contraception.

FORGING A NEW PATH—FROM AGITATION TO DIRECT ACTION

Sanger returned from Europe in October 1915 to find the birth control movement in good hands—her husband William occupied prime billing in the press for his arrest and subsequent grandstanding, and her contemporary Mary Ware Dennett successfully formed the first organization devoted to the cause known as The National Birth Control League (NBCL). Despite their relative success at agitation and organization, Sanger was convinced fighting for contraceptive information solely on free speech grounds was no longer tenable. Sanger explained in an undated document entitled "My Experiences in Holland," "Holland revolutionized my ideas regarding the future of the movement. No longer could I look upon birth control knowledge as essentially a free speech fight. . . . That was not enough. Personal instruction must depend upon physiological and anatomical knowledge."[28] According to historian James Reed, both Havelock Ellis and C. V. Drysdale encouraged her to disavow the "bourgeois do-gooders" of the Socialist Party in favor of courting social and professional elites requiring a shift in focus from civil liberties to contraceptive instruction. From this point forward, "she would offer feminist or pro-working-class arguments, but she never again saw her identity as mainly within a socialist, or even generally radical, movement."[29] This is not to say Sanger abandoned her resistance to the Comstock Act but rather that her newfound conviction led her to confront the law directly. As she explains, now was the time to fight; not by "wast[ing] our time and energy whining about our constitutional right to free speech," but by "speak[ing] out" and "assert[ing] the truth as we have found it."[30] In their open defiance of the law through very public discussions of birth control, early advocates such as Margaret Sanger, Emma Goldman, and Harold Cox enacted the right to free speech rather than simply requesting it, relying on supporters and the press to justify their actions on free speech grounds while they moved on to actually providing contraceptive information to the masses.

Sanger was not shy about her new ambitions and even used them as a justification for not joining the newly formed NBCL under the leadership of notable social reformer Mary Ware Dennett. Dennett recalls, "She was invited to be a member of the Executive Committee of the league. She declined stating that she did not think it wise to be officially a part of any organization, as she was likely to have to go to jail" as a result of her indictment over the *Woman Rebel.* Sanger explicitly told Dennett "she felt it her particular function to break the laws rather than to spend the effort at that time in trying to change them."[31] As would become typical of their relationship, Dennett extended an olive branch to Sanger only to be rebuffed. Scholars Melissa Doak and

Rachel Brugger identify 1916 as the turning point in the relationship between Sanger and Dennett, suggesting "Sanger's return from Europe in 1916 marked the beginning of the rivalry and animosity between Sanger and Mary Ware Dennett. . . . Dennett, a reformer who had previously been involved in the suffrage movement, believed strongly in fighting for birth control through legal channels, lobbying for repeal of federal and state statutes that defined birth control as 'obscene,' rather than engaging in direct action techniques."[32] Consistent with her confrontational nature, Sanger was unwilling to wait for the state's permission to dispense contraceptive information and embarked on a journey to counsel women directly through the establishment of clinics and the creation of the *Birth Control Review*, a monthly magazine devoted to advancing the movement's agenda.

By 1916, Sanger and Dennett had both published their own informational pamphlets on family planning but by and large focused their efforts on securing access to contraceptive information more broadly rather than advocating any one particular method. Focusing on general instruction rather than specific methods made sense for two reasons. First, whereas contraceptive devices were both cost prohibitive and sex-specific, general information was accessible and usable for all persons. In a report for the Motherhood Department of the American Birth Control League (ABCL), secretary Bertha Potter Smith noted that as of January 12, 1926, the league had received over 28,000 letters in the previous year alone from "all over the world [and] from all walks of life."[33] Given the diversity of contraceptive demands during this period, the provision of medically accurate information emerged as the only universal solution. Second, only through the provision of information could people begin to understand the variety of contraceptive options available to them. Mary Ware Dennett explained in a letter to the editor of the *New York Times* in 1922 that only after receiving contraceptive information can people "for the first time, be legally free to weigh the relative merits of unlimited and undetermined reproduction and self-determined parenthood achieved by the application of scientific knowledge."[34] For early advocates, a discussion of specific contraceptive methods was meaningless in a world where people remained ignorant of the basic principles of reproductive control.

These exigencies demanded the movement confront the Comstock Act directly as it was the nexus for all state and federal laws limiting the dispensation of contraceptive information. Dennett explains the foolhardy process by which contraception found its way into legislation addressing obscenity in the first place; she bemoans:

> Their error in judgement was to include in Section 211 of the Penal Code the two words 'preventing conception.' In their eagerness to abolish the promotion of the misuse of contraceptive knowledge in connection with morbid and

> irregular practices, they rashly framed the law so as to forbid all circulation of any knowledge whatever, thus making it in the eyes of the law just as much a crime for high-minded responsible married people to learn how to space the births in their families wisely, as for the low, vicious or perverted few to spread information about how to abuse knowledge in abnormal, unwholesome ways.[35]

Even though Comstock's death in 1915 facilitated greater public discussion on purportedly obscene topics like contraception, the legal statutes he worked tirelessly to implement kept a tight grip on those wishing to dispense contraceptive information. The movement's first priority was abundantly clear: forge a path for contraception by removing its largest obstacle.

Developing Divergent Strategies

Dennett and Sanger found a common enemy in Comstock but diverged dramatically in their preferred method of undoing the laws that bore his name. Committed to challenging the societal belief that discussions of sex and contraception were salacious, Dennett advocated for an open bill removing the phrase "prevention of conception" from federal obscenity laws. Sanger, however, compelled by the urgent need for widespread distribution of contraceptive information, pursued what she felt was the more expedient option in the form of a limited bill exempting physicians from the purview of obscenity laws without challenging their classification of contraception as obscene. Sanger and Dennett's disagreement over how best to secure legislative change was symptomatic of the ideological differences between the two; Dennett wanted revolution whereas Sanger willingly settled for progress. In parsing out their contrasting approaches, it's apparent that while Sanger's strategy secured critical victories, it simultaneously eroded the ideological underpinnings of the movement Dennett so desperately clung to. The following examination of their conflicting approaches seeks not to suggest what could have been under Dennett's leadership, although it does consider those possibilities, but instead pursues a more nuanced understanding of the decisions made during the movement's infancy and their lasting impact on the reproductive rights landscape in the United States.

Understanding Sanger's Strategy

Influenced by her trip to Europe, Sanger carefully clarified her intent only to promulgate information provided by members of the medical profession. Just as Ellis and Drysdale convinced Sanger to abandon her more radical allies, they also encouraged her to focus solely on scientific information as an overture to the medical profession whose endorsement was essential to legitimizing the movement. Writing in the *Birth Control Review* in October 1919, Sanger castigated the Comstock Act for keeping medically accurate information about contraception away from women suggesting, "the only practical effect—the real tragedy of the present law—is that it deprives us of the knowledge and skill of the only persons who are capable of instructing the masses."[36] Additionally, in 1921 Sanger explicitly demanded "scientific information be disseminated directly to the mothers through clinics by members of the medical profession, registered nurses and registered midwives."[37] More than a mere caveat, the use of the words scientific and medical functioned as rhetorical hedges to mitigate criticism. Communication scholars Vanessa Murphree and Karla Gower contend, "rational appeals put forward by respected doctors, economists, and sociologists gave the issue greater credibility and wider acceptance."[38] Repeated appeals to scientific information mobilized the opinion of trusted individuals in support of birth control without whom the movement had little chance of being taken seriously.

Other advocates quickly followed Sanger's lead by including rhetorical appeals to authority via the phrase "scientific information" in their own rebuke of the Comstock Laws. The 1921 response of Juliet Barrett Rublee, Vice Chairman of the First American Birth Control Conference, to Archbishop Hayes's labeling of contraceptive information as obscene is demonstrative; she remarked, "I agree with the Archbishop that it is right to prevent obscene and indecent literature from going through the mail, but I maintain that scientific information which will safeguard the health of women and children is neither obscene nor indecent."[39] Rublee's strategic use of "scientific information" creates a clear distinction between the obscene literature the Archbishop wished to curtail and the legitimate information desired by the birth control movement. Rublee's statement also demonstrates the prevailing rhetorical strategy adopted by Sanger and like-minded advocates who, unlike Dennett, willingly conceded the general question of regulating obscenity in order to secure support for scientifically based contraceptive instruction.

In addition to minimizing criticism, Sanger's focus on medical and scientific knowledge created a much-needed distinction between legitimate knowledge of contraception and folk science colloquially labeled as quack medicine. Popularized in the late 1800s by vendors such as Madame Restell, pills, potions, and purgatives claiming to prevent conception gave contraception a bad name among the medical community and repeatedly drew the attention of censors.[40] The rhetoric of Chicago Health Commissioner Herman N. Bundesen illustrates the conflation of birth control clinics and quack medicine the movement desperately needed to counteract. In his denial of the Illinois Birth Control League's permit request to open a clinic, Bundesen scoffed: "The establishment of one such clinic would open the way for an army of quacks."[41] Given the tendency of Bundesen and others to equate the birth control movement with quackery, advocates direly needed to distinguish themselves from quack medicine. To that end, speaking before the Connecticut legislature in 1923 endorsing a bill to overturn the state's version of the Comstock Act, H. F. Fletcher bluntly declared "the league did not represent patent medicine makers or 'quack doctors.'"[42] Fletcher's denouncement of quack doctors brought legitimacy to the movement by contrasting its educational goals with the primarily consumerist aims of the black market. *Current Opinion*'s 1915 assessment of the Comstock Laws was apt: "silence the scientist but do not shut the mouth of the ignorant midwife. The reputable physician does not like to risk imprisonment; the consicenceless quack will take a chance."[43] In juxtaposing reputable physicians with unconscientious quacks, an important distinction arose legitimating the cause as well intentioned, scientifically based, and medically superior to the unreliable and illegitimate means of preventing pregnancy peddled by opportunistic quacks.

Sanger's emphasis on scientific and medical knowledge also functioned as a much-needed overture toward the medical community—an emerging ally in the fight for birth control whom Sanger was desperate to court. Linda Gordon explains, most physicians in the early 1920s opposed contraception for a variety of reasons including a disdain for the movement's "affiliations with anarchism and quackery."[44] The successful juxtaposition of legitimate knowledge with quack medicine helped assure physicians they were a welcomed and vital part of the birth control agenda. The success of this rhetorical strategy is demonstrated by doctors who relied on this very same rhetorical tactic in their public defense of contraception. Gynecologist and obstetrician Dr. Joseph L. Baer explicitly compared science and quackery in 1922 when he pleaded, "The only difference in the majority of the cases is that the wealthy women use highly scientific methods, while the indigent women are forced to submit to the quack doctor."[45] In 1925, the *Chicago Daily Tribune* applauded the birth control movement for distancing themselves from the lurid contraception black market and proclaimed, "birth control now rates with respectables."[46]

Chicago physician Dr. Rachelle Yarros espoused the necessity of doctors to provide contraceptive information as a result of quack medicine's popularity; Yaross, who was tapped in 1923 to serve as the supervising physician for the Chicago Planned Parenthood Clinic, argued, because "a large number of remedies prescribed by quacks fail . . . the responsibility is the physician's. He should not let the quacks do what he should do conscientiously."[47] The early rhetoric of the birth control movement often antagonized the medical community—Sanger had after all blamed them for withholding information; yet, articulating birth control as a scientific issue distinct from quack medicine was crucial to legitimizing the movement among physicians who would eventually defend their right to provide contraceptive instruction utilizing these very same rhetorical tactics. Dr. Alice Hamilton of Harvard University even told the *Chicago Daily Tribune* in 1925 that "the fight for the scientific dissemination of the scientific facts of birth control is working its way slowly to a successful conclusion."[48]

Interestingly, the popularity of this strategy fueled the schism between Dennett and Sanger as concerns over the circulation of unscientific information also permeated Sanger's attack on Dennett's open bill which Sanger claimed would proliferate the spread of bad information. In a 1919 article in the *Birth Control Review* entitled "How Shall We Change the Law," Sanger bluntly states, "Personally, I object to the so-called 'unlimited bill'" because "If everyone is permitted to impart information, those who receive it have no guaranty that it is correct or suitable to the individual's physical requirements. Incorrect, unscientific information may bring good results in some cases, but it is more likely to cause a vast amount of disappointment and anxiety in others."[49] According to Doak and Brugger, Sanger castigated the Open Bill put forth by Dennett's Voluntary Parenthood League (VPL) for its potential to "'flood the mails' with unscientific and unreliable birth control information" as a means of establishing the superiority of doctors-only bills making physicians the sole distributors of contraceptive information.[50] Even in a document devoted to providing the details of her own Amendment, Sanger spends considerable time thrashing the open bill and makes a sensational comparison between non-medical instruction and the birth control black market. She portends, "the League is unalterably opposed to any change in the federal statutes that would lead to its commercial exploitation. The result of opening the mails to vendors of so-called preventatives of conception . . . [would be] a distinct set-back to the cause of Birth Control."[51]

Although aware of such a possibility, Dennett faithfully defended the marketplace of ideas, remaining steadfast in her conviction that scientific knowledge would crowd out quack medicine. Dennett rebuffed: "The implication seems to be that the repeal of the Federal ban would release *only* unreliable information, whereas it would likewise release all the best and most authoritative information. All knowledge has to compete with ignorance, and no laws can prevent the struggle. What knowledge needs is an open field in which to make its effort to overcome ignorance."[52] Dennett highlighted the preponderance of misinformation already available in the status quo that would only continue to flourish without legitimate contraceptive information as a direct competitor. Illuminating the failure of the Comstock Laws to prevent lurid advertisements, such as the Madame Restell's remedies, Dennett bolstered the value of reliable contraceptive information suggesting, "so long will that unwholesome atmosphere be reflected in vulgar advertisements, which cannot be properly antidoted by dignified decent advertisements of the proper sources for contraceptive information and means."[53] Scientific information was inherently more accurate and reliable than cultural lore or quack medicine giving little reason to believe women would continue to choose ignorance when presented with reliable sources of information.

Even more irksome to Dennett was the fact that Sanger herself once promulgated the very "misinformation" she now rebuked. In both her own pamphlet, *Family Limitation,* as well as the *Birth Control Review*, Sanger sought to bring clear contraceptive instruction to the masses despite lacking the professional qualifications she fought for in her limited bill. Clearly frustrated by Sanger's hypocrisy, Dennett scolded:

> And further, one of these contraceptives was recommended by name in Mrs. Sanger's pamphlet on family limitation, in which she described various methods. Since 1914 ten editions of this pamphlet have been sold or distributed. . . . The *Birth Control Review* reported the publication of it in England also, and protested most vigorously because it has been suppressed under the British obscenity law. In all this widespread circulation of contraceptive advertisement and instruction, there was not even the endorsement of any physician quoted, say nothing of "personal prescription." If the theory that there should be no information allowed except via a doctor's prescription for the individual, has been so little adhered to by the very people who advance it, is it not futile to try at the eleventh hour to embody that theory in legislation?[54]

The willingness of birth controllers, like Sanger, to openly defy their own standards demonstrated just how arbitrary the requirement for physician involvement was in the dispensation of reliable information. Sanger never directly answered Dennett's accusations of hypocrisy; but did subtly hedge back against her claims by including nurses in several of her articles discussing the limited approach. In a 1919 article in the *Birth Control Review,* Sanger explicitly empowers nurses to provide contraceptive instruction and applauds a measure proposed by the Legislative Bureau of Columbia University permitting both physicians and registered nurses to provide advice, instruction, and/or articles necessary for the prevention of conception. She concludes, "These are my personal opinions, based upon my experience as a nurse." Sanger invokes her credentials as a nurse to deflect Dennett's valid criticism and substantiate her own legislative efforts as stemming from a place of professional expertise.

Dennett's Ideological Defense of Contraception

Prior to her involvement with the birth control movement, Mary Ware Dennett boasted an impressive resume of activism as both a suffragette and an anti-war organizer. These experiences greatly influenced her preference for peaceful resistance and working within existing legal structures to seek change. Consistent with her advocacy for voting rights, Dennett believed contraceptive access at its core was a question of equality proclaiming: "men and women might provide special kinds of service to the family and to the state, but neither must play a superior role." Contraception was thus a prerequisite to the "self-determined, wisely undertaken parenthood" that makes equality possible.[55] Dennett saw the Comstock laws as an impediment to equality and self-determined reproduction not only because they prohibited family planning but, more importantly, because they silenced conversations at the cornerstone of equality. She asserts, "The function of law is to protect people's rights. As no one's mere feelings are an intrusion upon another's rights, it is no concern of the law to deal with them. The laws as they stand now are a gratuitous insult to the great mass of the people who do not consider the control of conception indecent. Do you want that legal insult maintained?"[56] Sheer access to contraceptive information proved insufficient for Dennett, as merely granting access did nothing to normalize conversations about sex and reproduction which are indeed the linchpin to self-determination. Comstock Laws were an affront to autonomy, and Dennett accordingly demanded their repeal.

Capitalizing on the arrest and subsequent exile of Margaret Sanger in 1914, Dennett formally entered the birth control movement in 1915 with the formation of the NBCL. Dennett was upfront about the new organization's focus on legislative efforts and although she, like Sanger, specified this information should be "scientifically sound," she concentrated the league's efforts on repealing obscenity laws rather than exempting medical professionals. Reflecting her concerted effort to alter the cultural conversation surrounding sex and reproduction, the declaration of principles adopted by the NBCL boldly proclaims: "This league specifically declares that to classify purely scientific information regarding human contraception as obscene, as our present laws do, is itself an act affording a most disgraceful example of intolerable indecency."[57] Almost immediately, the NBCL under Dennett's leadership set to work advocating for repeal of both state and federal obscenity laws through the circulation of literature, form letters to congressional representatives, and draft amendments composed for the league by a committee of lawyers. Interestingly, while Sanger returned from Europe convinced of the need for clinics, Dennett took the government's unwillingness to further prosecute Sanger as a sign that Comstock had lost its grip, suggesting, "A fair interpretation of this act would seem to be that the government itself did not deem the Comstock Laws in this regard, as worth enforcing."[58] Dennett feverishly proceeded with her plan to seek a full repeal of the Comstock Laws.

Dennett began her legislative work in the winter of 1917 but quickly discovered the movement's controversial start had left many legislators jaded and reluctant to clear a path for contraceptive instruction. Dennett's proposal was simple: amend Section 1142 of New York Penal Code by removing the phrase "for the prevention of conception" from the paragraph detailing what constituted an Indecent Article under the law. Her efforts proved unsuccessful, but the process was deeply instructive. In many ways, the experience confirmed Dennett's distaste for the sensationalist tactics that had thrust the movement into the national spotlight. Whilst lobbying for the amendment, legislators regularly voiced their reticence toward the issue altogether, given its association with radicalism—an association spearheaded by Sanger. Dennett recalls legislators expressed fear "that they would be made conspicuous in the newspapers if they got 'mixed up' with any of this 'birth control talk.' They had a horror of the possibility of flaming headlines that would somehow drag them into 'sensationalism.'"[59] Dennett grew increasingly frustrated with these legislators, many of whom willingly endorsed the bill in private conversations but refused to let the measure even leave committee. Sanger's subsequent arrest following the Brownsville Clinic raid only made matters worse for Dennett's crew in Albany. Dennett laments, "Some of them had no other knowledge of the birth control movement than that a woman named Sanger had 'made a rumpus' and gotten jailed."[60] Sanger eventually abandoned her controversial tactics in favor of pragmatic appeals to professional allies, but the damage to the movement's reputation was already done.

Dennett's efforts in Albany weren't a complete loss, however, as they did illuminate a promising path for change. After hearing the NBCL's proposed amendment, one member of the New York Legislature inquired, "Why do you come up here asking to consider a bill of this sort when our National laws set us the example they do on this subject?"[61] Dennett opted to tackle the New York Penal Code first largely as a matter of convenience as she was a longtime New York resident; coincidently Anthony Comstock was too, so the Penal Code was actually the first law of its kind on the books. This moment gave her pause and prompted her to reflect on whether a state-based approach was truly preferable to the pursuit of a federal repeal. She recalls, "It was undeniably true that the action of Congress in passing the Comstock bill in 1873 had influenced practically all of the States to follow suit."[62] Convinced a federal bill presented a more promising path to reform, Dennett created the VPL in 1919 with federal repeal as its primary objective.

THE RIVALRY REACHES A BOILING POINT

As the two ramped up their legislative efforts, tensions reached a boiling point between Dennett and Sanger—the irascible tone of their personal correspondence in 1921 is illustrative. In a letter addressed to the Editor of the

Birth Control Review but mailed directly to Sanger, Dennett bemoaned an article appearing in the March issue for giving "a misleading impression of the aims of those who are working for [the federal bill]" and including "an inaccurate statement of the effect of the repeal on State laws."[63] In addition to extolling the benefits of removing the phrase "preventing conception" from federal obscenity laws, Dennett took full advantage of the situation to assert her rightful place in the movement noting, "The Voluntary Parenthood League is the only national birth control organization in the country, and it has been working steadily and practically for nearly two years on the Federal Campaign."[64] Dennett remained transfixed on her legislative efforts and demanded Sanger respect, or at the very least accurately represent, her contributions to the cause.

Whether or not a federal bill would nullify existing state laws proved to be the biggest sticking point between Dennett and Sanger. Dennett was convinced that this was the case, noting in her initial letter that "in thirty states, by the passage of the Federal measure, the legal status of contraceptive knowledge will automatically be changed."[65] In her reply, Sanger summarily dismisses the claim and vows to acknowledge its veracity only if given proof; she quips, "If you, however, have legal opinion which bears out your statement, I will be delighted to publish such statement over the signature of such legal authority any time it is presented to me."[66] Dennett retorts with an identical claim in her response to Sanger on March 31, 1921: "If you will name any well-known lawyer or lawyers who will make a written claim that the passage of our federal bill will not automatically correct the legal status of contraceptives information in the thirty states which now have no special prohibition of the giving of knowledge, I will agree to furnish you with a list of lawyers whose opinion back our claims."[67] Unsurprisingly, neither party ever produced a list for the other (or at least not that we have record of) and the two continued to pursue their legislative agendas with little to no support from one another. Dennett was perhaps more frustrated with Sanger's harsh gatekeeping of her ideas than she was with Sanger's refusal to endorse the federal repeal. She laments in her last letter from this heated exchange: "If, as you say, it is the aim of the Review to impress upon your readers 'the larger aspects of Birth Control as an immediate world problem,' an authoritative presentation of the federal bill affecting the whole country, should have a place in the magazine quite as much as a limited bill for only one state."[68] Despite having once served on the editorial board for the *Birth Control Review*, Dennett never saw her legislative agenda printed in the paper. Instead, Dennett opted to publish her own book on the matter in 1926 entitled *Birth Control Laws: Shall We Keep Them, Change Them, or Abolish Them?*.

Like Sanger, Dennett believed in the value of scientific information to prevent conception and even went as far as to include it in her own definition of birth control, explaining it "consists of the use of intelligence and scientific hygienic knowledge to determine the wise time for conception to occur and to limit the possibility of conception to those occasions."[69] Yet, unlike Sanger, Dennett resisted the notion that medical professionals should be the sole purveyors of this information. Firmly situated within her ideological commitments to equality and equity, Dennett feared doctors-only bills would create a medical monopoly transforming contraceptive information into an economic privilege accessible only to doctors and those wealthy enough to procure private care.

Dennett detailed her vexation at the proposed doctors-only bill, boldly declaring such a measure would "create a complete medical monopoly of the dispensing of the information; would give doctors an economic privilege denied to anyone else; would treat this one phase of science as no other is treated, that is, make it inaccessible to the public, except as doled out via a doctor's prescription, as if the need for the knowledge were a disease."[70] Situating doctors as gatekeepers also transformed contraceptive access into an economic privilege. While a full repeal of the Comstock laws would enable the free flow of information, Sanger's limited bill "leaves the whole subject of knowledge about the control of conception, still in the category of crime and indecency. The doctor merely becomes a privileged character within this category."[71] For wealthy, predominantly white women with access to a private physician, doctors-only bills were an ideal solution; but then again, these women never truly bore the burden of Comstock's censorship. Famed British birth controller Marie Stopes, with whom Sanger and Dennett frequently jockeyed for favor, laments: "Meanwhile the rich and well-to-do all treat the law as a dead letter, but it is still effective in its operation against the poor and ignorant and against those who try to help them."[72] Clinics promised to rectify this economic disparity, but so long as contraception remained classified as obscene, advocates faced significant hurdles in legally opening and running clinics capable of distributing contraceptive information on a wider scale. Dennett left the suffragist movement with a disdain toward activism aimed primarily at the wealthy, and in her mind, doctors-only bills were just another iteration of that elitist ethos. Sanger castigated Dennett for suggesting that "information should be freely given by anyone to anyone"[73] and repeatedly presented free information and scientific instruction as oppositional. This juxtaposition was admittedly persuasive to physicians who sought to distance themselves from quacks and folk medicine; it also reified the very questions of access permeating Dennett's desire for an open bill.

Considering their reluctance to endorse contraception on its own merits, Dennett questioned the motivations of physicians suddenly voicing their support for Sanger's bill. A skeptical Dennett portends, "But the final beneficiary of this traffic would be the physician. The whole commerce would have no other lawful outlet than via the doctor's prescription."[74] Acutely aware of the medical profession's desire to bolster their respectability and Sanger's reassurances that a doctors-only bill would do just that, Dennett observed that "it is not exceptional to find only physicians who lean toward favoring a 'doctors-only' bill as a recognition of medical prestige, but this impulse is not at all synonymous with a mercenary desire."[75] Dennett's suspicions were confirmed when the VPL invited a group of physicians in support of doctors-only bills to speak at a league meeting. One unnamed physician explained, "he is really a firm believer in the ideal of clearing this subject from connection with obscenity, but because 'it *sounds* so safe' to say, 'keep it in the hands of the doctors,'" he would rather endorse Sanger's limited bill.[76] Sanger worked tirelessly to recruit doctors to support the birth control cause, but Dennett remained incredulous about their motives and was unwilling to support a bill positioning them as the primary gatekeepers of contraceptive information.

Dennett also struggled to understand how contraceptive information was any different from other widely available scientific or medical information. In her estimation, "Contraceptive methods are a part of hygiene, and the public should have access to knowledge about them just as to any other phases of hygiene" just as they have access to "instructions as to certain methods of brushing the teeth [and] to certain diets to produce certain effects."[77] On this point, Dennett enjoyed the support of numerous physicians that endorsed a federal repeal enabling the free flow of information. Speaking in support of the federal repeal at a congressional hearing in Washington, DC, Dr. Jerome Cook of St. Louis proclaimed, "No distinction should be made between this and other forms of medical knowledge, and no restriction should be placed upon the spread of knowledge."[78] Given the rudimentary nature of contraception at this time, the primary emphasis was on providing women with basic information concerning conception and recommending barrier methods such as condoms or diaphragms—neither of which truly necessitated the involvement of medical professionals.

Sanger's framing of contraceptive use as simple and easy proved equally contradictory to her push for a doctors-only bill further enraging Dennett. In an appearance before the New York Legislature Sanger boasted: "the Clinical Research Department of the American Birth Control League teaches methods so simple that once learned any mother who is intelligent enough to keep a nursing bottle clean can use them."[79] If the methods are indeed as simple as Sanger characterizes them to be, then why are doctors the only capable instructors? Dennett laments, "There is no need to make a medical mystery of this knowledge, or to assume that the public will be lost in hopeless ignorance unless a doctor prescribes specially for each individual.

The simplicity of some of the best methods makes such an attitude an absurdity."[80] Dennett felt immediate frustration at the suggestion only physicians could provide accurate contraceptive information. Frustration grew to outrage when the very proponents of doctors-only bills framed their efforts in such a way that doctors were relatively unnecessary. The hypocrisy of this stance solidified Dennett's view of doctors-only bills as ushering in a medical monopoly surrounding contraception. Speaking in support of Dennett's initiative, Dr. George Blumer contends, "I do not feel as a matter of principle that the regulation of birth control should be entirely in the hands of physicians. . . . [T]here are many cases where the problem is not a medical one at all."[81] Dennett's concern illuminates the long-term consequences of ceding control over contraceptive instruction to doctors explored fully in chapter 5.

SANGER'S STRATEGY PREVAILS

The disagreeable relationship between Sanger and Dennett passed its breaking point in the fall of 1921 when Dennett learned of her exclusion from the first American Birth Control Conference and Sanger's budding efforts to create a new national organization. A series of letters exchanged between the two during July and October 1921 are telling of the tumult both women felt toward the other. Dennett pleads on July 29, "There seems to be every reason for hoping that the time is ripe now, for a careful survey of the field and a great joining of forces instead of further splitting them by forming still another organization."[82] Dennett also voiced her dismay in a letter sent to the Board of Directors for the *Birth Control Review* writing, "none of these announcements has been sent to the League, nor has the League been asked to participate in the conference."[83] Although Sanger does issue a meek invitation for the VPL to attend the conference on September 23, her incredulous tone on October 10 reveals her true thoughts on the matter; she writes, "you say that the Voluntary Parenthood League 'has a record for achievement in educational work which is unprecedented in the Birth Control Movement,' it would be helpful if you would give an outline of your accomplishment."[84] The Conference commenced on November 11, 1921, and served as the perfect opportunity to announce the creation of the American Birth Control League (ABCL).

Dennett was justifiably furious. She had devoted years to the birth control movement, formed its first national organization, and performed the back-breaking work on legislative reform only to be summarily dismissed by Sanger. In a document entitled "A Special Message to the Council, Contributors and Friends of the Voluntary Parenthood League" dated November 18, 1921, Dennett lambasts the conference for failing to even read aloud the report submitted by the VPL and reiterates the fundamental differences between the VPL and the ABCL primarily concerning their divergent legislative efforts. In a section labeled "other straws," Dennett tersely writes: "Repeatedly, I heard her speak of organization and legislation as 'bourgeois,' 'pink tea,' 'lady-like' efforts etc., and of 'direct action' (i.e. getting the people informed regardless of the law) as the only work worthwhile. The only exception to this policy, until recently, was in 1919, when she approved a proposed 'doctors-only' bill in the New York State."[85] The two women would proceed as adversaries—working on their separate initiatives even after the VPL merged with the ABCL in 1925.

In 1928, Sanger resigned as president of the ABCL to form the National Committee on Federal Legislation of Birth Control (NCFLBC), and in 1929, Dennett received a moment of vindication when asked to speak at the Fourth Annual American Birth Control Conference. Aware of her audience and Sanger's surging efforts to pass limited bills across the country, Dennett reiterated her position with perhaps even deeper ideological commitments than ever before. She declared:

> I believe that the time has come to forward the clean repeal with quite a new emphasis, namely that birth control should be taken out of the law altogether; not only out of obscenity laws as such, but of any kind of law . . . and thus help to place it where it belongs; in the field of science so far as technique is concerned, in the field of education so far as access to knowledge is concerned, and in the field of private individual judgment so far as application of knowledge is concerned.[86]

Armed with a renewed conviction on the need for what she now called a "clean repeal," Dennett reached out to Sanger with a sense of humility that was no doubt a strategic ploy to finally win her favor. She writes in a personal letter on February 15, 1930: "You are now the one leader in the movement. . . . I am out of campaigning for good . . . [but] I hope you will decide to stand for the clean repeal. . . . I shall take great work in supporting your work in every way possible, if you will now give me the chance to do so."[87] Sanger acknowledged the "cordial" nature of the letter but doesn't quite extend the same genial tone to Dennett, instead asking for reassurance that Dennett is indeed ceding control of the movement; Sanger prods, "You had the field quite alone and you were a convincing and capable leader. . . . I think it only fair to ask that we who believe in the other kind of legislation have the field to ourselves without interference."[88] Ironically, it is only in asking her to leave does Sanger finally recognize Dennett's contributions to the movement.

Resigning to the reality of her schism with Sanger, Dennett shifted focus to her personal legal battle over the publication of *The Sex Side of Life*—a battle she fought since its initial censure in 1922. Backed fully by the American Civil Liberties Union, Dennett appeared before the U.S. Court of Appeals in January 1930 and diligently listened as presiding Judge Augustus Hand overturned her now eight-year-old conviction. Hand argued, "The old theory that information about sex matters should be left to chance has greatly changed. . . . [W]e hold that an accurate exposition of the relevant facts of the sex side of life in decent language and in manifestly serious and disinterested spirit cannot ordinarily be regarded as obscene."[89] Filled with vindication and a renewed optimism for a full repeal of the Comstock Act, Dennett pleaded with Sanger one last time in a personal letter on February 28, 1931. Dennett implored her to remember "a day back in 1915 when you lunched with me at my apartment, and the shine in your eyes when you talked of your determination not to rest till the people had the knowledge and the help they needed and birth control was rescued from indecency."[90] Sanger touted her own legal victory in 1918 as validation for her legislative approach, yet she refused to grant Dennett's triumph the same significance. This was the last straw for Dennett. The long-time birth controller soon cut ties with the movement and turned her attention to issues of global peace and stability, eventually serving as the chair of the World Federalists.

THE LASTING CONSEQUENCE: ACCOMMODATION OVER EMANCIPATION

What seemed to most as a mere power struggle, played out in dramatic fashion via petty exchanges in private, was actually an ideological dispute the resolution of which would forever alter the course of the birth control movement in the United States. Historian Peter Engleman suggests, "Dennett and Sanger's differing approaches to medical oversight of contraception provide the first attempt to map the perilous path through legal, medical and ethical mine fields on the way to achieving women's sexual autonomy."[91] Though united in their belief that women desperately needed both control and choice over their reproduction, Sanger and Dennett differed radically in their approach. Political scholar Gene Burns argues, "Dennett consistently distrusted professionalism and was suspicious about the compromise of principles," causing her to approach "chang[ing] the law on contraception [as] embedded within a broader conception of society and politics."[92] Though Sanger espoused birth control's potential to reshape social and political norms, Burns suggests that for Sanger "these other changes were indeed consequences, not prerequisites, of the use of birth control." Dennett, however, believed medicalization meant nothing "if one accepted the political and cultural notions of freedom and privacy" solely to provide contraceptive access.[93] Sanger prioritized *access* whereas Dennett fought to overhaul the very *system* that access was premised upon.

The lasting consequences of this dispute fall into harsh relief when sketched onto the reproductive rights framework at the core of the birth control movement. Within this framework, two specific rights emerge in relation to one's reproduction: control and choice. Control exists when women are given the ability to regulate reproduction through the use of contraceptive information and devices, whereas choice emerges from the individual freedom to voluntarily engage or reject parenthood. Securing both control and choice was essential to the birth control movement, for without the ability to regulate reproduction, it is impossible to enact choice over the matter. Despite their interconnectedness, advocates did not endorse the rights equally in their rhetorical choices and, as illustrated by the Sanger/Dennett dispute, were often willing to minimize, if not all together ignore, one right to secure the other.

Dennett's primary concern was with securing the right to choice by eliminating the social, legal, and political barriers preventing the voluntary acceptance and/or rejection of parenthood. Put simply, Dennett was concerned with the ideological function of contraception capable of liberating women from traditional modes of reproduction and motherhood. In a 1921 letter to the editor of the BCR, Dennett insisted, "Mere physical control of conception is not enough. There must also be a sense of self-respect and integrity in it, which is markedly lacking in the minds of thousands who have been the victims of perverse sex education."[94] Dennett's statement reflects a dedication to ameliorating the social conditions that robbed women of their reproductive autonomy as a prerequisite to securing access to the information and means necessary to exercise that very autonomy. Resulting in what feminist political theorist Lealle Ruhl calls "the willed pregnancy," birth controllers like Dennett sought to imbue reproduction with the values of responsibility, self-control, and, ultimately, choice.[95] Attaining individual development, relational satisfaction, and sexual liberation necessitated both adherence to the framework of "the willed pregnancy" and a rejection of the naturalist paradigm positioning reproduction outside the realm of human influence. Moving beyond the physical implications of control, such as mortality and overpopulation, the rhetoric of choice seeks to justify birth control by illuminating the benefits of adopting the framework of the "willed pregnancy" wherein parenthood is a choice rather than a consequence. The nuance of Dennett's conceptualization of choice has since been streamlined by modern advocates to fit within snappy monikers such as pro-choice, a woman's right to choose, and freedom of choice. Yet, these contemporary iterations put forth an essentialist view of women that obscures the very societal failures which

Dennett rightly perceived as the most pervasive obstacles not just to contraception but to society's recognition of women's bodily autonomy.

Dennett's ideological inclinations are consistent with her efforts to secure reproductive choice by localizing contraception within the realm of one's own private judgment and advocating for legislation aimed at restoring contraception's social acceptability. In doing so, Dennett was unwilling to accept legislative efforts that did not challenge the existing social order and was inimical to ceding power to external stakeholders, such as doctors, who did not share her emancipatory values. Commenting on this governing philosophy of her activism, Burns explains, "One did not have to advocate a broad reshaping of the social order in order to agree with Sanger's framing [but] Dennett refused to make such a narrow claim: for her, access to contraception was possible only in a fair society in which the law did not sanction special privilege."[96] In many instances, it would be a fair critique to say that such a brazen adherence to principles prevents *some* people from having meaningful access simply because access could not be secured for *all* people; however, in Dennett's case, it was well documented that wealthy women already had access to contraceptive information via private physicians, meaning that doctors-only bills provided minimal additional protection to those with existing access. Dennett's unwillingness to compromise wasn't just a matter of principle; it was a matter of genuine access.

Conversely, Sanger's primary concern was securing the right to control via access to contraceptive information and instruction resulting in her frequent elevation of the mechanistic function of contraception to regulate reproduction. She explained, "it is both our right and our duty, as intelligent beings, to control these for our own uses and our own good. This includes both the regulation of the number of children and the methods of regulation."[97] Supplemented by "the notion that reproduction ought to be managed and directed by human rationality," feminist political theorist Lealle Ruhl argues that the movement created "an instrumentalist view of pregnancy and child rearing."[98] Contrary to the prevailing naturalist paradigm positioning reproduction outside the realm of human influence, the framework of managed reproduction enabled advocates to boast outcomes such as the prevention of disease, decreased mortality, and population stability enabled by the widespread adoption of contraception. Less concerned with the secondary benefits of choice, such as individual development and relational satisfaction, the rhetoric of control seeks to justify birth control by illuminating the benefits of adopting the framework of managed reproduction wherein reproduction is closely regulated including decreased mortality rates, population control, and reduced public expenditures for dependent children.

Sanger's clinic initiatives, strategic partnerships with doctors and social workers, and ultimately her contribution to the development of hormonal contraception are all consistent with a mechanistic framework prioritizing the right to control, as each of these efforts focus on increasing access to different means of regulating reproduction. Yet, to secure such access, Sanger was often compelled to make compromises that eroded the promise of choice. The sequence of revisions Sanger willingly accepted for her own Federal Amendment are illustrative. In its earliest iterations, the doctors-only bill permitted *all* medical professionals including nurses and midwives to provide contraception information to *all* women; yet over time, nurses were removed, then midwives, and after countless alterations to the bill, the wording made it so that *only* doctors could provide information and *only* to married women.[99] It is true that this legislation provided contraception to women previously denied by federal law, but it also legitimated the denial of access to nonmarried women and/or those who could not afford a private physician. Burns argues that by medicalizing contraception and limiting its use to an acceptable swath of the population, "Sanger had charted a path that would frame contraception in a way that made practical change possible."[100] The efficacy of this strategy in the early years prompted Sanger to adopt a strategy of political accommodation more readily as the movement progressed. In doing so, Sanger willingly sacrificed key ideological commitments of early advocates to court allies whose cooperation could secure greater access to contraception.

Unfortunately, the adoption of a politically accommodating posture constrained the movement's ability to advance the emancipatory aims tied to birth control and forced advocates to couch their demands for reproductive rights in the benefits accrued through its adoption. Commenting on this strategic choice, Vanessa Murphree and Karla Gower contend that because the movement "sought to reach those in the middle and upper classes who could and would eventually use their influence to legalize birth control," advocates frequently "focused on birth control justifications . . . includ[ing] the reduction of poverty, maternal and infant mortality, child labor, tuberculosis, and birth defects."[101] Securing these benefits relied solely on the application of contraceptive measures, or the element of control, and could be accrued regardless of women's bodily autonomy or choice.

The tension between Sanger and Dennett is perhaps best understood as foreshadowing the inevitable conflict that produced the reproductive justice movement—a conflict made possible by the adoption of Sanger's strategy of political accommodation prioritizing the mechanistic right to control over the idealistic right to choice. Dennett's continued incredulity toward the social order and willingness to question the quality of access and the ability to voluntarily make reproductive decisions feature prominently in the work of today's reproductive justice scholars and activists. Reading the words of Loretta Ross and Rickie Solinger in this context is deeply enlightening. Ross argues, "Reproductive justice is rooted in the belief that systemic inequality has always shaped people's decision making around childbearing and parenting, particularly vulnerable women."[102] Dennett's characterization of the movement in 1921 shares a kinship with Ross's articulation of reproductive justice; she writes, "This [is] a humanist movement, a parenthood question, to be jointly solved by both men and women on the principle that it takes two to create a child and the responsibility should be jointly and consciously realized for both."[103] Dennett, like the reproductive justice advocates of today, acknowledged the complexity of reproduction as both a social and political act, and as Burns argues, "Dennett's frame anticipated late-twentieth-century law on privacy and sexuality much more than did Sanger's."[104] So while reproductive justice scholars often localize their work in opposition to early-twentieth-century advocates, perhaps Dennett should, at least partially, be exempted from their ire. We know Sanger emerged victorious in the struggle for leadership, but what is still left for us to consider is what this victory and subsequent adoption of a strategy of political accommodation means for the movement today.

NOTES

1. Sanger, *My Fight*, 52–53.
2. Ibid., 54.
3. Ibid.
4. Ibid., 56.
5. Ibid., 48.
6. Ibid., 58.
7. Tone, *Devices and Desires*, 67–68.
8. Burns, *The Moral Veto*, 40.
9. McLaren, *A History of Contraception*, 218. Sanger's focus on lower-class women was also influenced by British birth controller Marie Stopes, who founded the Society for Constructive Birth Control and Racial Progress in 1921 to pressure government officials to provide clinical services to the impoverished.
10. Advertisements in popular magazines such as *McCall's* and *Redbook* touted Lysol®'s power as a germicide, helping make it the most popular female contraceptive by the late 1930s (Tone, *Devices and Desires*, 158).
11. Sanger, "Suppression," 1. (When referencing articles from *The Woman Rebel Sanger* is listed as the author unless otherwise specified due to the lack of author identification for individual articles.)
12. Sanger, *An Autobiography*, 108.
13. Sanger, *My Fight*, 84.
14. McLaren, *A History of Contraception*, 217.
15. Sanger, *My Fight*, 62.

16. McCann, *Birth Control Politics*, 36. The first edition of *Family Limitation* explicitly framed birth control as necessary to both class struggle and women's liberation.
17. Gordon, *The Moral Property*, 139–50.
18. Engelman, *A History*, 32.
19. Ibid., 41.
20. "Bars Magazine," 19; "Bars Magazine," 1; "Can't Carry," 1.
21. Margaret Sanger Papers, 229968.
22. Engelman explains that William Sanger's arrest and trial generated far more publicity than Margaret Sanger's initial indictment likely because he was more easily portrayed as a victim in the press—"an unwitting accomplice entrapped by the crafty vice crusader" (Engelman, *A History*, 50).
23. "To Fight in Court," 8.
24. Engelman, *A History*, 49.
25. "Birth-Control and Aid," 4.
26. "Birth Control and Free Speech," 507.
27. Margaret Sanger Papers, 228424.
28. Margaret Sanger Papers, 236589.
29. Gordon, *The Moral Property*, 151.
30. Sanger, "The Fight against," 248.
31. Dennett, *Birth Control Laws*, 67.
32. Doak and Brugger, *How Did the Debate*, para. 3.
33. Margaret Sanger Papers, 238222.
34. Dennett, "Voluntary Parenthood," 12.
35. Dennett, *Birth Control Laws*, 19.
36. Sanger, "Meeting the Need," 14.
37. Sanger, "Morality and Birth Control," 14.
38. Murphree and Gower, "Making Birth Control," 226.
39. "Hayes Denounces," 1.
40. Gordon, *Woman's Body*, 26.
41. "Birth Control Clinic," 21.
42. "Birth Control Bill," 8.
43. "Social Aspects," 424.
44. Gordon, *The Moral Property*, 179.
45. "Sex Teaching," 5.
46. E. M., "Birth Control Now," 17.
47. Gardner, "Urges Doctors," 10.
48. E. M., "Birth Control Now," 17.
49. Margaret Sanger Papers, 226876.
50. Doak and Brugger, *How Did the Debate*, para. 7.
51. Margaret Sanger Papers, 236948.
52. Dennett, *Birth Control Laws*, 204.
53. Ibid., 57.
54. Ibid., 208.
55. Craig, "The Sex Side," 148.

56. Dennett, *Birth Control Laws*, 243.
57. Ibid., 68.
58. Ibid., 71.
59. Ibid., 101.
60. Ibid.
61. Ibid., 79.
62. Ibid.
63. Margaret Sanger Papers, 240406.
64. Ibid.
65. Ibid.
66. Ibid.
67. Margaret Sanger Papers, 240431.
68. Ibid.
69. Dennett, *Birth Control Laws*, 12.
70. Ibid., 201.
71. Ibid., 82.
72. Stopes, *Contraception*, 322.
73. Margaret Sanger Papers, 229968.
74. Ibid., 21.
75. Ibid., 253.
76. Ibid., 225.
77. Ibid., 210.
78. Ibid., 223.
79. Ibid., 253.
80. Ibid.
81. Dennett, *Birth Control Laws*, 223.
82. Margaret Sanger Papers, 240427.
83. Margaret Sanger Papers, 240429. The carbon copy of this letter found in the Margaret Sanger Papers collection indicates the margin notes and interlineations in the document were written by Sanger herself; the tone of these notes is unmistakably sardonic including short quips like "nerve!!," "cute," and "joke."
84. Margaret Sanger Papers, 240426; Margaret Sanger Papers, 240421.
85. Margaret Sanger Papers, 240419.
86. Margaret Sanger Papers, 201293.
87. Ibid.
88. Margaret Sanger Papers, 201296.
89. *United States v. Dennett*, 39 F. 2d 564 (1930).
90. Mary Ware Dennett to Margaret Sanger, February 28, 1931, ACLU Cases. As cited in John M. Craig, "'The Sex Side of Life': The Obscenity Case of Mary Ware Dennett," *Frontiers: A Journal of Women Studies* 15(3), 146–66.
91. Engelman, "The Rivalry," 2.
92. Burns, *The Moral Veto*, 116.
93. Ibid., 127.
94. Margaret Sanger Papers, 240406.
95. Ruhl, "Dilemmas of the Will," 642.

96. Burns, *The Moral Veto*, 126.
97. Margaret Sanger Papers, 236585.
98. Ruhl, "Dilemmas of the Will," 647.
99. Dennett, *Birth Control Laws*, 250.
100. Burns, *The Moral Veto*, 125.
101. Murphree and Gower, "Making Birth Control," 219–24.
102. Ross, "Reproductive Justice," 291.
103. Margaret Sanger Papers, 240419.
104. Burns, *The Moral Veto*, 127.

Chapter Two

Save the Mothers

I am thirty-three years of age, have been married a little less than fourteen years and have given birth to seven children, six of whom are living, one dying at the age of two years and four months from influenza, almost five years ago. Have also had three miscarriages during this time and am now pregnant again expecting to be confined in about one month.

I do not feel that I have shirked the responsibility of motherhood but do feel that I have all we can provide for and feeling that you can instruct me in what to use as a contraceptive I am writing to you begging for this information. My health is still good and I have a great desire to retain it for the balance of my lifetime in order that I may be able to raise my family and also enjoy life as I should like to.[1]

—Anonymous letter to Margaret Sanger
included in *Motherhood in Bondage*

These mothers may be fairly said to exemplify the typical American mother—the mother worshipped in our popular songs, stories, and motion-pictures. They reveal themselves heroically willing to make any sacrifice to their children. They work like slaves to provide food, clothing, shelter and education for the ever-growing brood. The majority of them are uncomplaining, long-suffering, thinking first of the well-being and the future happiness of the boys and girls they have brought into the world.

Yet for the greater part of their married life they are compelled to fulfill a double duty. For all the time they are 'slinging pots and pans,' milking cows, or engaging in the heavy manual and physical labor of farm-life, they are bringing an apparently endless stream of children into the world.

Pregnancy succeeds pregnancy in endless succession. Hardly is one child weaned than another is on its way. The double drain on the health of the mother is easy to imagine: she had neither the time nor the energy to devote to the living children in the most critical and delicate stage of their development. Nor can she, on the other hand, conserve her strength,

> *health and vital force to assure a rightful heritage of well-being to the unborn child she is carrying. From this slave mother is exacted a triple tax: her own health is broken down; the well-being of her older children is jeopardized; and the last-born infants are brought into the world with progressively decreasing chances of survival.*[2]
>
> —Preface to Chapter 3: "The Trap of Maternity"
> from *Motherhood in Bondage*

Childbearing in the early 1900s was a risky venture. In 1915, six women died for every thousand live births and one-tenth of all children born perished before their first birthday. This reality was even bleaker for women of color, who faced a maternal mortality rate of ten for every thousand live births and who buried almost 20 percent of infants in their first year of life.[3] Historian Mary Ladd-Taylor laments, "The most significant thing turn-of-the-century mothers had in common was fear of death, their own and their children's. Women from every social and economic group had personal knowledge of infant and maternal death, even though mortality rates were significantly higher among the poor and people of color."[4] In her 1928 book *Motherhood in Bondage*, Sanger acknowledges the ubiquitous feeling of dread felt by the women whose letters are featured in the book; she laments, "Repetition the readers will find, but significant repetition. It builds up the unit of this tragic communal experience. Despite all the differences, the story of motherhood in bondage is, by and large, the same story, the same pattern of pain, except here producing the same cry for deliverance."[5] Reviewers also honed in on the book's repetitive quality, remarking, "The result is monotonous, dreary reading, but a far more conclusive argument for birth control than columns of statistics."[6] Yet, within the dreary pages of *Motherhood in Bondage* the reviewer found an even more meaningful lesson about the current state of motherhood, writing, "There is no record of selfishness. Many of these mothers say over and over how they love their babies and they 'want to raise them right.' But they cry out either in fear of breaking health and puny offspring or in protest at children that come faster than income can care for."[7] The letters compiled in *Motherhood in Bondage* gave voice to the countless women suffering from perpetual pregnancies and, perhaps more importantly, provided context to their demands for contraceptive instruction—they wanted not to avoid motherhood altogether but to be better mothers for the children they already had and those yet born.

Motherhood in Bondage also represented the culmination of an intense effort to operationalize contraception within the agenda of progressive reformers concerned with issues of child and maternal mortality. In doing so, advocates framed motherhood as inevitable and positioned contraception as essential to elevating the status of mothers by alleviating the burdens of perpetual pregnancy. In this scenario, couples entered parenthood responsibly in accordance with the father's earning power and the mother's good health. The movement's attempt to professionalize motherhood stands in stark contrast to its initial rhetoric focused on agitation and free speech and thus represents the first major iteration of political accommodation. While birth controllers were certainly concerned with the welfare of mothers, they were equally concerned with their reputation. The use of motherhood as a terministic screen to advance their agenda helped establish the benevolence of the movement with influential parties; yet it did so by pushing a view of motherhood steeped in the heteronormative and whitewashed values promulgated in progressive circles. Birth controllers succeeded in elevating the status of motherhood, but only for those mothers adhering to a specific maternal ideal.

MATERNALIST RHETORIC IN THE BIRTH CONTROL MOVEMENT

Sanger wasn't the only one whose inbox overflowed with correspondence from desperate women as the recently created Children's Bureau also emerged as a source of potential succor for forlorn mothers. Established in 1912 under the guidance of the Department of Commerce and Labor, the Children's Bureau was tasked with investigating infant mortality and implementing educational efforts aimed at improving childbearing and rearing. *The Birth Control Review* applauded the department for bringing awareness to the mounting death toll of mothers and babies, proclaiming, "What this peace-time, year-in and year-out casualty list means in sorrow and suffering almost everyone knows from personal experience; what it means in loss to the nation has only been officially recognized since the establishment of the Children's Bureau at Washington."[8] Sanger capitalized on the efforts of the Children's Bureau and often cited their research as a justification for expanded contraceptive instruction in a clinic setting. Sanger portends in a 1919 editorial in the *Birth Control Review*:

> The Bureau advocated the establishment of clinics where the expectant mother could receive prenatal care and attention and adequate instruction on the proper care of the child when born, and thus still further increase its chances of survival. In addition, it seems obvious that if the Brockton babies, and all the rest of the babies born to the working classes all over the world, are to flourish and enjoy their undoubted right of belonging to the baby aristocracy, methods of scientific contraception should be included in the program of these clinics.[9]

Sanger long advocated for scientific instruction of contraceptive methods; however, her plea for its inclusion in the federally funded and operated programs of the Children's Bureau signals a shift in what was once a frigid relationship with state actors. Historian Robyn Rosen notes, "The Children's Bureau's place within the government and its commitment to federal activism was completely at odds with the ideological foundations of the birth control movement in America."[10] Yet, unlike the birth control movement, the Children's Bureau successfully secured government support for its initiative to reduce maternal mortality, and Sanger wanted in on the action despite her once caustic attitude toward the government.

Advancing this agenda required the careful courting of a powerful group of progressive women reformers known as maternalists. Ladd-Taylor explains, "Beginning in the 1890's, growing numbers of middle-class women, newly convinced that scientific information about child development could prevent most infant mortality, tried to turn their knowledge into action and save children's lives."[11] These women were not only responsible for creating the Children's Bureau, but they were also its primary employees and loudest advocates. Ladd-Taylor distills the ideological commitments of maternalists into four specific beliefs; she argues:

> Adherents held 1. that there was a uniquely feminine value system based on care and nurturance, 2. That mothers performed a service to the state by raising citizen-workers, 3. That women were united across class, race, and nation by their common capacity for motherhood and therefore shared a responsibility for all the world's children, and 4. That ideally men should earn a family wage to support their "dependent" wives and children at home.[12]

Scholars, including both Ladd-Taylor and Rosen, speak to the tumultuous relationship between birth controllers and maternalists which will play out in this chapter. Sanger, ever undeterred, recognized the strategic value in aligning her movement with the efforts of the Children's Bureau and soon began infusing her rhetoric with maternalists, sentiments. The passage quoted extensively here from a 1925 piece entitled "The Business of Bearing Babies" is illustrative. Sanger writes:

> Housekeeping nowadays has been put on a business basis and not even the most incorrigible sentimentalist regrets the passing of the day when "woman's work was never done." American women today revel in the discipline of housekeeping on the budget system. They delight in business like efficiency in the home. They have declared war on waste, dirt and slovenliness. They have gained more freedom, more comfort, more happiness. And so a new generation of American wives, a vast majority of whom have had business experience before marriage, is beginning to approach the central problem of life—that of motherhood—in a

> new manner. In a word, these women are trying to put the business of bearing babies and rearing children on a basis of intelligent efficiency. . . .
>
> Like all-important changes in civilization, this attempt to put the all-important profession of motherhood on a business basis has been denounced and decried. . . . To courageous, ambitious young husbands and wives today, parenthood is a problem that cannot be left to chance. Childbearing is too costly a venture—both in precious lives and in money, to be indulged in carelessly, incessantly, continuously, without thought of the lives of the mother and the child. No gallant, chivalrous, sane minded husband today would willingly ask his wife to descend into the valley of the shadow of death without taking every precaution for the health and well-being of his beloved and the new arrival. . . .
>
> Putting childbearing on a sound business basis—studying it, examining it, keeping the books of motherhood and starting budgets for babies, computing the cost of the overhead, and seeking to cut down waste and inefficiency—all this, I claim, does not mean that the mothers of the present generation are cold-blooded. It does not mean that we love babies less. It means that we love them more. We too can go into ecstasies over the adorable rosebuds—especially our own. But we modern mothers—and I have had some twenty years' experience in this business!—realize that we are not merely producing "better babies," but the men and women of tomorrow—the Americans upon whom the whole future of our civilization depends. Is it anything to wonder at, then, that the "business" mother today is insisting, in her whole particular inalienable field on "safety first" in motherhood? Is it not better for all concerned, the security of marriage itself, the health and economic well-being of the family, and the start in life of our young American in the making, that parents should stop, look and listen?[13]

Sanger praises the humble housewife for her fastidiousness in ensuring she can provide the best for her family and lauds the husband who dutifully provides for his dependents in service of creating the next generation of upstanding citizens, all the while making it clear that such efforts are possible only through the careful regulation of reproduction. In her pronouncement of the profession of motherhood, Sanger carefully clarifies that being meticulous and maternal are complimentary ambitions—that to calculate childbearing and rearing decisions is not cold but courageous and actually reflects a greater level of love for babies. In doing so, Sanger methodically inserts birth control into the maternalist agenda by co-opting both their reform efforts and their rhetorical framing of motherhood.

Through the inclusion of maternalist themes, Sanger transforms motherhood into a terministic screen by which we come to understand contraceptive use specifically and reproductive rights more broadly. Developed by renowned rhetorician Kenneth Burke, "terministic screens are conceptual vocabularies used to name and interpret the world . . . and as selections from among many conceptual vocabularies, they can lead to different conclusions as to what reality actually is."[14] Apart from the natural association of motherhood and reproduction, Sanger goes to great lengths to situate reproductive rights within a particular view of motherhood as natural, inevitable, and best carried out in a responsible manner. The mother who chooses to exercise control over her reproduction to preserve her maternal health in service of her family is the one that should be applauded. The potency of this terministic screen makes it impossible to divorce any conversation regarding birth control from its relationship to motherhood. The choice to prevent or delay pregnancy is also a choice to prevent or delay motherhood. Our understanding of reproductive rights is thus informed by the conceptual vocabulary of motherhood created to advance the movement's agenda in the twentieth century.

Zeroing in on the core values of maternalists, Sanger and her ilk strategically positioned contraception as an actionable step toward achieving the maternalist agenda in three specific ways. Initially, advocates presented contraception as a solution to maternal mortality caused by both perpetual pregnancy and abortion; yet, in both cases, the life of the mother was deemed worth saving because her survival meant increased survival and quality of life for her children. Second, advocates lionized mothers and sought to professionalize motherhood through the application of scientific principles enabling women to excel in the role of mother. More than just helping women become better mothers to their children, birth controllers argued that enacting control and choice over one's reproduction demonstrated the highest form of motherly love possible. Finally, advocates reinforced the primacy of the man's role as father and provider and capitalized on this logic to extend their recommendations regarding child spacing and family limitation. Taken together, advocates put forth the notion of responsible parentage to represent the conscious and controlled growth of the family in relation to the father's earnings and the mother's reproductive capacity.

CONTRACEPTION AS A SOLUTION FOR MATERNAL MORTALITY

Maternalists within the Children's Bureau situated infant and maternal mortality as a societal problem that all persons, and particularly women, had a responsibility to solve. In asserting the value of contraception as a solution to maternal mortality, Sanger borrowed heavily from the maternalists' themes of shared responsibility and the communal experience of motherhood. In a 1929 article in *The North American Review*, Sanger even directly quotes the first director of the Children's Bureau, Julia Lathrop, to bolster her articulation of contraception as central to the protection of maternity and infancy. Sanger portends:

> Whether Birth Control is right or wrong, moral or immoral, a need or a nuisance, one thing is certain. Mothers of ten or of one can no longer, by the mere exercise of a function common to all living creatures consider themselves exempt from social responsibility. As Miss Lathrop has expressed it: "One thing is in my opinion certain—only mothers can save this cooperative work for maternity and infancy. If prosperous, intelligent mothers do not urge the protection of the lives of all mothers and all babies, why should we expect Congress to come unasked to their aid?" Though Julia Lathrop is here making a plea only for Government protection of maternity and infancy, the same truth is applicable to the doctrine of Birth Control.[15]

Sweeping aside the contentiousness surrounding the morality of birth control, Sanger asserts contraception is concomitant with the work being done elsewhere to protect mothers and babies. The specific mention of Lathrop, known colloquially as America's First Official Mother, establishes a parallel between her efforts and the ambitions of the birth control movement to reduce maternal mortality. While maternalists worked to improve the health and safety of childbearing through education and outreach programs, birth controllers focused on effective child spacing as critical to curtailing maternal mortality and isolated two specific instances where women died due to lack of contraceptive information: childbirth and abortion.

Childbirth may seem like an obvious focal point for birth controllers, but this rhetorical focus stood in stark contrast to the child-centric messaging of the Children's Bureau. In a 1916 speech before the 48th annual convention of the National American Woman Suffrage Association, Julia Lathrop explains the Bureau's interest in maternal mortality as a mere by-product of their work to increase the welfare of children. She asserts, "In the Children's Bureau we have come to see the close connection between the welfare of mother and child. Because we are so concerned for the children, we asked a physician to take those vast, mysterious volumes of the census, and look up the facts about the mortality of mothers."[16] Whereas the Children's Bureau took up the issue of maternal mortality primarily because of its consequences for children, birth controllers centered their concern on the experiences of women often prioritizing women's health over that of children.

Advocates directly chastised efforts to reduce child mortality which failed to consider the life of the mother. An editorial comment in the July 1918 edition of the *Birth Control Review* declared, "Everyone is patriotically shouting 'save the babies.' But . . . [t]hose who work hardest to 'save the babies' look with coldness upon the least suggestion of saving mothers from hideously frequent births."[17] Sanger vocalized her frustration with the overwhelming focus on child mortality in a 1916 speech entitled "Chicago Address to Women." She scolds, "people, while awake to the claims of the unborn and even the unconceived, continue to be blind to the claims of the woman's health." She decried the myopic focus on children and the blatant disregard for the act that "eventually murders the woman who bears them."[18] The Children's Bureau, staffed primarily by upper- and middle-class white women, were particularly guilty of minimizing the consequences of unrestrained reproduction on maternal health. While they worked tirelessly to improve the conditions of motherhood through prenatal care and child-rearing classes, they remained largely unconcerned with the quality of life for mothers apart from its consequences for the child.

Meanwhile, birth controllers consistently reiterated the risks associated with childbirth particularly for women with multiple children. The John Price Jones Corporation explained in "1913 childbirth caused more deaths among women from 15 to 44 years of age than any other disease except tuberculosis."[19] Based on these findings, Sanger painted a grim picture for America's mothers lamenting in a 1923 speech, "22,000 mothers [pass] out of life each year from causes incidental to pregnancy . . . this means that two mothers every hour . . . pass into the great beyond from causes that might be prevented."[20] Directly connecting these dire findings to the work of the Children's Bureau, Sanger chided, "Until mothers have adequate knowledge to space, limit, or control their offspring, the Children's Bureau will continue to find the death rate . . . unchanged."[21] Whereas maternalists resisted any course of action likely to reduce the birth rate, birth controllers asserted the value of both child spacing and family limitation to reduce maternal mortality.

To further operationalize their concern for maternal mortality within existing maternalist discourses, advocates emphasized the connection between infant and maternal mortality by highlighting the importance of healthy mothers to healthy babies. The health of mothers was relevant to infant mortality in two ways: the transference of good health during pregnancy and the maintenance of health postpartum. Sanger articulates in the *Birth Control Review* in 1919, "The mother's health is more than likely to be wrecked and the later children are almost sure to fall short of that nervous and muscular health which might otherwise have been theirs."[22] The movement's argument was simple: women still recovering from a previous pregnancy, in poor health, or suffering from chronic illness were unlikely to birth healthy babies due to their inability to provide the necessary nutrients and stability to the child while in utero. This argument resonated with members of the Children's Bureau who observed a clear connection between the health of the mother and child. Robert Morse Woodbury, writing on behalf of the Children's Bureau in 1926, explained, "First in the underlying causes of these infant deaths was lack of health and physical vitality in the mother during pregnancy."[23] Even women fortunate to survive a difficult pregnancy often faced complications with labor and delivery which claimed their life before their child's first birthday. Woodbury furthers, "Infants whose mothers die within one year following confinement have a mortality rate four times as high as infants whose mother survives childbirth."[24] Contraceptive use promised to reduce the wanton loss of life directly related to poor maternal health fueled by perpetual pregnancy.

Thousands of women died carrying their pregnancies to term while countless others perished attempting to terminate theirs instead. Sanger lamented in 1916, "Abortion is the most common as well as one of the most serious disturbances of pregnancy. . . . It is roughly estimated that at least 250,000 abortions occur in the United States each year while 50,000 women die from their effects."[25] Influenced deeply by her experiences with Sadie Sachs, Sanger vigorously insisted contraception prevents the needs for abortions altogether by allowing women to prevent pregnancy in the first place. Writing for *Coronet Magazine* Sanger declared: "it isn't fair to deny to the vast majority of women in this country the child-spacing knowledge they desire. . . . It isn't fair to force them, often, to the sad alternative of abortion."[26] Sociologist Ray Erwin Baber touts the preventative capacity of contraception in 1932 proclaiming, "an adequate knowledge of birth control would wipe out most of this ghastly toll of adult life, to say nothing of the infinitely greater toll on half-formed life."[27] The proposition of giving women the ability to engage in conscious and controlled motherhood to eliminate the need for abortion proved particularly compelling to a medical community intimately familiar with the disastrous effects of illegal abortions. The testimony of Dr. Eric M. Matsner, executive secretary of the National Medical Council on Birth Control, before the Academy of Medicine in 1937 is exemplary. Without contraception, Matsner argued, women have no choice but abortion: "one-quarter of America's high maternal death rate is due to abortion and will be materially decreased by the extension of reliable contraception information."[28] Birth controllers introduced a new alternative—contraceptive instruction—and ardently defended its efficacy.

In addition to the lives claimed by illegal abortion in the early twentieth century advocates highlighted the lasting effect of abortion on women's health, including damage to the uterus, sepsis, infection, shock, and even sterility and barrenness. The illegal nature of abortion made the procedure risky and unsafe and also prevented women from seeking medical attention when complications arose, so that "the results of abortion are usually of far more serious effect on the woman's health than a full term child birth."[29] Even widespread knowledge of these risks failed to deter women desperate to avoid another child. The BCCRB's Committee on Public Progress explained in 1938, "Many women will risk not only their future health and welfare but their very lives rather than bring into the world an unwanted baby" or a baby they are unable to support.[30] Women who survived an abortion soon found themselves back at square one because without the ability to prevent conception it was only a matter of time before women found themselves contemplating abortion yet again. In 1925, the ABCL's Clinical Research Department revealed patients frequently admitted to multiple abortions, "varying from one to as many as 40 abortions in one particular case." They commented further, "It is not unusual to have women state that she has had 4, 5 or even 10 abortions performed."[31] Absent contraception, abortions were not the last resort, they were the *only* resort for women.

One striking similarity exists between the rhetoric of birth controllers and maternalists—the subordination of women's health to her children. Rather than advocating for the health and wellness of women as individuals, the urgency to prevent death or illness among women is directly tied to their maternal role. Under maternalist logic women's health deserves preservation because it is inherited by her children. Women's deaths are tragic only when configured into "maternal mortality" rates. Mourning occurs for the children left behind. Contraception as a solution to maternal mortality worked by ensuring women could plan their children in accordance with their health and promised to produce stronger and happier children. Healthy women were conduits for better babies. In effect, maternalism reduces women to their reproductive capacity and places a premium on the interconnectedness of maternal and infant health. Although well intentioned, this framework lays the groundwork for future spurious arguments advanced by eugenicists regarding who is "fit" for motherhood on the basis of health.

Despite claiming to place a higher priority on women's lives than their colleagues in the Children's Bureau, birth controllers commit the same rhetorical devaluation of women by deriving their justification for protecting women's health solely from her maternal role. The manuscript of Sanger's aforementioned "Chicago Address to Women" provides a disheartening glimpse into the real time prioritization of motherhood. The last stanza of the speech boldly proclaims: "We recognize the importance of safeguarding the dignity of ~~the individual woman~~ motherhood, and we want to raise her from the degradation of servility and sex slavery to a glorified privilege."[32] Sanger's silent interlineations speak volumes. Rather than appealing to the health of individual women, birth controllers couched their pleas in a simple demand to save the mothers! The individual woman is quite literally erased to make space for the mother.

PROFESSIONALIZING MOTHERHOOD

Maternalists strove to elevate the status of motherhood to a place of honor and prestige in hopes of fortifying the traditional role of mother. Historian Molly

Ladd-Taylor furthers, "sentimental maternalists were not only interested in child welfare; they also wanted to advance women's status. . . . [T]hey wanted to professionalize motherhood by bringing science and education to child-rearing . . . because they wanted women to be more content to stay at home in their traditional roles."[33] The introductory paragraph to Sanger's "The Business of Bearing Babies" is perhaps even more telling of her ideological allegiance to maternalism. She proclaims, "We are becoming a nation of business women as well as business men. No—I don't mean merely these women who are carving careers for themselves in the professional world, who are succeeding as shopkeepers, as artists, as doctors, decorators or as social workers. I mean the humble 'housewife' as well."[34] As explored in chapter 4, birth controllers readily encouraged women to pursue opportunities outside the home and asserted that doing so was impossible without contraception. Yet, rarely does their endorsement of these opportunities come without praise for women who choose to remain in the home and pursue motherhood. This rhetorical sleight of hand pays lip service to the emancipatory potential of birth control while simultaneously reinscribing the heteronormative and patriarchal assumptions inherent within maternalism. In addition to explicitly bolstering mothers in their rhetoric, advocates insisted contraception uniquely aided the profession of motherhood by enabling women to fully develop and in turn become better mothers.

Consistent with maternalist ideology, advocates sought to resurrect the role of mother from the diminished social position it assumed under the weight of unlimited reproduction. Writing from prison in 1917, Sanger proclaimed: "We hear so much of sacred motherhood. There are statues in plenty to kings, statesmen and generals who have led her sons off to the universal shambles of slaughter. But where are the monuments to motherhood?"[35] Responding to the prominent social and cultural troupes that lauded motherhood as the highest aim for women, birth controllers renounced these cultural platitudes as nothing more than hollow rhetoric—praising women for fulfilling their duties as mothers yet failing to assist them in these endeavors with meaningful policies making motherhood not just feasible but enjoyable. Sanger furthers, "For centuries she has populated the earth in ignorance and without restraint, in vast numbers and with staggering rapidity. She has become not the mother of a nobler race but a mere breeding machine."[36] Far from the honorific of motherhood bandied about in popular culture, the bleak reality of continual childbearing in the early twentieth century was in fact a death sentence for countless American women.

Though somewhat hyperbolic, birth controllers analogized society's view of motherhood to "servility and sex slavery" and suggested mothers have been "placed on the level of the nursemaid, permitted to care for man's offspring, allowed to compete with his animals as pack-horses whose honored destiny it was to suffer and serve."[37] These powerful analogies suggested society's treatment of mothers left them with the same level of control as a packhorse—which is to say none at all. Utilizing the imagery of chattel slavery, Sanger boldly warned in 1919: "A free race cannot be born of slave mothers. A woman enchained cannot choose but give a measure of bondage to her sons and daughters," signaling sex-bondage had implications on a societal level as well.[38] In one of the most explicit uses of slavery and emancipation as a metaphor, the National Council for Federal Legislation on Birth Control provoked, "In ignorance she brings forth her children and is enslaved as the black race never was enslaved. Where is mother Abraham Lincoln to free her?"[39] Considering Sanger's intended audience's likely ties to abolitionists, her analogy is both jarring and judicious in demonstrating the brutality inflicted on women burdened with constant childbearing. Sanger returned to the slavery analogy throughout her career; however, her rhetoric regarding motherhood noticeably softened alongside the rise of maternalism in the United States. Wesley Buerkle explains, "Where in 1914 Sanger calls motherhood a form of slavery, by 1922 she describes motherhood as the 'most important profession in the world' and 'woman's noblest career.'"[40] This rhetorical shift aligns with Sanger's uptake of maternalists' ideals intent on amplifying the profession of motherhood rather than illuminating the cultural conditions facilitating its degradation in the first place. The abandonment of the slavery analogy coincides with Sanger's strategic choice to eschew her previous radicalism in favor of milder rhetoric with broader appeal.

Birth controllers also professionalized motherhood in their existing reform efforts. Contextualizing the need to raise the status of motherhood within the movement's focus on maternal mortality, the 1923 version of the ABCL Bylaws, Aims, and Principles proclaims: "In addition to this grave evil we witness the appalling waste of women's health and women's lives by too frequent pregnancies. . . . It is essential that the function of motherhood be elevated to a position of dignity. And this is impossible as long as conception remains a matter of chance."[41] The ABCL makes two important rhetorical moves here. First, by linking the perception of mothers to existing concerns over maternal health, the ABCL demands society reconceptualize motherhood if it wishes to effectively combat maternal mortality. Second, the ABCL explicitly labels the provision of reproductive choice as a prerequisite to achieving both an elevated view of motherhood and decreased maternal mortality. Consistent with the maternalist desire to infuse motherhood with intentionality, the ABCL declares: "Instead of being a blind and haphazard consequence of uncontrolled instinct, motherhood must be made the responsible and self-directed means of human expression and regeneration."[42] Using the familiar strategy of juxtaposition, the ABCL effectively frames birth control as the linchpin to enacting reproductive choice and accruing the benefits of its application—responsible motherhood.

Although operating on different timelines, the Children's Bureau only concerned themselves with women once they transitioned into motherhood whereas birth controllers recognized the importance of allowing women to fully develop prior to entering motherhood, the end goal for both groups was largely the same. Stemming from the movement's well-established argument that birth control was not anti-life, advocates defended women's desire for children alongside the ability to blossom in their roles of woman, wife, and mother. In essence, the best mothers are those afforded the opportunity to mature into themselves and, more importantly, into their role as wife and eventually mother. Articulating the importance of both choice and family limitation to a woman's full development, Sanger exclaimed: "The woman of today wants something out of life for herself; she doesn't choose to be a drudge to motherhood. She wants to develop motherhood and womanhood so that she may be a better companion to her husband and a better guardian and playmate for her children. With two or three children she has this chance."[43] The desire to grow and develop as individuals—to embrace the potentialities of womanhood—prior to and throughout motherhood consistently emerged within the letters received by the ABCL requesting contraceptive information. Sanger laments, "This is all they ask—a chance to know their husbands . . . to be a real mother to their children . . . to be the real mothers that we want them to be."[44] Despite the emancipatory tone of Sanger's opening sentence, hinting at new possibilities for women, the remainder of the paragraph forecloses those possibilities by highlighting only her increased aptitude as a wife and mother. The ABCL is even more reductive suggesting that to excel in their roles as wife and mother is literally *all they ask.*

Reiterating the fact that allowing women to develop fully was not antithetical to motherhood, birth controllers characterized the children of these mothers as happier and healthier than those born to underdeveloped mothers. Rather than having motherhood thrust upon young women, advocates pleaded for "time to develop, time to attend to one or two children and to bring them up as they should be brought up," so as to raise children "better fitted for life and probably in every way better equipped than the children of very young girls."[45] Writer Jan Struther echoed this sentiment in the *New York Times* in 1941, proclaiming contraception enables reproduction "without impairing the mother's health or interfering with her and her husband's right to develop their own possibilities as human beings."[46] Contraception allowed women to delay pregnancy until they were ready, which according to advocates, transformed women into better mothers in the long run.

Taking this reasoning one step further, advocates proposed that a woman's maternal desire actually deepened as she developed, resulting in the birth of more *not* less children to fully developed women. Sanger proclaimed in 1923:

> One of the reasons today why I believe we have small families, sometimes only one child in a family, is because that child has come too quickly into that woman's life. She has never had a chance to develop herself; she has been first a girl, then a mother. The wife in her, the woman in her has never had a chance to evolve. If she had waited for a time after her marriage, if there had been a chance to develop that maternal instinct in her, motherhood would have been a joy to her and not a dread and a fear.[47]

Speaking of children and larger families as an inevitability for women given the option to postpone reproduction in their formative years helped mitigate concerns over stationary population growth and race suicide leveraged by opponents. However, note the order in which Sanger enumerates the losses for women not given time to develop—*the wife in her, the woman in her*—situating the identity of woman as deferential to wife.

Allowing women to fully develop prior to motherhood also held societal value in that it allowed women to better execute their maternal duties. Advocates paralleled the experience of motherhood with and without child spacing and again invoked the metaphor of slavery to amplify the dire experiences of women denied contraceptive instruction. Sanger writes in the *Birth Control Review* in 1921, "The potential mother is to be shown that maternity need not be slavery but the most effective avenue toward self-development and self-realization."[48] Sanger parallels the liberation of contraception with that of escaping slavery, but instead of advancing liberating women completely from their biological burden of childbearing insists that self-actualization is best achieved through motherhood. Connecting this development to the societal expectations of motherhood, Sanger boldly questioned in 1923: "Can any mother serve society when she died rearing another child? Can she serve society by having other children? I don't think so. I think that's the least we can do for these mothers."[49] Paying homage to the maternalist precept that mothers perform an invaluable service to the state through the raising of children, Sanger makes a case for contraceptive instruction as vital to woman's role in society. Note, however, the limited scope of that role to bearing and rearing children—actions that only lose their connection to slavery when infused with the self-determination made possible via contraception.

Birth controllers and maternalists found common ground in their mutual emphasis on the necessity to provide women with accurate scientific information regarding reproduction and child-rearing or what they called scientific motherhood. Noting the shift from traditional social medicine to modern medicine in the twentieth century, Ladd-Taylor explains, "disturbed by what they considered dangerous and ignorant practices of traditional mothers—maternalists educated themselves about scientific childbearing and . . . wanted to make the benefits of modern medicine and science available to all children."[50] This shift was reflected in the rhetoric of both parties who frequently drew stark comparisons between traditional and scientific motherhood. A 1909 article from *Vogue* announced "Scientific Motherhood [as] a Reform of the Near Future" and praised the "scientific study of child life" for creating a new generation of "truly intelligent mothers" who are "wise, as distinguished from merely sentimental mothers."[51] Charles Zueblin, president of the American League for Civic Improvement, mirrors the contrast made within the *Vogue* editorial and explicitly articulates contraception's place in this framework. Zueblin exclaims in the *Birth Control Review* in 1917: "Many scientific methods are being employed by intelligent women to control conception. . . . Defying fear, superstition, tradition, is the necessity of voluntary motherhood for the protection of mothers, children, and the race. Contraception commands the support of those who believe in MOTHERS FIRST!"[52] Consistent with the premium placed on scientific information and instruction explored in chapter 1, birth controllers aligned their efforts with maternalists committed to rescuing reproduction from quacks, untrained midwives, and folk science under the mantra of scientific motherhood.

FATHERS AS PROVIDERS

Undergirded by their ideological commitment to the separate spheres doctrine, maternalists firmly believed the father's primary obligation was to provide for his dependents so wives could focus exclusively on mother-work. Ladd-Taylor furthers, "Women's aptitude for caregiving was idealized while their social and economic contribution to the family economy was devalued, and they became more economically dependent on men."[53] Birth controllers shared these sentiments but were equally cognizant of the economic realities facing fathers who often struggled to make a living wage for themselves much less multiple dependents. Sanger received countless letters from fathers desperate for contraceptive information as a direct result of their inability to financially support their growing families; one letter writer bemoans, "I am a young married man thirty years of age and have one child and that is enough. Especially for a man such as me that can only earn forty cents per hour. . . . When a forty cent per hour working man raises several children it certainly means poverty."[54] Reflecting on these letters Sanger writes, "a new generation of men who enter marriage with a full realization of their responsibilities towards their wives and the children-to-be is certainly hope for the future."[55] In addition to being the primary breadwinners, fathers played an important role in family planning during this time period because their cooperation was required to utilize all existing methods of contraception. Barrier methods, withdrawal, and the rhythm method necessitated a willing male partner making fathers equally responsible for family planning.

Despite their shared commitment to the father as provider, birth controllers were the only ones who offered a tangible solution to the conundrum faced by families saddled with the possibility of children they could not afford. Writing in the *Birth Control Review* in 1919, an author known only as M. K. directly chastises Julia Lathrop and the Children's Bureau for their unwillingness to endorse family limitation despite openly acknowledging the relationship between poverty and infant mortality. After summarizing a pamphlet produced by Lathrop entitled "Income and Infant Mortality" wherein Lathrop highlights that "in all of the cities studied the lowest income groups were, in general, the highest in infant mortality," M. K. rebuffs:

> Miss Lathrop concludes by pointing out that among the essentials of a lowered infant mortality rate are . . . finally and fundamentally a general recognition throughout the country that a decent income, self-respectingly earned by the father is the beginning of wisdom, and the only fair division of labor between the father and the mother of young children and the strongest safe-guard against a high infant mortality rate. In presenting this summary of Miss Lathrop's report to the readers of the Birth Control Review we would like to suggest on our own account, that the only way in which a solution of the problems of wages, rent, babies, etc., can be permanently affected would seem to be some system of family limitation.[56]

Just as advocates voiced frustration with the Children's Bureau's myopic focus regarding the relationship between maternal and infant mortality, they also lambasted officials for failing to acknowledge the importance of family limitation especially among impoverished parents. Yet, even in their admonishment of the Children's Bureau, advocates such as M. K. demonstrate their commitment to the separate spheres doctrine by reiterating the father's wage as the family's only source of income. Far from a neutral reflection on the status quo, M. K.'s statement contains an unmistakable value judgment applauding the "self-respecting" father whose income supports the "only fair division of labor" within the household.

Assuming parents would choose to have more than one child, advocates expressed great concern over the ability of a man's wage to keep pace with the addition of new children to the home. The November 1915 edition of *Current Opinion* explicitly connected child mortality to earning ability, arguing, "The real reason why there are 300,000 unnecessary deaths every year among our babies is that the fathers cannot make enough money to keep them alive."[57] Speaking to the difficulty fathers face in supporting a growing family, Sanger explained in a 1935 radio broadcast: when a "father's wages remain the same and babies continue to arrive . . . the father soon feels the burden which falls too heavily upon his already bent shoulders, even when he is fortunate enough to have an average paying job."[58] Not only does the addition of children create more mouths to feed, house, and care for, but unless a father's wages increase proportionately with each new child, maintaining the same standards of living for the family over time becomes impossible. One father wrote to Sanger with this exact concern, pleading, "We intend to give our children an education which will enable them to maintain as high a standard as we have set for ourselves and if possible even higher. We feel that if we have any more children that we will not be able to do this."[59] Acknowledging this struggle, Sanger lamented in 1917 that as new children arrive the father "is obliged to reduce the expense for rent and the pleasant little home that he could maintain until after the second child was born has been relinquished for a crowded and shabby dwelling in a tenement region."[60] Where mothers primarily felt the physical toll of perpetual childbearing, fathers struggled under the monumental task of providing the basic necessities for their growing broods not to mention creating the financial stability to support their future endeavors.

Further compounding this problem, advocates noted an inverse relationship between increased offspring and the father's earning power which subsequently shrinks due to his inability to bargain for higher wages. In the early 1900s, strikes were a powerful mechanism for workers to attain increased wages; however birth controllers warned, "The man with a large family who is tied down by fear of losing his job [is] the last to fight for higher wages when a strike comes, and the first to crawl back at any price."[61] This situation was even more dire for men whose families were already poor, as they "must accept any wage that is offered. His very need for more than his fellow work man, who is young and single, compels him to accept less—in the fear that he get nothing."[62] Rather than merely demanding fathers provide for their families, as maternalists often did, birth controllers acknowledged the complex situation facing fathers whose fight for meager wages was simultaneously motivated and constrained by his family's needs. So, while advocates confirmed their ideological commitment to the father as sole provider, they also recognized the economic impossibility of providing a consistently high quality of life for each successive child absent the knowledge to space pregnancies and plan accordingly.

These concerns were magnified for the day laborers, factory workers, and contingently employed fathers whose lack of generational wealth prompted birth controllers to focus their efforts on impoverished communities. A report released by the Clinical Research Department of the ABCL in 1925 explained, "The patients applying to our clinic generally belong to the wage-earning class, and their families exist on meager incomes."[63] Confirming Sanger's assumption that wealthier women accessed contraceptive information via private physicians, the ABCL noted: "Only a small percentage of our patients come from the wealthier classes, and these are generally referred by their physicians who do not themselves prescribe contraceptive methods."[64] The unique need for contraceptive information among impoverished women also surfaced in the letters received by the ABCL. Alice C. Boughton, then Executive Director of the ABCL, highlighted the preponderance of letters from women who identified themselves as poor in her analysis of the 7,309 letters received between March 1931 and April 1932. Boughton observes, "The under-privileged letters were naturally much less self-assured; in fact, in many instances the writer was desperate."[65] Accompanying the desperate cries of poor women were numerous findings confirming their need for birth control. The ABCL's Annual Report in 1925 explained over 70 percent of women seeking birth control belonged to families whose weekly income ranged from fifty dollars to as little as fifteen and articulated a direct correlation between low wages and large family size. They conclude: "A tabulation made of 65 consecutive cases in each group show a living child rate of 3.1 for those with less than $20.00 and 1.8 for those over $100.00."[66] The relationship between income and quality of life was statistically undeniable and motivated Sanger to bemoan in 1925, "Poverty is the great enemy of baby life. Poverty means lack of proper food, lack of proper hygienic sanitation. Poverty means an overcrowded home; poverty means more babies than the mother can look after and more than the harassed father can support."[67]

Practicing contraceptive measures held the potential to reduce mortality across all demographics; however, advocates placed an additional emphasis on impoverished communities where maternal and infant death were often the highest. In his discussion of Sanger's pamphlet *Family Limitation* in 1915, Judge William N. Gatens of the Circuit Court in Portland, Oregon, argued, "The prevention of child mortality is, when boiled down, largely a problem in the prevention of poverty."[68] In her 1927 speech before the World Population Council, Sanger provided numerical support for Gatens's claim explaining that of the 250,000 children annually who died before they turned one, "90 percent of these die from causes due to poverty and neglect" despite the work of the Children's Bureau to provide free milk, food, and medical care for those unable to afford it.[69] The ABCL reached a similar conclusion in their 1925 review of clinic patients, explaining, "the relation of births and of infant deaths" as well as "the frequency of induced abortions" were directly related to income and were far more prevalent among the poorer classes.[70] Given the expense of raising children, Sanger suggested, "Abortion becomes therefore less a problem of morality than of economic necessity."[71] Poverty accelerated the desperation felt by women transforming abortion into a cost-effective solution to their untenable situation.

While economic impulses drove people to seek out abortion, the practice of birth control promised to alleviate these concerns and raise the standard of living for the entire family. A June 1935 Progress Report from the Birth Control Clinical Research Bureau proclaimed: "The physical health of mother, father, and children is improved by regulating the size of the family by means of spacing and planned pregnancies, which relieve the economic burden and allow a higher living standard."[72] The possibility of improved standards of living among poor families resonated with many of the movement's key stakeholders. An article jointly written by Dr. Antoinette Konikow, Dr. Evangeline W. Young, Reverend Monsignor M. J. Splaine, and social worker Mary K. O'Sullivan, demonstrates its wide appeal. Writing for the *Boston Daily Globe* in 1915, they implore: "the man of limited income should have only as many children as he can properly feed and care for, and that, therefore, he should have information as to harmless and intelligent methods for controlling the size of his family."[73] Adamant about a father's responsibility to provide for their dependent wife and children, advocates insisted all childbearing decisions be directly tied to income. These moves also rhetorically solidified the heteronormative family structure supported by the separate spheres doctrine as the ideal as fathers alone bore the financial burden.

RESPONSIBLE PARENTAGE

Considering the myriad factors contributing to maternal and infant mortality, advocates devised simple guidelines for child spacing to solve the frightful problems facing large families and bolster their concept of responsible parentage. Sanger enumerated these guidelines in her 1940 address at the Community Church of Boston, stating, "The first consideration should and must be the woman's health; the second, the father's earning ability; the third, the standards of living for the parents and children; the fourth, which [could] well be the first—the quality of life to be passed on to the children."[74] Advising reproduction only in situations where all four conditions were met mitigated the health and financial strain shouldered by large families, removed the desperation thrusting parents toward infanticide and abortion, and ensured children were conceived only when they were wanted and could be adequately cared for.

The refrain of responsibility also communicated the deference of women to the needs of their children and reiterated the benevolence of child spacing.

Dr. Douglas White suggested in 1930 that "responsible parenthood ought to consider both the spacing of children and the economics of the family."[75] *Los Angeles Times* columnist Fred Hogue reiterated Sanger's spacing recommendations and argued adherence "enables women to space their children, thus conserving their health and giving the greatest assurance that children will be born with a full endowment of health."[76] Hogue's statement also reaffirms the subservient relationship between mother and child established by advocates wherein a woman's life is more worthy of protecting because of the consequences its deterioration has on her children.

The movement's clear directives on child spacing buoyed its emphasis on responsible parentage by affirming the purpose of contraception to regulate and not eliminate reproduction. While advocating for the adoption of a "Mother's Bill of Rights" in 1931, Sanger explained the aim "was to amend federal laws so that motherhood shall be conscious and controlled."[77] Relying on an interpretation of motherhood as natural and inevitable, birth controllers pushed back against the countervailing narrative often perpetuated by religious conservatives of contraception as the province of selfish women wishing to live a life of leisure. Women seeking birth control weren't selfishly trying to stave off motherhood for personal reasons, they were desperate to avoid miscarriage, abortion, and death from yet another pregnancy. Sanger's disavowal of the selfish woman in 1935 is illustrative:

> To say that it is practiced for selfish motives is not true. The desire for birth control knowledge and its practice comes from a higher and much more permanent cause than that. It is due to increased respect for the sanctity of life and an increased regard for the welfare and education of children. Such parents are inspired by the hope that by having fewer children whom they can educate and properly care for, that they may help them escape the grinding poverty and hardships they themselves have endured due to the accident of birth.[78]

Appealing to the colloquial idea that all parents wish to provide a better life for their children than they had, Sanger pinpoints this motivation and not selfishness as the driving justification to practice birth control, thus demonstrating a higher regard for the sanctity of life. This attitude is not exclusive to "good" mothers either; Sanger argued in her 1917 prison journal, "Even the most inferior mother has too much mother-love to desire to bring into the world a child who will cause her grief instead of joy."[79] As will be further explored in chapter 4, placing the practice of birth control within a framework of benevolent and responsible parenthood allowed advocates to distance themselves from the opposition framing of birth control as anti-life by highlighting the respect for life motivating people to seek contraception.

The notion of responsible parentage resonated even with people traditionally opposed to the birth control movement. The defense of birth control offered by poet and Anglican priest G. A. Studdert Kennedy in 1927 points to the efficacy of this rhetorical strategy. Kennedy explains, "to thwart and starve the parental impulse [through] selfish and immoral birth control . . . is one of the chief reasons why moralists . . . [attempt] to prohibit birth control of any sort." Although Kennedy is unwilling to blanketly endorse birth control, he bluntly declares it essential for married couples to responsibly build their families. Kennedy furthers, "knowledge of the best, most effective, and most hygienic methods ought to be made easily accessible to every married couple [and] careful teaching as to the responsibility involved ought to be part of the preparation for marriage." Kennedy's rhetoric operationalizes the concept of responsibility and concedes the desirability of allowing "fathers and mothers [to] act together after careful consideration, and with sound medical advice, as seems to them best for their several families."[80] Others also took note of the distinction between regulation and elimination; in their report on a speech given by Sanger in 1917, the *Chicago Daily Tribune* applauded Sanger for "drawing a clear distinction between birth control and non-conception."[81] Alma Whitaker, staff writer for the *Los Angeles Times*, repeated the motherhood mantra almost verbatim, noting, "birth controllers claim that the normal woman wants children if she can have them under decent conditions, and not too many of them."[82] Taken together, advocates put forth a vision of responsible parenthood steeped in maternalists' ideology compelling to a broad audience. This rhetorical strategy paid dividends with groups once oppositional to the birth control movement by demonstrating their commitment to traditional values and the preservation of the heteronormative family unit.

FIGHT BETWEEN BIRTH CONTROLLERS AND MATERNALISTS

Despite their vocalized support for the maternalist agenda and repeated attempts to align contraceptive instruction with the goals of the Children's Bureau, Julia Lathrop and associates refused to recognize the upstream potential of contraception to alleviate infant and maternal mortality focusing instead on palliative measures and educational programs for mothers. Growing increasingly frustrated with the Children's Bureau's indifference, the BCCRB pleaded:

> As citizens and taxpayers we should ask the agency entrusted with the administration of the Maternal and Child Health services of our country to see

> that Birth Control information is given to those mothers who for physical or economic reasons ought not to become pregnant. It is a fundamental medical service which is most important for the health and happiness of this generation and the next. . . . Let us ask the Children's Bureau to include Birth Control in its fight for "Betterment of Mothers and Babies," as a means of reducing infant and maternal mortality through proper spacing of children; and to reduce the number of abortions for which women risk their health, welfare, and lives; and most important of all to give every child the priceless heritage of coming into this world a wanted child.[83]

Yet, even within this harsh rebuke of the Children's Bureau, the BCCRB performs important rhetorical work to explicate their value in the current political climate. In one succinct paragraph, the BCCRB defends both the practical value of contraception as "a fundamental medical service" with the "means of reducing infant and maternal mortality" and as societal necessity "for the health and happiness of this generation and the next" more fitting of taxpayer dollars than the current offerings of the Bureau.

The conflict between birth controllers and maternalists came to a head over the Sheppard-Towner Maternity and Infancy Protection Act (STA). Passed in 1921, the STA provided federal grants to states for the development of educational programs concerning prenatal health and infant care, many of which were facilitated by the Children's Bureau. The disagreement over the STA is indicative of the fragmented view of maternalism Sanger and others embraced. Whereas those within the Children's Bureau sought to eliminate the suffering of women and prevent maternal and infant mortality, they pursued interventionist strategies aimed at increasing the quality of care rather than the preventative measures preferred by birth controllers. Their reticence stemmed from widely held concerns about delayed marriages, childless marriages, and race suicide. Their hope was that in making motherhood a safer and more attractive enterprise via government assistance, women would continue to maintain high levels of childbearing but with lower levels of mortality. Sanger stood firm in her view of large families as dangerous and unsustainable for most American families.

Advocates of the STA demanded birth control information be excluded from Section 9, enabling organizations to provide nontechnical instruction on matters related to maternity, infancy, and related subjects, and going as far as to label contraceptive information as "propaganda." An article in the *Woman Patriot* defended proponents of the bill who "vigorously denied that there was any connection whatever between this 'Baby Bill' and the 'Birth Control' movement." At the heart of their objection was the belief that contraceptive instruction dramatically reduced the number of births by encouraging girls to delay motherhood. The *Woman Patriot* continues, "The 'Birth Control' movement, like all the other isms, pretends to benefit the human race. The fact that its propaganda is frequently carried on among young girls . . . shows just what it is."[84] Proponents of the STA loaded their criticism of contraception with well-worn attacks positioning birth control as a moral threat to the institution of marriage and an endorsement of childlessness. Katherine Mahoney, speaking on behalf of 35,000 Catholic women during a New York State hearing over the Sheppard-Towner Act in 1922 boldly proclaimed: "It opens the door to all kinds of vicious propaganda, including birth control and sex hygiene. It encourages sex immorality, for it induces young men and young women to defer marriage as long as possible. It fosters the empty cradle by pressing young people to prevent the coming of children whom they fear they cannot properly rear."[85]

Even as birth controllers persuasively presented contraception as a tool to facilitate the full development of women into better mothers more likely to have children and better suited to care for larger families, maternalists continued to vilify the birth control movement. Robyn Rosen speaks to the strategic importance of these actions and argues the passage of the STA was "at least partially predicated on its distance from the birth control movement throughout the 1920s."[86] Rosen elaborates, "maternal and infant welfare activists in the Children's Bureau decried any association with birth control. They had learned to fight for programs and privileges on the basis of the sanctity of motherhood and the family. Consequently, they took great pains to position birth control outside the parameters of legitimate programs and policies."[87] Even though the espousal of maternalist ideologies signaled a softening of the once radical tactics of advocates like Sanger, the reputation of sensationalism created by her early acts of agitation tainted the movement's ability to forge coalitions with progressive movements premised on the sanctity of motherhood and value of white womanhood. Maternalists, just as suffragists had previously, remained reluctant to endorsing the birth control agenda fearful that doing so would compromise their own agendas. This sentiment was echoed by the National League of Women Voters who explained to the *New York Times* in 1922, "The general feeling on the subject on the study of dissemination of birth control information was that it was not only not within the province of the league but also that any positive action might jeopardize the league's influence in fighting for Federal legislation similar to the Sheppard-Towner Maternity and Infancy act."[88] Not unlike the opposition Dennett faced with legislators unwilling to engage the topic given its lurid past, many progressive feminists shirked the birth control movement for fear that its reputation would hinder their own efforts.

Excluded from both the conversation and the funding stream, birth controllers funneled their energy into establishing a clinic initiative prioritizing contraceptive instruction. To this end, the National Birth Control League

(NBCL) provided financing to Dr. Robert Latou Dickinson, former president of the American Gynecological Society, to establish the Committee on Maternal Health in 1923 while the American Birth Control League (ABCL) established the Birth Control Clinical Research Bureau (BCCRB) later that year. These efforts mirrored the research focus of the Children's Bureau and channeled the movement's energy into the provision of services for women. Sanger boasted of the BCCRB's triumph, noting, "it has demonstrated the success of a new way to solve old problems. The old method of the printed word through leaflets, booklets and pamphlets has been abolished and the Clinic with a physician and nurse as instructor have taken its place."[89] This initiative, explored in detail in chapter 5, further augmented Sanger's push for doctors-only bills by cementing the role of medical professionals in the birth control movement. Perhaps more importantly, Sanger's inclusion of Dickinson and continued medicalization of contraception appeased the American Medical Association (AMA) who only reluctantly signed off on the STA in 1921 after the Children's Bureau agreed to provide educational resources only and not medical care in their clinics.

During the contentious renewal phase for the STA between 1927 and 1929, Sanger advocated on behalf of the STA but with her signature demand for contraception and insistence on medicalization. Sanger asserts:

> No branch of medicine needs public help so much as obstetrics, that "most backward of the medical sciences." The value of the public help already given is shown by the cut of more than ten percent in the infant death rate. The need of still more fundamental help, going back to the period before conception, is indicated by the fact that the mother's death rate has shown no such cut. That the mothers continue to die in practically the same proportions is brought sharply and often to the public attention. The next task before state and federal health authorities is to save mothers. This can be done by wiping out anti-Birth Control legislation and using the nationwide machinery of the Children's Bureau, now set up in forty-five states and one territory, to spread adequate, standardized methods of Birth Control.[90]

Sanger's claim is quite clever here in so far as she advocates for utilizing the "machinery of the Children's Bureau" not for the continuation of their programs, which she admits have been successful in lowering infant mortality, but instead for teaching preventative methods she deems as "more fundamental." The true tell in Sanger's statement is the invocation of the medical sciences and their expertise to best address maternal and infant health—both of which are a direct appeal to the very doctors who opposed the Sheppard-Towner Act and the Children's Bureau. Despite an initial agreement between the Children's Bureau and the AMA drawing clear boundaries for the services provided by the organization, as the Children's Bureau grew, so did the ire of the medical community. Rosen explains, "By the mid-1920s, obstetricians and pediatricians began to voice opposition to the continuation of Sheppard-Towner, suggesting maternal and infant mortality would best be reduced by improved medical training, facilities, and access to practitioners."[91] Sanger's recommendation to use the clinic infrastructure of the Children's Bureau to further develop doctor-led maternal and infant care was thus a well-timed olive branch to the medical community whose support was critical to furthering the birth control cause.

The AMA's opposition combined with growing skepticism of government-funded programs fueled by anti-socialist sentiments was enough to prevent the STA's renewal. Without matching funds from the federal level and oversight provided by the Children's Bureau, its initiatives slowly drew to a close. The inability to insert contraceptive instruction into the Children's Bureau's programs does not invalidate Sanger's strategic uptake of the maternalist agenda. On the contrary, the rhetoric of birth controllers specifically concerning mortality, abortion, and scientific motherhood enabled Sanger to further cozy up to the medical professionals responsible for the downfall of the Children's Bureau. While the AMA drew harsh territorial boundaries with the Children's Bureau, Sanger not only welcomed doctors in her clinics but gave them top billing in the provision of contraceptive information. These efforts, explored further in chapter 5, furthered the medicalization of both contraception and motherhood—a move which doctors greeted with open arms. Sanger's consistent deference to the medical community paid off in 1924 when then president of the American Medical Association (AMA) William Allen Pusey offered an official endorsement of birth control, albeit a mild one, at the International Neo-Malthusian and Birth Control Conference in New York City.[92]

Birth controllers recognized an opportunity to capitalize on the groundswell surrounding maternal and infant mortality created by the Children's Bureau and the Sheppard-Towner Act and strategically deployed maternalists' rhetoric to align their objectives. Yet, as the relationship grew increasingly tense, it became clear that advocates would need to repurpose their maternalist arguments to court a different audience—doctors. Historian Carole McCann elaborates, "The Birth Control Movement without great support among welfare feminists had little chance of [advancing their agenda] without some accommodation of physicians' interests."[93] The movement's deployment of motherhood as a terministic screen thus signals two different attempts at political accommodation—maternalists and doctors—and illuminates the malleability of the movement's rhetoric to accomplish its goals. In both instances, the emancipatory possibilities of birth control are shelved to make room for rhetoric that honors traditional femininity and male superiority.

WHERE'S MARY WARE DENNETT?

Despite her outspokenness on the legality of contraception, Dennett remained noticeably silent concerning the work of the Children's Bureau generally and the clinic initiatives of both the Children's Bureau and the Birth Control Clinical Research Bureau specifically. Dennett's silence does not reflect a waning interest in the movement, but rather a concerted focus on the legislative reforms described at length in chapter 1. As was the case with her derision toward doctors-only bills, Dennett's rejection of maternalism is indicative of her ideological commitments to equality, autonomy, and personal liberty. Her rhetoric during this time period merits examination as a counterpoint to the maternalist rhetoric prominent within the interwar years and, perhaps more importantly, as a foil to the use of motherhood as a terministic screen.

Dennett expressed disdain with maternalists and took umbrage with their reliance on the logic of separate spheres that, in her opinion, exacerbated the struggle for equality by emphasizing gender difference rather than sameness. In an opinion piece written for *The Century* in 1915 entitled "The Right of a Child to Two Parents," Dennett details her challenge to the separate spheres system and boldly questions its utility for both the family and society as a whole. She elucidates:

> Children are mostly brought up by their mothers, an arrangement which the world has accepted without question for centuries. But now, owing to the social ferment which, whether we like it or not, is disturbing women's traditional sphere, we find ourselves asking if that scheme of child-rearing is really best for the children, best for the mothers, and finally if it is best for the fathers. Everyone would admit the ideal way to be one that would be equally good for all three—good as to immediate results, and good in the long run as well. . . .
>
> As it is now, the father specializes on earning, the mother on personal service, with the result that the children get very false ideas in regard to the intrinsic and relative values of human effort. They cannot help acquiring the impression that the father's position is one of superiority and advantage, despite the polite effort made by all to envelop the mother's work so thickly in sentiment that its essential dependence and narrowness will not show. Earning money and rendering personal service are each admirable in their way, but it is possible to have too much of a good thing, and neither is satisfactory as an exclusive life work. . . .
>
> They do not, as we have vainly tried to assume, form the equal halves of a true domestic partnership, and that is why it will never do to have women devote themselves wholly to the one and men to the other. If they *were* comparable on a basis of equality, then it would not seem preposterous to men to turn things about, and to be economically dependent themselves and devote their own lives to personal family service. There is probably not a man in the country but would feel his self-respect affronted at the mere suggestion of such a thing, which of

> course only reveals the fact that there must be something radically wrong with the position of the average mother. . . .
>
> Social justice, then, would seem to be the one thing upon which the perfection of family life is literally and virtually dependent. Granted the possibility of securing it, think what it would mean to all concerned. It would give mothers their first chance in ages for a long breath and time to catch up; it would give men the surest guaranty in all history for deepening their own characters, for becoming truly civilized; and it would give children the untold benefit of fathering as well as mothering. . . .
>
> Child-rearing and home-making should be human work, not limited to either sex, but undertaken jointly and equally by both. If bringing up children is really a serious, inspiring work, as we are assured it is, then by all means the men should not be barred out from its beneficent reactions. It is not possible for the same work to be broadening and beautifying if women do it, and petty and inconsequential if men do it.[94]

Dennett's rhetoric here is quite incendiary and represents a marked departure from the praise lofted onto housewives and their provider husbands by Sanger. Not only does Dennett question both the practicality and desirability of the traditional arrangement espoused by maternalists, she boldly condemns it for inculcating patriarchal values eroding any semblance of equality between the sexes. While maternalists embraced a separate but equal posture to the division of labor within the home, Dennett astutely observes equality is impossible in this configuration because of the inevitable valuations assigned to each form of work. Taking her critique one step further, Dennett borrows a tool from the maternalists' playbook by centering the child's welfare and argues the best situation for the child is to have the untold benefit of mothering *and* fathering. Reiterating her humanist ideologies, Dennett insists child-rearing and homemaking are not the exclusive domain of women—they are not mother-work; they are *human work.*

Dennett acknowledges the grim reality facing American women and their families in the early twentieth century but in doing so, rarely deploys maternalist tropes. When discussing the consequences of unrestrained reproduction, Sanger focuses almost exclusively on the losses felt by women as mothers such as the inability to care for their children; even the phrase "maternal mortality" centers the woman's role as a mother in her death. Dennett, however, positions motherhood as the antagonist and even acknowledges a woman's role as a potential laborer writing, "had the woman known how to protect herself from further motherhood, she might have stood a chance for health, a fair earning capacity, and opportunity for her existing children."[95] Dennett's seemingly simple acknowledgment of a woman's earning capacity is significant in so far as it shatters the separate spheres doctrine undergirding the movement's articulation of responsible parentage and makes space for women who do not adhere to the maternal ideal advanced by the mainstream movement.

Although appealing to similar concerns as Sanger, namely health and future children, Dennett's language is plain and avoids inflating the status of motherhood. Dennett's rhetoric intensifies when discussing the societal toll of the problem; she bemoans, "One finds a fearful number of widows left with five to eight children, born so close together that the mother's strength and father's earnings have been so sapped that charity must step in to save the home. Many instances of the unwanted, abandoned babies who have unknown fathers and irresponsible mothers, an endless stream of misery that might have been avoided if the parents had only known."[96] To label a mother as irresponsible is a drastic departure from the maternalist ethos but one that reiterates Dennett's commitment to the concepts of individual autonomy and its accompanying responsibilities. Far from placing the sole source of blame on the parents, Dennett pinpoints a lack of knowledge as the culprit. She pleads, "the law stands in the way of their knowing. Changing the law cannot help most of these present unfortunates . . . but it can help innumerable thousands to avoid these tragedies next year."[97] Women and their families were suffering not of their own volition, but because society denied them the necessary information to improve their condition.

For Dennett, the question of contraception was not premised on what was best for mothers but rather on what was *right.* According to Rosen, Dennett made "a conscious decision to eschew maternalist politics" by framing her advocacy around "a fight for liberty, rather than a push for social welfare" and focusing "on questions of access rather than on demands for the provision of goods and services."[98] Unlike Sanger who relentlessly pushed birth control as the solution to issues of maternal and infant mortality, abortion, and poverty, Dennett rarely espoused the benefits of contraceptive instruction directly and instead steadfastly focused on legalizing access to information. At a special meeting of the National Conference of Social Work in Atlantic City on June 5, 1919, reformers including Helen Todd representing the *Birth Control Review*, Frances Bjorkman of the National Birth Control League, and Mary Ware Dennett of the Voluntary Parenthood Association were asked to speak regarding the issues. The two women espoused the need for increased clinics and medical instruction so as to "remove from the minds of women, particularly of the working class, the cloud of fear which hangs over them that they will be driven to reproduce the undernourished and the unfortunate"; Dennett, however, used her time to describe "the laws which prevent all intelligent understanding of the reproductive forces of life, and of the need for their removal."[99]Always the idealist, Dennett never missed the chance to drum up support for her legislative efforts.

In contrast to advocates like Sanger who openly promoted, and at times provided, contraceptive information, Dennett refrained from taking such a definitive stance. When pressed by legislators on methods to prevent conception, Dennett quickly clarified, "we make it plain that the question of methods is the sphere of the medical scientists, this it is not for us laymen to presume to teach, and much less it is possible for the laws to determine methods. All the laws can do is to give freedom to the scientists to give the world."[100] Even when contacted directly for guidance, Dennett refused and asked instead for their help in the fight for legalization. "It is absolutely illegal to mail any contraceptive information. . . . This is why it is time to repeal [the laws]. I hope you will help us accomplish it. . . . . I hope you will get [the information] in spite of the laws. Have you asked your own physician?"[101] Unwavering from her ideological commitment to autonomy and liberty, Dennett even refused to flatly endorse family planning and instead defended only the right to access information and not the desirability of its application. Dennett proclaims, "whether people make use of the information or not, is their own private concern. People can preach and teach and act exactly in accord with their own idea. But they can then, for the first time, be legally free to weigh the relative merits of unlimited and undetermined reproduction and self-determined parenthood achieved by the application of scientific knowledge."[102] Rosen concludes, "where maternalists and feminists homed in on women's suffering and women's rights respectively, Dennett's liberalism targeted more universal concepts such as democratic access to information and the setting of reasonable limits for state power."[103]

Dennett's activist history sheds light on her refusal to espouse maternalists ideas and reliance on systemic arguments premised on individual liberty. Dennett came to the movement with a long history of advocacy work in progressive organizations including the National Women's Suffrage Association and the Women's Peace Party. Though disparate in focus, Dennett's interest in these organizations stemmed from a deep ideological commitment to liberalism which propelled her to fight for individual liberty and against government intrusions into one's personal life. Even in advocating for woman suffrage, Dennett shirks traditional feminist refrains asserting the inherent value of women voters and plainly argues they meet all minimum qualifications to vote. Writing in the *New York Times* in 1914 Dennett retorts, "We could be kept busy overqualifying [*sic*] clean up to the millennium, for even then there would be some carping soul who would be sure that we were not yet quite ready for the vote," while at the same time "hordes of young men who had for years been casting their first votes, all unprepared, expected they were 21 and native or naturalized continue to vote."[104]

Prior to joining the battle for birth control, Dennett ardently defended the importance of voluntary motherhood and channeled her efforts into the

Twilight Sleep Association (TSA). Organized in 1915, the TSA advocated for widespread education about and use of the Frieburg Method of labor and delivery wherein women were anesthetized with a scopolamine-morphine mixture to alleviate the pain of childbirth. Dennett, who was elected to serve as the first vice president of the TSA, envisioned Twilight Sleep as "rested in women's desire for choice" and thus "a natural extension of the broader women's rights movement" with whom she had been actively involved.[105] As was often the case with Dennett, her advocacy for Twilight Sleep was not so much about the actual experiences of women, in this case the excruciating pain of childbirth, but was focused on expanding the autonomy of women to make their own choices regarding their bodies. So, while Dennett frequently invoked the experiences of motherhood in her rhetoric, she separated herself from Maternalists by focusing on the needs of women as autonomous individuals rather than helpless mothers.

With Dennett committed to securing individual bodily autonomy via legislative reforms and altogether unconcerned with the work of The Children's Bureau, Sanger again assumed top billing in the movement and readily adopted maternalist rhetoric to strategically align with progressive reformers. Buerkle's work synthesizes this maternalist focus and points to the messy consequences of Sanger's prevailing strategy. He ponders, "The quandary that Sanger's rhetoric raises is the expense women can afford by engaging a rhetoric of good motherhood as a means to gaining freedoms that carry personal benefit. The maternal themes Sanger uses temper an otherwise dramatic reordering of women's status in society, yet the challenges to restrictions on birth control remain alive and well."[106] In her rejection of the separate spheres doctrine and demands for individual liberty, Dennett defended the dramatic reordering of women's lives while Sanger fortified the traditional division of labor and aggrandized motherhood. Dennett's bold advocacy won her favor within liberal circles like the ACLU but did little to move the needle on birth control, whereas Sanger's enshrinement of mothers curried favor with maternalists and doctors willing to help mothers but altogether resistant to broader social change.

THE LASTING CONSEQUENCE: MOTHERHOOD AS A TERMINISTIC SCREEN

The divergent stances of Dennett and Sanger on maternalism and the mobilization of contraceptive information in the interwar years further exemplifies their dissimilitude regarding the mechanistic and idealistic functions of birth control discussed in chapter 1. Reading Sanger's "The Business of Bearing Babies" alongside Dennett's "The Right of a Child to Two Parents," it's hard to believe that the two authors were even fighting for the same cause. While both women write of fanciful familial situations they believed tangible with the help of contraception, the worlds they envision are remarkably different and reveal each author's respective commitment to either control or choice. Dennett, enthralled with the idealistic function of contraception, speaks of the heroism required to rebalance the caregiving responsibilities between mother and father and reminds willing parents of "the inspiration and compensation of helping to erect a milestone on the road to civilization marked, 'At this point children began to have two *real* parents.'"[107] Moving beyond the immediacy of reproduction, Dennett conceptualizes a new reality wherein the iniquity and inequality of the existing heteronormative system are ameliorated by the ability to make different choices. In this way, Dennett's rejection of maternalist rhetoric serves as an extension of her ideological commitment to the willed pregnancy. Sanger, enamored with the mechanistic function of contraception, glorifies heightened levels of control within the family that now operates like a business complete with "keeping the books of motherhood and starting budgets for babies, computing the cost of the overhead, and seeking to cut down waste and inefficiency."[108] Just as she did with maternal health and mortality, child welfare, abortion, and a father's earning power, Sanger emphasizes the tangible benefits accrued through regulating reproduction, making her maternalist rhetoric an extension of the instrumentalist view of reproductive rights.

The birth control movement's uptake of maternalist rhetoric signaled a new phase of political accommodation, this time to a growing group of advocates concerned with maternal health and child welfare. Although unsuccessful in winning over maternalists in the Children's Bureau, this strategy paid dividends with both doctors increasingly troubled by mortality rates and with detractors distressed by contraception's anti-child mythos. The efficacy of these rhetorical tactics validated Sanger's choice to transform the movement's once antagonistic message into a commonsense plea steeped in the dominant discourses of utilitarianism, societal welfare, and the preservation of traditional roles within the family. As explored in later chapters, these discourses quickly became a template for advocates seeking to forge coalitions with conservative allies largely unconcerned with women's bodily autonomy but deeply invested in the principles of population control and the preservation of the maternal ideal.

Yet, the movement's use of motherhood as a terministic screen through which we understand reproductive rights is deeply problematic in so far as it invites a singular understanding of contraceptive users as wives who want children but not yet and/or not too many. It elevates the traditional heteronormative family structure as ideal. It presents children as an inevitability rather than a possibility. It establishes the value of women's bodies in service not to themselves but to their children. It suggests that concern for women's health is governed almost exclusively by her reproductive capacity. This terministic screen occludes other considerations for contraceptive use and depreciates the experiences of women not directly tied to motherhood and stands in direct opposition to one of the foundational tenets of reproductive justice which "posits that intersecting forces produce differing reproductive experiences that shape each individual's life" thus "requiring different considerations to achieve reproductive justice."[109] Ultimately, the terministic screen of motherhood functioned as a tool of essentialism obscuring the nuanced experiences of women produced by structural and systemic inequities in favor of a universalist image of women whose lack of contraceptive information was the only hinderance to their ascension to the maternal ideal.

The ideal of motherhood crafted by birth controllers reflected a deep commitment to heteronormative value structures that relied on the gendered division of labor wherein child-rearing was the exclusive province of women. Albeit motivated by a desire to restore honor to the profession of motherhood, this narrow conceptualization of women's role within the family unit reinforces the very patriarchal structures that devalue women's work and codifies the inevitability of motherhood. Birth controllers labeled maternal desire as innate and motherhood as the most natural state of being for women. Even as she matures and develops, she does so with the implied ambition of excelling as a wife and mother. The Supreme Court's rhetoric when deciding the landmark case *Griswold v. Connecticut* legalizing contraception for married couples is illustrative. The words woman/women appear only once. Instead, women are exclusively referred to as "wife." The court's ruling that the government shall not interfere with "the marital right to bear children and raise a family" deploys the same deterministic rhetoric affirming both the heteronormative relationship and the inevitability of children. Legal scholar Martha Fineman elucidates the lingering consequences of the legal primacy given to traditional mothers in this context. She contends:

> Paramount among these is, of course, the strong preference for formally celebrated heterosexual marriage that functions as a reproductive unit and is thus the "core" upon which all else is founded. This preference places responsible reproduction (indeed, responsible sexuality) solely within the context of the traditional family—a context in which legal consequences are clear and decisions will be considered and controlled. Motherhood outside this family unit will be punished and stigmatized. Nonmothers will also be disciplined, pressured and pitied.[110]

Implicit within Fineman's statement is the prescient reminder that women are always defined by their maternal status—future mothers, mothers, or nonmothers. The maternalist rhetoric of birth controllers not only facilitated this categorization, it capitalized on it to craft an image of women suited to its strategic goals to the detriment of women's full autonomy as human beings regardless of their reproductive capacity.

The remaining chapters go beyond maternalism to explore the other rhetorical strategies and stakeholders that comprise the birth control movement, yet even those disparate discourses cannot escape the terministic screen of motherhood crafted by advocates in the interwar years. The discussion in chapter 3 is about the new opportunities for women facilitated by contraception being inseparable from the terministic screen of motherhood as the choice to pursue these opportunities is simultaneously a choice to reject the idealized view of motherhood put forth in this chapter. New ways of being are imagined, but the lingering exaltation of motherhood haunts these possibilities and serves as a mechanism to police women's sexuality, ambition, and identity. The reduction of women to their reproductive capacity seeps into the discussions of children and their supposed right to be wanted and well born that takes place in chapter 4. The solidified relationship between maternal health and infant health is weaponized to facilitate the dangerous eugenic conversations concerning which women are "fit" for motherhood explored in chapter 5. And in chapters 6 and 7, motherhood remains a salient framework used by the state to both demarcate the boundaries of reproductive rights and inform their limited efforts at expanding contraceptive access. In her attempt to free motherhood from bondage, Sanger inadvertently created new bonds for women that still tie her worth to her motherhood potential.

NOTES

1. Sanger, *Motherhood in Bondage*, 54–55.
2. Ibid., 41.
3. Linder and Grove, *Vital Statistics Rates*, 49.
4. Ladd-Taylor, *Mother-Work,* 18.
5. Sanger, *Motherhood in Bondage*, xlvi.
6. "The Bookshelf," 34.
7. Ibid.
8. "What We Do," 15.
9. Sanger, "The Editor's Uneasy Chair," 12. The phrase "Brockton babies" is a reference to babies born in the small town of Brockton, Massachusetts, wherein specific conditions were required of parents prior to bearing children. These requirements included financial stability, access to medical care, literacy of both parents, and a clean not overcrowded residence for the family. These conditions are consistent with those later advanced by Sanger in her "Children's Bill of Rights" and are regularly discussed as preconditions for responsible parentage.

10. Rosen, "Federal Expansion," 55.
11. Ladd-Taylor, *Mother-Work*, 33.
12. Ibid., 110.
13. Margaret Sanger Papers, 236170.
14. Blakesley, "Terministic Screens," 1745.
15. Sanger, "Women and Birth," 533.
16. A. B. S., "Saving the Mothers," 300.
17. "Editorial Comment," 9.
18. Margaret Sanger Papers, 236132.
19. Margaret Sanger Papers, 229968.
20. Margaret Sanger Papers, 236021.
21. Margaret Sanger Papers, 236022.
22. Sanger, "Birth Control and Racial," 11.
23. Woodbury, *Maternal Mortality*, 24.
24. Ibid., 26
25. Margaret Sanger Papers, 236132.
26. Sanger, "Sexual Adjustment," 1.
27. Baber, "Birth Control," 295.
28. "Physicians Split," 25.
29. Ibid.
30. Margaret Sanger Papers, 227560.
31. Margaret Sanger Papers, 232979.
32. Margaret Sanger Papers, 236132.
33. Ladd-Taylor, *Mother-Work*, 45.
34. Margaret Sanger Papers, 236170.
35. Margaret Sanger Papers, 236502.
36. Margaret Sanger Papers, 224706.
37. Margaret Sanger Papers, 236132; Margaret Sanger Papers, 236141.
38. Margaret Sanger Papers, 226268.
39. Margaret Sanger Papers, 236191.
40. Buerkle, "From Women's Liberation," 30.
41. Margaret Sanger Papers, 222421.
42. Ibid.
43. Margaret Sanger Papers, 237335.
44. Margaret Sanger Papers, 236021.
45. Margaret Sanger Papers, 237335; Margaret Sanger Papers, 224706.
46. "U.S. Security Seen," 12.
47. Margaret Sanger Papers, 236021.
48. Sanger, "The Eugenic Value," 5.
49. Margaret Sanger Papers, 236021.
50. Ladd-Taylor, *Mother-Work*, 33.
51. "Scientific Motherhood," 994.
52. Zueblin, "MOTHERS FIRST," 4.
53. Ladd-Taylor, *Mother-Work*, 4.
54. Sanger, *Motherhood in Bondage*, 250.

55. Ibid., 246.
56. M. K., "Income and Infant," 9.
57. "The Battle over," 340.
58. Margaret Sanger Papers, 239180.
59. Sanger, *Motherhood in Bondage*, 251.
60. Margaret Sanger Papers, 224706.
61. Margaret Sanger Papers, 236191.
62. Margaret Sanger Papers, 201364.
63. Margaret Sanger Papers, 236089.
64. Ibid.
65. Boughton, "What 7309 Mothers," 10.
66. Margaret Sanger Papers, 232979.
67. Margaret Sanger Papers, 236170.
68. "The Battle over," 340.
69. Margaret Sanger Papers, 236134.
70. Margaret Sanger Papers, 223089.
71. Margaret Sanger Papers, 236390.
72. Margaret Sanger Papers, 229659.
73. Young et al., "Do the Poor," 46.
74. Margaret Sanger Papers, 226564.
75. "Birth Control Held," 7.
76. Hogue, "Social Eugenics," I19.
77. Sanger, "Birth Control Steps," 1.
78. Margaret Sanger Papers, 236179.
79. Margaret Sanger Papers, 224706.
80. Kennedy, "Is Birth Control Right?" 14–15.
81. "Mrs. Sanger May," 17.
82. Whitaker, "The Birth Controllers," II4.
83. Margaret Sanger Papers, 227560.
84. "'Birth Control' Propaganda," 4.
85. "Women Urge State," 17.
86. Rosen, *Reproductive Health*, 81.
87. Ibid.
88. "Women in Clash," 12.
89. Margaret Sanger Papers, 2297.
90. "Editorial," 99.
91. Rosen, "Federal Expansion," 61.
92. Gordon, *The Moral Property*, 182; McCann, *Birth Control Politics*, 94. The AMA refused to endorse the clinic movement and reaffirmed its position that contraceptives should only be prescribed when medically necessary.
93. McCann, *Birth Control*, 68.
94. Dennett, "The Right of," 108.
95. Dennett, "'Not Fit to Print,'" 17.
96. Dennett, "Voluntary Parenthood Bill," 16.
97. Ibid.

98. Rosen, *Reproductive Health*, 107.
99. "Hard Facts," 12.
100. Dennett, "Legislators, Six-Hour,"4.
101. Dennett's response is quoted in Rosen, *Reproductive Health*, 93–94.
102. Dennett, "Voluntary Parenthood," 12.
103. Rosen, *Reproductive Health*, 73.
104. Dennett, "Fitness for Suffrage," 10.
105. Thompson, "The Politics of Female," 71.
106. Buerkle, "From Women's Liberation," 33.
107. Dennett, "The Right of," 108.
108. Margaret Sanger Papers, 236170.
109. Ross et al., *Radical Reproductive*, 19.
110. Fineman, "Masking Dependency," 2197–98.

Chapter Three

Think of the Children

On November 12, 1915, Anna and Allen Bollinger gave birth to their fourth child, John, at the German American Hospital in Chicago, Illinois. Unlike the joy accompanying her previous deliveries, this time she felt only distress. Moments after what was by all accounts a standard delivery, Mrs. Bollinger was informed of her child's dire medical condition. Baby Bollinger, as he came to be known, arrived with numerous congenital issues which the attending physician, Dr. Henry J. Haiselden vividly described in The Detroit Times. *Haiselden laments, "a child has been born without one ear; the ear it has will never hear, there being no auditory canal; the head is set deep into the shoulders without sign of a neck; it would take the most delicate of operations to permit the abdominal organs to perform their functions."*[1] *Anna was heartbroken and equally concerned about the quality of life possible for her child. After agonizing over their options, the Bollinger's agreed to follow Dr. Haiselden's advice to forego the risky, and likely ineffective, surgical intervention and allow the infant to pass away on its own terms. Anna Bollinger mournfully explained: "I love the poor deformed little one. With tears and breaking heart, I gave my consent to its death. Left to itself, it has no chance to live. No one need think me cruel or an unnatural mother. My heart is full of mother love for all my children. But this poor little one if allowed to live, would be for years only a burden to itself. . . . I am willing that nature should correct its errors by my baby's death."*[2]

Denied the space to grieve privately, the Bollinger family was thrust into the spotlight as word of Dr. Haiselden's actions quickly spread. Reaching even the farthest corners of the United States, articles about "Baby Bollinger" appeared in the papers of bigger cities, like The Seattle Star, *and small-town papers, such as* The Waxahachie Daily Light, *alike.*[3] *Some sought charges against Dr. Haiselden for violating the Hippocratic Oath while others, including Helen Keller, praised him for acting in the best long-term interest of the child. In an article written for* The New York Call, *Keller lauded the doctor's judgement and suggested that the controversy unearthed critical questions facing society writ large noting, "When Dr. H. J. Haiselden permitted the Bollinger baby to die in a Chicago hospital he performed a service to society as well as to the hopeless being he spared from a life of misery . . . but that baby has lived not in vain because its death has brought us face to face with the many questions of eugenics and control of the birth rate—questions we have been side-stepping because we were afraid of them."*[4]

Keller wasn't the only one to discern a more pressing issue lurking. Prominent medical scholar Dr. Frederick H. Robinson, managing editor of the Medical Review of Reviews *of New York, swiftly jumped to Haiselden's defense and redirected the focus to the conditions which thrust Mrs. Bollinger into the spotlight in the first place—her fourth pregnancy in just a handful of years and this time mired by a life-threating bout with Tuberculosis. Robinson argued, "The Bollinger case has no direct bearing on birth control . . . but the publicity with which the case has received has at last swept away these barriers of silence which hitherto have kept the subject of childbirth from consideration by her Great American public. . . . There is no single measure that would so positively, so immediately, contribute towards the happiness and progress of the human race as teaching people the proper means of birth control."*[5] *Whether due to the desolation of John's passing or something altogether unrelated, Anna Bollinger followed her son in death just two years later in 1917. Their story far outlived them remaining a cautionary tale frequently peddled by birth controllers hoping to give women the tools to prevent the duplication of this nightmare scenario in their own lives.*

Sadly, Baby John Bollinger's death, despite the sensationalism surrounding it, was not an anomaly. In the early 1900s, death frequented many children during infancy or their early childhood years. According to the Department of Commerce's Bureau of the Census report of Mortality Statistics for 1915, children under one year of age accounted for 16.3 percent (148,561) of all recorded deaths while children under five accounted for an additional 22.4 percent (203,233). As with John, the cause of death for a substantial portion of these children, 41.1 percent (61,082), was either congenital malformation, congenital debility, or "other causes peculiar to infancy." Even healthy children faced insurmountable odds often struggling to survive illnesses that by today's standards typically amount to a mild nuisance such as whooping cough, which claimed the lives of 8,290 children, or diarrhea and enteritis—a fatal diagnosis for a staggering 40,099 children in 1915.[6] Rudimentary medical care certainly played a significant role in transforming common illnesses into death sentences but so did physical and financial barriers to medical professionals, cleanliness and hygiene, malnutrition, and of course the health of the mother.

Cognizance of this bleak reality is precisely what prompted Mrs. Bollinger and Dr. Haiselden to pursue their drastic course of action with John. He reflects, "The mother's condition was undermined by illness (Tuberculosis) and no vitality to give the child. She feared it would be subnormal, and expressed this fear as soon as the baby was born, though she never saw it, she said: I know there is something wrong."[7] Haiselden matched his strong sense of grief for the Bollingers with a commitment to prevent other families from facing the same hardship. He continues, "If I could have legally prevented the birth of the child, I would have done it. I am not her physician; I was not asked for advice. Parents rendered defective, even temporarily defective, by disease, should prevent the birth of children."[8] With little concrete understanding of how, or even if, diseases such as tuberculosis or meningitis, could be passed to children during pregnancy, Haiselden and others turned to contraception as the only viable means of preventing the spread of disease to otherwise healthy babies.

Concomitant with their efforts to cozy up to the Children's Bureau explored in chapter 2, birth control advocates readily accepted the endorsement of medical professionals who positioned contraception as a desperately needed solution to the ghastly death tolls facing infants and young children in nineteenth-century America. When asked specifically about the Bollinger case, Mary Ware Dennett emphatically stated, "I think the physician has done a big, humanitarian thing! Since there is no way of curing defectives at the present time, I don't see how anyone can fairly criticize Dr. Haiselden. The position he has taken is the bravest, frankest and most honest thing he could have done."[9] Although unfolding in 1915, when the movement was still very much finding its footing, Baby Bollinger served as the perfect opportunity for birth controllers to frame their advocacy efforts as deeply, and uniquely, focused on children.

Over time, rhetoric surrounding the health, needs, and rights of children grew into a cornerstone of the movement's discourse in three distinct ways. First, the movement labeled child welfare as a primary justification for disseminating contraception information with an intensified focus on eliminating large families whose size jeopardized their ability to provide a high quality of life to all children. Second, birth controllers spoke on behalf of children to argue that all children should be wanted and, perhaps more importantly, should be guaranteed certain rights upon birth. Finally, advocates intensified their rhetorical claims through a personification of the unborn that sought to highlight the moral superiority of voluntary parenthood. Taken together, these tactics elevated the perspective of the child in conversations about contraception and ultimately laid the framework for contemporary rhetorical disputes over fetal personhood and the right to life.

THE WELFARE OF CHILDREN

The movement's attempt to align themselves with the Children's Bureau, although technically a failure in terms of formal integration into the agency's work, demonstrated the efficacy of foregrounding the well-being of children in their discursive strategies. Yet, as illustrated in the case of Baby Bollinger, birth controllers had long heralded the value of contraception to producing healthier and happier children. In its earliest instantiation, contraception was constructed as an antidote to the obvious threats posed by abortion and infanticide. The advertisement for Sanger's first birth control clinic, opened in Brooklyn in 1916, boldly proclaimed: "DO NOT KILL. DO NOT TAKE LIFE, BUT PREVENT."[10] Almost exclusively framed in preventative terms, contraception was positioned as a viable solution to abortion, infanticide, and orphaned children. Going beyond these obvious threats, advocates spoke of the need to increase survival rates among children, many of whom, as reflected in the Mortality Statistics for 1915, perished in their first five years of life. Advocates zeroed in on the threats to child welfare posed by large families, particularly in impoverished communities where scant resources failed to keep up with an unrelenting flow of hungry mouths to feed.

Threats to Life

Abortion, as explored in chapter 2, was the most potent threat to life articulated by individuals on all sides of the debate; however, in addition to the ghastly loss of life attributable to illegal abortion, high maternal mortality rates, due to both pregnancy-related complications and abortion, introduced yet another existential threat to children—becoming orphaned. Sanger observes in an address to the Tucson Mothers Health Center that of the women who sought abortions, "90 percent are young married women, who leave families of small children behind them. They induce abortion because . . . [i]n many cases they cannot feed the children they have and another is something they cannot face."[11] A 1934 report from the Philadelphia Maternal Health Centers validated Sanger's claim and pleaded, "NINE-TENTHS of all those women who died left ORPHANED FAMILIES," the deaths of which could be prevented "by giving women like these, 90 percent of whom were already mothers, the opportunity to secure skilled contraceptive instruction."[12] Speaking directly to the maternalists who identified child welfare as their top priority, birth controllers situated contraceptive instruction as an immediately viable alternative to abortion with the additional benefit of reducing the incidence of orphaned children. In 1938, Mrs. Richard J. Bernhard of the Joint Home-Finding Committee for Jewish Foster Children in New York proposed the "wider use [of contraception] would also avert some of the family catastrophes which leave children homeless, their faith in the adult world and in society badly shattered."[13] The constellation of consequences associated with a rudimentary abortion in the early 1900s necessitated its eradication made possible through contraceptive instruction.

Birth controllers identified a similarly avoidable but real threat to children—infanticide. Thinking about infanticide from a twenty-first-century perspective understandably rattles the nerves a bit, but it is important to recognize its existence as a cultural practice manifested in response to the very existential factors contraception promised to alleviate. Norman Thomas, Executive Director of the League for Industrialized Democracy, explains in 1929: "[H]uman society has always had a rough and ready sense of the maximum population which it thinks desirable. In all sorts of ways, some of them infinitely cruel, our race has sought to control population. Abortion, infanticide and war are among the commonest of those measures."[14] Categorized alongside war and abortion, infanticide is rightly identified as a deeply undesirable outcome of a society whose decisions have produced unmanageable situations shouldered by the individual and not the state. Recognizing the immense weight felt by parents facing an unwanted pregnancy with a perceived lack of viable options, Viscount John Morley laments in 1927: "Infanticide is, of course, merely the primitive methods of limiting families. It is possible that, in countries where infanticide is common, the parent thinks no more of preventing a baby from continuing to live than people in civilized communities think of preventing a baby from being born. In both cases economic necessity—or at least economic convenience—presses, and for economic necessity men and women will do almost anything."[15] Morley's statement speaks not only to the economic reality of desperate parents but also the cultural reality of a society, one that he bitingly refers to as primitive, that fails to provide a means to prevent pregnancy. In their report for the BCCRB in 1930, the John Price Jones Corporation noted, "despite the law, religious canons, public opinion, and penalties ranging all the way from ostracism to death, women have for ages practiced infanticide" and will continue to do so as a result of "woman's instinctive urge to freedom."[16] Infanticide wasn't just an act of the deranged, it was the only seemingly feasible solution for forlorn women denied the option to prevent conception.

Rates of infanticide were not regularly reported in the early twentieth century; yet its use as a referent was nonetheless powerful, as it painted a grim picture of children literally dying at the hands of their forlorn parents. Although it would be easy to dismiss infanticide as a practice of a bygone era, The John Price Jones Corporation provides a prescient explanation for its decline arguing, "Infanticide tends to disappear as skill in producing abortions" spreads, suggesting infanticide has only decreased because abortion made the process possible prior to birth.[17] In addition to the literal problem of infanticide, Sanger analogized unrestrained procreation, resulting in the death of a quarter of a million children, as a form of infanticide via exposure. She bemoaned: "The Western World which has long professed horror at the ancient Oriental practice of exposing unwanted infants for the purpose of their destruction has now been brought to a sharp realization that there was a justification of that action on the part of starving parents in a famine ridden country, whereas there is no moral excuse for the richest country in the world to commit a quarter of a million children to preventable death. Is not our crime greater?"[18] By analogizing the preventable death of children in the United States with the long-condemned practice of infanticide, Sanger implies the two are similarly problematic, as both entail the willful destruction of life. The question Sanger leaves us with is chilling—how can the United States claim the moral high ground on infanticide when it condones the same wanton loss of life just on a different time frame?

While organizations such as the Children's Bureau lionized their efforts to bolster the health and wellness of children and mothers, neither milk banks nor maternity education programs could resolve the underlying economic and social issues driving women toward abortion and infanticide. Even if the existence of these programs assuaged some concerns women had regarding their impending pregnancy, they did nothing to ensure the long-term vitality of children or the mothers who bore them. Refusing to settle for these palliative measures, birth controllers sought to solve the root causes of infant mortality by ameliorating the desperation driving women toward abortion and infanticide. The goal of the movement, printed plainly and in all caps on the door of the nation's first birth control clinic, couldn't have been more clear: "DO NOT KILL. DO NOT TAKE LIFE, BUT PREVENT."[19]

The Dangers of Large Families

Large families presented an equally ominous threat to child welfare. The challenging allocation of resources in large families created a best-case scenario filled with unnecessary suffering and a worst-case scenario marked by the inevitable death of later born children. Deploying a Darwinian argument, Sanger proclaimed in her 1916 *Chicago Address to Women*, "even nature tends toward birth control," using famine, disease, and disaster to eliminate the weakest members of a population. She continues, "The death rate of the seventh is 350 a thousand [and] the twelfth is 600 a thousand. So that when nature has its way and twelve children come . . . nearly 60 percent of these later ones die."[20] Rather than simply letting nature run its course, claiming the lives of millions in the process, the BCCRB sought to "eliminate the vast misery and suffering accompanying nature's method of holding the population in check."[21] Rather than having twelve children and seeing only five mature to adulthood, advocates advanced spacing guidelines crafted to ensure all children born into a smaller family actually survive.

The large family hypothesis received statistical validation from a 1925 study conducted by The Children's Bureau which found "the death rate for infants is highest when they are born at short intervals. It was found that the infant death rate increases with the increase in the amount of congestion and overcrowding in the home."[22] The obvious consequences of resource disparities within crowded homes such as malnutrition and lowered sanitation standards only exacerbated the likelihood of illness and disease within the household. Helping to contextualize the deaths of more than 40,000 children due to diarrhea and enteritis as well as more severe illnesses such as tuberculosis, Dr. Adolphus Knopf explains in 1919:

> The larger the family, the more congested will be the quarters they live in and the more unsanitary will be the environment. Last, but not least, with the increase of the family there is by no means a corresponding increase of the earning capacity of the father or mother, and as a result malnutrition and insufficient clothing enter as factors to predispose to tuberculosis or cause an already existing latent tuberculosis to become active. What is the result of this condition in relation to tuberculosis—one single disease? Out of the 200,000 individuals who die annually of tuberculosis in the United States, 50,000 are children. Of the economic loss resulting from these early deaths I will speak later on, but in continuing along the medical and sanitary lines of my subject, I must call your attention to the fact that according to some authors 65 percent of women afflicted with tuberculosis, even when afflicted only in the relatively early and curable stages, die as a result of pregnancy which could have been avoided and their lives been saved had they but known the means of prevention.[23]

Knopf's research illuminates a harsh reality that is almost incomprehensible from a modern vantage point. tuberculosis was a serious diagnosis for even the healthiest of persons in the early twentieth century, but for families without contraceptive access necessary to ensure the continued health of the mother and maintain a family size conducive to sanitary and stable living conditions, tuberculosis was more often than not a death sentence.

In line with these findings, advocates cautioned against ignoring the standards of living in the home wherein children were often "born in conditions that make cruelty inevitable."[24] *Current Opinion* reiterated this position in their June 1915 edition stating: "A small family of children can have proper food and warm clothing where double the number would suffer from malnutrition and go always ragged."[25] Size was only part of the equation. Families also needed to space their children accordingly to avoid the physical and financial burdens of children born in rapid succession. If mothers are subjected to another pregnancy too soon after the birth of one child then "both the new born baby and the [fetus] still in the formative stage, suffer from malnutrition and are often permanently stunted for the duration of their lives."[26] Ray Erwin Baber, writing in *Forum and Century* in 1932, added numerical force to this argument contending, "Close spacing also means higher infant mortality. A recent study shows the death rate of infants born less than two years after the preceding child to be fifty percent higher than for those born after a longer interval."[27] *The Birth Control Review* revealed the ultimate benefit of child spacing in June 1921, proclaiming: "It was soon discovered that a lower birth rate brought with it a lower death rate, especially a lower infant mortality rate. Fewer children were born, but more of them survived."[28] As explored later in this chapter, these arguments laid the foundation for the moral framework espoused by the birth control movement prioritizing quality of life, both for living children and those yet born, over potential life. The survival rates of later born children as well as the overall strain placed on families through the addition of unsupportable offspring made a compelling case for this moral framework and codified the movement's interest in preventing the suffering of children even if doing so prevented their birth as well.

The movement's emphasis on small families drew the ire of eugenicists, worried a widespread uptake of contraception would produce a "race suicide" among predominantly white middle- and upper-class families. The allegation of "race suicide" encapsulates the murky relationship between birth controllers and eugenicists explored extensively in chapter 5 but is worth briefly addressing here given each party's divergent stance on optimal family size. An agitated Paul Popenoe, former editor of the *Journal of Heredity* for the American Genetic Association, cautioned advocates against making "unfounded claims of the merit of small families and delayed parenthood. The quality of a child is determined much more by the character of his ancestry than by the number of brothers and sisters."[29] Popenoe, like many eugenicists, feared emphasizing small families would produce population stagnation particularly with those deemed most fit for parenthood. Dr. Anna Blount aptly synthesized the conflict in the *Birth Control Review* in 1918: "There is no more hotly disputed question in the world than the relation between large families and mental and physical ability. Roosevelt is proclaiming loudly on the one hand that fine families cannot be too large, and that degenerate ones cannot be too small; while most of us are willing to admit that women are entitled to choose how many children they will bear, and not, like a salmon, spawn as copiously as possible, and then die."[30] Dr. Blount keenly illuminates the hypocrisy of people, such as Popenoe and Theodore Roosevelt, who demanded unrestrained reproduction from some while marking any reproduction at all from others as abhorrent. Blount's hyperbolic analogy of spawning salmon paints a vivid picture of the need for responsible limits on reproduction from even the most desirable stocks.

Attempting to shirk demands for advocates to articulate an optimal number of children in a family, birth controllers reiterated their argument that even though fewer children were born, more of them survived to adulthood—resulting in a temporary and acceptable lull in population growth. Sanger retorted in 1923: "[T]he stationary population of the well to do is not an immediate problem. . . . They may have perhaps two, three or four children . . . [but] those children are brought up to full maturity."[31] The emphasis on survival rates resonated with demographers concerned with the overall stability of the population, as illustrated by American demographer and sociologist Kingsley Davis's deployment of a similar version of this argument in the *New York Times* in 1957. Davis contends, "The old attitudes that encouraged prolific childbearing—necessary when death took most children before adulthood—thus persists even when high fertility no longer makes sense."[32] Recognizing society had outgrown the need for rapid reproduction, Davis echoed the movement's prioritization of the survival of fewer children over the birth of many in hopes of improving the quality of life for all children. As such, advocates justified the practice of birth control as an additional solution to the massive loss of infant and child life, leading the John Price Jones Corporation to declare: "The conclusion claimed by the friends of birth control that the use of contraceptives avoids a frightful toll of mortality, particularly of infants, which is the inevitable consequence of an unrestrained birth rate, seems to be borne out by the facts."[33] At the risk of oversimplifying the nuanced demands of the movement when it came to children, advocates prioritized quality over quantity and remained tethered to contraception as an upstream mechanism to improve the quality of life for children by eliminating the threats to life posed by their membership in large and, more often than not, unsustainable families. Appeals to "quality" venture into deeply problematic beliefs in the context of eugenics explored in chapter 5, but in its earliest form was a seemingly earnest appeal to protecting children from superfluous suffering and potential death.

The Looming Threat of Child Labor

Even children who lived to see their fifth birthday, the common milestone for child mortality statistics, remained susceptible to the fate of poverty and its frequent accompaniment of child labor. Contrary to the popular bootstrap mythology painting economic prosperity as the glorious by-product of hard work, Sanger was attuned to the realities of poverty which often precluded people's assent up the class ladder. Sanger protested in 1939, "The argument is often used that poverty and hard work strengthen and toughen people; that some of our finest citizens have risen from such circumstances to be leaders of the nation. That is true only in a small minority of cases."[34] Appeals to the bootstrap mythos were frequently used to bolster the opposition's claim that birth control threatened to eliminate genius from the population. Renowned journalist Arthur Brisbane wielded this logic in the following hypothetical from *The Washington Times* in 1920: "You might imagine Nancy Hanks and her husband, Lincoln, saying to each other: 'Let us wait until we covered this dirt floor with boards, until we have one or two windows to let in the sunlight. It would be unfair to bring children into the world in such a place as this.' If that conversation had occurred and birth control had been understood the world might not have had Abraham Lincoln."[35] Lincoln wasn't the only example trotted out to validate large families with opponents seemingly uncovering any notable person with ample siblings as proof of concept for unlimited childbearing. "Physicians have found that, on the average, successive children in a family are stronger up to the fifth or six in succession, and that those marked with special genius are very often born after the fifth in the family. The 7th child has been regarded traditionally with some peoples as the most favored by nature. Benjamin Franklin was the 15th child, John Wesley the 18th."[36] Despite the fact that Lincoln had only two siblings and himself buried two young children, opponents routinely speculated about the extraordinary members of our society who might have never come into being had their parents practiced family limitation.

In response to these obviously cherry-picked examples, American Civil Liberties Union cofounder Crystal Eastman reiterated the unlikely odds of genius emerging from families plunged into deep poverty. Writing for the *Birth Control Review in 1918*, Eastman argued: "We all know that it would be a different matter to be one of two children living on fifteen dollars a week, from being one of ten, on the same income. . . . The slum environment breeds children that can withstand the conditions of the slums. They are selected because they can resist dirt and germs, and poor food. A genius may appear among them, but they are not selected for genius."[37] Two elements of Eastman's argument are noteworthy. First, Eastman aptly distinguishes between supporting two children versus twelve on a meager salary—suggesting neither family size nor income alone are ruinous, but their confluence eradicates the potential for genius. Second, Eastman co-opts the opposition's argument that strong children may eventually rise out of poverty by attributing this occurrence to the rare feat of surviving the harsh environment of the slum. In this way, advocates effectively positioned the practice of birth control as a mechanism to mitigate the personal and societal consequences of poverty by focusing on the particularized relationship of poverty and large families.

Born of an entirely different era, the examples of Lincoln and Franklin also failed to account for the economic realities facing large families during the continued industrialization and urbanization of the early 1900s, which motivated the abhorrent but financially necessary practice of child labor. *The Birth Control Review* argued in 1918, "desperately poor parents need the extra wages that their little tots can earn and so they join hands with employers in opposing all legislation that would take these pennies away." The continued addition of children diminished both the father's earning ability and the overall strength of the labor pool as well. Radical labor rights activist and poet Ida Wright Mudgett explains in July 1918, "surplus population determines the economic status of the wage-earning class. . . . Where there are a large number of wage-earners competing for a limited supply of jobs, the wage scale is bound to be forced down to the limit of subsistence."[38] As swaths of children reach the eligible employment age and enter the labor pool, employers are able to reduce wages across the board in relation to the increased supply of laborers. The decrease in wages, felt especially hard by large families, perpetuates the use of child labor to supplement their income. Sanger laments, "So runs the vicious circle—large families forcing more workers into the labor market, and more workers causing lower wages, which again increases the number of workers through the forcing of women and children into the labor market."[39] The desperation of large families and the capitalist aims of the market worked in tandem to sustain the vicious cycle of wage deflation.

Despite increased attention and vocalized outrage from organizations comprised primarily of middle-class activists, such as the Children's Bureau and the National Child Labor Committee, little was done to legally stem the flow of child laborers. Journalist and activist John Boyle O'Reilly chided these organizations for their lack of action in 1919, writing: "[T]hat the awakening is still sentimental rather than real is startlingly evidenced by the fact that there are, according to the estimate of the National Child Labor Committee, nearly 3,000,000 child laborers in the United States."[40] Mudgett intensified her criticism and laid the blame squarely on the privileged classes who she believed resisted legislative solutions to child labor as a means of retaining their own privileged status. She scoffed, "The desire of the privileged classes (clerical or secular) to keep in subordination the masses, upon whose helplessness their special privileges and opportunities depend, is one reason why these classes are so vehement in their opposition to birth control."[41] Labor organizer Mary Kenney O'Sullivan echoed Mudgett's sentiments observing a hypocritical bent among the affluent who practice birth control themselves but reject its use among the poor "because of an unwritten law that the children of the poor must be plentiful enough to feed the mills and the factories with young, cheap workers."[42] No amount of impassioned advocacy could obscure the economic truth of child labor whose widespread use, necessitated by massive income inequality, kept the engines of industrialization running—allowing the rich to get richer and the poor to get poorer.

Just as they did with infant and maternal mortality, politicians and organizations opted for palliative programs aimed at treating the symptoms of child labor rather than addressing its root cause. Writing for the *Birth Control Review* in 1919, Ellen Keenan proclaims, "well intentioned ladies and benevolent gentleman spend all their days trying to bring order out of chaos with an endless chain of compulsory attendance laws, factory laws, free milk laws, tenement house laws" but refuse to recognize that "so long as we maintain an economic system that condemns children to a life of slavery," these efforts are pointless.[43] Akin to their rebuke of the Children's Bureau explored in chapter 2, birth controllers regularly chastised programs aimed at treating the problems attendant with large families for their failure to address the root cause of the problem—the unsustainability of perpetual childbearing facilitated by a denial of contraceptive information. Owen Lovejoy vehemently declared in the *Birth Control Review* in 1919, "The country is agreed that child labor in factories, mills, and mines is destructive to human and even industrial efficiency. . . . [T]he state which keeps women from the knowledge which would enable them to give opportunity to a few children instead of the heritage of want and ignorance to a large family, is as guilty towards its citizens as the state that implicitly allows exploitation of its children in industry."[44] Lovejoy's bold statement not only blames the state for its denial of contraceptive information as a preventative measure but equates the maliciousness of this denial with permitting child labor in the first place.

Having established the horrors of child labor and the insufficiency of existing remediation efforts, birth controllers positioned contraceptive information as the only viable solution to address the root cause of child labor. Lovejoy continues, "This fact lies back of the economic pressure to which 1/3 of the body of child laborers are attributed. If we are to get down to fundamental forces, birth control must be viewed frankly and sanely in its relation to child labor."[45] Even organizations that once drew the ire of advocates eventually espoused contraception as necessary to eradicate child labor. While advocating for a charter of childhood prohibiting child labor, the National Child Labor Committee (NCLC) proclaimed, "we must have birth control teaching . . . for the protection of the child against enforced labor" and ensure "that the child is cultivated physically, morally, intellectually, and spiritually."[46] In her plea for working-class families to adopt the practice of birth control Sanger portends, "until [the limitation of families] is done, and done by the workers themselves, other remedies for low wages, long hours, and oppressive conditions are palliatives."[47] Birth controllers advocated for smaller families as a way of restoring power to the worker by alleviating the major cause for their disenfranchisement—the continued flow of laborers who entered the labor pool out of sheer necessity to survive despite the fact that doing so ultimately undermined their ability to earn a wage capable of supporting their growing families.

Birth controllers grounded their advocacy for children in the existential threats facing children born into untenable circumstances brought about by mothers desperate to avoid yet another pregnancy, fathers struggling to make ends meet, and a society who continually failed to look out for their best interests. Although these threats manifested within the family unit, advocates localized the blame for these issues on the societal forces permitting, and often accelerating, their existence. Parents couldn't be solely to blame for their misfortune when the government deprived them of the very solution to the problem—contraception. The labeling of existing programs as mere palliatives exposed the true intent of the state to remedy the costly side effects while altogether ignoring the root cause. Exposing the government's half-hearted attempts to ameliorate the deleterious conditions facing children and placing the blame on the state for their failure to eliminate barriers to contraceptive instruction laid the foundation for the movement to advocate for the rights of children.

THE RIGHTS OF CHILDREN

With the establishment of milk banks and the promise of child labor laws, the federal government signaled a willingness to enact measures to improve the welfare of children; although these never materialized at the level promised, birth controllers seized the opportunity to make a case for the rights of children. Birth controllers defended the negative rights of women or the right to make reproductive decisions free from governmental interference insisting that giving women control and choice required nothing more from the government than to change its absurd laws restricting contraceptive access. However, when it came to children, advocates asserted the existence of positive rights or rights "that impose a duty on the state to provide certain goods and services."[48] In the eyes of the movement, the state had a responsibility to ensure children were born only in conditions conducive to their long-term health and prosperity; they had a positive obligation to ensure the rights of children were upheld.

In 1919 Sanger outlined the specific rights children ought be guaranteed in the *Birth Control Review*; she postulates, "the first right of the child is to be wanted [by] both parents." Further, parents must be able to ensure "the material rights" and "spiritual rights of the child" which "are far more easy to enumerate and to obtain when children are scarce."[49] Writing with even more specificity in a 1932 piece for *Church and Society*, Sanger enumerated the material and spiritual rights children ought to be assured at birth:

> Every child born into the world has a right to assurance of six competencies: 1. Emotional competency—assurance of a welcome. 2. Physical competency—assurance of a sound body. 3. Economic competency—assurance of support during childhood and of remunerative work in maturity. 4. Intellectual competency—assurance of education. 5. Cultural competency—assurance of a degree of leisure and of access to the cultural inheritance of the race. 6. Religious competency—assurance of the possibility of belief in divine justice and love.[50]

Beyond simply being wanted and consciously conceived, birth controllers considered it equally important for parents to procreate only when confident in their ability to provide a high standard of living for all children. Although advocates made a diversity of claims regarding the needs of children, what Sanger labeled as competencies, their core argument established two key rights all children were entitled to: to be wanted and wellborn.

EVERY CHILD A WANTED CHILD

Cognizant of the opposition's framing of the movement as anti-child, advocates reiterated their endorsement of children so long as they were welcomed additions to the family. Unlike their pro-birth counterparts who recklessly encouraged all pregnancies regardless of the parent's actual desire for another child, advocates stressed the right of the child to be wanted and framed parental desire as a prerequisite to providing a high quality of life. Sanger laments in 1919:

> The tragedy of the unwanted child, of the accidental child, only begins with whatever evil prenatal effect the emotional condition of the mother may have upon it. The right to be wanted is its first right but only the first of many that are ignored. Usually it suffers a further handicap by being carried by a mother who is physically ill or overworked. Fear of pregnancy is frequently inspired in the mind of the mother by the burden of too many children, or by want or by both. When it arrives, the accidental child usually finds itself in the ranks of the millions of hungry and neglected infants. Often it is merely a candidate for an item in the infant mortality statistics. We have before us always the horrible spectacle of hundreds of thousands of children dying miserably before they have lived 12 months, of other hundreds of thousands dying just as miserably before they reach the age of five. Where still, is the lot of those other millions who after the age of five take their places among the toilers in Mills and factories.[51]

Sanger's statement does significant rhetorical work by outlining the cascading consequences accompanying the birth of an unwanted or accidental child and connecting those consequences to the salient issues of the day including maternal health, infant mortality and child labor. Eviscerating the blissful overtones often accompanying the birth of a baby with a blunt description of the unwanted child's eventual reality created a compelling case for contraception as a solution to other urgent problems facing the nation. Even religious leaders, many of whom led the anti-child charge against the movement, acknowledged the peril of bringing unwanted children into the world. Speaking at the Modern Churchmen's Conference, Dr. Douglas White conceded: "[B]irth control must have its place in determining the future of the family and the nation in spite of its dangers" because "unwanted children, whether in or out of marriage, are undesirable productions, misfortunes alike to themselves and their parents."[52]

Aside from the looming threats to the child's welfare, advocates acknowledged the unique toll placed on women experiencing an unwanted pregnancy. Numerous letters featured in *Motherhood in Bondage* spoke of the fear, anguish, and dread accompanying the thought of another pregnancy. One letter writes pleads, "I have six children, my youngest two months old and I am just scared to death for fear I will get that way again for I never can live to go through with it again. I came near dying this time. . . . But I live on the banks of [a] Lake and just as sure as I get in the family way again I will end my troubles and be at rest."[53] Her harrowing words illuminate the utter despair felt by women denied contraceptive information. A joint report of the Birth Control Clinical Research Bureau and National Committee for Federal Legislation on Birth Control in 1930 identifies another distressing outcome for women unwilling to undergo yet another pregnancy, explaining, "For the pregnant woman, terror-stricken at the prospect of another child, the abortionist is the only recourse and, if she be ignorant of the use of contraceptives, the same prospect faces her in the future."[54] Even when women chose not to pursue an abortion in the wake of an unwanted pregnancy, the fear associated with the prospect of added children was likely to disrupt the stability of the family. Sanger explained, "Babies who are brought into the world by mothers afraid of childbirth and fathers who resent offspring face many more than the ordinary perils of life. They inherit a legacy of fear [surrounded by] nervous and emotional discord."[55] Given the difficulty of providing for even a small family in the early twentieth century, such discord and fear was both understandable and infuriatingly avoidable had they simply been given basic contractive information.

Taken together, this rhetoric functioned as a powerful retort to the accusations of selfishness hurled at women mentioned in chapter 2. By inviting critics to think of the situation from the perspective of either the unwanted child or the deeply anguished mother, advocates reframed the emotional tone of the phrase "unwanted child" to reflect the complexity of the situation. For many women, especially those facing financial instability, wanting a child is not a simple question of desire but a deeply complex question of feasibility requiring an evaluation of one's ability to provide the kind of life the child deserves. In foregrounding this complexity, advocates resisted the narrative of the selfish mother and demanded critics also consider the lasting consequences for the child forced into existence by a system that wants it even when the mother does not.

To be certain, not all unexpected children are unwanted, and not all new parents are unprepared; however, without reproductive options, parents have little opportunity for preparation, and children are born with no guaranteed inheritance of health or happiness. Those women fortunate enough to secure access to basic contraceptive information, either through word of mouth or private doctors, extolled the value of having children only when ready. In 1935, the American Birth Control League held a letter contest for "the best letter from a mother telling how birth control helped her to plan her family for health and well-being," and the winning entry written by Mrs. Leland F. Stone masterfully illustrated the value of contraceptive instruction. She writes, "I had time to train one to independence before the next one came, and proper spacing has made babies a joy and a most welcome event. I have borne my three with willingness and pride, and the result has been healthy children full of joy and living."[56] Contrasted with a life of fear, "[t]he physical health of mother, father, and children is improved by regulating the size of the family by means of spacing and planned pregnancies" resulting in "improved mental health, better marital adjustment, and more perfect family harmony."[57]

These improvements were noticeable too. Jennie Haxton, an elementary school teacher and member of the New York Kindergarten Association, cheekily remarked on the value of wanted children in 1938, noting, "It would seem that by advocating birth control [our school] is slowly putting itself out of business. Quite the contrary is the case" because "we see that the family having children because the parents want them is the family that taps every source to secure the betterment of its children. That is why the level in our nursery schools is higher than it was before thought was given to controlled birth."[58] Haxton's comments speak to the downstream effects of contraceptive instruction heralded by advocates and serves as a powerful testimonial of birth control's power to restore "self-direction, self-decision, [and] self-determination of the parents to advance the family" by recognizing "the desire on the part of the husband and wife to build up a healthy, happy family [and] accept responsibility" for their growing families.[59]

It was in the context of ensuring all children were wanted that the movement first offered up the mantra "children by choice not by chance." Pitted against the alternative of leaving childbearing to chance, the right to exercise control and choice over one's reproduction gained traction as a preferable method of regulating the population. Geneticist Edward Murray East argued in a 1927 issue of *Forum* that "the idea of children by choice instead of chance has made so much headway . . . to show that conscious regulation of the birth rate is a highly ethical proposal."[60] Dr. Louis L. Mann explicitly embeds this phrase in his 1932 definition of birth control, writing, "Let me define birth control. . . . It means that children shall come into the world by choice and not by chance."[61] Drawing a distinction between choice and chance proved so successful for the movement that Planned Parenthood later used the phrase "Children by Choice, Not by Chance" as a slogan in 1947 and again in 1981.[62]

CHILDREN DESERVE TO BE WELLBORN

Given the vulnerability of children to death and disease in the early twentieth century, merely being wanted wasn't enough for birth controllers who simultaneously demanded children be assured of their right to be wellborn. Admittedly, the standards of what it meant to be "wellborn" shifted over time in relation to numerous factors most of which were reducible to two major categories: health and environment. Dr. Thomas Wingate Todd, a well-known physician and professor at what is now Case Western Reserve University explained in 1933:

> What is it to be well born? We cannot yet make a complete answer. Human traits are numerous, human heredity is complex, and our social organization greatly multiplies the intricacies of the problem. Much careful investigation is still needed upon the details of human heredity, upon conditions making for fertility and sterility, and upon the issues which involve not only the child but the home in which the child is born. The general principles of heredity and the influence of environment have been established and are presented in every section of this report, but much work still remains to be done to qualify the details of their operation, particularly in regard to the human race. We must face this pressing human problem with true devotion to the interests of the children yet unborn, whose lives and usefulness, who's very souls depend upon our pledged faithfulness. The physical and spiritual worlds are but two aspects of the same thing. Our efforts must be directed to see the problem whole, not split up into separate parts, and to frame our investigation with all human values uppermost in thought. We must seek the truth, the whole truth, and nothing but the truth.[63]

Todd's remarks, although offering little in the way of a concrete definition, provide critical context for conversations concerning heredity, the transmissibility of disease, and environmental determinants of health all of which became intense subjects of inquiry and debate in the mid 1900s. The reminder of how woefully inadequate our understanding of these issues was at the time is essential and factors heavily into the discussion of eugenics featured in chapter 5. Although lacking in precision, Todd's claim aptly contextualizes the movement's preoccupation with the health of children as encompassing far more than just ensuring children were wanted, seeking instead to ensure that their physical and spiritual needs were met as well.

Advocates insisted neither parental desire nor the all-coveted mother love could overcome the challenges faced by children when born into situations of poor health, economic instability, or both. Commonly labeled as a child's "birthright," advocates situated the health of children as an equally pressing concern to being wanted. Physician Carl G. Roberts remarked in 1938, "Here were two young people starting out with the usual hopes and aspirations with which newlyweds build their air castles and, in a few years, swamped beyond rescue with the results of uncontrolled reproduction. . . . The children born without choice into poverty and deprivation, destined to belong to the last generations who never have a chance for their share of the health, happiness and educational opportunities which should be the assured birthright of every child."[64] The storyline sketched by Roberts was familiar to many couples in the first half of the twentieth century illuminating the frightful downward spiral of an eager young couple whose dream of building a family turned ruinous without the means to properly plan and space their children.

Contraception, on the other hand, allowed parents to reproduce only when confident in their ability to provide these competencies for their children—the actualization of which functioned as a foil to the reality of compulsory parenthood wherein parents could not guarantee even the most basic needs of their children. In defense of his choice to knowingly violate the Comstock Act by dispersing contraceptive information, Boston-based birth control advocate Van Kleeck Allison argued, "the folly of withholding this information from married people . . . [are children] born into the world unwanted, unloved, or with a physical defect which would make them a lifelong burden to society."[65] In a 1932 form letter to its members, the BCCRB proclaimed, "birth control enable[s] mothers to raise their families with the assurance of strength and health. It gives each living child its birthright; a mother's care and affection."[66] Dr. Roberts went as far as to label the withholding of contraceptive information as a "crime against civilization" and invoked the birthright rhetoric to lambast opponents to the movement. Roberts proclaimed, "In this crime against the birthright of the unborn, those who dogmatically fight against the establishment of a scientific, ethical system of birth control are participating partners whether they realize it or not."[67] Roberts's statement cuts through the thinly veiled concerns about obscenity and moral licentiousness offered by opponents to establish their complicity in the suffering of children through the denial of contraceptive information.

Advocates parlayed these accusations of complicity into a full-blown attack on the state for failing to protect the rights of children. Maude Durand Edgren, an editor for the *Birth Control Review*, explicitly questioned the moral underpinnings of a government who would shirk its responsibility to its most vulnerable citizens. Writing in the *Review* in 1917, Edgren scoffs, "a state that allows its citizens already born to suffer privations and become exposed to unhealthful and criminal environments is immoral. A state that does not protect the rights of helpless baby citizens is immoral."[68] Advocates frequently spoke of children as vulnerable, disenfranchised, and in dire need of the protection afforded via the recognition of their rights. An anonymous article in the *Birth Control Review* entitled "Is Birth Control a Constitutional Right?" extended the movement's positive rights claims arguing the denial of contraceptive information to parents "violate[d] the right of the child to be born of that emphatically purposeful parentage which is necessary if the child is to be the perfect result of the creative impulse."[69] *The North American Review* advanced this plea via a comparison to the struggle for women's rights, suggesting in 1922: "[I]t will soon be the turn of the last remaining unenfranchised class of human beings to claim their rights—the children . . . and as women depended for their enfranchisement upon the all-powerful male voter, so the helpless child must await its liberation."[70] On the heels of the victorious suffrage movement, birth controllers optimistically advanced similar claims on behalf of children hoping to garner the same level of support.

The use of rights-based rhetoric to advocate for birth control through the lens of a child resonated widely. Demonstrating the strength of these arguments on a global scale, The League of Nations adopted the Declaration of the Rights of the Child in 1924 with a commitment from all signatories, including the United States, to work toward ensuring all children were guaranteed the birthright of health, safety, and prosperity. *The Birth Control Review* accordingly lauded the comprehensiveness of the Declaration and summarized its mandates, noting: "The child a birthright shall inherit for natural growth in flesh and spirit. Children should be fed when hungry, nurtured when sick, led with patience, kept from sin, surrounded by kin, and always loved."[71] Harnessing the momentum generated by this impressive moment, birth controllers turned their attention to then presidential candidate Herbert Hoover who had already taken a keen interest in the work of the Children's Bureau and the larger project of improving child welfare.

Hoover rose to prominence as a member of the Wilson administration and was well known for his efforts as Secretary of Commerce to create a minimum wage and prohibit the use of child labor and was even asked to serve as president of the American Child Health Association in 1920. Given these predilections and their obvious alignment with the goals of the birth control movement, advocates optimistically felt Hoover would push the issue of child welfare and subsequently birth control to the top of the agenda. An editorial in the *Birth Control Review* in 1929 explains, "we have reasonable grounds for expecting that President Hoover will be favorable to any measure or legislation which will forward the cause of birth control. The Child's Bill of Rights enunciated by him as president of the American Child Health Association, contains seven clauses, each one of which states a right which is absolutely dependent on birth control."[72] These clauses enumerated by Hoover bear a striking resemblance to the very rights articulated by the birth control movement, including the "birth right of a sound mind and body" and "the encouragement to express the fullest measure of the spirit within." The author of the editorial also noted the uncanniness between Hoover's rhetoric and the movement's, quipping, "The child's Bill of Rights might well have been enunciated by Margaret Sanger in support of her fight for birth control. It was put forth by Mr. Hoover and again and again in his campaign speeches, broadcasted over the length and breadth of the country, he emphasized it's importance, and his concern that every child should enjoy its birth right a birthright which [in] every clause hinges on birth control."[73] Hoover's rhetorical uptake of children's rights signaled to advocates that perhaps, for the first time, they had an ally in the White House.

Despite their optimism, Hoover remained reluctant to formally endorse contraception and focused his energies on strengthening programs within the Children's Bureau until the economic stresses of the Great Depression wiped out virtually all funding for programs aimed at improving child welfare. That didn't stop advocates from using Hoover's rhetorical endorsement of the birthright of children as a springboard to extol the benefits of family planning and contraceptive instruction. In 1931, the American Birth Control League passed a series of resolutions specifically addressing the foolhardiness they saw in programs, like Hoover's, seeking to help children without providing parents the means to prevent conception. In the preface to the adopted resolution, the ABCL questions, "President Hoover has declared that 'there should be no child in America that is not the complete birthright of a sound mind in a sound body, and that has not been born under proper conditions.' But can such a millennium ever be obtained under our present economic regime without resort to birth control?"[74] In the resolution proper, the ABCL guarantees its full support to the president in carrying out the ambitions of the Children's Charter but also "called upon the president to more seriously consider the importance of contraceptive measures as part and parcel of his objectives" and more specifically asserted, "Voluntary Parenthood is a means to this end, when based upon prerequisite instruction on the importance of normal well born children to the home, the family, and the nation."[75] Regardless of Hoover's reluctance, his uptake of the movement's rights-based rhetoric served as much-needed validation.

Hoover wasn't the only prominent figure whose rhetoric mirrored the movement's rhetoric. In 1922 Mary Vida Clark, a leading social worker within the Central Council of Social Agencies where she served as the chair of the Committee on Children for several years, boldly pleaded for the recognition of "the innumerable rights to which the child is entitled as corollaries of his inalienable constitutional rights to life, liberty, and the pursuit of happiness."[76] Clark's article critiqued the indiscriminate use of contraception by all; however, her appeal to the rights of children in conjunction with birth control demonstrates the salience of the argument that, if nothing else, the rights of the child and not just the parents are relevant considerations. Given their growing role in the post-WWI welfare state, it is unsurprising that numerous religious groups in the early 1930s vocally supported the birth control movement citing the rights of children as their primary justification. The *Chicago Daily Tribune* reported in 1931, "Approval of voluntary parentage through birth control was formally given by The National Council of Congregational and Christian Churches [who] stood resolved [in] the right of children to be wanted."[77] Similarly emphasizing the welfare of both children and parents in their choice to support the birth control agenda, the Presbyterian Church stated in 1932: "[C]hildren have a God-given right to be well born and to this end the spiritual and bodily fitness of parents is enjoined."[78] These endorsements marked a significant shift in the often tense relationship between birth controllers and religious institutions and exposed the common ground between them, children, the protection of which relied on securing contraceptive access.

Beyond simply convincing once tentative groups to support birth control, the emphasis on children's rights broadened the scope of the movement to include the needs of children—both living and those yet born. Feminist and journalist Genevieve Parkhurst explained this shift in a 1936 article for the *North American Review*: "With the growth of the movement, its purpose has grown." Birth control emerged "as a doctrine of human rights [including] the right of the child."[79] The positive rights extended to children are commensurate with the reproductive rights framework espoused by early birth controllers that sought to give women control and choice in reproductive matters. Control, the mechanistic function of contraception, ensured the proper spacing and planning of children preserving their right to be wellborn. Whereas choice, the ideological function of contraception, empowered women to enter motherhood voluntarily in accordance with the right of children to be wanted.

Yet, in positioning the negative right of unrestricted contraceptive access as the solution to the child welfare crisis, birth controllers unintentionally undercut the government's positive burden to ensure the welfare of children. Under this framework, the government can shirk its responsibility to ameliorate the social conditions rendering children vulnerable merely because they have given parents control over the terms of their reproduction. The lingering consequences of this framework are explored later in this chapter and again in the concluding chapters of the book as we dissect the legal frameworks governing reproductive rights and subsequently the government's role in securing access to contraception. Positive rights are rare and although myriad parties willingly recognized their existence in the context of children, including President Hoover, few were compelled to take action to secure the contraceptive access needed to actualize these rights for all children.

BUILDING THE MORAL HIGH GROUND

Working within the framework of child welfare, birth controllers built a rhetorically strong and logically sound case for the provision of contraceptive information as a downstream solution to the neglect, malnutrition, and poor health associated with large families and unwanted children. However, as highlighted in their fruitless efforts to convince President Hoover, advocates grew increasingly frustrated at the ease with which common people and politicians alike dismissed their sensible plea for contraception. Remarking on a hearing held by the New York State Legislature in 1923, Sanger scoffed: "When it came time to reply to the exponents of Birth Control, in support of which we had mobilized and marshalled the finest forces of reason, logic, science, public health, idealism and ethics, our opponents resorted to the weapons of vulgar personal abuse" dismissing the case "with a gesture that lacked even the redeeming merit of dignity."[80] Searching for some kind of justification for this behavior, scientist Edward Murray East chided, "These arguments are typical. They are endeavors to rationalize irrational prejudices. And they mask the real issues. Down deep in their hearts the antagonists of Birth Control are merely oppressed with fear for their miserable souls."[81]

Repeated attempts at commonsense legislative change made it abundantly clear to advocates that advancing the birth control movement couldn't rely on logic alone. As such, advocates infused their rhetoric with two emotionally driven arguments aimed at counteracting the opposition's characterization of the movement as anti-child and anti-life. First, advocates positioned their goal of preventing the wanton suffering of children via contraceptive instruction and family limitation as reflective of a higher respect for human life. Second, birth controllers foregrounded the experiences of children through the personification of the unborn. By literally giving voice to the needs and wants of hypothetical children, advocates brought opponents face to face with the very children they claimed to protect. Taken together these arguments sought to give birth controllers the moral high ground by framing opponents as negligent, hypocritical, and self-serving.

A HIGHER RESPECT FOR LIFE

When it came to children, advocates faced tough opposition who labeled their initiatives as immoral and anti-child; one critic went as far as to call birth control advocates "apostles of infanticide."[82] Taking a strong stance against any attempt to restrict reproduction, opponents labeled contraception as an immoral threat to the sanctity of life—a rhetorical tactic resurrected decades later by anti-abortion advocates in the 1980s whose purportedly pro-life stance was carefully crafted as a foil to the pro-choice movement formed in response to *Roe v. Wade*. To be clear, for much of the early twentieth century no real consensus existed regarding when life begins. Bearing in mind the rudimentary nature of medicine and the dearth of doctors or researchers specializing in obstetrics and gynecology, women were not even considered pregnant until the moment of quickening or the first felt sensation of movement in the womb. Historian Beth Gibson explains, "Pregnancy was not considered to exist until the fetus was able to move and the mother was aware of such activity. . . . Before the instance of quickening the woman's condition was indistinguishable from the absence of menstruation" and subsequently "[l]aw and society did not recognize fetal life before that moment of animation."[83] The following discussion thus lacks much of the rhetorical nuance afforded to contemporary disputes over the point at which life begins facilitated by technical terms (like fetus) and gestational markers (such as in-utero) to signify ideological differences. Children were discussed in the abstract, often encompassing both living and potential offspring, and the term "life" was used less tactically to describe both the quality of being alive and the actual life one lived. Interestingly enough, it is this very linguistic ambiguity that makes the rhetoric of early birth controllers easily co-opted by people with contradictory ambitions, as we'll see in the concluding pages of this chapter.

Havelock Ellis explains the dominant moral backdrop advocates faced, noting, "In order to understand the morality of the present [we] should be able to put ourselves in the place of those for whom birth control was immoral" and so "we must remember that, throughout the Christian world, the divine command 'Increase and multiply' has seemed to echo down the ages from the beginning" and made perfect sense when "addressing a world inhabited by eight people." Ellis recognizes the salience of the biblical tradition encouraging unrestrained reproduction and acknowledges its initial usefulness as a guiding principle; however, Ellis also provides an important caveat: "[T] he old religious command has become a tradition which has survived amid conditions totally unlike those under which it arose."[84] In responding to accusations of immorality, advocates advanced two specific counterarguments to demonstrate the deep moral commitments of the movement. First, birth controllers relied on the rhetorical tactic of juxtaposition to highlight the true moral failings of a system permitting unrestrained reproduction. Second, extending their focus on the quality of life inherited by children, advocates provocatively questioned whether it was better to be born into suffering or not at all, challenging the notion of protecting "potential life" as a flawed endeavor.

First, whereas prevailing norms, often influenced by Judeo-Christian morality, placed a premium on the sanctity of a child's life, birth controllers prioritized the quality of a child's life and defended the moral superiority of their position by comparing the realities attendant with each worldview. A March 1920 article in the *Birth Control Review* titled "Wasting Our Human Resources" argues: "We have wasted [life] prodigally because we have had an unlimited supply. . . . When our numbers are cut down, these human resources will appear to us in their true light—as the most precious of all our possessions."[85] Utilizing the principles of supply and demand, birth controllers blamed unrestrained reproduction for a decreased respect for human life by reducing the value, or preciousness, of children as more came into existence. Extending this line of reasoning, advocates specifically admonished the church who vocally denounced contraception for frustrating the natural laws of God and nature. John Haynes Holmes, a preeminent Unitarian minister and cofounder of both the American Civil Liberties Union and National Association for the Advancement of Colored People, offered a scathing rebuke of the church's stance on contraception:

> The church, oblivious of its high spiritual function, is utterly materialistic in its contention that production is the one standard to be observed in married life. It is the husband's business to beget and the wife's business to bear children. As many children as possible, the more the better, regardless of the mother's health, the child's perspective life, and proper upbringing, the rights of other children, the economic condition of the family, and other conditions which would seem to have some relation to the problems as to whether a couple shall fructify or not this is the dictum solemnly laid down by the church! Production, quantity—as though human life were on no higher level than that of early tribesmen, or of pigs and rabbits, or for that matter, of automobiles and cotton cloth. If such a standpoint is not materialism, I frankly know not what materialism is. Certainly, it goes far toward making of the home a factory, of parent's machine, and have children and economic product! To anyone who has any sense of what we know as human values, it seems an elementary proposition that there is something

> else involved in the facts of conception and birth than the mere problem of large-scale production. Not quantity but quality, not how many children but what kind of children is a question that takes us straight for the basis of the material to that of spiritual standards. . . . What the church needs is comprehension of the significance of its own essentially spiritual attitude toward life. It needs to discover moral values as related to the institution of marriage. When this is done, the church will advocate and not deny contraceptive Birth Control.[86]

Holmes masterfully summarizes the movement's purported morality premised on ensuring children receive a high quality of life and places it in harsh relief against the moral stance of the church seemingly concerned with the mere existence of the child. Couching the church's moral framework in terms of materialism raises valuable questions about the church's motives casting doubt on the value structures underlying their rejection of contraception. Perhaps more importantly, Holmes calls into question the utility of valuing life without a consideration of the conditions under which that life is lived.

An unsigned editorial in the *Birth Control Review* narrows Holmes's biting criticism to the Roman Catholic Church and unequivocally proclaims, "The Roman Catholics say birth control is immoral. We claim that for us birth control is of high moral value."[87] The author sketches the details of this moral standard and argues, "It includes the rights of little children, the right to be well born, to have a reasonable chance to live and develop; The right of men and women to happiness and harmony in the home; The right of the nation to protect itself against decadence and disaster; The right of all humanity to have sufficient space on earth, that one nation shall not crowd another into war, and that there shall be enough food for all."[88] When compared to the myopic view of morality established by the church, the comprehensive value structure supported by the birth control movement attains even greater significance.

Despite contraception's potential to save the lives of millions of women and children, opponents reiterated the underlying premise of the birth control movement was anti-life. Sanger acknowledged this belief stating, "Some of those who take their stand against birth control do so by the thought that we have no right to destroy potential life."[89] Oregon-based doctor Ella K. Dearborn questioned the veracity of this statement given the daily atrocities permitted by society. She scoffs: "A student of history will search long for any evidence of the sacredness of life, either remote or modern. Ancient history is page after page of war, theft and rape, men, women, and children killed, virgins taken captive, and trophies carted away. Modern history is the same. Our daily paper shows us that human life is the cheapest thing on the market." After working through a laundry list of ways society already shows its blatant disregard for human life, Dearborn forcefully concludes: "No, LIFE isn't sacred, never has been, never will be till birth control has taught the world that ideal motherhood means welcome babies then and only then, are mother and babe sacred, and home a sanctuary."[90] Dearborn's statement highlights the implicit contradiction of a stance that fails to categorically advocate for the lives of people and suggests that a moral framework concerned with the sanctity of life must embrace birth control to ensure new lives are brought into the world only when wanted and wellborn.

Advocates couldn't deny contraception prevented conception and subsequently new life from entering the world—that was their explicit aim after all—but they could indict the categorical prioritization of potential life as antithetical to the long-term preservation of life. Sanger protested: "For the supposed sake of the one or two of these myriad sperms which must naturally and inevitably die, they insist on the production of babies in rapid succession which are weakened by their proximity."[91] Sanger's retort mitigated the opposition's argument in two ways. First, the clarification of *potential life* as merely sperm and ova that inevitably die in accordance with the natural cycles of men and women makes contraception no greater of a threat to potential life than everyday living. Second, Sanger illuminated the end result of prioritizing potential life, weaker babies, to demonstrate the fallacious aims of protecting the sanctity of life. A 1922 article in the *Birth Control Review* succinctly articulated this position as a concern for the child's ability to subsist rather than exist. Whereas opponents assert "the right of the child not only to 'life, liberty and happiness,' and the right to 'legal parents,' but also the right of the next generation to 'Exist.' . . . The right of the child, born, to subsist is the categorical demand" of the birth control movement.[92] By reframing concerns for life in terms of subsistence rather than existence, birth controllers upended the dominant moral framework and espoused the moral superiority of planning and prevention over amelioration. The John Price Jones Corporation noted in 1930, "one of [contraception's] most promising and recent developments is the control of conditions before birth" which demonstrate "not only a responsibility for the human lives that are, but for the new human lives that come to be."[93] Enabling parents to prevent conception when they are unable to support new life actually places potential life on a pedestal ensuring it is only brought to fruition when it can thrive. In 1935 Sanger heralded this evolved perspective as "a new moral responsibility, a higher regard for life, not only after birth, but even before life has been conceived."[94] The mother who delays pregnancy or prevents conception isn't anti-child or anti-life—far from it. The society denying women the ability to regulate their reproduction, on the other hand, has demonstrated its disregard for the child's quality of life.

These arguments effectively redirected the ire of many religious objectors. As explained earlier, leaders in both the National Council of Congregational and Christian Churches and the Presbyterian Church endorsed contraception as a necessary measure to protect children. According to historian Daniel K. Williams, even the Catholic Church abandoned their vocal opposition to birth control as a result of changing public perception of the movement's orientation to child welfare generally and abortion more specifically. He explains, "Catholic prelates were well aware that the birth control controversy had exacerbated the difficulties they faced in winning Protestants to their position on abortion. . . . They quickly disbanded their campaigns against birth control legalization, which they now viewed as quixotic" and focused their efforts on "the distinction between contraception and abortion."[95] Although the reproductive rights movement writ large would face continual opposition from the Catholic Church, particularly on the issue of abortion, their acquiescence to the birth control movement in the 1930s was truly remarkable.

WHAT DO THE CHILDREN WANT?

Opponents spoke tirelessly of "unborn children" advancing emotional pleas about their inherent divinity. New York–based Archbishop Hayes proclaimed, "Children troop down from Heaven because God wills it. . . . To take life after its inception is a horrible crime; but to prevent human life that the Creator is about to bring into being is satanic. . . . Sin not against children who, after all, are the noblest stimulus and protection to marital affection, fidelity, and continency."[96] Setting aside Archbishop Hayes's casual comparison between actual murder and contraception, his rhetoric exemplifies the intensity with which opponents questioned the morality of birth control. Building on their own moral framework prioritizing quality of life, advocates countered this caustic rhetoric with a bit of sensationalism of their own in the form of personification. Rather than claiming to speak on behalf of children, advocates wrote detailed dialogues and poems from the perspective of the potential child. Ranging from simple questions posed from the child's point of view to poems written in the voice of the unborn child, this tactic reframed common concerns for child welfare voiced by activists into powerful pleas from the very group opponents supposedly sought to protect through the prohibition of contraception—children.

Harkening back to the tragic story of Baby Bollinger, Dr. Robinson charged critics to consider the situation from the perspective of the baby, pleading, "Do you think that defective baby in Chicago would have consented to live if it has been consulted? What future could it have? At best a precarious existence in a Coney Island tent, or as the Wild Man of Borneo in a tank-town circus."[97] Coupled with the powerful imagery of the freak show, a now defunct venue for people seen as physical oddities, Robinson's comment seeks to evoke empathy from those who demanded the child be allowed to live prompting them to consider the child's long-term quality of life. Furthering the notion that many children would not choose the life they are forced to inherit, Sanger utilizes personification when she boldly writes from the perspective of destitute children: "We are the victims of an irresponsible parenthood. Few of us have any hope of living full and useful lives. We are a care on our parents, relatives, and many a burden upon the taxpayers of the nation. We did not ask to be born, and had we anything to say to the summons which called us from the realm of the unborn, we would have said no."[98] The notion of consent features prominently in these discourses as advocates foregrounded the child's inability to consent, or even be consulted, about their desire to live when facing dire conditions. Advocates co-opted the concept of innocence utilized by opponents to justify the morality of evaluating the subsistence of the child brought into the world not of their own volition.

Foregrounding the wants and desires of children was also a favored rhetorical strategy of Sanger who frequently pondered what it would look like if children were given a say over who became their parents. Sanger explained the impetus for this particular rhetorical move writing, "In attempting to draw up a fair and equitable code for the children of tomorrow, I have been compelled to go back and put myself in the position of those unborn children who have not been yet called into the realm of earthly reality. . . . If, in imagination, we do this, we may easily set down the sort of questions these Children-to-be might put to us."[99] The following list of questions appeared frequently in Sanger's speeches and writings throughout the 1920s and 1930s and were always posed from the perspective of the child:

> "How do you live? Where do you live? How many rooms have you got, and how is mothers health; Is she a happy, comfortable, jolly mother, or is she a nervous, worn out, drudge, a wreck?"[100]

> "Shall we come as the undesired, unwanted progeny into a country where already millions of children are already wandering the highways and roads looking for food and work?"[101]

> "How do you plan to bring me up? Have you any plans for my life and my development? Am I had to be a chimney sweep thrust on out to earn my own living, or am I to have possibilities of perhaps being a President?"[102]

Sanger extends this thought exercise to contemplate the creation of a "Baby Bureau" wherein "prospective parents would have to apply and answer the questions of the unborn."[103] Operating just like an employment bureau, applicants provide references and reassure their prospective child of both their desire for a baby and their ability to provide for them as well. Sanger paints a stark picture of what this type of placement interview might look like from the perspective of the child. "'What's that you say? Five children already? Two dark rooms in the slums? No! Thank you! I don't care to be born at all if I cannot choose to be well born. Goodbye.' So the interview might be abruptly terminated if all parents had to apply for babies at a sort of Bureau of the unborn."[104] Rather than advocating on behalf of children, Sanger utilizes this thought experiment to generate empathy for children afforded no say over the life they are born into. In doing so, Sanger shifts the discourse from generalized statements about child welfare to a pointed inquiry into the wants and needs of children.

Personification was perhaps most powerful in showcasing the hypocrisy of opponents advocating for the life of children while ignoring the circumstances surrounding their birth and the subsequent impact on their right to be wanted and wellborn. One such poem reads:

> Mother of mine, mother-to-be,
> Oh, bear me not unwillingly!
> I ask not life, but if you give,
> Oh, grant me then the chance to live"
> "If blows and curses be my fate,
> Oh, you can turn my love to hate!
> Mine is the right to love and joy.
> Create not, if you must destroy![105]

The author, identified only as "A Friend," speaks directly to the longing of children to be wanted and in just a few short lines encapsulates a number of prominent arguments advanced by the movement including the prioritization of subsistence over existence and the desire to prevent pregnancy rather than resort to abortion.

Other writers spoke much more bluntly of the frightful situation facing unborn children and imbued their work with a palpable sense of frustration at those claiming to protect the unborn. In an essay appearing first in the *New York Post* and reprinted by the *Birth Control Review* in 1935, Ernest L. Meyer writes:

> I am a stilled voice. I have not yet been heard, but I am speaking. I am a germ plasm that has failed of growth. I am one of the unborn. . . . We have been denied the right of fruition, the right of birth, the right of fulfilling our destiny. We have been destroyed by a sin against biology. So say the prophets and we listen, and in the eternal darkness where we abide we indulge in a faint protoplasmic laugh. We have been denied the right to add our millions of unborn souls to the 130 million born souls in this great nation, and thus increase by so many millions the

> army now standing with idle hands before the factories and shops, or toiling in the farmlands for a pittance, or hungering in the cotton fields among the plentiful crops. We have been denied the right of shivering on windy corners selling apples and pencils or pawning in the alleyways for scraps of food or freezing the nights through wrapped in newspapers which carry stories about the sin of contraception and the glory of being born. Prepare the way for us, you born, before you weep over our fate. Prepare the way for us. Look to the soil before you plant the seed. In the world you have made for us we would find scant nourishment. We would be stunted, blasted, whipped by the winds or uprooted by stupid or hateful hands. You proclaim the right of the unborn to inherit the drought and the dust and the barren earth, but for the veriest cabbage you prepare the loam.[106]

Meyer's work is a scathing review of those who oppose birth control under the guise of protecting the unborn. Not only does the unborn child laugh at the false prophecy offered by opponents, but they literally keep themselves warm by swaddling in the hollow rhetoric of these prophets who naively speak of the glory of being born while shunning the material needs of the child after birth. Against a backdrop of brazen hypocrisy, the unborn child issues an important demand: "Prepare the way for us, you born, before you weep over our fate" reiterating the movement's emphasis on quality of life as a more important consideration than life itself.

These dueling discourses on behalf of unborn children are emblematic of the broader conversation surrounding fetal rights, abortion, and eugenics which dominated the 1920s. Historian Sara Dubow impeccably traces the meanings ascribed to the fetus throughout American history and argues: "[C]ompeting fetal stories and contested fetal meanings have occupied an important place in the public sphere and collective imagination of the United States throughout the modern era."[107] These stories, according to Dubow, advanced claims regarding both "the physical fetus and the metaphorical unborn" to create a compelling narrative based in reality but steeped with overwrought emotional appeals suiting the agenda of the storyteller. The birth control movement's use of personification certainly fits this description. Birth controllers meticulously reframed the anti-life accusations of opponents to demonstrate the inherent morality of contraceptive use. Opponents to birth control framed the movement as cold and calculating comprised of selfish women seeking smaller families out of convenience or self-indulgence. They questioned the morality of a movement whose core demands frustrated the laws of nature and god. And they claimed to safeguard the sanctity of life by demanding all potential life be brought to fruition. Birth controllers directly confronted these charges, but rather than denouncing their moral underpinnings, advocates co-opted them arguing the movement's framework facilitated a higher level of respect for human life. Less children were born, but more survived. In doing so, the movement established family planning as a morally superior alternative to injudiciously adhering to the laws of nature with no regard for the children who inherit the consequences.

THE LASTING CONSEQUENCE: CONTESTED PERSONHOOD

Emphasizing the rights of children fulfilled a strategic need for the movement. Commensurate with their rhetoric elevating and professionalizing motherhood explored in chapter 2, the movement's focus on the welfare of children and their rights to be wanted and wellborn provided a necessary counterpoint to prevailing perceptions of the movement as a radical rejection of motherhood. The bold and caustic actions of early leaders such as Margaret Sanger, her sister Ethyl Byrne, and her anarchist mentor Emma Goldman propelled birth control into the public discourse; however, it also created an image problem for the movement resulting in the reluctance of public officials to entertain, let alone endorse, the repeal of existing barriers to contraceptive information. Meanwhile, women continued to die in droves due to pregnancy-related complications stemming largely from multiple pregnancies in short succession, pre-existing health conditions with which pregnancy was contraindicated, and unsafe termination efforts. Children too suffered facing an inheritance of poor health from weak mothers, overcrowded and unhygienic living conditions, and the daunting likelihood of child labor. These issues were alarming to birth controllers but also presented a unique opportunity to advance their movement in the name of saving mothers and their children. Under the leadership of Sanger, advocates shifted their efforts away from the ideologically motivated battle over contraception's obscenity classification and toward the goal of establishing the functional utility of contraception to reduce maternal and infant mortality.

The shift in focus to children precipitated an unavoidable foray into the politics of fetal rights which inadvertently laid the rhetorical foundation for the contemporary pro-life movement. Dubow, while not writing about the birth control movement specifically, contextualizes the slippery slope implicit within the child-centric rhetoric of many Progressive-era reforms; she explains, "Those strategies began by claiming to protect the 'right to be well born' and quickly moved to debate the meaning of fetal life and define the relationship between the mother and fetus."[108] These discourses continue to animate contemporary reproductive politics; Dubow furthers, "Recent efforts to protect 'fetal rights' and fetal citizenship echoed but did not replicate late nineteenth-century efforts to protect the 'right to be well-born.'"[109] These echoes are palpable when exploring the similarities between the rhetoric of early birth controllers and today's pro-life movement. Both place a premium on preventing abortion. Both claims to have the child's best interest at heart. Both weaponize the wants and needs of the "unborn" to justify their actions. Both utilize the sensationalist tactics of personification to create an emotional plea hyperbolizing the logic of their argument. How is it possible that these two diametrically opposed groups separated by both time and space could utilize such similar rhetoric to advance such different ambitions?

The short and admittedly reductionist explanation for the similarities between early birth controllers and current pro-lifers is context. In the early twentieth century, abortion was equally abhorred and understood as an act of total desperation for women denied the option of preventing another pregnancy. It was truly a last resort. Despite its illegality, doctors, advocates, and law makers alike broached the subject as an inevitability. This attitude is precisely why birth controllers featured abortion prevention so prominently in their rhetoric. Stemming the flow of the illegal abortions threatening the lives of both mothers and children was perhaps the movement's most salient opportunity to establish common ground with the stakeholders necessary to secure contraceptive access. Contraception was the first viable solution presented to curtail abortion, and advocates worked tirelessly to prove this fact to potential allies who, if for no other reason, listened to advocates because of their shared desire to halt abortions. So, while the contemporary reproductive justice movement defends abortion as a necessary option for women, which it is, vehement opposition to abortion was required of early advocates to secure acceptance of contraception as a preventative measure.

In the twenty-first century, however, abortion is no longer accepted as inevitable and instead is perceived as the most extreme contraceptive option for women afforded a litany of methods to prevent pregnancy. Existing at the top of the contraceptive hierarchy, a concept explored in chapter 4, abortion no longer carries the empathetic connotation of a last resort it did in the early 1900s instead viewed as an irresponsible Hail Mary for those whose previous contraceptive efforts failed. Abortion remains abhorred by many precisely because early advocates did such an impeccable job framing contraception as a preventative measure. By their very their own logic, the supposedly unfettered access to contraception granted to most women today should have eradicated the practice of abortion, and yet it remains. To be clear, contraceptive access has never and will never be unfettered in this country so long as countless women face enormous social, political, and economic barriers regarding their reproductive decisions. Yet, the mere existence of these options provides ammunition for the pro-life movement to vilify women seeking an abortion as irresponsible and immoral. Pro-life activists ignore barriers to contraceptive access and erase the complexities of an unplanned pregnancy often necessitating abortion, condescendingly suggesting women wouldn't need abortions if they would have just utilized the contraceptive options available to them.

Additionally, in the early twentieth century abortion was only one of many threats facing unborn children whereas today it has been reduced to virtually the only threat. This doesn't mean that twenty-first-century children don't face the same harsh realities accompanying being unwanted or born into unsuitable conditions, but rather that those realities have been muffled by the prevailing notion of individual responsibility holding parents, particularly women, accountable for their reproductive actions. Poverty and unplanned pregnancies are subsequently categorized as personal failings with abortion no longer accepted as an act of desperation but a sign of moral depravity. Whereas birth controllers effectively blamed the government for withholding contraceptive information and the attendant consequences of large families, high mortality rates, and child labor, the progress in removing barriers to contraception in today's society has allowed pro-lifers to shift the responsibility for these consequences to women. This shifting context enables pro-life activists to exploit the positive rights framework built by birth controllers to present abortion as the only significant threat to a child's right to be wanted and wellborn.

The longer and more nuanced explanation stems from the inevitable tension between women's negative rights and children's positive rights. The initial rights framework espoused by the birth control movement sought to establish women's negative right to make reproductive decisions free from governmental interference as a means of securing unrestricted contraceptive access. The provision of this right, explored more fully in chapter 6, granted the state considerable latitude to interfere in cases where they demonstrated a compelling state interest such as preventing the use of harmful or unregulated medical substances, and although there has been little to no encroachment on women's negative right regarding contraceptive use, the same cannot be said when it comes to abortion. In fact, the pro-life movement has relied almost exclusively on the court's willingness to renegotiate women's negative rights in line with a state's interest to protect children and have built their moral position on fetal personhood around the assumption that women's rights are secondary to those of the fetus. Kristin Luker, director of the Center for Reproductive Rights and Justice at Berkeley, argues:

> Concretely, a decision about the moral status of the embryo is an implicit statement about the role of children and women in modern American society. If the status quo of the embryo has always been ambiguous, as argued here, then to attribute personhood to the embryo is to make the social statement that pregnancy is valuable and that women should subordinate other parts of their lives

> to that central aspect of their social and biological selves. Conversely, if the embryo is held to be a fetus, then it becomes socially permissible for women to subordinate their reproductive roles to other roles, particularly in the paid labor force.[110]

Contemporary reproductive justice advocates engaging this moral positioning are haunted by the rhetoric of early birth control advocates whose strategic deployment of the terministic screen of motherhood valorized women for making choices which centered their role as mother and the needs of their children.

As medical advancements largely resolved threats to the child's right to be wellborn, pro-life advocates focused in on the right of the child to be wanted. In *Roe v. Wade* the court meaningfully acknowledged the mother as the arbiter of this right as well as the complexities associated with an unwanted pregnancy. Bearing a stark resemblance to the rhetoric of early birth controllers, Justice White notes:

> The detriment that the State would impose upon the pregnant woman by denying this choice altogether is apparent. Specific and direct harm medically diagnosable even in early pregnancy may be involved. Maternity, or additional offspring, may force upon the woman a distressful life and future. Psychological harm may be imminent. Mental and physical health may be taxed by child care. There is also the distress, for all concerned, associated with the unwanted child, and there is the problem of bringing a child into a family already unable, psychologically and otherwise, to care for it.[111]

Yet, in 1992 when the court was asked to reevaluate *Roe* based on newly implemented restrictions on abortion in the state of Pennsylvania, their decision was notably devoid of the same level of empathy for the mother facing an unwanted pregnancy. The court writes:

> Even in the earliest stages of pregnancy, the State may enact rules and regulations designed to encourage her to know that there are philosophic and social arguments of great weight that can be brought to bear in favor of continuing the pregnancy to full term and that there are procedures and institutions to allow adoption of unwanted children as well as a certain degree of state assistance if the mother chooses to raise the child herself. "[T]he Constitution does not forbid a State or city, pursuant to democratic processes, from expressing a preference for normal childbirth."[112]

The movement of the court in the years between *Roe* and *Casey* is significant and demonstrates the implicit tension and subsequent vulnerability of women's negative rights given their orientation to children's positive rights.

Glen Halva-Neubauer and Sara Zeigler isolate the court's decision in *Casey* as a critical turning point in propelling fetal personhood legislation. They explain, "Casey allowed pro-life advocates to assert the state's interest in protecting fetal life in a more forceful way than in the past" and "allowed pro-life sympathizers to pursue other forms of legislation designed to establish fetal personhood as a legal principle indirectly and encourage a public perception of the fetus as a baby, rather than as something that will become a baby."[113] Today, fetal personhood laws are one of the most insidious tools utilized by pro-life activists and legislators to restrict abortion access. According to the Guttmacher Institute, there have been more than seventy-five attempts to pass fetal personhood laws at the state level since 2015; these bills substantially limit, and in some instances outright ban, abortion.[114] Contraception doesn't appear to be safe either, as legal scholar Joseph Rebone argues, "conferring personhood on the unborn child may also outlaw some contraceptives. Because contraceptives in some cases act not to prevent fertilization but rather to destroy the fertilized ovum, this could be tantamount to the killing of a person."[115]

Claims of personhood are rightfully infuriating to contemporary reproductive justice advocates who view them through the same lens of hypocrisy early birth controllers saw the Catholic Church's condemnation of contraception. Channeling this infuriation, legal scholar Katie Gentile scoffs, "Personhood and fetal rights have little to do with the health of the fetus and everything to do with containing and controlling" women and their choices, leading many contemporary activists to accuse the pro-life movement of really being pro-birth.[116] This accusation is reified by the court's opinion in *Casey* lauding adoption and the right of the state to express a preference for "normal childbirth." Yet, it was early birth controllers who first asserted the rights of children to be wanted and wellborn and demanded the state play an active role in ensuring these rights are protected. In the eyes of the pro-life movement, the state is simply meeting its burden.

The birth control movement's rhetoric regarding children enabled them to make significant headway in changing perceptions of the movement as anti-life. As explored in chapter 5, statements about the quality of life inherited by children at birth and the duty of the state to protect the rights of unborn children drew the support of eugenicists who used these arguments to fuel their negative eugenics agenda and empower the state to take drastic steps to limit the reproduction of women problematically deemed dysgenic. Their moral framework prioritizing subsistence over existence and demanding consideration of the quality of life inherited by the unborn demonstrably moved the needle for law makers, doctors, and religious figures who once ardently opposed contraceptive instruction. By the late 1930s, the movement had secured both key legal victories enabling the distribution of contraceptives as well as the support of many within the medical community, including the American Medical Association, all of which translated into the establishment of over 800 clinics by 1942.[117] Accordingly, the movement shifted its rhetorical focus from the mechanistic functions of birth control at the core of their arguments regarding the welfare of children to a more concerted defense of women's right to choose—or rather her ability to make good choices as explored in chapter 4.

Yet, in prioritizing the rhetoric of choice, the birth control movement essentially abandoned the moral and rhetorical high ground they worked so hard to establish in the first three decades of the movement by allowing the discussion of reproductive rights to be reduced to pro-choice or pro-life. Lost within these binary labels is the nuanced discussion of quality of life that was once so prominent in the discourse of early advocates. Lea Ivey argues, "Fetal rights advocates have used language much more effectively to suit their purposes than mainstream pro-choice feminists. Fetal rights advocates notoriously refer to fetuses as 'unborn children.' By deliberately using language that denotes embodied subjectivity, they confer the status of personhood upon fetuses and implore society to protect these vulnerable subjects."[118] Yet, birth controllers were the first to make such arguments—and convincingly so. The pro-life movement's rhetoric is effective today for the very same reasons birth controllers were rhetorically persuasive in the early twentieth century.

Formulated as a response to the undue emphasis placed on the concept of choice, the reproductive justice framework is uniquely suited to reintroduce nuance to the binary landscape of contemporary reproductive politics. Unlike the reproductive rights framework utilized by early advocates, reproductive justice recognizes "the right to have a child, to not have a child, and to parent the children we have in safe and healthy environments."[119] This move, explains Andrea Smith, is essential to "develop[ing] a framework that does not rest on pro-choice versus pro-life" which "would enable us to fight for reproductive justice as a part of a larger social justice strategy."[120] Operationalizing choice within the full spectrum of women's reproductive decisions is essential to swaying pro-life sympathizers by reminding them that women's choices are rarely selfishly motivated. That even though women and children have more options and support available to them than perhaps at any other time in history, subsistence must still be prioritized over existence. That protecting the sanctity of life means acknowledging each of these rights. That women's rights are not a threat to children's rights, but rather they are the primary mechanism for ensuring they are actualized in our modern neoliberal world.

NOTES

1. "Parents Will Let," 7.
2. Ibid.
3. "Birth Control Subject," 1.
4. "Helen Keller," 13.
5. "Battle Is Started," 8.
6. Department of Commerce, "Mortality Statistics," 409.
7. "Dr. Haiselden," 7.
8. Ibid.; The term "defective" used here by Haiselden and shortly after by Mary Ware Dennett was frequently used to discuss children born with congenital issues, such as John, as well as those who inherited poor health from their mothers at birth. Over time, the term assumed a much more insidious meaning as eugenicists deployed it far more liberally to describe persons deemed "undesirable." See chapter 5 for a more nuanced discussion on this topic.
9. "Defective Baby," 5.
10. Reynolds, *Women Advocates*, 58.
11. Margaret Sanger Papers, 236022.
12. "The Mother's Need," 4.
13. Bernhard, "Child Welfare," 102.
14. Thomas, "A Socialist's," 255.
15. Morley, "Primitive Methods," 267.
16. Margaret Sanger Papers, 229968.
17. Margaret Sanger Papers, 229968.
18. Margaret Sanger Papers, 213371.
19. Reynolds, *Women Advocates*, 58.
20. Margaret Sanger Papers, 236132.
21. Margaret Sanger Papers, 229968.
22. Margaret Sanger Papers, 236120.
23. Knopf, "Birth Control," 11.
24. Margaret Sanger Papers, 236134.
25. "Social Aspects," 424.
26. Margaret Sanger Papers, 236170.
27. Baber, "Birth Control," 297.
28. Sanger, "Birth Control—Past," 5.
29. Popenoe, "Birth Control," 6.
30. Blount, "Large Families," 3.
31. Margaret Sanger Papers, 236021.
32. Davis, "Analysis of the Population," 227.
33. Margaret Sanger Papers, 229968.
34. Margaret Sanger Papers, 223091.
35. Brisbane, "Birth Control," 1.
36. "Birth Control," 8.
37. Eastman, "Birth Control," 3.
38. Mudgett, "The Crying Need," 7.

39. Margaret Sanger Papers, 224706.
40. O'Reilly, "The Progress," 12.
41. Mudgett, "The Crying Need," 9.
42. O'Sullivan, "Sickness and Death," 46.
43. Keenan, "The Child," 11.
44. Lovejoy, "Birth Control," 3.
45. Ibid.
46. "Rights of the Child," 11.
47. Margaret Sanger Papers, 224706.
48. Ezer, "A Positive Right," 4.
49. Sanger, "The Tragedy," 5.
50. Margaret Sanger Papers, 223063.
51. Sanger, "The Tragedy," 6.
52. "Birth Control Held," 7.
53. Sanger, *Motherhood in Bondage*, 240.
54. Margaret Sanger Papers, 229968.
55. Margaret Sanger Papers, 228414.
56. "The Best Letter," 8.
57. Margaret Sanger Papers, 229659.
58. Haxton, "Child Welfare," 102.
59. Margaret Sanger Papers, 236042.
60. East, "Tabu," 222.
61. "Birth Control Debated," 16.
62. Browning, "The Better Half," G8; Phillips, "Planned Parenthood," K1.
63. Todd, "The Well-Born," 1.
64. Roberts, "The Birthright," 87.
65. "Appeal Now," 11.
66. Margaret Sanger Papers, 222765.
67. Roberts, "The Birthright," 89.
68. Edgren, "The Spiritual Aspect," 6.
69. "Is Birth Control," 6.
70. Clark, "The Rights of Children," 411.
71. "The Children's Charter," 290.
72. "Editorial," 69–70.
73. Ibid.
74. Bromley, "Birth Control," 21.
75. "Resolutions," 36.
76. Clark, "The Rights of Children," 405.
77. "Congregational Group Approves," 3.
78. "New Marriage Plan," 2.
79. Parkhurst, "Children Wanted," 93.
80. Sanger, "Intelligence Test," 107.
81. East, "Tabu," 222.
82. "Says Birth Control," 17.
83. Gibson, "The Termination," 1.

84. Ellis, "Birth Control," 6.
85. Sanger, "Wasting Our Human," 12.
86. Holmes, "The Church," 228.
87. "Editorial," 169.
88. Ibid.
89. Margaret Sanger Papers, 236132.
90. Dearborn, "Birth Control," 88.
91. Margaret Sanger Papers, 236132.
92. E.F.R., "Letter to," 230.
93. Margaret Sanger Papers, 229968.
94. Margaret Sanger Papers, 236141.
95. Williams, "No Happy," 48.
96. "Archbishop Hayes," 16.
97. "Dr. Haiselden," 3.
98. Margaret Sanger Papers, 236465
99. The exact date of this document is unknown as the only noted date on the original is "193?." Margaret Sanger Papers, 236465.
100. Margaret Sanger Papers, 236021.
101. Margaret Sanger Papers, 236465.
102. Margaret Sanger Papers, 236021.
103. Sanger, "Passports for," 142.
104. Ibid.
105. A Friend, "Hymn of the," 16.
106. Meyer, "The Unborn," 6.
107. Dubow, *Ourselves Unborn*, 9.
108. Ibid.
109. Ibid., 190.
110. Luker, *Abortion &*, 7–8.
111. *Roe v. Wade*, 410 U.S. 113 (1973).
112. *Planned Parenthood of Southeastern Pennsylvania v. Casey*, 505 U.S. 833 (1992).
113. Halva-Neubauer and Ziegler, "Promoting Fetal," 103.
114. Guttmacher Institute, "State Legislation Tracker."
115. Rebone, "Personhood and," 581.
116. Gentile, "Using Queer," 38.
117. Margaret Sanger Papers, 227219.
118. Ivey, "Deconstructing, Reclaiming," 4.
119. Ross, "Trust Black," 63.
120. Smith, "Beyond Pro-Choice," 167.

Chapter Four

Responsible People, Responsible Parents

In season two of the hit Netflix show Orange Is the New Black, *the beloved character Black Cindy blew her fellow inmates' minds when she declared "My grandma used to douche with disinfectant. This was the original birth control. It's cheaper than condoms and it leaves the koochy crack smelling lemony fresh." Though the show is fictional, Cindy's declaration is anything but. While Cindy, battling an outbreak of bedbugs in the episode, happily douses herself in disinfectant, chances are it was one of the only readily available options for her grandmother. Unlike other early contraceptive devices found on the black market, disinfectants like Lysol® could be purchased virtually everywhere. Lehn & Fink, the makers of Lysol®, capitalized on this captive audience and directly marketed their product to women through a series of ads entitled "calendar fear" which appeared in everyday publications including the Sunday edition of the* New York Daily News. *Used as a douching solution, Lysol® promised to eliminate a woman's "calendar fear" by ridding the "delicate, tender tissues" of germ-life, making it "truly a revelation to the fear-worn wife in its dependable contributions to marital health and happiness." Although the Comstock Act prevented the company from explicitly labeling the Lysol® douche as contraception, nothing stopped them from touting the benefits of their signature product for the purposes of "marriage hygiene."*[1] *Oh, and in case you were worried about the safety of literally douching with Lysol®, they wanted you to know it was druggist and doctor approved! These campaigns combined with the accessibility of Lysol® made it the best-selling feminine hygiene/contraceptive product until well into the 1960s.*[2]

The prominence of Lysol® douching as a contraceptive method is admittedly jarring to modern readers accustomed to roaming drug store aisles with expansive sections devoted solely to feminine hygiene and family planning. Equally jarring is the rhetoric utilized by Lehn & Fink to market their product. Unlike modern contraceptive marketing showcasing the empowered woman living life on her own terms, the women targeted by these advertisements were neither empowered nor permitted to live life exclusively on their terms. Instead, as Andrea Tone argues, these advertisements "were designed to inculcate and inflate apprehensions in the reader's minds. They conveyed the message that ineffective contraception led not only to unwanted pregnancies but also to illness, despair, and marital discord."[3] *Rather than a stroke of marketing genius, Lehn & Fink seem to have taken their cues directly from the rhetoric of early birth controllers. Butting up against dominant depictions of contraceptive users as selfish, promiscuous, anti-child, and race saboteurs, advocates carefully constructed the image of an ideal contraceptive user. She was a devoted wife who sought the assistance of contraception to plan her family in accordance with her husband's earning power and with the goal of providing the best quality of life for her growing brood. She was, as Lehn & Fink brilliantly put it, "the fear-haunted wife."*

Sanger formally established the movement with her publication of *The Woman Rebel*, but quickly realized advancing its goals necessitated a far less rebellious woman. In their earliest attempt to form a strategic alliance, birth controllers courted suffragists whose shared goal of emancipation seemed like an obvious fit. Suffragists, however, remained wary of the movement's far more radical vision of female empowerment particularly as it related to the sexual liberation of women. Their reticence reverberated widely as doctors and politicians similarly refused to endorse the movement, citing its questionable morals, and clinging to the assumption that promiscuity and licentiousness would increase if couples could freely engage in nonprocreative sex.

Convincing wary allies of the value of birth control to the lives of women and their husbands necessitated new rhetorical strategies justifying the ideological functions of contraception. Unlike the mechanistic function of birth control which directly benefits society, such as decreased mortality rates and improved child welfare, the ideological benefits of birth control exist primarily at the individual level. These benefits, including sexual liberation and expanded opportunities, also signaled a huge cultural shift. Despite the passage of the Nineteenth Amendment, or perhaps because of it, the emerging notion of "the new woman" threatened to destabilize the existing family structure, and contraception would surely accelerate its decline.

Continuing the trend established in previous chapters, advocates accordingly abandoned their radical framing of contraception in favor of persuasive appeals to traditional norms and values. Operating from a defensive posture, advocates worked diligently to assure critics of contraception's role in preserving, not eroding, traditional family values as they related to the development of girls into wives and mothers for dutiful husbands.

Advocates lauded the independent, well-educated modern woman as a symbol of contraception's emancipatory power but rarely featured this woman's story prominently in their rhetoric, instead focusing on the downtrodden woman desperate for contraceptives merely to survive. Giving only a passing mention to the education and employment opportunities made possible by contraception, advocates emphasized the need for young girls to fully develop prior to motherhood—to grow as people and partners capable of being excellent parents. Motherhood remained a foregone conclusion. Men also stood to benefit from contraception; they could now plan their children in accordance with their income and enjoy the marital bliss connected to the removal of fear. The institution of marriage was perhaps the biggest winner as contraception promised to facilitate early, happier, and more sexually fulfilling marriages for both partners.

Perhaps what is most striking about the movement's rhetoric espousing the ideological benefits of birth control is how little the needs of women actually factored into this rhetoric. Although birth controllers initially position contraception as the linchpin to the full liberation of women, they routinely articulated this liberation in terms of its benefit to her life as a married woman and mother. This framing provided crucial inroads to rebuff opponents who propagated a narrative of contraceptive users as selfishly motivated and anti-child and scaffolded nicely with their moral defense of family planning as morally superior to involuntary parenthood. Taken together, this rhetoric seeks to position women as trustworthy of making sound decisions regarding their reproduction—as responsible reproducers. In isolation this is clearly a valid premise, but in the context of the larger discourse surrounding reproduction the notions of responsibility and trustworthiness are easily weaponized against women presumed incapable of embodying these traits. Resulting in what I call the contraceptive hierarchy, these discourses work to discipline women into making choices deemed responsible by a system which implicitly biases traditional heteronormative standards of morality.

EMERGING IN THE SHADOW OF SUFFRAGE

Despite its emergence in the waning years of the fight for women's suffrage, the birth control movement often experienced a contentious relationship with suffragists. Historians Heather Munro Prescott and Lauren McIvor Thompson argue, "The ideological connections in both movements cannot be reduced to merely schematic understandings or a simplistic relationship. . . . Rather, we find that reformers' demands comprised a series of overlapping and often competing arguments for bodily autonomy as part of a broad spectrum of rights."[4] Many suffragists kept their distance, fearful the inclusion of contraceptives into their political agenda might be both a distraction and a political liability. The reticence of Carrie Chapman Catt, a key player in the suffrage movement, is emblematic: "[P]lease be assured that I am no opponent even though I do not stand by your side. . . . [Y]our reform is too narrow to appeal to me and too sordid."[5] Conversely, birth controllers framed suffrage as a partial victory and, as historian Linda Gordon explains, quickly set out to "transform the nature of women's rights—indeed, of human rights—to include free sexual expression and reproductive self-determination."[6] This framing of contraception troubled many suffragists who relied on appeals to traditional standards of appropriateness for women, especially sexual standards, to win popular support for suffrage. Suffragists faced a difficult choice: endorse birth control and jeopardize their own movement or reject birth control despite ideological sympathies.

Searching for Common Ground

Although suffragists fought broadly for equality between men and women, they localized their fight in terms of access to the ballot whereas many birth controllers, especially Mary Ware Dennett, took umbrage with this myopic view of equality. A proud suffragist herself, Dennett rejected arguments premised on the unique value of women voters, such as those stemming from the temperance movement instead defending women's right to vote from the basis of their shared humanity. Dennett cautioned, "So it behooves us to go slowly with our bragging of what we have done and our promising of what we will do with our votes and to turn the attention of our audiences to the fact that we are asking for the vote just because we are people, units in the community, and, as such, must be counted in when the affairs of the community are arranged."[7] Dennett rejected the instrumentalist logic of suffragists who lobbied for the ballot solely on the grounds that women would do great things with their enfranchisement.

For Dennett, the issues facing women, including suffrage and contraceptive access, were structural issues unlikely to be fixed through the addition of rights without a reconsideration of the underlying causes. Using the fight against poverty as an example of the need to reject systemic oppression, she explains, "Undeserved poverty is the daily curse of vast portion of womankind. . . . Our proposal is not to treat the symptoms of poverty but to strike a blow at its root which we believe is the unequal right to the earth."[8] Dennett was not alone in her focus on the structural components that had disenfranchised women for generations. Suffragist and social worker Edith Houghton Hooker poignantly acknowledged the immense weight of these structural forces situating the full embrace of voluntary motherhood as the key to actualizing women's freedom. She proclaims:

> It is interesting to observe that even the most radical feminist organizations in America do not include birth control in their programs. Expediency doubtless is in large measure responsible for this negative policy. . . . As involuntary motherhood is the taproot of the subjection of women, so will its final uprooting the last symbol of their emancipation. . . . Ours has been a voluntary subjection, not born of nature, nor created by man, but entered into in the sacrificial spirit of motherhood. While the race required it, women with generous, though unknowing hands, placed her life upon the altar. But now the need is no longer there. The full cup, life, love, children, personal fulfillment, stands ready to her lips. She and her mate will drink of it together and be glad, when the courage to be free quickens her sleeping soul.[9]

Hooker's statement vocalizes the feelings of frustration shared by advocates, like herself and Dennett, who failed to understand the broader suffrage movement's nonacceptance of birth control while also, and perhaps more importantly, identifying ingrained cultural patterns and practices as an explanation for their reluctance to embrace the movement's bold promises of emancipation and liberation.

As explored in chapter 1, Dennett clung tightly to her ideological commitments pursuing reforms addressing systems of oppression rather than those merely granting women increased access to a flawed system. Dennett's articulation of what feminism means to her is illustrative; she clarifies, "Feminism has nothing to do with suffrage. It is the rebellion against being ticketed and treated as somebody's female relative. It began with women's claim to an education, to her own property and to equal guardianship of her children. There are as many phases of feminism as there are ways of making coffee, for every woman's revolt takes a different form."[10] This view gained traction with many reformers who failed to see significant changes to their daily lives despite passage of the Nineteenth Amendment. According to the *New York Times* in 1926, "many once ardent suffragists see that feminism means something else than adopting the ways of men . . . that the process can be achieved only in the transformation of society as a whole."[11] Just as Dennett fought obscenity laws in the name of civil liberties, she approached suffrage specifically and feminism more broadly with a distinctly humanist perspective necessitating structural changes to the systems oppressing women.

Dennett's commitment to feminist ethics often put her at odds with her fellow activists in the suffrage movement. When the National League of Women Voters (NLWV) refused to endorse contraception in 1921, a clearly frustrated Dennett reiterated its importance to achieving the larger ambitions of the women's movement. Acknowledging the organization's reticence stemmed from a desire to placate conservative and Catholic members as well as preserve their existing efforts with the Sheppard-Towner Act, Dennett pleaded with NLWV leaders "to understand that birth control was 'the very basis of child welfare,' and that the 'service' provided by Sheppard-Towner would be 'incomplete' without teaching women how to 'space births by regulating conception.'" [12] The inability or unwillingness of other reformers to acknowledge the role of contraception in the struggle for equality was a recurring source of frustration for birth controllers in the early twentieth century. A 1928 editorial in the *Birth Control Review* tells a similar story regarding the National Women's Party:

> They do work for blanket equal rights in marriage, but at the same time they push very definite concrete legislation for such partial rights in marriage as those concerning property, earnings, equality in divorce and equal guardianship of children. If women work for a law giving them equal rights to children born, why should they not work for a law, even more vital, giving them the right to determine whether or not children shall be born to them? If the aim of the National Woman's Party is complete equality between men and women it cannot consistently appear in a legislative hearing in support of an equal guardianship law, while it absents itself from the hearing on a birth control bill.[13]

As explored in previous chapters, birth controllers hoped to find a sympathetic audience with like-minded reformers—socialists, suffragists, labor activists—but despite similar ideological underpinnings, none of these groups proved to be a fruitful alliance for the movement.

Rather than working together to secure enfranchisement and contraceptive access, the two movements continued to wrestle for both power and issue supremacy. Crystal Eastman, a well-known lawyer and activist for both suffrage and birth control, sought to temper this dispute by acknowledging the interconnectedness of the movements. Writing in 1918 she pleaded: "[W]e are surely agreed, that birth control is an elementary essential in all aspects of feminisms. . . . if feminism, conscious and bold and intelligent, leads the demand, it will be supported by the secret eagerness of all women to control the size of their families, and a suffrage state should make short work of repealing these old laws that stand in the way of birth control."[14] The valiant efforts of Eastman and Dennett to unite suffragists and birth controllers resulted in a stalemate with both sides demanding deference from the other. Two articles appearing in the same 1928 issue of the *Birth Control Review* showcase the continued tensions felt between the movements. An editorial on page 5 chastises national organizations representing women for collectively ignoring the birth control cause, noting, "There never was offered in a woman's program a fundamental demand for freedom and self-realization on which so large a body of women of so many shades of opinion were ready and waiting to agree."[15] Yet, an article tucked in the back of the issue includes a bold statement from the National Women's Party expressing their frustration with the ABCL: "We believe that women cannot exercise the right to limit their families if they choose unless they have Equal Rights in all the relations of life. Thus, we might ask the American Birth Control League to place Equal Rights in its programs as an essential part of its demands."[16] The circularity of their logic left both sides claiming primacy while also seeking collaboration—an obvious exercise in futility.

Advocates grew increasingly frustrated with the reluctance of suffragists to support the birth control movement. A clearly exasperated Sanger remarked in March 1920: "We promised when we sought the ballot that we would make use of it . . . [yet] in none of those states where women have for years had the ballot, has there been any attempt to amend or repeal the laws against birth control."[17] An unsigned editorial in the *Birth Control Review* directly confronted the League of Women Voters and questioned their commitment to the rights of women, chiding, "If the women of America had been as timorous as this in the last decade, would they ever have got the vote? Nowadays their policy seems to be determined by considerations of expediency rather than rights."[18] Leaders were equally flummoxed by the perceived hypocrisy among key suffragists who themselves had small families or no children at all. Sanger pointed out in a 1933 speech that "only because [of] its practice among themselves could [women] have battled for suffrage or any other social and cultural movement during their childbearing years."[19] If suffragists relied on family limitation to enact their own democratic participation, wouldn't other women need the same opportunity?

Birth controllers also pointed to the privileged status of suffragists, often the result of both race and class, which afforded them a level of political and personal autonomy inaccessible for poor women. A 1917 editorial in the *Birth Control Review* asserts: "There are hundreds of thousands of mothers who are so submerged beneath the burdens of childbearing that they will not have the time to even cast their vote, much less to take an intelligent interest in the problems of the society."[20] Dennett advanced a similar allegation in her 1921 critique of the NLWV and "urged League members to note the disservice that they, as the 'more or less privileged, sophisticated, resourceful women of the country,' would be doing to 'the great mass of poor and ignorant women' by refusing to support the cause of legal contraception."[21] An obvious overlap existed between prominent suffragists and the privileged classes of women able to circumvent contraception's illegality through access to private physicians. Dennett and Sanger rightfully chastised suffragists for failing to use both their privilege and enfranchisement to secure the same access to contraceptive information they clearly already enjoyed.

Despite their differences, birth controllers could not afford to completely shun suffragists or denounce their contributions to the movement's trajectory.

Suffragist and birth control advocate Florence Guertin Tuttle explained the primary commonality between the two movements in the *Birth Control Review* in 1921: "Each movement has had the same enemies to fight, the ancient foes of tradition and prejudice, of ignorance and superstition, and in both causes, to fight these foes, courage, vision, endurance and consecration to a higher racial ideal have been required."[22] The "racial ideal" referred to by Tuttle is that of a free and equal human race which she explains was not achieved solely through the passage of the Nineteenth Amendment. She continues, "It is true that the granting of the franchise was supposed to emancipate woman in some total and miraculous way. And so it did emancipate her mind to express itself in political terms. But the complete emancipation of woman cannot be affected while unjust laws in regard to her body are on the statutes."[23] Ever the opportunists, birth controllers capitalized on the momentum of suffragists through the strategic co-optation of the salient discursive strategies of suffragists. In doing so, the movement engaged in what communication scholar Jennifer Peeples calls appropriation; she explains, "once an articulation becomes successful . . . the constructs begin to appear in the rhetoric of other like-minded or oppositional groups that see these articulations as a means of gaining the material and/or symbolic rewards momentarily attached to that discourse."[24] Through appropriation, birth controllers used the early victories of the women's movement as a springboard to advocate for contraceptive control and choice, extending the constructs of emancipation, freedom, liberty, and equality popularized by suffragists to build a case for reproductive rights.

Appending and Appropriating the Suffragist Movement

Initially, birth controllers applauded the efforts of suffragists while judiciously reminding audiences of the deficiency of enfranchisement alone. Florence Guertin Tuttle bluntly pleaded with her fellow suffragists to recognize the emptiness of extending voting rights to women without also ridding the law of measures limiting women's bodily autonomy. Tuttle scolds, "She is not free when the law bars her from that science which should shield the birth of every child. This is a fundamental truth the sooner all suffragists comprehend the better. The granting of a scrap of paper to be used once a year cannot emancipate woman so long as other scraps of paper hold them in legal physical bondage to a mistaken idea."[25] In addition to securing the right to vote, the women's movement made significant strides in reforming laws undermining women's autonomy such as coverture; yet even these efforts fell short in the eyes of the birth control movement. Writing for the *Birth Control Review* in 1921, Sanger labeled these victories as merely steps in the right direction, cautioning, "she has claimed the right of suffrage and legislative regulation of her working hours, and asked that her property right be equal to those of the man. None of these demands, however, affected directly the most vital factors of her existence."[26] It was true that women in the early twentieth century possessed more rights and freedom than any other time in history, yet they still lacked the basic ability to make unfettered decisions regarding their own reproduction.

Birth controllers rightly scrutinized the utility of achieving social and political equality in a world where women remained constrained by their biological burden of childbearing. In a 1933 speech entitled a "New Deal for Women," Sanger proclaimed: "Woman has struggled upward for her rights and she has won them, one by one, but until she has won biological freedom over the laws of childbearing, her other prizes so hardly won can do little for her onward march in civilization. The function of procreation must be under her control for the woman who is constantly submerged in the fears of pregnancy can never be equal in social or political efficiency to man."[27] Accordingly, advocates situated contraceptive freedom as concordant with legislative moves toward women's autonomy and a prerequisite to enacting the full rights of women. Building on the successful repeal of laws prohibiting women from owning property, activist and journalist Lily Winner positioned reproductive control and choice as the next logical step toward the complete freedom of women. She explained in the *Birth Control Review in* 1917, "now that the law recognizes her as a self-centered individual, not incorporated in another personality . . . she must fight for her own body, to own it and care for it and use it according to her own high desire and purpose."[28] Winner's statement also highlighted the need to build on the more pragmatic victories of the women's movement, such as property ownership and suffrage, by pushing for more intangible rights such as self-fulfillment. Such demands facilitated a shift in the movement's rhetoric away from the mechanistic benefits of birth control toward the ideological justifications for its widespread adoption.

In addition to appending contraceptive control and choice to the established feminist agenda, birth controllers strategically adopted the rhetoric of previous movements to harness their momentum for social change. Prescott and Thompson explain, "Since the beginning of the women's movement, their activism encompassed not only the quest for the vote but the right to bodily control as well. . . . Early birth control activists had seized on this old idea and used it as part of a series of strategies to popularize the idea of making contraception legal."[29] Recognizing the rhetorical salience of concepts such as freedom, liberty, equality, and emancipation, birth controllers co-opted this language to position contraception as a complementary goal. Asserting the foundational nature of birth control to women's freedom, Sanger declared in 1921: "[B]irth control is the means by which woman attains basic freedom; [it] is for woman the key to the temple of liberty."[30] This logic reverberated in reformist circles as illustrated by the bold statement of famous socialist Eugene V. Debs in the *Birth Control Review*. Debs proclaimed:

> She demands the whole of freedom for the whole of womankind. The ballot is but a paltry concession to her revolutionary aspiration and determination. The right to vote, to a voice in human relations is elementary, and it is the shame and reproach of man that he robbed woman of her birthright and gloried in her humiliation and in his own brutal conquest. . . . FREEDOM, COMPLETE FREEDOM, is the goal of woman's struggle in the modern world, the struggle in which she must persist at any cost until she is absolutely free from man's insolent and debasing domination. She, the mother of man, shall be the sovereign ruler of the world. She shall have sole custody of her own body; She shall have perfect sex freedom as well as economic, intellectual and moral freedom, and she alone who suffers the agony of birth shall have the control of the creative functions with which she is endowed. Speed the day when woman shall be free! Then, too, shall man be free and they together, emancipated from the degrading ignorance and superstition of the past, shall walk into the Highlands of vision, mate in perfect love, and people the earth with a race of gods.[31]

In one paragraph, Debs does a great deal of heavy rhetorical lifting; he identifies the right to vote as insufficient, establishes bodily autonomy as a prerequisite to full freedom, and connects the emancipation of women with the larger social good. Sanger extends these connections in a 1933 speech explicitly labeling contraception an instrument to secure equality between the sexes. She proclaimed, "only through the emancipation of woman's creative energies, her sex force, can humanity redeem itself" and asserted the foundation for the movement should be to make motherhood a "voluntary and conscious undertaking in order to be approximately equal to man. Upon this foundation only can she strive for equal rights."[32] Previous reforms sought to establish greater parity between the sexes in terms of property ownership and enfranchisement under the auspices of creating equality; however, true equality remained contingent on an equalization of the biological burden between males and females or at the very least the provision of bodily autonomy for women to choose the biological burden of childbearing.

The movement intensified the rhetorical linkages between contraception and emancipation through comparison to other historical struggles for freedom. Initially, Sanger proclaimed in 1916 that women were subjected to "the same powers of oppression which wrought from us the liberties [of] our forefathers. . . . Today we are engaged in a relentless struggle for woman's liberty . . . for her release from the domination of church and state."[33] Localizing the struggle as a battle for freedom from church and state resonated within the deeply held values of a nation birthed by revolution. Building on this analogy, Sanger suggested just as Great Britain used America for resources to selfishly build their empire, women have "been the stepping stone of oligarchies [and] kingdoms" who have "thrived on her enslavement."[34] This overtly patriotic rhetoric became increasingly salient amid the backdrop of two ongoing world wars with advocates pleading for a renewed sense of urgency to safeguard all forms of liberty—including reproductive freedom. Sanger demanded in 1942:

> At no time in history has it been so important that we here in the last remaining stronghold of human liberty keep that eternal vigilance that is the price of freedom; that we be ever alert to preserving our human rights—our civil liberties—in their full vigor . . . [including] the right of free men and free women to undertake the deep and satisfying act of parenthood, not by chance or ignorance, but in full knowledge of their responsibility to the child, to themselves and to the nation. Only on this foundation can a free, sturdy, and independent people build their collective life and maintain intact their liberties.[35]

The use of historical parallels further aligned birth controllers with suffragists who had frequently deployed an identical rhetorical strategy. The Declaration of Sentiments drafted by suffragists at the Seneca Falls Convention in 1848 repurposed the Declaration of Independence to establish a parallel between woman suffrage and the American Revolution. Noting the importance of the Declaration of Sentiments as the "first important feminist document in this country," journalist Mildred Adams suggested that birth control may finally "move [women] into the enlarged sphere which her great creator has assigned to her," fulfilling the ultimate objective established by those in attendance at the Seneca Falls Convention.[36] Adams's use of rhetoric from the Declaration of Sentiments situates birth control within the historical progression of revolution in the United States and demonstrates the salience of the established connection between the fight for birth control and previous struggles against oppression.

Additionally, birth controllers extended slavery and bondage as a metaphor to explain the oppression resulting from the denial of bodily autonomy to women. Prescott and Thompson elaborate, "White female abolitionists and women's rights reformers drew explicitly on the connections between slavery and marriage, arguing that both enslaved people and women had unfree bodies and were civilly dead, unable to participate in the public sphere."[37] While exploring the question of whether or not birth control was an issue for parents or simply women, Sanger argued, "She is still in the position of dependent today because her mate has refused to consider her as an individual apart from his needs . . . she is exploited, driven and enslaved."[38] Historian Walter Adolphe Roberts extended this argument when he wrote in 1917 that "it is essential to women to know how to prevent conception. Without this knowledge, she cannot . . . emerge from the sex-bondage in which she has been held."[39]

Birth controllers were not the first group to analogize the oppression of women with slavery. Historian Laura Mayhall argues suffragists and abolitionists in the 1800s such as Lucretia Mott used the concepts of slavery and tyranny within their rhetoric to "connect family, state, and citizenship within the realm of the political, and [offer] remedies for their political exclusion."[40] The use of slavery and bondage as a metaphor for the denial of reproductive rights functioned in much the same way by suggesting women, and subsequently humanity, could not be free as long as they remained in the bondage of unrestrained childbearing inflicted on them through the tyranny of church and state. This metaphor held strategic value as well helping white birth controllers forge connections with both abolitionists and Black suffragists by connecting their struggles for freedom.

The passage of the Nineteenth Amendment dramatically altered the landscape of the birth control movement producing a rupture between mainstream feminists, afraid to push their luck on additional legal reforms, and radical birth controllers committed to a continued legal battle for birth control. Historian Carole McCann contends the passage of the Nineteenth Amendment split feminist coalitions into diverse single-issue groups, leading to what she describes as a "chilly relationship" between feminist organizations and birth controllers who futilely sought the official endorsement of both the National Women's Party and the League of Women Voters.[41] Historian Elaine Tyler May explains, "as the women's rights movement gained momentum in the early twentieth century . . . birth control advocates promoted contraceptive as a radical idea linked to political change as well as personal emancipation."[42] The birth control movement soon found itself in a tricky position which illuminates the strategic differences between Dennett and Sanger.

Dennett, ever the ideologue, pushed suffragists to expand their often myopic view of equality beyond the ballot. Reformers like Dennett "considered legal and political advancement important, but they thought that the way to accomplish these goals was through the reformation of society to recognize woman as free actors, in charge of their own destiny, rather than directly through the reformation of laws."[43] Analogous with her rejection of doctors-only bills in favor of removing obscenity laws, Dennett remained committed to destroying the systems and structures responsible for women's oppression rather than merely amending them to give women the semblance of equality. Yet, "in a period of enormous legal change and constitutional transformation, radical demands to upend traditional marriage and family were at odds with the postbellum focus of the suffrage movement."[44] The result was a rhetorical strategy premised on demonstrating the interconnectedness of birth control and women's suffrage utilizing concepts already rooted in the public consciousness such as bodily autonomy, freedom, and emancipation.

Yet, leaning too heavily into this rhetorical strategy also carried the implicit risk of isolating other key allies, namely the medical community, who supported birth control as a public health measure but not as a mechanism for liberation. Jessie Ashley, an advocate who was arrested in 1916 for dispensing contraceptive information, explained in the *Birth Control Review*:

> They discussed [birth control] as a measure calculated to replenish the race, to multiply the number thereof. It was just like talking about democracy, perfectly proper and safe, until this misguided member of the board of the National Birth Control League happened to suggest that birth control would be a boon to women by giving them protection and a little freedom by helping them to control their own bodies. Horrors! The worthy doctors grew cold. That they gravely answered would be personal individual liberty; we cannot consider personal freedom.[45]

Professionalizing the movement to gain the allied support of doctors, social workers, and policy makers was a top priority for the movement particularly as envisioned by Sanger. These stakeholders, however, concerned themselves almost exclusively with the mechanistic functions of contraception related to maternal mortality, child welfare, and the economic implications of large families. Women's bodily autonomy was, and in many ways remains, an irrelevant consideration for those interested in the benefits accrued through managed reproduction. Accordingly, Sanger tempered her demands for liberty arguing in 1924: "The philosophy of birth control insists upon the maximum of personal liberty in every sphere of human behavior that is compatible with the maxim of personal responsibility. Rightly or wrongly, it throws back upon the individual full responsibility [to] act upon the basis of reason, experience, and prudence."[46] Sanger uses the well-worn appeal to personal responsibility, outlined in chapter 2, to mediate the movement's liberatory rhetoric suggesting that liberty only extends to those responsible enough to use it properly.

The emancipated woman, even in its tamest iterations, marked a significant departure from the generations of women who had come before her. She now had the right to vote, own property, have dual custodianship over her children; yet laws classifying contraception as obscene and a threat to morality prevented her from enacting bodily autonomy over her most basic human function. Birth control promised freedom from the biological enslavement of unrestrained reproduction and subsequently the full benefits of her emancipation. Challenging these laws meant bucking centuries of tradition prohibiting women from acting autonomously and justifying the lifestyle of the emancipated woman—one characterized by choice.

THE EMANCIPATED WOMAN CHOOSES

Under the leadership of Sanger, the movement went to great lengths to establish the mechanistic functions and benefits of managed reproduction facilitated by the dissemination and use of contraceptive information. The wide scale adoption of contraceptive methods promised to dramatically reduce maternal mortality, infant mortality, and abortion as well as significantly improve child welfare and maternal health. These benefits directly correlated to the control side of the reproductive rights equation as they relied on the actual application of contraception. As demonstrated in previous chapters, these arguments enjoyed broad uptake and produced tangible victories for the movement in terms of both decreased regulation and increased popular support. Yet, securing these outcomes required the movement to continually defend itself against attacks conflating regulation with elimination and branding the movement as selfishly motivated and anti-child. Advocates rebuked these claims in nuanced ways reflecting the specificity of the opposition argument; however, at the heart of each of these retorts exists a basic assumption of motherhood as a natural and inevitable desire for women or what is described in chapter 2 as the terministic screen of motherhood.

The terministic screen of motherhood also filtered into the movement's discourse surrounding the emancipation of women made possible through contraception. Speaking more to the ideological functions of birth control including expanded opportunities, bodily autonomy, and sexual liberation, these rhetorical strategies justified the uptake of contraception based on an adherence to the philosophy of voluntary parenthood. Resulting in what feminist political theorist Lealle Ruhl calls "the willed pregnancy," birth controllers sought to imbue reproduction with the ideas of responsibility, self-control, and, ultimately, freedom of choice.[47] Sanger's rhetoric reflected these commitments almost verbatim. She writes, "It is constructive from the educational point of view because it stimulates habits of intelligent self-direction and control, gives parents the autonomous conduct of their own lives, and awakens a sense of their responsibility in bringing children into the world."[48] Attaining individual development, relational satisfaction, and sexual liberation necessitated adherence to the framework of "the willed pregnancy" and a rejection of the naturalist paradigm, positioning reproduction outside the realm of human influence. In this framework, choice is dependent on control as one cannot make a choice without both a variety of options and the ability to freely select the option that best fits their needs. Yet, the rhetoric itself moves beyond the physical implications of control, such as mortality and overpopulation, to address the new possibilities for women and their partners when parenthood is a choice rather than a consequence.

In one of her boldest explanations of the right to choose, Sanger vehemently defends the right of women to decide not only when, but if, they shall have children and staunchly insists women be the sole decision makers regarding reproduction. She proclaims:

> Woman must have her freedom—the fundamental freedom of choosing whether or not she shall be a mother and how many children she will have. Regardless of what man's attitude may be, that problem is hers—and before it can be his, it is hers alone. She goes through the valley of the shadow of death alone, each time a baby is born. As it is the right neither of man nor the state to coerce her into this ordeal, so it is her right to decide whether she will endure it. That right to decide imposes upon her the duty of clearing the way to knowledge by which she may make and carry out the decision. Birth control is a woman's problem. The quicker she accepts it as hers and hers alone, the quicker will society respect motherhood. The quicker, too, will the world be made a fit place for children to live.[49]

At first glance this statement reads as an unflinching endorsement of women's autonomy irrespective of her desire, or lack thereof, to be a mother. Yet, even at her boldest, Sanger's pronouncement of women's right to decide remains tethered to motherhood with women assigned the unique responsibility of restoring society's respect and making the world suitable for children. This muddled statement is emblematic of the movement's larger rhetorical strategy concerning women's autonomy and freedom of choice—bold statements accompanied by frequent caveats.

Caveats of this kind were recurrent among birth controllers who spoke of choice almost exclusively in terms of its relationship to motherhood. The explanation of choice provided by Alice Drysdale Vickery is illustrative. Vickery explains, "The adult daughter should consult with their respective partner, as to their mutual claims. The wife who agrees to retire from industrial or professional employment in marriage, will only do so on the recognition by her husband of her claim to be considered an equal participator in all his acquisitions in emoluments. This is essential to our self-respect and personal dignity."[50] For Vickery, the power of choice comes not in the pursuit of opportunities outside the home but in the freedom to choose motherhood from a position of equality in the marriage. Birth control expanded women's choices but did not free them from the societal expectations of marriage and motherhood.

For centuries, women deployed a variety of techniques hoping to prevent or postpone pregnancy including abstinence, the rhythm method, withdrawal, and prolonged breastfeeding; yet the fallibility of these methods made them much more of a gamble than a guarantee. Absent the ability to meaningfully plan for pregnancy, women lacked the ability to vigorously pursue opportunities outside the home. At the most basic level, scientific information regarding conception enabled women to delay pregnancy until they reached full maturity. Sanger explained in 1917: "As soon as pregnancy begins the mother's own development is arrested. The child mother is therefore stunted in growth both in mind and body." She furthered, "Every breeder of animals understands this natural law, and keeps his young heifers or mares from breeding until they are grown and developed and ready for the strain."[51] Though opponents suggested faster maturation among females meant they were capable of childbearing at a much younger age than males, advocates rejected the forced maturation brought about by parenthood uniquely robbing women of the opportunity for education and other valuable life experiences. Sanger laments, "The American boys and girls who are given longer education and freedom from responsibility shed considerable light on the forced process which has for so long made women out of really immature girls."[52] The BCCRB detailed the benefits of full physical and psychological development in their June 1935 progress report concluding, voluntary parenthood enables "spiritual, physical, and emotional fulfillment" by making it possible "for persons to marry and lead a normal sex life while completing their education and professional training."[53] Although women stood to benefit greatly from the ability to control their reproduction, the BCCRB's statement reflects the two primary areas emphasized by advocates: expanded opportunities outside the home and increased sexual satisfaction.

In laying out the two major ideological functions of contraception—expanded opportunities and sexual liberation—birth controllers imbued their rhetoric with idealistic optimism while simultaneously reassuring critics these benefits were compatible with existing societal norms and expectations of women and the mothers they would eventually become. Opportunities for women were framed as additions to and not replacements for motherhood. Sexual liberation for women existed solely within the confines of monogamous marriage. The movement's rhetoric articulating a woman's right to choose was less about the actual choices she would make and more about making the very existence of her choice acceptable. The movement's rhetoric is accordingly preoccupied with statements assuaging the concerns of opponents and defending the morality of women as agentic actors. The following analysis of the movement's rhetoric reads less like an unflinching declaration of women's autonomy and more like a timorous plea for recognition with the promise of compliance. Nevertheless, it is upon these rhetorical foundations that the right to contraception, and subsequently all reproductive rights, were won, so it behooves us to understand why the movement opted for restraint and the lasting consequences of that decision.

New Opportunities for Women

Justifying the pursuit of opportunities outside the home necessitated advocates challenge the existing societal norms and structures demarcating the public and private domain as belonging to men and women respectively. Assuming a correlation between these spheres and the biological burden borne uniquely by females, Sanger labeled pregnancy as "the greatest handicap that woman has had to overcome in order to develop her talents and to express her individuality."[54] Over time, this biological burden cemented into the social fabric and emerged as the prevailing basis of inequity between men and women. Feminist and legal activist Doris Stevens laments, "This over-emphasis of woman's reproductive ability, this social exclusion from diverse expression of her creative abilities, is too universal to have been accidental. It is as if man, not being the race bearer, had elected to compensate himself by usurping all other power."[55] For centuries, constant childbearing made women dependent on their male partners for financial and physical assistance. Journalist and advocate Lily Winner explained in 1918, "man has for centuries held his power over his mate through her own ignorance and dependence upon him, and consciously, as evolution wrought its inevitable awakening process, man has struggled to keep that power by nursing prejudice and superstition."[56] From an evolutionary standpoint women were victims of circumstance forced to rely on their male counterparts; however, as progress eliminated the environmental factors necessitating such dependence, prejudice and fear stepped in to maintain the imbalances between the sexes in both spheres. Dennett offers a blistering critique of the assumed division of labor between mothers and fathers:

> In the wage slave class both the men and the women share the same stupid fate, the women always getting the worst of it, however. For childbearing is added to their own other laborers. Men have been apt to assume that their responsibilities to women and children were wholly discharged by merely paying over cash, without much personal service. Both men and women had meant well, but the men have been rather stupidly selfish, and the women stupidly unselfish.[57]

Consistent with her harsh criticism of the separate spheres doctrine offered in chapter 2, Dennett resisted the bifurcated view of emancipation seeking women's entry into the workforce without calling upon men to assume greater responsibility in the home.

Even with a dissolution of the separate spheres, true equality was unlikely absent a woman's ability to ameliorate the undue burden of pregnancy. Sanger argued in 1933: "The woman who is constantly in the condition of pregnancy, or who is submerged in fears of pregnancy, can never be equal in economic or social efficiency to man. Even with great expectations of wealth and cars, she cannot keep step with him under these conditions."[58] Sanger's statements demonstrate the movement's willingness to challenge the existing power dynamics between men and women attributable to their uneven biological burdens—the control of which for women enabled them to explore the full range of their identities. Taken in even their most modest form, birth controllers warned of the shifts in familial life attendant with the uptake of contraception. "The pattern of home living suitable for modern conditions needs more than ever to be questioned and planned. To this end, women and men need new kinds of services designed to favor family life—in education, in health, in recreation, in housing."[59]

The push for women to pursue educational and employment opportunities was not unique to the rhetoric of the birth control movement; rather, it was a by-product of the changing social and political currents producing what historian Caroll Smith-Rosenberg calls the "new woman." Smith-Rosenberg explains, "Education constituted the New Woman's most salient characteristic. . . . [M]any young women saw in higher education an opportunity for intellectual self-fulfillment and for an autonomous role outside the patriarchal family."[60] Education was the cornerstone of the new woman, but even prominent thinkers in education recognized the infeasibility of this path for women without contraception. Renowned philosopher and education reformer John Dewey aptly stated in 1932: "I have no hesitation in saying that no matter what educators may say and do on behalf of better development of individuals as individuals, their ideals cannot be realized unless there is intelligent control of the size of families."[61] Sanger, a new woman herself, capitalized on the droves of women venturing outside the home for the first time and positioned contraceptive access as essential for women to thrive in the public domain.

As to be expected, the suggestion that women can and should harness birth control to pursue ventures outside the home was regularly met with hostility. Opponents leveled two charges against the expansion of women into the public sphere. First, despite repeated reassurances that birth control didn't inhibit maternal desire, opponents framed educational and employment opportunities as a drain on women's willingness to pursue motherhood. A 1921 article in the *New York Times* carrying the felicitous headline "Is the New Woman a Traitor to the Race?" is emblematic. The article reviews the book *The Trend of the Race* published by Samuel J. Holmes, a professor of zoology at the University of California. Holmes makes several caustic conclusions concerning the implications of women's entrance into the public sphere:

> There can be no doubt that the race is losing a vast wealth of material for motherhood of the best and most efficient type. Many of the women who are nowadays most prone to sacrifice motherhood to a career are just the ones upon whom the obligation of motherhood should rest with the greatest weight[;] it

> may be seriously doubted if the growing independence of women, despite its many advantages, is an unmixed blessing. Thus far it has worked to deteriorate the race in the interests of social advancement, a process which is bound to be disastrous in the long run.[62]

In addition to stunting the emancipation of women, arguments such as those put forward by Holmes bolstered the eugenic demand for college-educated people to prevent a race suicide by having more children. *Los Angeles Times* columnist Marjorie Dorman boldly labeled women's colleges as "stronghold[s] of aged virginity" making "the baby unfashionable" and risking "the extinction of valuable stocks."[63] The accusation of race suicide, explored fully in chapter 5, reflected the moral panic associated with upending traditional family norms particularly among the middle class. Meanwhile, poor women had long worked to support their families out of sheer necessity with little acknowledgment of their suffering or concern for their children's well-being, but the thought of affluent women doing the same was unconscionable.

These same opponents also questioned the quality of mothering possible among women who worked outside the home. Rebecca Stiles Taylor details the opposition's assumption of mutual exclusivity, explaining, "They point out that the woman who tries to manage a home and an outside position, frequently does a poor job of both, therefore it is concluded that the only thing for her is to give up the outside job and go back in the home. That has always been her place."[64] Amplifying their erroneous depiction of working mothers, opponents articulated a variety of grave consequences befalling women who tried to have it all. Holmes furthers, "employment of women, upon whose physique it has an unwholesome effect, while also diverting from marriage and motherhood the better endowed. When married women are employed in industry to any extent, the rate of infant mortality always rises."[65] There is some truth to Holmes's claim in so far as child mortality rates were indeed higher in homes where both parents worked; however, the supposed causality he draws solely between working mothers and infant mortality completely obscures the predominant cause of death being abject poverty. Julia Lathrop of the Children's Bureau explains in 1919: "[W]omen do not go out to work unless driven by necessity," with only 9.5 percent of mothers whose husbands earned a livable wage pursuing outside work. Lathrop concludes, "These figures show impressively the connection between income and infant mortality."[66] The arguments advanced by Holmes, and others like him, are merely red herrings hoping to drum up resistance to the expansion of women's opportunities under the guise of protecting children and the human race when in reality children were already dying in droves due to the prohibition of contraception.

Birth controllers openly acknowledged the imperative for women to work outside the home and the consequences of doing so when unable to postpone pregnancy. Maintaining their emphasis on the eventuality of motherhood for most women, advocates spoke of the need for women to achieve the financial stability necessary to support their future families. Based on her analysis of mother letters received by the ABCL, Alice C. Boughton explained in the *Birth Control Review* in 1933 that many letters "came from newly married women, who, because of present conditions, were obliged to continue working to help establish a home. They wished to postpone rearing a family until in an economic position to do so."[67] In contrast to the rhetoric of opponents shaming women for their pursuit of opportunities in the public sphere, birth controllers acknowledged the interconnectedness between a woman's public and private life and created a space for their coexistence.

The harsh economic realities of the Great Depression and the need to offset lost wages after WWI exacerbated the issue as women were thrust into the work force in order to support their families with no mechanism to manage their reproduction. Lily Winner warned in the *Birth Control Review*: "Birth Control! That will be the greatest problem for the women" forced into the workplace during the war.[68] If women were expected to fulfill their patriotic duty by taking up the jobs left behind by brave soldiers, advocates argued, then they must be given the means to control their reproduction. Sanger explained in the 1943 *Britannica Book of the Year*, "Absenteeism, due often to pregnancy or induced abortion, became an acute problem in many areas as millions of women went into work" motivating law makers to reconsider their stance on birth control in relation to economic productivity.[69] In stark contrast to the opposition narrative of the selfish woman, advocates highlighted the imminent need of contraception for female workers whose employment was vital to both their own financial stability as well as the nation's.

The flood of women into the work force during WWII largely driven by necessity produced an unexpected ideological shift toward female employment. Historian Annie Rehill argues, although "Rosies who remained in the workforce were once again pushed into lower-ranking and lower-paying positions," many chose to retain these positions as "the experience had given more women a taste of the independence afforded by working outside the home—which smaller families would eventually enable on a widespread scale."[70] In the short term, reproductive control secured women's economic productivity in a time of dire need, and in the long run, reproductive choice enabled women to find balance between their public and private lives in a way that negated well-established assumptions of mutual exclusivity between motherhood and employment. This sentiment reverberated in the discourse surrounding birth control as evidenced by journalist Rebecca Stiles Taylor's 1942 proclamation in the historically black newspaper the *Chicago Defender*.

Stiles proclaimed: "[I]t is time that the world gave up the infantile attitude that a woman must choose between marriage and a career. . . . [T]here is no reason why she should surrender all personal proclivities" solely to raise children.[71]

Sexual Liberation

The advent of the contraceptive pill is often credited with sparking the sexual revolution when in reality advocates heralded the benefits of birth control to the private sexual lives of its users long before the 1960s. In contrast to abstinence, continence, and withdrawal, three prominent methods of preventing conception, the use of barrier methods and later hormonal interventions allowed heterosexual couples to fully engage in sexual intercourse without the risk of pregnancy. As such, contraception uniquely enabled couples to enjoy sex recreationally and not just for procreation. Frank Hankins, former president of the American Sociological Society, directly credited the early birth control movement for the creation of a sexual revolution in 1929. Hankins remarked: "[T]he spread of contraceptive information [has] made the sexual revolution possible. Here is a tremendous tribute to the fundamental social and human significance of the birth control movement."[72] The ability to negate the reproductive function of sexual intercourse was arguably one of the most important benefits of birth control and also one of the most controversial. Famed feminist and birth controller Charlotte Perkins Gilman suggested in 1927, "It is mainly this phase of the birth control movement which brings upon it wide condemnation and the attempted suppression of its message. Yet the matter is of such vital importance to society that it commands growing attention."[73] In the face of opposition, advocates defended the separation of sex and reproduction—both ideologically and literally—by emphasizing the naturalness of sexual urges and extolling the benefits of this separation, most notably the preservation of the marital union.

Setting aside the early black-market drugs and devices masquerading as contraception, couples wishing to prevent conception in the early twentieth century essentially had three basic options: avoid sex altogether via abstinence, time their sex in accordance with a woman's menstrual cycle via the rhythm method, or interrupt the sex act to prevent insemination via withdrawal. These options were not only profoundly unreliable; they were also unrealistic. Yet, without the option to prevent pregnancy, every instance of sex carried the possibility of procreation. Advocates drew a clear delineation between sex and reproduction to rebuff the framing of sex propagated by social conservatives wherein sex was intended solely for procreation and not pleasure. Sanger argued in 1923 that if sex takes place only for procreation then "the average normal people who can only afford to have two or three children . . . shall [have sex] but two or three times," which Sanger concludes "is unduly harsh and unnecessary and is also a condition that cannot be lived up to by the average normal people."[74] Albeit hyperbolic, Sanger's statement highlights the impracticality of restricting sexual intercourse solely to its procreative function; even those concerned with birth control's supposed promotion of sexual licentiousness would be hard pressed to admit married adults should only have sex a handful of times over the course of their lives.

To ideologically separate reproduction from the sex act, advocates needed to reframe procreation as the result rather than the purpose of the sex impulse. Sanger proclaimed in 1933: "The day has passed to consider that the sexual urge has procreation as its primary purpose. Rather this is the result and not the purpose of the urge. This frank and scientific attitude must be faced and accepted before we can go forward in any attempt to evaluate sex behavior."[75] Just as motherhood was a feature of womanhood and not its exclusive aim, procreation was a by-product and not the exclusive aim of the sex act. Hedging back against the opposition's well-worn appeals to nature, advocates differentiated between human relationships and those among animals, noting, "While for Nature and the animal kingdom the sex relation is only a means, for man and woman it is the first and most important part of the end."[76]

The separation of sex and reproduction was a direct affront to the value structures of many, particularly within religious circles, as evidenced by Anne Kennedy's 1926 interview with P. J. Ward of the National Catholic Welfare Council. Ward explained the position of the Church toward nonprocreative sex: "Birth control interferes with the plan of God, who intends that people who marry may do so for the purpose of procreation. . . . Marriage without the desire and responsibility to procreate, and not lived in strict continence, is adultery."[77] A "desire to procreate" admittedly serves as a motivator for sexual intimacy, but birth controllers insisted, "It's the exception, rather than the rule."[78] The underlying assumption of solely procreative sex was also troublesome for the birth control movement. In 1923, Sanger boldly questioned, "We call it prostitution when one sacrifices personal choice and love in the sexual relation, for monetary gain; why should it be less prostitution when the end is the propagation of the species?"[79] Sanger's clever analogy calls into question the inherently transactional model of exclusively procreative sex endorsed by the puritanical point of view. Additionally, advocates pointed to the inherent hypocrisy of the Catholic Church's position for "even good Catholics are not always forbidden to perform the sexual act for other purposes than procreation."[80] The Catholic Church's approval of nonprocreative sex during the safe period of a woman's cycle as well as in cases of barrenness, sterility, or menopause directly contradicted their rejection of non-procreative sex by permitting sexual intimacy in cases where procreation was impossible.

Advocates reiterated the naturalness of the urge for sexual expression. Sanger explained at the 1922 International Neo-Malthusian and Birth Control Conference in London: "From the dawn of humanity, and even the dawn of civilization, we have recognized that there are two fundamental urges which have prodded mankind forward. These have been hunger and sex." While society recognized the immediacy of the hunger urge, the same could not be said for the sexual urge, prompting Sanger to conclude it was time to "recognize it as fully fundamental and equally dynamic and fateful in its consequences as hunger."[81] The John Price Jones Corporation extended this analogy in 1930: "The sex impulse is one of the few dominant human urges. Along with hunger it is one urge which, in all normal people, demands satisfaction."[82] By analogizing sex and hunger, birth controllers framed the sex impulse as an innate human characteristic not an indecent urge experienced by morally questionable persons.

Emphasizing the normalcy of the sex urge also functioned as a critique of the most commonly promulgated method of regulating one's reproduction—abstinence. Ida Wright Mudgett extends the analogy of hunger and sex to highlight the infeasibility of abstinence, writing, "There are two fundamental functions inseparable from organic life; they are food desire and sex desire. . . . It is as profitable to ask the race to refuse expression to the former as to ask it to refuse expression to their latter desire."[83] Abstinence, the only form of contraception endorsed by the Catholic Church, was both impractical and ill-advised for married couples. The John Price Jones Corporation furthers, "While continence may be practicable among certain people of highly developed will power, it is expecting too much of the average person to carry out such a program over a long period of time."[84] More than just unworkable for married couples, the practice of abstinence threatened their marital stability. Sanger warned in 1917: abstinence "offers no solution for the great problem of the too-large family because it is a course of conduct utterly impossible to enforce, and highly detrimental to health and happiness if it could be consistently adhered to."[85]

Yet, abstinence wasn't universally rejected by the birth control movement. The rhetoric above initially appears to be a wholesale rejection of abstinence, but on closer examination only invalidates abstinence within the context of marriage. In fact, birth controllers frequently recommended abstinence for unmarried couples. Dr. Rachelle Yarros, prominent birth controller and founder of the Chicago-based Hull House Clinic, explicitly cautioned unmarried people to refrain from sex prior to marriage. When asked for her recommendation regarding unmarried persons specifically, she counseled: "The advice to be given cannot be other than strong warning against promiscuity and prostitution, because of the menace of venereal diseases and the moral deterioration resulting from such relationships. This should be accompanied by the strongest possible advice to seek real love and family life with all its joys and responsibilities."[86] Yarros was not alone in her recommendation. Howard K. Hollister offered a nearly identical warning regarding premarital sex in the *Birth Control Review* in 1931; he cautioned, "The question of illicit relationships before marriage is frankly discussed. It is explained that aside from the physical hazards such relationships usually result in serious emotional dislocations, if not in disaster, and that remaining within the bounds of social convention is a far-sighted policy which proves the wisest in the long run."[87] In the context of unmarried persons, abstinence is juxtaposed to the morally treacherous outcomes of venereal disease, promiscuity, and prostitution to frame premarital sex as undesirable, morally hazardous, and irresponsible. In doing so, the rhetoric of the mainstream birth control movement demarcates the boundaries of appropriate sexual expression firmly within the confines of monogamous marriage.

Altogether ignoring unmarried persons, the mainstream birth control movement spoke of the disparate desires for children and sexual fulfillment almost exclusively in the context of monogamous marriage. Edith Houghton Hooker explains, "In considering birth control and its relation to monogamist marriage, it is of fundamental importance to recognize the dual nature of sex, first in its relation to the racial life, and second its relation to the happiness and productivity of the individual."[88] Sanger directly asserts the value of indulging both desires, separately and together, in a press release for the National Council on Federal Legislation for Birth Control in 1931: "There is nothing whatsoever unnatural in the conduct of married couples who deliberately respond to the sexual urge on some occasions for the 'cultivating of mutual love' and on other occasions for the same purpose plus the intention of begetting children."[89] Unlike abstinence, contraception enabled couples to fully express their innate desire for sex apart from their desire, or lack thereof, to procreate. Sociologist and cofounder of the Planned Parenthood Federation of America Henry Pratt Fairchild argues, "Contraception enables man to differentiate between the two disparate desires for sexual pleasure and for offspring, and to pursue the realization of one or the other, or the two conjointly, as reason and emotion may dictate."[90] Fairchild's statement advances two important notions: first, the desire for sexual pleasure and offspring are distinctly different impulses, and second, although the two desires are not mutually exclusive, contraception uniquely enables individuals to pursue them both separately and in tandem.

The literal separation of sex from reproduction facilitated by contraception was critical to transforming the sexual act into a fulfilling experience for women and a satisfying element of the marital union. Contraception promised to alter the current sexual order by transforming sex into a fulfilling experience for women. Havelock Ellis explained in the *Birth Control*

Review in 1918, "the sexual order thus established . . . had an unnatural and repressive influence on the erotic aspect of woman's sexual life. It fostered the reproductive side of woman's sexual life, but it rendered difficult for her the satisfaction of the [sex] instinct."[91] Other readily available methods, such as withdrawal, also resulted in sexual frustration for both partners. *The Birth Control Review* cautioned in 1919: "The lack of sexual satisfaction aggravates nervous and hysterical troubles. . . . This method, in the opinion of the best informed of modern birth control advocates is unscientific and dangerous."[92] Additionally, whereas men faced little immediate risk from sexual intercourse without contraception, women were forced to risk an unwanted pregnancy to attain sexual gratification. As a result, women faced a catch-22 wherein, as Sanger contends, "virginity or motherhood were the only two states of respectable womanhood."[93] Explicitly contrasting man's ability to reap the full benefits of his sexuality, Ellis praised contraception for placing women on "the same human level as men" by giving them "the right to the joy and exaltation of sex, to the uplifting of the soul" possible only through "the intimate approach and union of two human beings."[94] The biological burden placed on women through reproduction robbed them of the ability to engage in sexual intercourse recreationally without the assistance of contraception. Giving women this option provided couples a previously nonexistent pathway to intimacy.

Unsurprisingly, birth controllers also linked the sexual liberation of women to the betterment of marriages. Women experienced sexual liberation alongside and with the cooperation of their male partners and ultimately in service of protecting the marital union from internal discord and infidelity. Henry Pratt Fairchild explains, contraception "permits the union in legitimate marriage of two persons who are sincerely attracted to each other and opens the way to all the benefits of that general fulfillment of personality that is associated with affectionate home life."[95] Other methods of family limitation permitted couples to engage in sexual intercourse, but the methods' questionable efficacy meant couples couldn't remove the biggest barrier to sexual satisfaction—fear. A reliable contraceptive device coupled with accurate medical instruction, on the other hand, "takes away fear and releases the joy and love energy in both man and woman, giving greater power to be gained from each to the other."[96] The movement's focus on improving the sexual relations of married couples resonated in popular discussions of birth control. In 1929 *Forum* proclaimed: "Fundamental to a true marriage is complete biological fulfillment. Man and wife should have physical delight in each other" and that in order to do so they "should seek to safeguard themselves against overwhelming offspring."[97] Contextualizing sexual satisfaction in terms of improving the marital relationship counteracted the puritanical views of sex characteristic of early-twentieth-century America and situated sexual fulfillment as equally important to marital harmony as procreation.

Changes to the family structure directly connected to urbanization as well as women's emancipation presented new challenges to the institution of marriage for which contraceptive instruction proved essential in resolving. Ernest Mowrer, author of the 1927 book *Family Disorganization: An Introduction to Sociological Analysis*, provides a deft analysis of the central role of contraception in preventing domestic discord. He argues:

> The importance of birth control in the prevention and treatment of domestic discord grows directly out of the changed conception of marriage and the family in the United States. The historical family was chiefly a status-giving, property conserving institution. To belong to a family gave one immediately the status of that family and the community. Family pride made the perpetuation of the family name of paramount importance. Sexual adjustment was relegated to a position of minor concern in the pattern of an accommodation. Social taboos dictated repression of the sex impulse along with other individual wishes in the interests of preserving the family unit. The emancipation of woman however has changed our conception of marriage. It has become not simply a convenient arrangement for the control of sex relations and the support of the wife and children, but a cooperative relationship for the mutual satisfaction and stimulation of the personalities involved. Sex relations are no longer looked upon by many as unclean and exclusively for the propagation of the species. Individuals are coming more and more to feel that they have a right to say how many children they shall have and to determine the interval between births in such a way as to work with the best interests of the parents as well as those of the children. And while the newer outlook is not always as clearly formulated in the minds of both those who are marrying and those who are married, much of their conduct indicates that their expectations are not far different. The result is that domestic discord not infrequently develops out of the lack of a satisfactory plan for regulating sex relations in such a way as successfully controlled conception.[98]

Well aware of the social changes accompanying women's emancipation and adoption of voluntary motherhood, advocates like Mowrer went to great lengths to demonstrate the commensurability between these changes and the preservation of traditional institutions like marriage. Mirroring their rhetoric elevating the status of motherhood explored in chapter 2, advocates sanctified marriage, heralding contraception as a tool to preserve and even improve marriages. Specifically, advocates identified contraception as a solution to the sense of fear prompting couples to delay marriage and even lauded contraception as a catalyst for couples to have larger families than they otherwise would.

Akin to their arguments regarding the full development of women, advocates pinpointed the removal of fear as an opportunity for couples to strengthen their relationship prior to bringing children into the home. In a 1923 speech, Sanger touted the benefits of contraception for young couples, explaining that if "finer companionship in the home after marriage" is desired, then "no young couple should have parenthood thrust upon them" without the chance to "buil[d] up the home in preparation, as a nest for the coming of the children that are wanted."[99] Just as women needed time to develop themselves in preparation for motherhood, couples needed the opportunity for relational development made possible through the removal of fear and the postponement of children. This argument appeased social conservatives worried about the denigration of monogamous relationships in a world of purportedly unrestrained sexuality. Ethicist and cofounder of the New York Society for Ethical Culture, Algernon D. Black, actually praised contraception's influence on marriages in 1932: "The spiritual significance of birth control lies in the possibilities it affords of improving human life. Although the good life cannot be crystallized into words it may not be irrelevant to say that it must include a freedom accompanied by a sense of social responsibility; and it must be a life in which human beings further their mutual development through their relations with one another."[100] Taken together, the removal of fear and the possibility of enhanced sexual fulfillment promised to resolve the major sources of marital discord experienced by couples in the early twentieth century.

Advocates connected the removal of fear to an increased likelihood of early marriages particularly in terms of their economic feasibility. Though opponents, especially those concerned with women's pursuits outside the home, argued reproductive choice would cause women to delay or avoid marriage altogether, birth controllers suggested just the opposite was true. Sanger highlighted the fear felt by young men, particularly in terms of their ability to support a family, in the *Birth Control Review* in 1918: "The ever ascending standard and cost of living, combined with the low wage of the young men today, tend toward the postponement of marriage."[101] Citing the financial barriers of unexpected and unrestrained childbearing, William F. Ogburn, Professor of Sociology at Columbia University, suggested: "[M]any who now hesitate through fear of burdens greater than their means warrant would marry were the fear removed."[102] Giving couples control over their reproduction equipped them to enter marriage at a point in their lives when the prospect of an unwanted pregnancy would have halted such a decision. American physician and sexologist William J. Robinson argued in 1931:

> The causes of the increase in the percentage of marriages are many, but without doubt the spread of the knowledge of prevention or birth control is one of the most potent factors. Anybody who is an earnest student of the subject will

> acknowledge that the fear of a large family was one of the most restraining influences, one of the most powerful brakes on marriage. Now that all intelligent men and women know about birth control, there is less hesitation in entering the institution of marriage. And it is well my considered opinion that with the further spread of prevention knowledge and with divorce becoming easier, the number of marriages will go on increasing. Instead of taking place at a later and later age, as was the case a generation or two ago, marriage will take place at a considerably earlier age.[103]

Absent the ability to prevent pregnancy, young couples delayed marriage until they felt ready to assume the financial burdens of children. Sanger contends in her 1925 speech "The Business of Bearing Babies," "To courageous, ambitious young husbands and wives today, parenthood is a problem that cannot be left to chance. Childbearing is too costly a venture—both in precious lives and in money, to be indulged in carelessly, incessantly, [and] continuously."[104]

The salience of this argument is demonstrated by Harvard biologist Edward M. East's 1925 proclamation in the *New York Times*: "[F]reedom from involuntary parenthood will do a great deal toward making marriage more of an idealistic co-partnership. . . . As a result, we may also expect earlier marriages."[105] Freedom from fear motivated couples to marry sooner while insulating them from the pitfalls associated with delayed marriage. A 1935 progress report from the BCCRB explained: "Marriage is made possible at an earlier age when fear of unwanted pregnancies is removed, thus preventing promiscuity, prostitution, and venereal disease."[106] The moral hazards of promiscuity, prostitution, and venereal disease feature prominently in the discourse of the movement as rhetorical catch-alls to describe the undesirability of sexual relations outside of marriage. Whereas abstinence is the preferred solution for unmarried persons who should refrain from premarital sex, contraception is the preferred solution for married persons who can eliminate the need for extramarital activities by seeking responsible sexual fulfilment with their partners from an early age.

Similarly, advocates argued giving couples reproductive freedom diminished the fear of pregnancy often at the root of marital dissatisfaction. Jessie A. Rene, a local activist based in Detroit, pleaded in the *Birth Control Review* in 1918 for couples to avoid the "consuming wasteful mental anxiety, and bring instead peace within the marriage bond" through the application of contraceptive information.[107] In fact, the relational benefits of contraception proved compelling enough for martial experts to call for the widespread implementation of contraceptive instruction. Harriet Mowrer, a domestic discord consultant for the Jewish Social Service Bureau in Chicago advised in 1936 that "much of the conflict centering around sex could have been avoided or modified early in the marriage relationship through a thoroughgoing program of scientific birth control and sex hygiene. In the writer's experience as a domestic discord consultant."[108] Birth controllers championed the preservation of marriage and directly promoted contraception's ability to eliminate "the element of fear which is so frequently the cause of marital unhappiness."[109]

This argument appeased those concerned with growing divorce rates in the United States as evidenced by Judge J. C. Ruppenthal's 1918 letter to the *Birth Control Review*; Ruppenthal concludes, "My very thorough inquiry in divorce cases leads me to conclude that quite an amount of domestic infelicity come by reason of the ills that flow from uninvited motherhood. . . . Because of wrought-up nervous conditions in apprehension of possible pregnancy."[110] Beyond the interpersonal benefits accrued by husband and wife, society stood to gain immeasurably from the preservation of harmonious and, perhaps more importantly, monogamous marriage. Dr. Eric Matsner, a practicing obstetrician and gynecologist, espoused the societal benefits of birth control in 1931. He opines:

> It is society's business to see that this is attained by providing proper conditions of married life. Civilization can be built only upon satisfactory family life. I do not mean to intimate that happiness and family life are dependent altogether upon sexual gratification. We know that under extraordinary conditions satisfactory marital unions can be built upon the higher aspirations and tastes alone. But one is willing to say bluntly that sexual life is the elemental fact upon which satisfactory family life as a rule depends, and without satisfactory sexual life, marital life is irreparably damaged. And it is here that the importance of birth control comes in. Is it possible to have satisfactory marital relations by having sex relations only for the purposes of procreation? Is it conceivable that a satisfactory relationship can be maintained in the shadow of a constant fear and constant dreaded pregnancy?[111]

Matsner masterfully rebukes abstinence and asserts the value of sexual gratification as the cornerstone of family life upon which civilization is built. The fact that both Matsner, a physician, and Ruppenthal, a judge, adopted the rhetoric of birth controllers regarding sex and marriage to espouse the need for contraception is demonstrative of the movement's rhetorical efficacy.

Beyond the resolution of marital discord, a worthy goal in and of itself, birth controllers identified an even more admirable goal of strong marital bonds—intensified parental desire. Sanger explained in 1923, giving couples a chance to "know each other, to play together, to read together, to develop their love lives" creates "a finer, and a stronger bond between them" that ultimately "intensif[ies] the desire for maternity."[112] Sanger leveraged this sentiment in her 1940 address at the Community Church of Boston to position birth control as a catalyst for the large families so cherished by the Catholic Church. She boasts: "If the first year or even two years can be free from pregnancy children invited into these homes come wanted before they are conceived. Here we lay the foundation for happy marriages and large wanted families. All of these arguments have been brilliantly stated by Catholic leaders in support of the so-called rhythm method."[113] In this succinct statement, Sanger deftly demonstrates the surprising compatibility between the movement's agenda and that of its harshest critics. Couples given the ability to develop individually and jointly possess a strong parental desire that when informed by contraceptive instruction leads to large families full of wanted children.

Despite the efficaciousness of these arguments, many in religious circles saw contraception, and feminist reforms generally, as an immediate threat to their core values. A 1915 article in the newspaper associated with the National Association Opposed to Women Suffrage, *Woman's Protest*, written by Mrs. Simeon H. Guilford, illuminates the perceived threat of feminist movements to traditional value structures. In the article entitled "Woman's Emancipation—from What?" Guilford bluntly states: "This is the real menace of Woman Suffrage—its diabolic alliance with Socialism and Feminisms, which it attempts to conceal whenever it think it can fool the people. . . . Feminists seem to be fighting, really for moral emancipation from the principles of CHRISTIANITY AND MONOGAMY [*sic*]."[114] Journalist Isabelle Keating more tactfully explains the genesis of this perceived threat writing, "[R]eligious conditioning went far toward maintaining women and their specific interests—marriage and the home—on an inferior plane. And it is probably true that the present emancipation of women has, for that very reason, been in direct ratio to the declining influence of the church. Christianity, in the minds of thousands of women today, is synonymous with bondage."[115] For generations, religious doctrines prescribed women's subservience to their husbands and enactment of traditional gender roles as the correct moral order. Subsequently, efforts to reshape the existing power dynamics through the emancipation of women produced a rupture between women and the church despite the fact that many feminists clung tightly to the normative moral codes fostered in conservative religious contexts.

Reframing the emancipation of women and the application of contraceptive methods as a solution for marital discord directly refuted the moral panic circulating within religious communities and proved to be quite persuasive over time. Polish National Church (Pennsylvania) priest T. V. Jakimowicz passionately articulated the value of contraception in 1920:

> Emancipation and equal suffrage will not make a free woman. Freedom has to be attained and this attainment will be realized only when woman will not be

> an unwilling but a willing mother and when maternity will not be forced upon her. Woman enduring forced maternity cannot be free, she may be emancipated politically and economically but remains a slave of superstition and to the lore of marriage as a trade in a factory to produce children. Woman will attain her freedom by birth control. . . . From the spiritual and religious view, birth control is plausible, because it will give time to a mother to recuperate her forces and to conceive by the spirit of intelligence before she conceives in flesh and blood. From the philosophical view the intelligent life should not be forced into manifestation by the law, but by love. A humanitarian view is that if a being is to be born, it has the right to be born well.[116]

Beyond merely endorsing contraception as a tool of emancipation, Jakimowicz directly confronts the problematic view of marriage facilitated by involuntary motherhood paying homage to the rhetoric of the birth control movement through his reiteration of their most prominent arguments. During a speech at the 1922 International Birth Control Conference, Minister Frederick W. Betts echoes Jakimowicz's praise for the principles of voluntary motherhood, proclaiming, "Children and motherhood are the crowning glory of every real home" but "only when the act is voluntary, joyous, the free expression of the deliberate choice." Betts's endorsement doesn't stop there, but rather transforms into a call to action for religious entities to reevaluate their caustic relationship to the movement and embrace the new morality facilitated by voluntary motherhood. He portends: "Morality and religion have everything to gain and nothing to lose by getting back to reality, beginning with facts, and building codes and ideals, on the freedom, the choice, the glad desire of womanhood which finds in motherhood the finest and divinest expression of its own personality."[117] As explored in previous chapters, the birth control movement made significant headway in religious circles by emphasizing the mechanistic benefits of contraception specifically relating to abortion, maternal health, and infant mortality. These statements signal an uptake of the ideological underpinnings of the "willed pregnancy" as well and thus represent a significant shift in the adversarial relationship between birth controllers and the church.

The statements of Jakimowicz and Betts weren't just bluster either. Keating explains, "Throughout the country, classes in sex education, preparation for marriage, marital adjustment, and family problems are being organized within the sacred precincts" with many relying on the works produced by Dennett and Sanger to share with congregates the message that "the careful and restrained use of contraceptives by married people is valid and moral."[118] To be clear, marital counseling and contraceptive instruction scantly appeared in the most orthodox churches, but their inclusion in a broad swath of religious institutions during the early twentieth century was, as Keating puts it, "the most courageous if not revolutionary steps [churches have] ever taken."[119] Moving beyond the adversarial relationship once propagated by religious zealots, church leaders altered their position on contraception as a direct result of the movement's localization of family planning within the traditional confines of marriage.

Marriage remained a rhetorical constant in the discourse of the mainstream birth control movement. Edith Houghton Hooker makes the movement's focus on preserving heterosexual marriage abundantly clear when she writes in 1928:

> There is in the state one institution of Supreme importance and that institution is the home. The most important defense for the home in this age, in my opinion, is birth control. If this institution—and this means monogamous marriage, the marriage of one man and one woman—is to be continued, it must be made feasible and I contend that it is not feasible if we do not have birth control. . . . It is said that the number of divorces and legal separations is coming almost to equal the number of marriages. I think that with birth control, divorce would be checked, the home unit would become better marked, love between husband and wife would be permitted expression, instead are being ever denied, and monogamist marriage would be conserved.[120]

Birth controllers were keenly aware of the lurid associations frequently attached to contraception, framing it as a threat to monogamy and subsequently marriage. As such, advocates strategically positioned contraception exclusively within the confines of the traditional family structure and characterized it as a necessary tool to maximize the health and happiness of both parents and their eventual children. Dr. Ira S. Wile extends Hooker's characterization to articulate the broader societal benefits of contraceptive use as they relate to the maintenance of the traditional family. He explains, "In general, it may be said that the social advantage of contraception lies in the improvement of family morale, the promotion of economic competence, the satisfaction of social ideals, the sustaining of spiritual goals, and the conservation of all the social equilibrium that constitutes normality and family life."[121] Rather than upending the traditional values and norms surrounding marriage and family, birth controllers worked meticulously to frame their efforts as essential to the maintenance of these norms. Taken together, the movement's emphasis on the innate sexuality of people is subdued through its utilitarian application in service of ending marital discord. Contraception was predominantly framed as a protection against unwanted pregnancy and the fear it produced among married, or soon to be married, couples. The sexual liberation of women was merely a convenient by-product.

THE MORALITY OF BIRTH CONTROL

Considering the emergence of the movement as a response to the labeling of contraception as an obscene topic, advocates found themselves constantly atoning for both the decency and morality of birth control. Dennett resented the morality claims built into the Comstock Act and bluntly questioned the law's efficacy, writing, "Let me ask the committee, in all fairness, if the morality of this country is strikingly superior now to what it was before 1873. . . . Certainly the insertion of this proviso in our statutes has not noticeably increased the morality of the United States."[122]Although Dennett and Sanger both defended the respectability of medically accurate contraceptive instruction, as explored in chapter 1, opponents still questioned the morality of birth control on the grounds that it was unnatural, frustrated the will of god, and if misused, would increase licentious behavior.

Clinging to their insistence that sex is intended solely for procreative purposes, moralists and conservatives opposed contraception because it disrupted a natural human process. Dr. William J. Robinson, sexologist and editor of the *American Journal of Urology and Sexology*, explained this counterargument in the *Birth Control Review* in 1918. Robinson notes, "The adjective 'unnatural' is doing fine service in the hands of our conservative and reactionary friends." Frustrated by the opposition's reliance on this trope, Robinson foments, "Why is it unnatural? Because it is artificial, because none of the lower animals do it, because we never did it when we were savages, when we lived in a state of nature."[123] Advocates conceded that contraception intervened with the natural reproductive process but argued it was no different than any other device giving humans control over the natural environment. The BCCRB posits: "The advocates of birth control admit this willingly but inquire, what of it? So are devices to improve the eyesight, the hearing, or the teeth. . . . So, too, is cooking and shaving, houses, radios, automobiles. . . . By its very nature every attempt to adjust man to an environment radically different from that [of] the early world must be 'unnatural.'"[124] Comparing contraception to uncontested inventions such as clothing and cooking effectively demonstrated the frivolity and futility of preserving nature when it had been so readily shirked in other areas of human development. Dennett had little patience for this line of reasoning and bluntly chided in her 1922 book: "We hear a great deal about 'interference with nature' and the 'right of the child to be born.' To speak perfectly frankly, for a scientist this is nonsense, for in the light of the facts it leads to the reduction ad absurdum."[125] Speaking in Massachusetts in 1940, Sanger lambasted the state's deference to morals over scientific advancement as an impediment toward improving societal welfare. She protested, "Vaccination against smallpox, immunization, the germ theory of disease, the use of anesthesia, the cell theory of life—all these were opposed once in the name of morality. These instances seem incredible to us now; yet once again today we are faced with the same distortion of fundamental morals to impede the progress of human welfare."[126]

Advocates expanded this analogy by suggesting birth control, like most human interventions in the natural world, equipped people to more fruitfully engage with the spiritual realm of life by allowing them to control it. Writing in the *Birth Control Review* in 1917, Havelock Ellis explains, "We at no point enter the spiritual save through the material. . . . Eye-glasses and contraceptives alike are a portal to the spiritual world for many who, without them, would find that world largely a closed book."[127] Just as glasses allowed people to conquer their natural deficiencies by giving them the power of sight, contraception allowed people to conquer the reproductive process by giving them the power of control. These comparisons provided a platform to argue for an increased emphasis on contraceptive development. Sanger warned in 1933, "before we congratulate ourselves too complacently upon all these achievements of modern science," we must ask ourselves why "countless millions are born in conditions of disease, ignorance and misery."[128] Science was hard at work making virtually every aspect of life easier but was embargoed from the realm of reproduction in the name of nature.

Religious opponents also demonstrated a proclivity for preserving the laws of nature which they frequently labeled as the will of God. Demonstrating its regularity within the rhetoric of religious opponents to birth control, Justice Breitbart of the New York City Court of Appeals cautioned in 1948 raising the cost of rent for couples with large families fearing it would "foster and encourage birth control, which is a violation of the law of God and nature."[129] Isolating the Catholic Church as the main source of this argument, Sanger explained in 1931, "The Pope maintains that any performance of the sexual act in a way which frustrates procreation is a sin against nature." However, in an attempt to highlight the illogical nature of such a claim, Sanger quipped: "that to say sin against nature is only a manner of speaking. All of us, the Pope included, are habitually defeating the ways of nature; the advance of civilization has been achieved largely by triumphing over nature."[130] Appeals to naturalism held little weight with advocates who found the natural state of perpetual pregnancy uniquely savage. Akin to the arguments explored in chapter 3, birth controllers refused to capitulate to the laws of nature when doing so risked the lives of countless women and children whose needless suffering was easily preventable through contraception.

Advocates also questioned the very laws of nature proffered by the church. French surgeon and social anthropologist Robert Briffault revealed the true source of these laws in a 1932 article in the *Birth Control* Review; he posits, "All restrictions and restricted values on sex relations are social artifacts.

There exist no 'natural instincts' corresponding to them. Those restrictions and values have originated either as superstitious taboos" resulting in "what hitherto has been termed 'morality' in reference to sex relations, and of the consecrated importance of conventional marriage in particular."[131] The hypocrisy of the Church's simultaneous endorsement of abstinence and rejection of contraception is proof of concept for Briffault's claim. Rather than negating the Church's spurious interpretation of nature, birth controllers reiterated their own view of nature as including the innate human desire for sexual intimacy apart from a desire for children, which subsequently made abstinence both unnatural and uniquely harmful. Frederick Blossom characterizes abstinence as an "unnatural asceticism" which degrades marriage "by implying that there is something bestial and reprehensible about the normal expression of affection between husband and wife. We will elevate the race, not through trying to crush out the physical basis of life, but by laying stress upon its spiritual meaning."[132] Contraception admittedly thwarted the laws of nature but so too did denying the human desire for sexual intimacy—the latter of which was far more consequential for the marital bond.

Even though birth controllers advocated for contraception almost exclusively within the confines of marriage, opponents frequently spoke of the potential misuse of information to facilitate promiscuity and infidelity. States too hid the moral agenda of their obscenity laws behind the façade of preventing misuse or abuse of contraceptive information. Reflecting on her legislative efforts, Dennett explains, "A somewhat common type of Senator is he who fears that making contraceptive knowledge legally accessible will result in its abuse, particularly by the young."[133] Advocates heartily mocked this argument for its speciousness. Sanger pointedly observes: "[W]e don't stop the progress of humanity because of the few who misuse things. Automobiles can be misused; certainly razors can be misused, and as a matter of fact, when razors were first put on the market there was just the same objection."[134] Dennett's version of the argument cut even closer to the quick: "Even reading, writing, and arithmetic are abused, by forgers, embezzlers and the like, but that is no reason for not teaching the pre-requisites of civilization to everyone."[135]

Similarly, opponents labeled the separation of sex and reproduction via contraception a potential catalyst for immorality. Dissenters feared that making sex safer by removing the possibility of pregnancy would prompt people to engage in riskier sexual behavior. The John Price Jones Corporation summarizes this erroneous claim articulating the accusation of opponents that "the main check on sex immorality is the fear of consequences in the shape of an illegitimate child."[136] Even if promiscuity accompanied the increased availability of contraception, advocates framed this as preferable to the existing problems of venereal diseases, divorce, and illegitimate children. Dr.

S. Adolpohus Knopf explained in the *Birth Control Review*, "The benefit derived from a diminution of venereal diseases [and] a greater number of happy and successful marriages among the younger people . . . would more than outweigh the isolated instances of sexual intercourse prior to marriage."[137] Knopf's shockingly rare acknowledgment of premarital sex serves only to highlight the benefits of contraception to early marriages and is characterized as a regrettable, yet comparatively acceptable, consequence of expanded access to contraception.

The implication that consequences alone shaped the moral choices of women infuriated birth controllers. Sanger chastised opponents for their offensive logic, proclaiming, "it is an insult to suggest that our women will become promiscuous if they have not the fear of the result to keep them moral."[138] Other advocates also took umbrage with this ridiculous argument. Writing in 1922, Rabbi Sidney Goldstein, a board member of the ABCL and later the PPFA, scolded: "No fouler indictment could be framed against the virtue of women. Women are virtuous not because they fear the consequences of sin, but because they reverence the right. No knowledge that we can place in their hands will shake the foundation upon which their ethical life is built."[139] Even if the fear of pregnancy did prevent individuals from engaging in immoral acts, birth controllers "pointed out that there cannot be much to say for the inherent righteousness of those who are restrained from an immoral act merely by fear of the consequences."[140]

The distinction between imposed and intrinsic morality was a vital part of the movement's rhetoric, particularly as it related to the purported impropriety facilitated by contraceptive access. Dennett effectively used the fear of licentiousness expressed by reluctant legislators as a springboard to indict the moral underpinnings of a cultural system wherein mere knowledge shattered existing moral standards. She asserts:

> Then again we reassure them by citing the other countries which have no shocking repressive laws like ours, but which nevertheless do not show any records of general promiscuity and unbridled excess, or of sexual laxity among the young. We go further, and remind them that if it be true that the mass of our American young people would have so little moral anchorage that we should fear to trust them with knowledge, then something is awfully the matter with us of the older generation to have reared them, and that it is for us to hasten to develop a keener sense of responsibility for the education of all young people, as well as those of our families. And they all respond to this appeal. They would obviously feel ashamed not to.[141]

Advocates questioned the efficacy of external attempts to preserve moral standards noting the failure of prohibition to alter the morals or behaviors of the county. Writing for the *Bombay Chronicle* in 1935, Sanger retorted, "knowledge does not cause immorality. . . . We are not truthful because there [are] jails and other methods of punishment. We are not moral because of the fear of venereal disease, or of pregnancy."[142] By framing sexual morality as a choice, birth controllers reiterated their position that reproductive freedom did not entail an abdication of responsibility but rather called for a more conscious understanding of the sexual relationship divorced from its reproductive function. *The Birth Control Review* proclaimed in 1923: "Contraceptives call for foresight and demand a sense of responsibility—qualities that tend toward the maintenance of a higher rather than a lower standard of morality."[143]

Lurking beneath the thinly veiled concerns of moralists lies the true question they grappled with in response to women's reproductive freedom: could women be trusted? Trusted to pursue motherhood when no longer relentlessly thrust upon them. Trusted to prioritize their roles as mothers amid a plethora of new opportunities. Trusted to maintain their purity when given the ability to engage in sex recreationally. Camouflaged as legitimate concerns about child welfare or increased licentiousness, the spurious claims advanced by opponents of birth control wreaked of skepticism that women would continue to uphold their traditional societal norms if relieved of the biological burden holding them captive in the private sphere. Unfortunately, birth controllers defended the trustworthiness of women not as agentic actors but as potential wives and mothers. The movement's reliance on the terministic screen of motherhood and continued prioritization of monogamous marriage allowed advocates to skirt the insidiousness of the moralists' true concern by aligning women's reproductive freedom with the very values moralists saw in jeopardy. Monogamy and motherhood weren't in any danger, but instead would be *more* revered in a world where children were welcomed and married couples could enjoy one another fully. Additionally, the movement's continued reliance on the trope of responsibility eased moral panic surrounding women's reproductive freedom. At every turn, the rhetoric of the movement reassured critics that women could be trusted to act responsibly by engaging in abstinence before marriage and practicing family planning once married in accordance with her status as both wife and mother. The preceding analysis highlights the defensive posture inherent within the movement's early rhetoric concerning choice which justified women's ability to make sound decisions consistent with the traditional values and expectations of women.

THE LASTING CONSEQUENCE: THE CONTRACEPTIVE HIERARCHY

By modern standards, the movement's articulation of women's right to choose can best be described as timid—chock full of caveats, overtures to conservative religious opponents, and deeply wedded to traditional heteronormative assumptions. Yet, this timidity served a strategic purpose given the movement's emergence in a time of great social upheaval. The newly emancipated woman emerging from the private sphere to claim her rightful spot in educational institutions and the workforce represented an afront to centuries of traditions, so couching reproductive freedom as nonthreatening was essential to its broad uptake. Critics needed constant reassurance women would still choose to bear children and prioritize their roles as mothers. They needed to know the new woman could still be controlled, if not legally through the denial of her fundamental rights, then socially through the maintenance of institutions such as marriage whose normative assumptions policed women's choices in service of traditional norms.

Accordingly, a woman's right to choose is specifically articulated within a moral framework defined by responsible sexual expression. This framework, informed by the principles of the "willed pregnancy," suggests women gain the freedom to full sexual expression through a demonstration of their responsibility—first to remain abstinent prior to marriage and then subsequently to engage in procreative sex only when capable of shouldering the physical and financial burdens of a child. Under this framework, contraception becomes the means "by which parenthood is taken out of the sphere of accident" and transformed into "a matter of conscious knowledge, of deeper satisfaction, of ready and eager acceptance of responsibility."[144] Hidden within this framework is an implicit hierarchization of contraceptive choices, or what I call the contraceptive hierarchy, premised on the functionality of each contraceptive method in terms of control, responsibility, sexuality, and morality.

Abstinence resides at the bottom of the hierarchy, because even though it provides adherents full control over their reproduction, it does so by prohibiting the full expression of their sexuality. Steeped in the mythos casting non-procreative sex as immoral, the choice to remain abstinent is thus imbued with a perception of responsibility and morality not ascribed to contraceptive methods permitting non-procreative sex. Barrier methods and hormonal contraceptives occupy the middle rungs of the hierarchy and accordingly function as a middle ground for individuals wrestling with the discordant aims of the hierarchy. These methods provide women control by separating sex from reproduction which subsequently increases their burden to act responsibly. The morality of women choosing to engage in non-procreative sex stems exclusively from her ability to do so responsibly—ideally in a monogamous, heterosexual relationship. Emergency contraception and abortion reside at the top of the hierarchy as these options provide women the highest levels of control over their reproduction but are also assumed to be the result of one's moral failing to act responsibly. The following section explores the foundations of the contraceptive hierarchy within the rhetoric of early birth controllers and explores its lingering influence on contemporary discourses surrounding contraception.

Abstinence

Contemporary rhetoric on the subject of abstinence is punctuated by sharp echoes from the past, particularly in terms of Abstinence Only Until Marriage (AOUM) sex education programs. The U.S. Federal Government formally initiated funding streams for these programs in 1981 and has continued funding them at a significantly higher rate than their comprehensive counterparts. Yet, the critique of AOUM offered by contemporary advocates is eerily familiar. Samantha Hart of Planned Parenthood of Metropolitan Washington, DC rebukes AOUM programs for using "scare tactics and lack of information as a weapon," suggesting, "When abstinence-only sex education is employed, it leaves a population of sexually active people vulnerable and uninformed."[145] Hart's plea for accurate information is an unfortunate callback to the very same demands for information first advanced by the birth control movement in 1914. Given the progress of the movement over the last 100 years, this demand feels perplexing, but only initially. On closer look, the demand for information makes perfect sense in the trajectory of a movement that has long denied the legitimacy of sexual expression outside of marriage.

Early advocates secured popular support for their agenda by restricting their advocacy of contraception to married couples and recommending abstinence for unmarried persons as a supposedly necessary check on promiscuity, prostitution, and venereal disease. Even Dennett, whose controversial book *The Sex Side of Life* was one of the earliest sex education texts aimed at adolescents, advocated premarital abstinence as the morally righteous course of action. In the overview to the text she articulates a need for young people "to have some understanding of the marvelous place which sex emotion has in life . . . to give them the self-control that is born of knowledge, not fear, the reverence that will prevent premature or trivial connections, the good taste and finesse that will make their sex life, when they reach maturity, a vitalizing success."[146] Although Dennett believed in giving adolescents medically accurate information regarding sex and reproduction, she carefully contextualized the application of that knowledge purely to situations of mutual love and marriage. She continues, "For the idea of sex relations between people who do not love each other, who do not feel any sense of belonging to each other, will always be revolting to highly developed, sensitive people. People's lives grow finer and their characters better, if they have sex relations only with those they love."[147]

The information presented in *The Sex Side of Life* lives on today in the AOUM curriculum. In their 2017 position paper on AOUM policies and programs, the Society for Adolescent Health and Medicine explains the ideological underpinnings of government-funded AOUM programs, noting, "funding requirements suggest that abstinence from sexual intercourse is 'the only certain way to avoid out-of-wedlock pregnancy, sexually transmitted diseases, and other associated health problems.'"[148] The official definition of abstinence education included under Title V further specifies "a mutually faithful, monogamous relationship in the context of marriage is the expected standards of sexual activity" with "sexual activity outside the context of marriage likely to have harmful psychological and physical effects."[149] The rhetoric of contemporary AOUM advocates bears a striking resemblance to that of early birth controllers because for all intents and purposes, it is the same.

As contemporary activists fight to secure funding for comprehensive sex education, they face a deeply entrenched enemy of their own movement's making. Abstinence is heralded as the best framework for adolescents not because of its efficacy, which is notoriously lacking, but because of its purported moral value. Its position at the bottom of the contraceptive hierarchy reflects both its lack of sophistication as a contraceptive method and its primacy in our societal norms surrounding sex. Abstinence technically offers women the most control over their reproduction by eliminating the chance of pregnancy altogether and accordingly demands the most discipline from users who exercise their responsibility by refraining from intercourse. Whereas other contraceptive options decouple sex from reproduction, abstinence prevents either from occurring and therefore is the only form of contraception capable of preserving the conservative ideal of strictly procreative sex.

Barrier Methods

In the early twentieth century, barrier methods, also known as prophylactics, were the most common form of contraception utilized to prevent pregnancy. Yet, birth controllers had a somewhat tumultuous relationship with prophylactics. Sanger initially advocated for both condoms and diaphragms in her 1917 instructional pamphlet *Family Limitation*, presenting them as an added level of protection when paired with postcoital douching. She notes, "But there is always the possibility that the sperm has entered the womb before the solution can reach it. It is safer therefore to prevent the possibility of the contact of the semen and the ovum, by the interposition of a wall between them."[150]

Yet, as the movement sought mainstream acceptance, their discussion of prophylactics took on a markedly different tone. Condoms are scantly mentioned in the pages of the *Birth Control Review*, and the use of diaphragms came to be known simply as "the method" with almost no detail provided to readers as to what this mysterious method entailed. This censorship, although deeply frustrating to readers desperate for practical advice, represented a strategic choice for the movement as they tried to secure passage of doctors-only bills and create an image of respectability.

Given their lurid associations, condoms didn't quite fit the narrative of responsibility promulgated by the movement. Historian Linda Gordon explains, "one reason for neglect of the condom was fear of licensing sexual immorality. The condom was well suited to be, as it became, the chief contraceptive for 'sinners.' It was easy to get and required no doctors or special instructions."[151] The double standard surrounding the different prophylactics used by men and women was not lost on advocates. The alarming rates of venereal disease during WWI pushed condoms and chemical prophylactics for men into commercial spaces and, curiously, without the accompanying moral panic surrounding contraception for women. Remarking on this very situation, The John Price Jones Corporation queried: condoms are "purchasable at almost every corner drug store. But we do not appear to be overwhelmed by a wave of sex immorality."[152] The movement's repeated references to venereal disease undoubtedly carried a bitter undertone toward the readily available condom granting men a level of sexual freedom inaccessible and impermissible to women. Sanger made her frustration on the matter clear, bluntly stating: "She is still bound because she has in the past left the solution of the problem to him. Having left it to him, she finds instead of rights, she has only such privileges as she has gained by petitioning, coaxing, and cozening."[153] Yet, this double standard also revealed the way forward for birth controllers. In order to overcome the moral qualms uniquely leveled at women, contraception would need to be presented as an aid to the marital relationship and infused with a sense of responsibility facilitated by the involvement of doctors.

From both a functional and ideological standpoint, the diaphragm was the ideal contraceptive to simultaneously suit the needs of individual women and the broader birth control movement. On a functional level, its efficacy, especially when properly fitted and integrated into a strict douching regimen, far exceeded that of the rhythm method or withdrawal. Its use had a negligible impact on the pleasure of the sex act and its durable construction meant that, if properly cared for, it could be used repeatedly for upwards of a year. But the real value of the diaphragm was how neatly it fit within the movement's moral framework of responsible sexual expression. Unlike condoms which could be used impetuously, diaphragms required forethought and preparation making their use far more consistent with the aims of family planning than recreational sex. For context, merely obtaining a diaphragm required a gynecological exam, a fitting performed by a physician, and a nurse-facilitated practice session requiring women demonstrate their ability to successfully insert and remove the device. Just to be sure a woman could be trusted to use the device properly, "she is asked to practice at home and return in a week's time, so that we may assures ourselves that she is proficient."[154]

Unlike the readily available condom, diaphragms were, and still are, heavily regulated as a subversive check on women's sexual behavior, requiring she seek consultation with her doctor before use. Linda Gordon explains the ideological appeal of this cumbersome process: "Indeed, it is *because* the diaphragm was a medical device, requiring fitting and instruction in a clinic, that its distribution could be controlled."[155] Reiterating their commitment to traditional values, clinics only saw married women and more specifically sought to reach women who were already mothers. The intent of these clinics was not to liberate women sexually but to give them the tools of responsible motherhood. "The method" obtained an air of respectability in large part because of the involvement of doctors who served as gatekeepers ensuring access solely to married women for the purpose of regulating their reproduction. In this way, the diaphragm was the first contraceptive method to rely on medicalization for legitimacy—a phenomenon explored more fully in chapter 5. Female-specific barrier methods, especially given the option for insertion hours before sexual intercourse, finally enabled women to separate sex and reproduction and thus gain some semblance of control over their reproductive capacity. Yet, the involvement of doctors meant the control was not solely theirs. Additionally, the requirements of the process—time, money, and sanitary living conditions—made the method inaccessible for impoverished women who needed it most. Situated just above abstinence in the reproductive hierarchy, barrier methods increased control, required high levels of responsibility to use properly, and attained moral approval via their strict association with married women desiring reproductive control.

Modern Contraceptives

The 1960s ushered in a new era of contraceptive methods beginning with the oral contraceptive pill in 1960, followed by a wave of Long-Acting Reversible Contraception (LARCs) beginning with the IUD in 1968, and culminating with the approval of emergency contraception in 1998. With each successive development, women gained increasingly more control over their reproduction as these methods not only solidified the separation of sex and reproduction, but also decoupled sex and contraception. Whereas barrier methods required extreme foresight or the cooperation of a willing partner during the sex act or both, hormonal interventions could be deployed long before the initiation of sex or in the case of emergency contraception after sexual intercourse. Yet, accompanying the rollout of each new method was the familiar script of opposition arguments questioning the responsibility and morality of further separating sex and reproduction, met with assurances from advocates that women could still be trusted to use these new technologies in accordance with established norms. These scripts form the basis of the U.S. Supreme Court's successive decisions concerning contraception, as explored in chapter 6, and are also readily apparent in the public discussions following the emergence of each new method.

Although the first oral contraceptive pill, Enovid, was initially approved only for the treatment of gynecological disorders, news spread quickly of its contraceptive capability and ignited a familiar debate. In 1962, when the Illinois Public Aid Commission proposed incorporating oral contraceptives into its public welfare policy, they were roundly rebuked because "over 80 percent of the women and girls on relief are either unwed or separated from their husbands, it would foster irresponsibility and downgrade public morals."[156] Despite the Catholic Church's warming toward contraception as a marital aid in the 1940s, the development of the pill resuscitated its hostility. Monsignor Kelly, the director of the Family Life Bureau of the Roman Catholic Archdiocese of New York, trotted out their well-worn critique in a 1963 article in the *New York Times*. He scolds, "the time indeed has come to take a good look at the increasing promiscuity, not only of the young, but the married as well, and to see their intimate connection with contraception."[157] Oral contraceptives offered women an unprecedented level of control and freedom by replacing the cumbersome process of the diaphragm with a convenient pill taken days or even months prior to the sex act providing constant protection regardless of the intention to actually engage in unprotected sex. The confluence of control and convenience reignited concerns about the misuse of contraception and made the fallacious myth of the promiscuous woman a more realistic possibility in the eyes of moralists.

In responding to these criticisms, the movement relied heavily on its previous rhetorical strategies opting to placate opponents and reiterate the values of monogamy and responsibility instead of directly defending the sexual liberation of women. When explicitly questioned about the pill's impact on sexual morality, then PPFA president Dr. Alan Guttmacher balked, stating, "contraceptives had contributed relatively little to the sexual revolution" and even if there was a resulting increase in "extramarital intercourse," it was "a small price to pay for the elimination annually of 250,000 illegitimate births and one million abortions."[158] Guttmacher's response is packed with staples from the early movement's rhetorical toolkit—a minimization of sexual liberation, a denouncement of extramarital relationships, and a statement of comparative benefit in relation to abortion. Old scripts were also put to good use to explain the benefits of oral contraceptives—not to women but to families. Writing for the *New York Times* in 1966, noted reproductive rights advocate Jane E. Brody proclaims, "it has revolutionized family planning and relieved a traditional source of family tension: the fear of having unwanted children. With the pill, newlyweds are confident that their first child will not catch them emotionally and financially unprepared."[159] Although there were certainly proponents of oral contraception, particularly within Women's Liberation, who ferociously defended the sexual freedom granted women as a result of an easier method of contraception, these arguments rarely found their way into the mouths of mainstream birth control advocates like Guttmacher. In terms of the contraceptive hierarchy, hormonal interventions isolated contraception from the sex act and gave women a unique level of control in comparison to their male counterparts. This newfound level of control carried with it an even greater demand that they act responsibly—in part because these methods shifted the presumed locus of control for contraception almost exclusively to women and in part because the ease and efficacy of these methods left little room for women to justifiably experience an unintended pregnancy. These developments also precipitated a shift away from the married woman as the sole contraceptive user and reignited concerns with promiscuity and licentiousness historically used to question the morality of women and discredit their ability to make responsible reproductive decisions.

The lengthy political battle for emergency contraception is also replete with familiar rhetorical strategies from both opponents and advocates. Despite the fact that the process of preventing pregnancy via hormonal interventions after the sex act, known first as the Yuzpe method and later colloquially as emergency contraception, was first developed in the 1960s, it would take almost three decades to secure FDA approval and an additional eight years for the authorization of over-the-counter sale. Dr. Caroline Wellberry of the Georgetown University School of Medicine succinctly describes the opposition to emergency contraception in a 2004 brief for the *American Family Physician*; she explains, "Opponents argue that over-the-counter access will deprive users of the benefit of a physician encounter. . . . In addition, some opponents state that over-the-counter emergency contraception would encourage high-risk behavior, particularly in adolescents, and increase reliance on this method rather than use of other contraceptive methods."[160] Unsurprisingly, in response to a contraceptive method allowing women increased control over reproduction, opponents regurgitated the familiar false flags of promiscuity and moral licentiousness used to classify contraception as obscene a century prior.

Of deep concern, these fallacious sentiments had the ear of individuals directly involved in the FDA decision regarding over-the-counter availability of emergency contraception. In 2004, Dr. Janet Woodcook, then Deputy Commissioner for Operations at the FDA, "worried that approval of the OTC switch application could potentially lead to 'extreme promiscuous behaviors such as the medication taking on an urban legend status that would lead adolescents to form sex based cults centered around the use of Plan B.'"[161] Dr. Galson the FDA official who wrote the 2004 letter denying over-the-counter approval later that year cited his agreement with Woodcock's concern as a motivating factor despite the numerous scientific studies dispelling the link between emergency contraception and promiscuity. Rather than getting bogged down in yet another debate about the potential for promiscuity, birth controllers relied on decades of evidence disproving the link between increased contraceptive access and licentiousness. Citing a litany of convincing evidence finding no correlation between access to emergency contraception and unprotected sex, Dr. David Grimes scoffs, "This is analogous to suggesting that a fire extinguisher beneath the kitchen sink makes one a risky cook."[162] Grimes's analogy pays homage to the movement's early comparisons to eyeglasses and further dismisses the offensive suggestion that women act "morally" only when faced with the possibility of pregnancy.

Yet, emergency contraception did present an interesting challenge to the long-standing rhetoric of the movement emphasizing prevention. Unlike previous methods utilized preemptively to prevent pregnancy, emergency contraception is deployed after the sex act making it, in the eyes of many, more akin to an abortifacient than a contraceptive. Admittedly, scientists aren't 100 percent sure how emergency contraception works in all instances, as there are a variety of ways it interferes with the reproductive process including preventing ovulation, slowing ovulation, increasing cervical mucus to prevent fertilization, and in rare cases preventing implantation.[163] Additionally, the very premise of a reactionary method of contraception created tension with the movement's reliance on the trope of responsibility. Under their own framework, responsible women used contraception preemptively to manage their reproduction. Opponents exploited this framework to label women using emergency contraception, a reactionary method, as irresponsible for either failing to use preventative methods or failing to abstain from risky sex.

To tamper these concerns, advocates continually emphasized the validity of emergency contraception solely as a secondary method of contraception and reiterated the need to prevent abortions through any means possible. Firmly cementing the placement of emergency contraception in the contraceptive hierarchy, Jane Brody cautions, "Every woman must realize that emergency contraception is a backup, not a substitute for more reliable precoital contraception. Emergency contraception is not as effective in preventing pregnancy, as, say, oral contraceptives, implants, or the copper IUD."[164] A 2013 PPFA fact sheet reiterates the supplementary status of emergency contraception, explaining, "Every woman deserves every chance to prevent an unintended pregnancy. Emergency contraception (EC) provides women with a second chance at prevention in cases of unanticipated sexual activity, contraceptive failure, or sexual assault."[165] It's worth noting here that sexual assault was commonly used as a rhetorical shield of sorts because opponents were less likely to defend the denial of emergency contraception to survivors.

Advocates lauded this second chance as critical to preventing abortions. Felicia Stewart, co-director of the Center for Reproductive Health Research & Policy at the University of California in San Francisco explained the utility of emergency contraception to preventing abortions in the *Guttmacher Policy Review* in 2002. She proclaims: "Wider access to emergency contraception is perhaps the single most promising avenue for reducing this country's high rates of unintended pregnancy and abortion. . . . The regimen is used in the most risky of all settings, when many women, if they were to get pregnant, would have an abortion." Stewart further speculates, "If women heard about emergency contraception from their doctors and saw it in pharmacies, many would use the method and wouldn't have to experience an unintended pregnancy."[166] Drawing on the rhetorical strategies discussed in previous chapters, advocates positioned emergency contraception as preferable to abortion—a uniquely valuable tactic given the popular misconception that emergency contraception functioned as an abortifacient.

In terms of the contraceptive hierarchy, emergency contraception gives a woman immense control—allowing her to retroactively prevent a pregnancy up to five days after intercourse. Yet, in the eyes of many, the sheer need for emergency contraceptive proves that women are not responsible actors. To those who deny the reality of contraceptive failures or unanticipated sexual activity the litany of preemptory options afforded women should remove any need for emergency contraception. In reality, the only reason why emergency contraception exists today is because it is framed as the last line of defense against abortions. On this point, and perhaps only this point, can opponents and advocates agree.

ABORTION AND THE CONTRACEPTIVE HIERARCHY

Abortion remains a stigmatized decision precisely because of the sense of responsibility imbued into the use of contraception. Women who pursue an abortion are assumed incapable of acting responsibly, and thus morally, by preventing an unwanted pregnancy regardless of their unique circumstances. This dynamic results in a familiar battle between reproductive justice advocates demanding improved contraceptive access and moralists who point to both abstinence and barrier methods as simple, easily accessible, and morally superior options of preventing an unwanted pregnancy. Conservative political analyst Ross Douthat summarizes this dynamic in the *New York Times* in 2012. He writes:

> Even the most pro-choice politicians, for instance, usually emphasize that they want to reduce the need for abortion, and make the practice rare as well as safe and legal. Even the fiercest conservative critics of the White House's contraception mandate—yes, Rick Santorum included—agree that artificial birth control should be legal and available. And both Democrats and Republicans generally agree that the country would be better off with fewer pregnant teenagers, fewer unwanted children, fewer absent fathers, fewer out-of-wedlock births. Where cultural liberals and social conservatives differ is on the means that will achieve these ends. The liberal vision tends to emphasize access to contraception as the surest path to stable families, wanted children and low abortion rates. The more direct control that women have over when and whether sex makes babies, liberals argue, the less likely they'll be to get pregnant at the wrong time and with the wrong partner—and the less likely they'll be to even consider having an abortion. . . . The conservative narrative, by contrast, argues that it's more important to promote chastity, monogamy and fidelity than to worry about whether there's a prophylactic in every bedroom drawer or bathroom cabinet. To the extent that contraceptive use has a significant role in the conservative vision (and obviously there's some Catholic-Protestant disagreement), it's in the context of already stable, already committed relationships. Monogamy, not chemicals or latex, is the main line of defense against unwanted pregnancies.[167]

These two competing narratives seek to accomplish the same objective—reduce and ultimately eliminate abortion. While social conservatives stress the bottom tier of the hierarchy with its heavy emphasis on responsibility and moral superiority, cultural liberals favor the middle rungs of the hierarchy giving women more control over their reproduction in consideration of factors outside the scope of responsibility such as contraceptive failures and sexual assault. Ultimately, the contraceptive hierarchy works in tandem with the terministic screen of motherhood to shame women for ever needing an abortion undergirded by the long-standing framing of abortion as a last resort, as something that should be "safe, legal, and rare."

Each successive rung in the contraceptive hierarchy offers women a higher level of control over their reproduction beginning with preemptive measures, such as condoms and hormonal birth control, and culminating in the reactive measures of emergency contraception and abortion. Yet, because the entire rhetorical legacy of the birth control movement has preached prevention, the reactionary measures remain heavily stigmatized—shrouded in the assumption of irresponsibility. Women who seek an abortion are heavily questioned about their contraceptive practices prior to the unintended pregnancy as well as what changes they will make moving forward. These questions assume a level of irresponsibility prior to pregnancy and seek to establish a more responsible practice of pregnancy prevention. Even pro-choice positions are not immune to this logic particularly concerning women who've had multiple abortions. Kristen Luker explains, "The first abortion presumably represents the lesser of several evils. . . . But since most women are given contraceptive services after an abortion, every abortion after the first represents a case where a woman had the option of avoiding pregnancy and did not. Except in extraordinary cases, pro-choice people see this bringing of an embryo into existence when it could have been avoided as morally wrong."[168] The phrase contraceptive failure, often cited as a primary reason for abortion, implies not only a malfunction in the contraceptive method but user error as well. If they weren't going to practice abstinence, then they should have at least used a condom. The condom broke? Well then you should have used emergency contraception. Women who find themselves in need of an abortion have thus made a series of irresponsible choices reflecting a deep moral failing on their part.

The moral framework of early birth controllers and the resulting contraceptive hierarchy reverberates within the rhetoric of even the most ardent defenders of women's reproductive rights. In 2005, House Democrats introduced the Putting Prevention First Act which, among other things, would have expanded federal appropriations for family planning services, mandated contraceptive coverage under insurance plans, expanded access to emergency contraceptives, and funded sex education programs. Speaking just days after the thirty-second anniversary of *Roe v. Wade*, then Senator Hillary Clinton offered a compelling endorsement of the bill littered with rhetoric demonstrating the salience of the contraceptive hierarchy. She proclaims:

> We should all be able to agree that we want every child born in this country and around the world to be wanted, cherished, and loved. The best way to get there is do more to educate the public about reproductive health, about how to prevent unsafe and unwanted pregnancies. . . . Research shows that the primary reason that teenage girls abstain is because of their religious and moral values. We should embrace this—and support programs that reinforce the idea that abstinence at a young age is not just the smart thing to do, it is the right thing to do. . . . But we have to do more than just send the right messages and values to our children. Preventing unwanted pregnancy demands that we do better as adults to create the structure in which children live and the services they need to make the right decisions. . . . The use of contraception is a big factor in determining whether or not women become pregnant. . . . So by preventing unintended pregnancy, contraception reduces the need for abortion. . . . One bill that provides a comprehensive approach to the problem of unintended pregnancies encapsulates many of these efforts. It's called "The Putting Prevention First

> Act." It provides a road map to the destination of fewer unwanted pregnancies—to the day when abortion is truly sage, legal, and rare.[169]

The influence of the contraceptive hierarchy on Clinton's remarks is palpable. Not only does she work through the various contraceptive options facilitated by the bill in their hierarchical order, she makes her claim by borrowing heavily from the rhetoric of early birth controllers. She defends abstinence as both the right and moral choice for young girls, heralds the value of contraception in preventing unwanted pregnancies, and justifies the use of emergency contraception all in service of the ultimate goal of making abortion "safe, legal, and rare." Missing from her speech are many of the hallmarks contemporary advocates come to expect in a speech about reproductive rights, including an acknowledgment of women as sexual beings and an unfettered defense of women's bodily autonomy.

Clinton faced backlash from many pro-choice advocates who felt her speech "soften[ed] their stance on protecting women's reproductive health and freedom."[170] Yet, Clinton revealed the intent of her speech in both the first line of the segment above and in the concluding stanza: "So my hope now, is that whatever our disagreements with those in this debate, that we join together to take real action to improve the quality of health care for women and families, to reduce the number of abortions and to build a healthier, brighter more hopeful future for women and girls in our country and around the world."[171] The demands in Clinton's speech were softened just as early birth controllers softened their rhetoric to make the movement palatable to a broad audience. It's difficult to blame Clinton for her calculated rhetoric. Afterall, decades of discourse demonstrated the efficacy of political accommodation as a strategy to secure support for reproductive freedom. Instead, Clinton's timid advocacy and shrewd call for common ground illuminates the relatively unchanged cultural context surrounding women's reproductive freedom; despite decades of progress, advocates are still trying to convince opponents that women can and should be trusted to make their own decisions concerning their reproduction.

NOTES

1. "Calendar Fear," 23.
2. Tone, *Devices and Desires*, 160.
3. Ibid., 157–59.
4. Prescott and Thompson, "A Right," 543.
5. Gordon, *The Moral Property*, 162. Catt's endorsement of continence and abstinence also made it difficult for her to endorse birth control, for if couples could

embrace self-restraint in these ways there would be no need for contraceptives. James Reed discusses the tensions between birth controllers and feminists at length, noting that "a certain uneasiness [existed] among many women reformers in dealing with sex" (Reed, *From Private Vice*, 131).

6. Gordon, *The Moral Property*, 13.
7. "Women Should," 14.
8. "Women's League," 5.
9. Hooker, "The Tap-Root," 234.
10. "Nurseries in," 11.
11. "Ellen Key," E8.
12. Prescott and Thompson, "A Right," 552.
13. "Editorial," 5.
14. Eastman, "Birth Control," 3–4.
15. "Editorial," 5.
16. "Feminism and," 21.
17. Sanger, "Has Suffrage Reached," 3.
18. "The League," 177.
19. Margaret Sanger Papers, 236141.
20. "Editorial Comment," 1917, 16.
21. Prescott and Thompson, "A Right," 552.
22. Tuttle, "Suffrage and," 5.
23. Ibid., 6.
24. Peeples, "Downwind," 252.
25. Tuttle, "Suffrage and," 6.
26. Sanger, "Woman's Error," 1.
27. Margaret Sanger Papers, 236127.
28. Winner, "Woman Rebellious!," 3.
29. Prescott and Thompson, "A Right," 553.
30. Sanger, "Woman's Error," 1.
31. Debs, "Freedom Is the Goal," 7.
32. Margaret Sanger Papers, 236141; Margaret Sanger Papers, 236168.
33. Margaret Sanger Papers, 236132.
34. Margaret Sanger Papers, 224706.
35. Margaret Sanger Papers, 236505.
36. Adams, "Woman's Future," SM8.
37. Prescott and Thompson, "A Right," 544.
38. Margaret Sanger Papers, 226268.
39. Roberts, "Birth Control," 7.
40. Mayhall, "The Rhetorics of Slavery," 494.
41. Gordon, *The Moral Property*, 167; McCann, *Birth Control Politics*, 26. McCann explains that between 1920 and 1930 Sanger and the ABCL made repeated requests for support from the NWP but were refused on the grounds that birth control was too controversial and would erode their focus on the Equal Rights Amendment.
42. May, *American and the Pill*, 17.
43. Prescott and Thompson, "A Right," 546.

44. Ibid.
45. Ashley, "Editorial Comment," 2.
46. Sanger, "The Fight against," 248.
47. Ruhl, "Dilemmas of the Will," 642.
48. Sanger, "The Need," 227.
49. Sanger, "A Parents'," 7.
50. Vickery, "Endowment of," 15.
51. Margaret Sanger Papers, 224706.
52. Margaret Sanger Papers, 224706.
53. Margaret Sanger Papers, 229659.
54. Margaret Sanger Papers, 236127.
55. Stevens, "Birth Control," 122.
56. Winner, "A Parents Problem," 5.
57. "Men and," 5.
58. Margaret Sanger Papers, 236168.
59. Gruenberg, "The Positive," 216.
60. Smith-Rosenberg, *Disorderly Conduct*, 247.
61. Dewey, "Education and," 34.
62. "Is the New," 36.
63. Dorman, "The Weeping Stork," X20.
64. Taylor, "Activities of Women's," 18.
65. "Is the New," 36.
66. M. K., "Income and," 9.
67. Boughton, "What 7309 Mothers," 10.
68. Winner, "The Triumph," 9.
69. Margaret Sanger Papers, 233644.
70. Rehill, "Hearth and Home," para. 9.
71. Taylor, "Activities of Women's," 17.
72. Hankins, "The Sexual," 239.
73. Gilman, "Progress Through," 622.
74. Margaret Sanger Papers, 236021.
75. Margaret Sanger Papers, 236168.
76. Margaret Sanger Papers, 236585.
77. Margaret Sanger Papers, 234585.
78. Margaret Sanger Papers, 236191.
79. Margaret Sanger Papers, 236585.
80. Margaret Sanger Papers, 236637.
81. Margaret Sanger Papers, 213557.
82. Margaret Sanger Papers, 229968.
83. Mudgett, "The Crying Need," 6.
84. Margaret Sanger Papers, 229968.
85. Margaret Sanger Papers, 224706.
86. Yarros, "Birth Control," 199.
87. Hollister, "The Disappearing," 315.
88. Hooker and Thomson, "Birth Control," 156.

89. Margaret Sanger Papers, 236637.
90. Margaret Sanger Papers, 229968.
91. Ellis, "The Love Rights," 4.
92. Sanger, "Are Birth Control," 3.
93. Margaret Sanger Papers, 236168.
94. Ellis, "The Love Rights," 6.
95. Margaret Sanger Papers, 229968.
96. Margaret Sanger Papers, 237335.
97. Murray and Young, "Modern Marriage," 22.
98. E. Mowrer, "Birth Control,"189.
99. Margaret Sanger Papers, 236021.
100. Margaret Sanger Papers, 223063.
101. Sanger, "Morality and Birth Control," 14.
102. "Scientists Plead for," XX6.
103. Robinson, "The Future," 211.
104. Margaret Sanger Papers, 236170.
105. "Scientists Plead for," XX6.
106. Margaret Sanger Papers, 229659.
107. Rene, "The Waste," 6.
108. H. Mowrer, "Birth Control," 5.
109. Margaret Sanger Papers, 229968.
110. "A Judge on," 11.
111. Matsner, "The Physician's," 70.
112. Margaret Sanger Papers, 236021.
113. Margaret Sanger Papers, 226564.
114. Guilford, "Woman's Emancipation," 5.
115. Keating, "The Church," 426.
116. Jakimowicz, "A Priest," 12.
117. Betts, "A Christian," 198–99.
118. Keating, "The Church," 430.
119. Ibid., 435.
120. Hooker, "Birth Control," 251.
121. Wile, "Birth Control," 199.
122. Dennett, *Birth Control Laws*, 127.
123. Robinson, "Is Birth Control," 14.
124. Margaret Sanger Papers, 229968.
125. Dennett, *Birth Control Laws*, 137.
126. Margaret Sanger Papers, 236357.
127. Ellis, "The Objects," 8.
128. Margaret Sanger Papers, 236141
129. "Court Rules," 29.
130. Margaret Sanger Papers, 236766.
131. Briffault, "Will Monogamy," 207.
132. Zueblin, "MOTHERS FIRST!," 4.
133. Dennett, *Birth Control Laws*, 103.

134. Margaret Sanger Papers, 236021.
135. Dennett, *Birth Control Laws*, 185.
136. Margaret Sanger Papers, 229968.
137. Knopf, "An Arsenal," 8.
138. Margaret Sanger Papers, 236021.
139. Goldstein, "Control of," 196.
140. Margaret Sanger Papers, 229968.
141. Dennett, "Legislators, Six-Hour," 5.
142. Margaret Sanger Papers, 236046.
143. Sanger, "Facing the New Year," 3.
144. Margaret Sanger Papers, 236357.
145. Hart, "The Reality," para. 6.
146. Dennett, *The Sex Side*, 8.
147. Ibid., 19.
148. Society for Adolescent Health and Medicine, "Abstinence-Only," 401.
149. Ibid.
150. Sanger, *Family Limitation*, 9.
151. Gordon, *The Moral Property*, 218.
152. Margaret Sanger Papers, 229968.
153. Sanger, "A Parents'," 6.
154. Society for the Provision of Birth Control Clinics, *Annual Report*, 8.
155. Gordon, *The Moral Property*, 218.
156. "Illinois Divided," 84.
157. "Dr. Rock," 9.
158. Wehrwein. "New Moral," 12.
159. Brody, "The Pill," 1.
160. Wellberry, "Emergency Contraception," 656.
161. *United States v. Christmas*, 222 F.3d 141, 145 (4th Cir. 2000). *Tummino v. Torti*, 603 F. Supp. 2nd 519 (E.D.N.Y 2009).
162. Grimes, "Emergency Contraception," 220.
163. "What kind of emergency contraception should I use?," Planned Parenthood, accessed May 25, 2021. https://www.plannedparenthood.org/learn/morning-after-pill-emergency-contraception/which-kind-emergency-contraception-should-i-use.
164. Brody, "The Politics," F7.
165. Planned Parenthood Federation of America, *Emergency Contraception*, para 1.
166. Boonstra, "Emergency Contraception," 13.
167. Douthat, "The 'Safe," para. 3–4.
168. Luker, *Abortion &*, 180–81.
169. Clinton, "Preventing Unwanted Pregnancy."
170. Healy, "Clinton Is," para. 14.
171. Clinton, "Preventing Unwanted Pregnancy."

Chapter Five

Alliances and Accommodation

On October 25, 1915, an unusual parade took to the streets of New York with colorful floats and jubilant crowds nowhere in sight. In their place, "Half a dozen derelict, poverty stricken, poorly clad, underfed men" donned "poster signs asking all to read whether these poster carriers should be allowed to become fathers."[1] *Calling attention to their own personal deficiencies as proof of their "devitalized heritage" for which reproduction was contraindicated, one man's sign queried, "Would the prisons and asylums be filled if my kind had no children?" Another asked, "I cannot read this sign, by what right have I children?" Yet another definitively proclaimed, "I have no opportunity to educate or feed my children or myself; they may become criminals."*[2] *Press dubbed the spectacle put on by Frederic H. Robinson, president of the Sociological Fund, "The Horrible Examples Parade," and the* Intelligencer *on October 30, 1915, suggested the parade was certainly a "novel publicity campaign in favor of birth control."*[3] *Victor Robinson of the Voluntary Parenthood League lauded the spectacle of "human wrecks" plucked from the "the bottom strata of life" as an unconventional ploy to literally place "the issue of birth control in the path of society" where "the authorities and the man on the street could dodge the issue no longer."*[4]

Frederic H. Robinson wasn't formally affiliated with the Voluntary Parenthood League, but he was part of a growing crowd taking note of the movement—progressive social reformers with a penchant for eugenic thinking. As president of the Sociological Fund for the Medical Review of Reviews, *Robinson championed eugenics and even used the organization's funds to establish a $1000 prize to "the ideal eugenically man and woman who will marry" and raise a large family.*[5] *Yet, Robinson was also the only publisher willing to print Mary Ware Dennett's 1918 pamphlet* The Sex Side of Life, *and as birth controllers struggled to win over the medical community, Robinson repeatedly came to their defense. Directly chastising doctors for their willful ignorance on the subject of contraception, Robinson scolded, "Apparently a regrettably large percentage of the profession requires time to* *think, or the courage to think out loud, and birth control is merely a type of topic that shows one weakness that demands a remedy."*[6] *Despite his jarring tactics and ideologies, Robinson proved useful to the movement giving them both a visible platform and much needed validation.*

Having exhausted their attempts at agitation and legislative change to little success, the birth control movement pivoted toward an agenda of professionalization in the interwar years characterized by the pursuit of strategic allies whose involvement promised to bring legitimacy to the movement. Dr. Harriette M. Dilla, a faculty member in Economics and Sociology at Smith College, explained at the First American Birth Control Conference in 1922: "It is a fact that no movement by itself is self-sufficient, and as members of the movement for birth control I am sure that we do not claim that it alone is adequate to the tremendous needs of society. We must be largely dependent upon, and certainly cooperate with, all the splendid agencies that are working at present."[7] Note the type of cooperation sought by Dilla—"splendid agencies"—who, unlike the Socialist Party, provided the movement an air of respectability and the promise of resources. Subsequently, the movement worked during the interwar years to forge relationships with three specific groups: doctors, eugenicists, and Black activists.

This chapter, while cumbersome in length, performs the critical task of dissecting the movement's coalition-building strategy which dominated its efforts between 1920 and 1940. During this time, advocates under the leadership of Sanger diligently courted groups who could help rebrand the once sensationalist movement into a well-reasoned cause. In doing so, birth controllers sought the acceptance of doctors, the endorsement of eugenicists, and the uptake of prominent Black leaders. There is enough to say about each of these alliances on their own to fill entire chapters, and even entire books, but addressing them collectively yields unique insight into the guiding strategy and accompanying rhetorical tactics utilized by the movement during this time. Yet, as this chapter illuminates, the alliances forged by birth controllers in the interwar years are remarkably similar in both form and function as advocates consistently drew from the same stable of rhetoric to court external stakeholders to the movement in hopes of expanding its reach and professionalizing its reputation. Returning to a framework of managed reproduction, these alliances crystallized around the mechanistic benefits of birth control—improved health outcomes, heartier populations, racial uplift—and articulated a societal right to contraception that empowered external stakeholders to subvert the individual needs of women in the name of societal welfare.

The theme of a collective societal right to contraception resonates within the rhetoric of each of the alliances explored in this chapter. Doctors acknowledged a societal obligation to prevent the spread of disease and decrease pregnancy-related mortality; eugenicists ardently defended their discriminatory policies as protective mechanisms to ensure future prosperity; and Black activists emphasized the need for racial uplift within their community. In each instance, birth control is positioned as the means to an end the efficacy of which relied on its broad application. Couching contraception within the framework of societal benefit left little room for the empowered woman whose choices may be at odds with maximizing the social value of practicing contraception. This tension is most prominent in the following discussion of negative eugenics but is characteristic of each of the alliances forged by early birth controllers. To actualize these relationships, birth controllers ceded control to a litany of external stakeholders including doctors, eugenicists, and public health officials whose supposedly expert guidance took priority over the lived experiences of their female patients. In doing so, birth controllers embraced an agenda that was unabashedly oriented toward population control the success of which would permanently shape their efforts moving forward. As explored in chapter 7, advocates repurposed this logic to lobby for the inclusion of family planning services in federally funded programs and continue to rely on utilitarian justifications for expanding contraceptive access. The movement would never be the same again.

The true embodiment of political accommodation, these alliances brought respect, visibility, and power to the movement, but at what cost? Linda Gordon observes, "Beginning in the 1920s birth control as a cause was taken over by male professionals, many of them physicians, in a 'planned parenthood' campaign that made women's equality and autonomy a secondary issue" and was undergirded by a belief "that some individuals were more valuable to society than others."[8] In addition to obscuring the needs of women, these alliances corrupted the movement's once benevolent goals. Angela Davis laments:

> When Margaret Sanger severed her ties with the Socialist Party for the purpose of building an independent birth control campaign, she and her followers became more susceptible than ever before to the anti-black and anti-immigrant propaganda of the times. Like their predecessors, who had been deceived by the race suicide propaganda, the advocates of birth control began to embrace the prevailing racist ideology. The fatal influence of the eugenics move would soon destroy the progressive potential of the birth control campaign.[9]

In many ways, this chapter picks up where chapter 1 left off, with the movement embracing Sanger's strategy of political accommodation to secure the endorsement, support, and validation of professional groups. Although building these alliances necessitated the rhetorical strategies explored in previous chapters, they also demonstrate the pervasiveness and efficacy of a new rhetorical strategy—deference. In their attempts to convince doctors and court eugenicists, birth controllers softened their once defiant posture and surrendered much of their control to government sanctioned stakeholders. Black activists who joined the cause during this period mimicked the rhetoric of the mainstream movement, including its deference to professional allies, and subsequently undercut the unique value of contraception within their own communities. Taken together, the interwar years marked a period of acquiescence for the movement. Bodily autonomy was subsumed by public health, voluntary motherhood was supplanted by hygienic reproduction, and birth control was exchanged for population control. These discourses worked conjointly to constitute our earliest understandings of contraceptive access, and their influence continues to animate current struggles for reproductive justice. The movement would never be the same again.

CONVINCING THE MEDICAL PROFESSION

Doctors, despite their reluctance to join the movement, played a vital role in the approach of mainstream birth controllers under Sanger's broad strategy of political accommodation. As explained in chapter 1, Sanger perceived the emphasis on scientific knowledge and the involvement of doctors as necessary steps toward respectability for the movement, particularly in light of its radical association with outspoken socialists like Emma Goldman and the early use of sensationalist stunts like Ethyl Byrne's 1917 hunger strike. Dr. George Kosmack's characterization of the movement in the *Journal of the American Medical Association* is representative of many physicians' attitude at the time. Kosmack, who later served as a director of The American Committee on Maternal Welfare, bluntly characterized the birth control movement "as a vicious propaganda movement, developed and continued by false sentiment and inadequate reasoning."[10] Morris Fishbein, the editor of the *Journal of the American Medical Association*, vocally opposed contraception insisting "not even the physicians, have ever perfected any method of birth control that is physiologically, psychologically and biologically sound in both principle and practice."[11] Historian James Reed contextualizes Fishbein's resistance as "part of a larger concern with the defense of a profession just coming into its own after years of struggle with quackery and with public indifference to the needs of the ethical practitioner."[12] As the dispute with the Children's Bureau in chapter 2 illustrates, physicians denounced any and all external efforts to provide health information to the general public and took specific umbrage with birth controllers, midwives, and popular healers for spreading what they dismissed as folk knowledge.[13] Often hiding behind the excuse that contraceptive instruction lacked 100 percent efficacy, the medical community busied itself with an endless slew of committees and studies to determine what advocates already knew—contraception, even if at times faulty, was vital to the health of the nation.

The Brownsville Clinic—A Test Case for Doctors-Only Laws

Not easily deterred, birth controllers fought tirelessly to alter the legal framework surrounding contraception in hopes of enticing doctors to join the cause. Unlike Dennett's open bill declassifying contraception as obscene and permitting the widespread dissemination of information, Sanger's doctors-only bill gave physicians exclusive control over the dispensation of contraceptive information—an obvious appeal to the medical community's quest for professionalism and authority. Suggesting legal barriers and not their own biases inhibited the medical community's involvement, Dr. Harriet Dilla proclaimed: "When our federal and state laws confer upon the medical profession the necessary freedom to develop the vital subjects of sex science and obstetrical practice, may we not confidently trust it to measure up to the excellent progress it has made in other fields where it has been free from legal limitations?"[14]

Despite Dilla's optimism and the movement's offer of exclusive control over contraceptive instruction, much of the medical community, with a few notable exceptions, remained unmoved. Dr. Abraham Jacobi, former president of the American Medical Association and cofounder of the *American Journal of Obstetrics*, was one such exception. Jacobi, an early adopter of contraception, proclaimed in the *New York Times* in 1916: "It is right to allow every licensed physician to give advice to married people on the question of birth control." Yet, according to the *Times* Jacobi's colleagues at the New York Country Medical Society felt "change to both the obscenity laws and the accompanying penal code should come from laymen and not physicians."[15] Although individual doctors like Jacobi readily defended birth control, the major organizational players in the medical community refused to engage and dismissed the movement as pure propaganda involvement with which was unbecoming.

With doctors-only bills failing to gain traction with either legislators or doctors, Sanger returned to her days of direct action in hopes of forcing the hand of both the law and the medical community. In October 1916, Sanger opened the Brooklyn-based Brownsville Clinic with help from her sister Ethel Byrne but without the supervision of a physician as required by New York state law. Within only nine days, the Brownsville Clinic examined and collected information from 450 women, including undercover police officer Margaret Whitehurst. Whitehurst visited the clinic under the guise of seeking contraceptive information only to return with an arrest warrant for both Sanger and Byrne. The 1916 raid brought immense publicity to the cause fueled in large part by Byrne's subsequent hunger strike while imprisoned for her complicity in the clinic's operation. Byrne spent thirty days at Blackwell Island and was eventually subjected to force-feeding after forgoing food and water for more than seven days. The *New York Times* provided daily updates on Byrne's condition referring to her as the "birth control prisoner" and even reported her efforts to share contraceptive information with her fellow inmates.[16] It was a brilliant publicity stunt for the movement.

The choice to proceed with the clinic was calculated—helping call attention to both the absurdity of the law and the need for the medical community to increase their involvement.[17] In his liberal interpretation of section 1142 of the Penal Law, Judge Frederick Crane held that although Sanger and Byrne indeed violated the state's version of the Comstock Law by disseminating contraceptive information, the intent of the law was not to deny doctors from dispensing contraceptive information for the cure or prevention of disease. In his written decision, Crane includes the *Webster's International Dictionary* definition of "disease" to explain that because pregnancy produces "an alteration in the state of the body, or of some of its organs, interrupting or disturbing the vital functions, and causing or threatening pain and sickness" contraception is no different than other accepted means of treating disease.[18] In doing so, Crane squarely situated contraception within the purview of the medical profession and validated Sanger's argument for exempting doctors from existing obscenity laws.

The Birth Control Review printed Crane's decision in full in its February-March, issue accompanied by an unsigned editorial comment noting the significance of his decision; it contends: "By construing the case as it did, the Court spared birth control advocates the time, expense, and labor of repeating the entire process with a physician as the appellant."[19] Sanger had not anticipated such an interpretation, yet, as a joint report for the BCCRB and the NCFLBC proclaimed: "[B]y going to jail two women established for the medical profession a right which it had neglected to establish for itself."[20] Sanger herself acknowledged the irony of the decision: "It is indeed a strange task for me to seek for the medical profession a right which has been neglected to claim for itself. None knows better than I, perhaps, the indifference neglect and evasion which has so generally characterized the attitude of physicians toward Birth Control." Doctors too seemed keenly aware of the precedent set by Crane. Writing in *The Medical Times* in 1918, Brooklyn-based physician Arthur C. Jacobson argues, "It clearly behooves the reputable wing of the profession to establish clinics for hygienic birth control advice. The language in which the court's decision is framed leaves no doubt as to the propriety of scientifically informed and well-intentioned physicians giving information as to birth control in select cases."[21] By contextualizing birth control within a medical framework, contraceptive instruction operated as an extension of the rights already granted to doctors to help women deal with matters of life and death for which pregnancy clearly qualified.

Sanger found a great deal of validation in Crane's decision and its subsequent uptake in the medical community—it was the proof of concept she needed for her insistence on scientific information and the inclusion of doctors to legitimize the birth control movement. With the endorsement of the New York Court of Appeals in hand, Sanger moved full speed ahead on her initiative to pass a doctors-only bill legally solidifying the role of doctors in the birth control movement. As explored in chapter 1, these efforts were far more persuasive to the medical community than Dennett's open legislation because they allowed physicians to establish control over the dissemination of contraceptive information complementing their own agenda to separate themselves from midwifery and quack medicine.

Yet, in situating contraception as necessary for the "cure or prevention of disease," Crane's decision established a specific and limited framework for contraceptive instruction that would prove troublesome for the movement over time. This limited interpretation was entirely predictable reflecting the long-standing feud between Sanger and Dennett over doctors-only bills. Sanger frequently invoked the disease framework and began her first major *Birth Control Review* article discussing doctors-only bills in 1919 with a statement that explicitly connects contraception and disease, declaring, "Appalling situations revealed every day indicate all too plainly that in cases where a woman's disease is affected by pregnancy, the medical institutions and clinics of New York State are accomplishing nothing to relieve those diseased conditions."[22] Pregnancy was and still is an avoidable accelerant for those battling disease, but disease itself constitutes just one of many circumstances justifying contraceptive use.

Dennett, however, vocally opposed the association of pregnancy and disease, vehemently defending contraception as an invaluable form of preventative medicine rather than a treatment for disease. Dennett bluntly labeled "contraceptive knowledge [as] part of general hygiene and education, and not a physician's prescription for disease."[23] Dr. William Bayliss, Professor of General Physiology in London, echoed this sentiment in his introduction to Marie Stopes's 1923 book; Bayliss portends, "If I may venture to say so, it seems to me that the question should be looked upon as one of normal physiological behavior, and for that reason, practical instruction should be distinct from the cure of disease."[24] Amid staggering maternal mortality rates, situating contraception within a disease paradigm constituted a powerful persuasive appeal to both physicians and the public; yet, doing so also obscured the complex sociopolitical motivations for contraceptive use that have nothing to do with health. Crane's decision, which quickly became the guiding legal framework for providing contraception, failed to account for these motivations and carved out a narrow set of conditions for the appropriate and legal provision of contraception.

Energized by the court's historic ruling, advocates vigorously pursued doctors-only bills and further developed their clinic initiative with the help of a small group of willing physicians. These efforts succeeded in convincing once reticent doctors to revisit the question of contraception as part of their medical practice. One notable example comes from the Chicago Gynecological Society who wrote to the *Journal of the American Medical Association* in 1923 in hopes of "giving proper publicity to its stand on the subject of the regulation of conception." The letter summarized the resolution adopted by the Society expressly recommending contraceptive instruction "wherever indicated to husbands and wives by physicians" in light of the "risk to the mother, based on ill health, whether due directly to existing diseases or to the drain of too frequent childbirth under unfavorable home conditions" suggesting that the latter was "the essential indication for instruction in the prevention of conception."[25] Even the *Birth Control Review* recognized the spectacularism of the statement, commenting, "It is a stand which gives great encouragement to the advocates of responsible and deliberate parenthood. It shows that the Society recognizes its responsibility for the health and life of the mothers and infants that come under the care of its members, and it also shows a readiness to introduce Birth Control instruction into clinics and dispensaries designed for the use of the poor."[26]

Of course, the Chicago Gynecological Society had no actual plans to expand its efforts into clinics and made as much apparent with the third clause of their statement, declaring, "Special clinics for the dissemination of this information are neither necessary nor desirable, nor should nursing organizations be utilized to give out such instruction." They also directly lambasted the use of female-centric contraceptive methods bluntly stating, "All mechanical devices used by the wife, as well as strong chemical douches, are discountenanced."[27] The *Review* noted its "serious exception" to these statements and the Society's "impression that the doctors were not willing to put into the hands of the wife the power to protect herself against pregnancy."[28] Yet, advocates remained optimistic praising the resolution as "a long way in advance of the mass of New York Physician" and framing the resolution an opportunity to coalesce support within the medical community.[29]

The BCCRB—A Push to Professionalize

Despite the skepticism of the medical profession toward specialized birth control clinics Judge Crane's 1918 decision made their legality clear and prompted a renewed interest in their use. Remarking on the significance of the decision for the clinic initiative, the *Birth Control Review* explained: "[It] opened the way for the giving of birth control information by physicians" and "ever since this decision it has been Mrs. Sanger's aspiration to take advantage of this decision."[30] In an obvious push toward professionalization and respectability, Sanger established the Birth Control Clinical Research Bureau (BCCRB) in January 1923 with the dual aim of providing contraceptive information and conducting rigorous research into the need for and use of contraception. Sanger hired Dr. Dorothy Bocker, a physician and former Director of the Child Hygiene work of the State Health Department of Georgia, to serve as Medical Director of the BCCRB.

Ever fearful of ceding ground to those outside the medical establishment, the New York Obstetrical Society, the New York Academy of Medicine, and the American Gynecological Society sponsored the creation of its own initiative known as the Committee on Maternal Health (CMH). Under the leadership of Dr. Robert L. Dickinson, the committee set to work researching the effectiveness and safety of contraception.[31] According to their governing documents, the objective of the CMH was "To determine what may be practicable and scientific in dealing with problems in the field of fertility and sterility, beginning with the problem of therapeutic prevention of conception. To collect and examine case records in relation to the questions under consideration, and so to obtain data on the practical aspect of these subjects. To maintain an office of record and reference, but not for treatment or professional advice."[32] Envisioned solely as a research institute, the CMH was clear about its agenda in relation to the larger birth control movement, stating, "This organization has no plans at present for alliance or affiliation with any other existing organization. Being a strictly medical and public health project and its medical policies being outlined and controlled by physicians of recognized standing, it will strictly avoid general publicity."[33] Despite Crane's decision granting physicians the legal authority to dispense contraception, most doctors remained reluctant to do just that, opting instead to research contraception with an apparent air of skepticism about the efficacy of giving women control over their reproductive lives. Simply put, doctors weren't yet convinced of either the need for contraception or its efficacy.

The BCCRB and CMH stood in stark contrast to one another, and their respective results reveal a sharp ideological chasm between birth controllers and physicians regarding who was eligible to receive contraceptive information. In their first year of operation the BCCRB collected the case histories of approximately 900 women whereas the CMH collected a meager 34.[34] By 1926, the chasm widened with the CMH totaling only 124 case histories compared to the 1,655 completed by the BCCRB.[35] Why the huge difference? Was the BCCRB circumventing the law and providing advice to women lacking medical indications? Surprisingly no—both the BCCRB and the CMH vouch for the clinic's strict adherence to New York law. Dr. Bocker explained that although women often came to the BCCRB "as the result of one woman passing on the good news. Many who had applied had been refused, because they did not come within the limits of the law."[36] Dickinson confirmed: "Five visits on the part of six members of our committee have given an impression of a desire to live up to the law and to stand wide open to inspection."[37] Although both organizations adhered to the letter of the law, the BCCRB operated under a much more liberal interpretation of its spirit. Historian James Reed explains, "[Sanger's] direction meant that the phrase 'for the cure or prevention of disease' was interpreted by the standards of a feminist rather than by those of middle-aged gentlemen" to include consideration of the economic and social indications of good health and not strictly medical. *The Birth Control Review* provides further clarification: "The limits of this phrase are narrow and many women who are 'not diseased enough' have to be turned away. The League recognizes not disease alone, but nine reasons for the use of contraceptives."[38] Essentially, physicians focused on curing women with existing diseases, while birth controllers sought to prevent the needless suffering of women ravaged by multiple pregnancies now tempting the fate of disease and death. These disparate definitions characterized the struggle between birth controllers and physicians and served as the major roadblock to cooperation.

The dichotomy between cure and prevention is evident in the description of services provided by the CMH and BCCRB respectively. Dr. Harold Bailey, chairman of the Committee on the Regulation of Conception supervising the CMH's efforts, outlines precisely who they intended to treat: "Such patients to be accepted must be referred with the diagnosis over the signature of one or more physicians of recognized standing. . . . [A] patient will furnish a statement regarding the condition for which contraceptive advice or treatment is necessitated for the maintenance or protection of the patient's health of the saving of life."[39] By limiting their services to married women with pre-existing conditions, the CMH refused to acknowledge the potential health consequences of too frequent or poorly spaced pregnancies. Dr. Bocker's narrative of a typical case treated at the BCCRB illuminates the striking differences in each organization's treatment paradigm. Bocker recounts the story "of a woman of 29 with one weak child as the result of three difficult and dangerous births. In the hospital where her third child was born, she was told that she would die if she had any more children, but contraceptive advice was refused to her."[40] Whereas the CMH clung to the notion of "curing" existing diseases, effectively denying women a solution until they were already knocking on death's door, the BCCRB fully embraced the prevention mandate of Crane's decision and prescribed contraception in cases where its use alleviated the wanton suffering of women.

Despite their disparate approaches, the CMH and BCCRB continued their parallel work in New York. As part of his efforts with the CMH, Dickinson meticulously observed the work of the BCCRB—a formative experience that significantly altered his view of the movement. In regular reports to his supervising agencies Dickinson complimented the BCCRB: "Dr. Bocker is particularly well informed on contraceptive matters, and her pamphlet is a clear and explicit brief publication. Whatever its imperfections, this work is carried and reported with a research idea—which is novel in propaganda work."[41] Dickinson's dismissive use of the phrase "propaganda work" is telling of the tense relationship felt between physicians and advocates at the time. Like most physicians, Dickinson was leery of advocates who he believed "were giving birth control a bad name through their irresponsible behavior."[42] However, a 1924 CMH report in the *Journal of the American Medical Association* written by Dickinson suggests a change of heart likely informed by the movement's conscious shift in tone and resulting focus on scientific information disseminated by doctors. Referencing the dispute over the open legislation known as the Cummings-Vaile Bill, Dickinson writes, "The Sanger group seems to have taken no part. On the contrary, the league's literature shows it is working for the 'doctors-only' amendment. In conference with our committee's legal advisers the American Birth Control League agreed to push such amendments as the one passed in May by the American Gynecological Society."[43] Dickinson's statement, published in the *Journal of the American Medical Association*, validated the movement's strategic choice to abandon Dennett's more liberal legislative efforts in pursuit of cultivating professional relationships with the medical community.

Dickinson's honest appraisal undoubtedly assuaged his contemporaries about their promised role in the birth control movement influencing them to reconsider their opposition to contraception. Dickinson admitted as much in a letter to the editor of the *Birth Control Review*, writing, "The application of over 7,000 doctors to the League for information; the attendance of some 700 at the International Conference, and the sixty or more engagements of your Medical Director to speak before official medical bodies are evidence of the interest of the medical profession in your work."[44] Among those showing interest in the birth control movement was Dr. William Pusey who, as sitting president of the American Medical Association, made waves in the medical community when he acknowledged birth control in his 1923 Presidential Address. Pusey proclaimed: "The point I am undertaking to emphasize is that the subject is of vast importance to the welfare of man; that it is one which should have scientific guidance; that for this medicine must be looked to and that medicine should undertake to approach its responsibilities here by beginning to give the subject the continuous serious thought it justifies."[45] Yet, despite Pusey's caged endorsement of contraception little, if any, substantive effort from the mainstream medical community followed. A 1928 editorial in the *Birth Control Review* lamented the unfulfilled hope brought about by Pusey's supposed change of heart, noting:

> Three years ago the American Medical Association put itself on record as favoring "the alteration of existing laws, wherever necessary, so that physicians may legally give contraceptive information to their patients in the regular course of practice." The passage of this resolution and the outspoken advocacy of birth control by doctor William Allen Pusey in his presidential address, the previous year inspired the hope that the medical profession was about to put itself at the head of a great medical movement in favor of contraception. Since 1924–1925, the birth control movement has made enormous progress, but very little help has been given by the organized doctors of this country.[46]

Despite warming relations between the movement and a handful of supportive physicians, the mainstream medical community kept its distance continuing to internally debate contraception but refusing to formally recognize the potential benefit of its wide scale application.

They might not have said it publicly, but doctors were acutely aware of the BCCRB's efficacy and secretly clamored for more information about contraception. In 1929 Dr. Earl C. Sage, Nebraska State Leader of the Joint Committee on Maternal Welfare, took note of the massive demand for contraceptive information among his colleagues, revealing: "One doctor in every eight in the country has written to the American Birth Control League for information. Over two hundred county medical societies, covering every state, have asked for talks on birth control."[47] These inquiries fueled the efforts of the American Birth Control League to expand their clinic network across the country with the hope of recruiting the very doctors reaching out for advice. Sage furthers, "Medical advice on birth control can now be obtained by married people with a proven need in 28 organizations, in 12 cities, in 10 states of the United States."[48] Perhaps most importantly, Sage's endorsement of the clinic initiative speaks directly to the influence of the BCCRB and its emphasis on contraception as prevention. He explains, "Medicine today strives not merely to be curative. Its ultimate aim is to be preventative; and scientific, intelligent contraceptive advice is, in innumerable cases, the highest-expression of modern preventative medicine."[49] Sage recognized the value of contraception to preventative medicine and gave hope to the movement others would soon follow suit.

The Second Raid—Clearing a Path for Clinics

The limits of Sanger's liberal interpretation of Judge Crane's disease framework were put to the test in 1929 when police raided the BCCRB. Entering under the suspicion of clinic staff fitting women with diaphragms without demonstrated medical need, police officers made two key errors which inadvertently aided the movement's cause.[50] First, even though the female officer selected to go undercover was not legitimately seeking a diaphragm for medical reasons, an examination revealed she suffered from pelvic abnormalities which, ironically, justified fitting her for a diaphragm. In an April 24 hearing, Magistrate Abraham Rosenbluth heard the testimony of numerous prominent physicians who, to the surprise of the police, ardently defended the sanctity of the clinic's operations. Among them was Dr. Louis Harris, a former Commissioner of Health, who boldly proclaimed:

> Having children too often may precipitate invalidism and result in ill health to the next child. As Health Commissioner, I have officially investigated this clinic to see its mode of procedure conformed with Section 1145 of the penal code. I found that the work of the Bureau was quite in keeping with the spirit and purpose of the law, and the spirit and purpose of the practice of medicine. I consider this public health work in the sense in which the word has been used today, I should say it is a prevention of disease.[51]

Persuaded by the audacious testimony of Harris and his peers, Rosenbluth excoriated the raid and declared: "[P]hysicians and nurses who act upon their instructions are absolved from the prohibition of Section 1145 of the penal law, provided they act in good faith. . . . Good faith is thus made the test of guilt or innocence."[52] Disregarding the disease framework established by Judge Crane, Rosenbluth acknowledged the myriad conditions necessitating contraception and accordingly expanded a doctors ability to provide instruction so long as they did so in good faith. *The Birth Control Review* acknowledged the significance of the ruling remarking, "The result of the raid on the Clinical Research Bureau on April 15 was fully to vindicate the Clinic and its work" and provided "the stamp of approval to a somewhat wider interpretation of the Section 1145 than had been attached to it before the Clinic was open."[53] This was the validation Sanger needed to pressure the mainstream medical community to adopt contraception as a standard part of their medical practice for *all* women rather than just those with a diagnosis in hand.

Blunders made by police officers during the process created yet another silver lining by inadvertently emboldening doctors to defend the BCCRB. When conducting the raid, officers confiscated most of the patient records housed at the clinic without any assurance of confidentiality, committing, according to Sanger, a huge "tactical error." Sanger explains, "doctors throughout the land, the world in fact, [were] highly sensitive about the sanctity of case records."[54] In seizing patient records in hopes of proving the clinic's illegal prescription of contraceptives, "the clinic raid forced physicians to come to [Sanger's] aid in order to protect the right of their own patients to privacy."[55] The mishandling of confidential records combined with the fact that the nature of the raid called into question a doctor's ability to correctly assess the medical necessity of contraception created a perfect opportunity for doctors to express their concerns. The Council of the New York Academy of Medicine immediately voiced their support for the clinic staff arrested in the raid. In a scathing rebuke of the whole affair, the council chided: "[T]he conduct of the prosecution threatened the freedom of the medical profession" by fallaciously questioning the "competency and honesty of physicians to arrive at conclusions concerning diseases," and in doing so posed a "threat against the public good and a serious menace to the rights and privileges of the medical profession as granted by law."[56]Although the medical community frequently disparaged clinics as inferior, the shocking conduct of the police forced doctors to defend their sanctity because in the eyes of the law, clinics functioned no differently than a private doctor's office or hospital.

Not only was the raid a tactical error, as Sanger suggested, the following trial further galvanized the medical community's demand for the right to provide contraception at their own discretion. Remarking on the success of the raid to solidify support for contraception among physicians, the *Birth Control Review* proclaimed: "The medical profession aligned itself more definitely than ever before on the side of Birth Control. The raid proved a veritable boomerang."[57] Shortly after the raid, the New York County Medical Society (NYCMS) validated Rosenbluth's expanded interpretation and pushed to formally recognize the right of doctors to provide contraception at their own discretion. In a resolution prepared by Dr. Foster Kennedy, the organization defended "the right of physicians giving birth control information to determine from their own experience the meaning of the cure and prevention of disease for which purpose birth control teaching is legal."[58] Advocates greeted these initiatives optimistically expressing their hope for more substantive change in the mainstream medical community. A 1929 editorial in the *Birth Control Review* pleads, "Individual physicians are overwhelmingly in favor of birth control, but it has been difficult to get the Medical Societies to act on the question. We may reasonably hope that the recent action of the Academy of Medicine and of the New York County Medical Society presages more decided action in favor of birth control."[59]

The raid was undeniably a turning point for the movement, reigniting conversations within the medical community surrounding contraception as preventative medicine and sparking a renewed fervor for clinics. In perhaps an unlikely turn of events facilitated by their close working relationship over the last seven years and accelerated by the raid, Dickinson joined the BCCRB's advisory board in 1930 with an explicit focus on aiding the clinic initiative. Not coincidentally, Dickinson's rhetoric markedly shifts after joining the BCCRB, reflecting an uptake of the movement's liberal treatment paradigm and commitment to securing contraceptive access for all women. Dickinson portends in 1931:

> And the Doctor who does not help to prevent the start of a pregnancy that he is persuaded will run his patient down further—how does he excuse himself for neglect of ordinary health protection? Shall his patient, mother of two or three, without means, and married to a chronic alcoholic, go on bearing? Or this worn-out wife of a hopeless incompetent, just because she has not yet gotten tuberculosis, or because her strained heart muscle still compensates? We doctors are afraid of the words "social and economic grounds" for birth control advice.[60]

It's almost hard to believe these words were uttered by the same man who once referred to the birth control movement, almost exclusively, as propaganda. Yet, that is precisely why they are so significant. By acknowledging the failure of the disease paradigm to fully account for the health needs of women and children, Dickinson's statement reflects a radical departure from the position advanced by the very medical societies who sponsored his initial research. In a sharp about-face, Dickinson embraces the preventative powers of contraception and explicitly chastises his colleagues for their unwillingness to recognize the "social and economic grounds for birth control advice" dismissing their actions as neglectful and fear driven.

Remarkably, Dickinson wasn't the only doctor singing a different tune in the early 1930s and was actually joined by several of his esteemed peers in calling on the medical community to reconsider its hostile stance toward contraception as a form of preventative medicine. In addition to his bold testimony at the 1929 trial, Dr. Louis Harris offered a scathing criticism of his fellow physicians in the *Birth Control Review* in 1931. Echoing Dickinson's rhetoric of neglect and fear Harris exhorts, "Indeed, medical men must come to play a more distinctive role in the spread of contraceptive knowledge, and they must do so not in an apologetic or fearful way, as if they were possibly offending against some unwritten statute or social canons, but they must do so with that courage which is the proud tradition of real preventative and therapeutic medicine."[61] In acknowledging the historical reluctance of the medical community to associate itself with the birth control movement, one largely premised on false pride and misconceptions, Harris pleaded with his colleagues to prioritize their initial commitment to medicine by actively involving themselves with the dissemination of contraception. Dr. Eric M. Matsner, the executive secretary of the National Medical Council on Birth

Control, advances a similar argument, noting, "As a physician my chief interest is in the medical aspect of birth control. Three of the greatest strides that have been made in medicine have been in the fields of control." Matsner pleads with his colleagues to take seriously the role of contraception in their medical practices, urging: "From a medical point of view it seems to me that the emphasis at this time should be laid upon the proper spacing of children rather than upon any other factor."[62] Matsner would take over for James Cooper as Medical Director of the ABCL in 1931.

The AMA Balks

As more prominent physicians leant their voice to the birth control movement, attention again turned to the American Medical Association. In 1933 the AMA introduced yet another lackluster resolution, this time noting, "The problems and methods of Birth Control are of vital concern to the health as well as the social and economic welfare of our American people" and acknowledging "A demand has been made by various groups for dependable evaluation of methods of contraception and of the conditions that justify their employment." Unsurprisingly, the AMA eschewed true involvement in favor of yet another committee to study the efficacy of various contraceptive methods. The AMA remained adamant on one thing: "The appointment of this special committee shall in no way be construed as an endorsement of birth control on the part of the American Medical Association."[63]

Unlike with past resolutions this time doctors vocalized their frustration at the AMA's diffidence. Some were demure in their critique, endorsing the resolution but calling on the AMA to consider contraception "in preventative medicine as well as in the advancement of therapeutics."[64] While others, such as Dr. Frank Ebaugh, openly called on the AMA to endorse contraception beyond its accepted disease paradigm. Ebaugh lamented, "We have encountered in our work numerous instances where birth control measures would have lessened considerably the social and economic stress both by many individuals and communities. It seems at this time more than at any other that such measures should be given the approval of the organization."[65] Perhaps the most scathing rebuke of the resolution came from Dr. Stuart Mudd, chairman of the Department of Bacteriology at University of Pennsylvania Medical School, who declared:

> So many of us feel that the American Medical Association is in danger of drifting into a very false indeed ludicrous, position by insisting that contraception is essentially a medical matter and then refusing to give it investigation in the spirit of scientific medicine. Growth of public interest in the medical practice of contraception can hardly be stopped at this late date, whatever attitude any

> organization takes with reference to it; is it not more dignified to meet this situation fearlessly and in the spirt of impartial investigation rather than to let it be forced on the medical profession through public pressure?[66]

Dr. Mudd's frustration is palpable and reflects almost two decades of inaction on the part of the AMA under the guise of pursuing additional research which yielded no tangible results.

As clinics proliferated across the United States and continued to be effective in England and Holland, it became clear the movement was forging ahead with or without the support of the mainstream medical community. Individual physicians worried about losing their grip in the fledgling field of obstetrics and gynecology demanded the AMA stop wavering and offer their full backing to contraceptive instruction. The most pointed criticism of the AMA's inaction came from the very committee they created to carry out this research—the Committee on Maternal Health. In a 1934 letter to the editor of the *Journal of the American Medical Association*, the Committee itself directly pleaded for the AMA to increase their involvement and assert their control over contraception in the name of preventative medicine. They entreat:

> Our ultimate objective is the development of a reference and standardization service, and consequent control of the practice of contraception by the medical profession, through its duly constituted authorities. We have accordingly been studying the existing laws and agencies that might be involved in the plan for control. . . . [S]ince 1924 the committee has repeatedly urged on the board of trustees of the American Medical Association, and especially the council on pharmacy and chemistry, that it take these matters into serious consideration and furnish guidance in the choice of materials and methods. Until now the trustees have declined any such undertaking. . . . [O]nly the American Medical Association or national governmental agency would function with the requisite scope and authority. The committee therefore welcomes the expression of interest by the American Medical Association, especially the final statement that the situation now prevailing is warrant for some type of action leading to scientific control. . . . These mark the beginning of a program for the control by the medical profession of contraception as a recognized part of preventative medicine, for the primary object of such selective advertisement is not the negative one of censorship at the positive one of informing the doctor of reliable measures.[67]

The CMH goes well beyond a request for additional research or a plea for an official endorsement and boldly demands the AMA assume a regulatory role over contraception so as to give the medical profession "control of the practice of contraception." Although they should be commended for rightfully identifying "contraception as a recognized part of preventative medicine" their choice to imbue the AMA, an organization who actively distanced itself from the birth control movement, with sole control over contraception is infuriating.

Unwilling to wait for the AMA, the movement proceeded with its own project to standardize contraceptive instruction across clinics affiliated with the ABCL. Under the guidance of Dickinson, who joined the BCCRB's advisory board in 1930, the ABCL launched its clinic certification program in 1935.[68] This project served both a functional purpose establishing standard operating procedures for the rapidly growing network of clinics and a strategic purpose demonstrating their professional veracity to the ever-skeptical medical community. Functionally, the program reaffirmed the movement's commitment to providing only scientifically based accurate medical instruction. Advocates utilized the certification process to draw a sharp contrast between themselves and disreputable commercial enterprises, explaining, "Because patients applying for contraceptive advice are entitled to the most reliable information available, the certified clinics are asked to report to the league's medical board any deviation from the standardized clinical techniques. . . . [T]heir certificate differentiates the reputable, scientific centers from the commercial enterprises, outlets of manufacturers for their products, which masquerade as 'birth control clinics' in a number of cities."[69] By all measures, the program was a massive, and unexpected, success. Mrs. Louis Deb Moore, chairman of the board for the ABCL, noted the surprisingly quick uptake of the initiative in 1937: "The minimum standards and certification of clinics announced in 1935 was something of an innovation and we were prepared for slow development. A movement so comparatively young as ours would need to digest the effort towards standardization with deliberation. . . . Today I'm glad to report that 159 clinics hold the ABCL certificate and these include 26 hospital clinics."[70]

Clinic certification also served the strategic goals of the movement by demonstrating an adherence to the principles of standardization and oversight revered in the medical community. *The Birth Control Review* explicitly acknowledged the value of this strategy in 1937, writing, "The first standardization of clinic procedure and management was instituted by the League to interest medical and lay sponsors in developing better standards of social service and medical administration," and again in 1938 suggesting the program "advance[d] the common objectives of securing maximum inclusion of birth control in medical education, in medical practice, in institutions and in public services for maternal and infant health and family welfare."[71] As a key member of the AMA, Dickinson was acutely aware of the negative perception of clinical work held by many of his colleagues. A 1935 report in the *Journal of the American Medical Association* bluntly questioned the efficacy of contraceptive instruction promulgated by "nonmedical groups," stating: "[U]nder the stimulus of large nonmedical groups, the general use of contraceptives is being advocated and encouraged . . . [even though] the ultimate effect of these measures on the health and general welfare the population of the United States is unknown if not questionable."[72] Clinic certification reassured doctors of their role by asserting the medicalized work of clinics. Rachelle Yarros, a Chicago physician and early advocate for birth control, explains the utility of this strategy, arguing the movement needs "to make every effort to enlist interest and cooperation of the physicians" and "one of the most valuable means of removing such apathy as it exists is the systematic reporting of findings based on experience with large numbers of cases, such as are treated by the birth control clinics."[73] Although Sanger's first clinic in Brownsville admittedly intended to provoke and disrupt reluctant lawmakers and doctors, almost twenty years later the goal had shifted. Under the guiding framework of political accommodation, Sanger pursued clinic standardization to firmly situate contraception within a medical framework best aided by the dutiful oversight of physicians.

United States v. One Package

The course of the movement was forever altered in 1936 when the U.S. Court of Appeals issued what the *Birth Control Review* aptly called an "epoch-making decision."[74] The case itself, *United States v. One Package*, was the long-pondered brainchild of Sanger and ACLU lawyer Morris Ernst who previously represented Sanger after the 1929 raid. Seeking a test case to challenge the 1930 Tariff Act, a by-product of the Comstock Act prohibiting the importation of contraceptives, Sanger and her colleagues at the BCCRB imported a variety of contraceptive devices from around the world including England, Germany, and Japan, many of which were, as expected, seized in port by Customs. As with the 1929 trial, Ernst relied on the testimony of prominent physicians to challenge the statute by asserting the medical necessity of contraception. Presiding Judge Moscowitz cited this testimony in his decision, explaining, "The testimony adduced on behalf of the claimant . . . all recognized physicians and surgeons, indicates from a medical viewpoint there are various types of cases in which it is necessary to prescribe a contraceptive."[75] As with previous decisions, the testimony of doctors articulating the value of contraception firmly within a medical framework undeniably influenced in the court's decision.

Unsurprisingly the decision was appealed and sent to the U.S. Circuit Court of Appeals for the Second Circuit where Justice Hand would liberate contraception from the restrictive grasp of obscenity laws. Dismissing the sham argument of moral propriety used to justify all such statutes labeling contraception as obscene, Hand unequivocally proclaimed: "It's design, in our opinion, was not to prevent the importation, sale, or carriage by mail of things which might intelligently be employed by conscientious and competent physicians for the purpose of saving life or promoting the wellbeing of their patients."[76] Although the decision was critical to expanding contraceptive access, it's important to recognize the rationale offered by Justice Hand dealt exclusively with the credibility and intelligence of doctors and not the importance of contraception itself. The ruling wasn't so much an acknowledgment of contraception as much it was a defense of the medical profession.

Yet, the court's monumental decision represented the final nail in the coffin for the Comstock Laws and expanded the acceptability of birth control beyond the disease paradigm. *The Birth Control Review* heralded the decision:

> The dead hand of Anthony Comstock is powerless today to keep birth control information from any married woman who physicians feels that she needs it for the purpose of saving life or promoting well being. Thus the 63-year-old federal statutes on contraception were interpreted in turn with modern public opinion and clinical practice through a unanimous decision handed down on December 7, 1936 by the United States Circuit Court of Appeals for the Second Circuit. The decision stands out as a landmark in birth control history. It upholds views held over a period of years by the American Birth Control League, whose policies have been based upon previous court decisions of a like nature and upon the practical observation that the federal laws did not interfere with the work of medically directed birth control centers. Undeniably, however, the laws have retarded clinical extension. With their added clarification, the movement can push forward with even greater confidence in the task of making medical birth control available to poor mothers. [77]

The pivotal connection between health and contraception also echoed in the press with the *New York Times* explaining in 1937, "the primary purpose of medically prescribed contraceptives is for the protection of the lives and health of mothers and children."[78] After almost two decades spent espousing the preventative powers of birth control, advocates finally received vindication.

The court's ruling in *One Package* was also the linchpin for the long-awaited endorsement from the AMA. At the June 1937 meeting of the AMA in Atlantic City, the American Neurological Association put forth a Resolution on Contraception declaring: "[T]he United States Circuit Court of appeals has handed down to the medical profession a Bill of Rights in the field of contraceptive medicine, and because the decision marks the termination of a struggle begun in 1873 to make clear that the federal obscenity laws do not apply to the legitimate activities of the physician, and that he may now prescribe a contraceptive in the interest of life and health."[79] Despite the obvious piety of the resolution written as if to suggest the AMA actively rallied against the Comstock Act themselves, word of the AMA's new stance spread quickly in the popular press and was of course emblazoned on the front page of the *Birth Control Review*.

Yet, a closer reading of the Atlantic City conference proceedings reveals the medical community's true motivation for finally endorsing contraception—control. In the paragraph immediately following their pronouncement of the medical profession's right to contraceptive medicine, the AMA reveals the reason for their sudden change in disposition. It reads:

> That the American Neurological Association urged the American Medical Association again to consider seriously the inroads that are being made on the prestige of organized medicine by the rapid advance of popular thought in the matter of social medicine science as evinced by the success of lay organizations in carrying out their program for greater medical freedom in the matter of contraception. It is come to the pass at which the road for medical advance is blazed by laymen assisted by the law. Unless organized medicine as directed by farseeing and freethinking leaders untrammeled by the age and antiquated fetters of Sophism, it will most certainly come to pass that organized medicine will in the not distant future come entirely under the control of lay and legal administration assisted by their political allies. The American Medical Association is further urged to take up at once the matter of the proper teaching of contraception at the medical schools in the organization of medically supervised contraceptive clinics in hospitals. The time has passed for discussion and debate. The fact remains that the physician is now free to use contraceptives in his practice and should be educated in their use.[80]

Simply put, the AMA's reluctance to assume a meaningful role in the birth control movement compromised its leadership on the issue creating a vacuum in medical instruction eagerly filled by birth control clinics. For years, the AMA willingly abdicated its role in the movement and now, in the wake of a strong clinic initiative from the ABCL, it was desperate to regain control. The report of the Reference Committee spoke urgently of the need for the AMA to assume the regulatory role currently fulfilled by the Clinic Certification Program, demanding "information and advice concerning the prevention of conception given in dispensaries, clinics and similar establishments should be given only in such dispensaries, clinics and similar establishments legally licensed to treat the sick and under medical control."[81] After years of busying themselves with research while advocates built the critical infrastructure needed to disseminate contraceptive information, the mainstream medical community was finally ready to get involved so long as they could assume their customary position of authority.

Advocates not only acknowledged the AMA's increased involvement; they welcomed it. A 1937 article in the *Birth Control Review* exclaimed:

> With the sanction of the high courts and of the American Medical Association, just where do we stand? What course will the movement take? On the firm foundation of legal and medical acceptance, we now enter the most constructive era of the movement. Every effort and every dollar can produce vastly greater results. . . . While the American Medical Association's action will afford the powerful protection the public needs against the vast industry of harmful and fraudulent contraceptives. . . . Responsibility rests upon lay leaders in birth control to make the public aware of medically directed service and of the protection to be expected from the American Medical Association. . . . Contraception is a medical problem. It may go only so far as doctors will or can guide it. . . . We welcome the progressive leadership of the American Medical Association.[82]

In an obvious callback to the shared concern over quack medicine motivating the initial push for doctors-only bills, the movement affirmed the regulatory role of the AMA to protect people from potentially harmful contraceptive devices. The statement also outlines the path forward for both doctors and birth controllers—doctors will assume a leadership role while "lay leaders" will focus on the advocacy work necessary to expand proper contraceptive use. The rhetoric of the statement reveals a clear, yet disheartening, truth about the nature of the movement moving forward. The very women and brave advocates who fought tirelessly to legalize contraception are resigned to the role of "lay leader" while the physicians, who for decades obstinately resisted their efforts, are lauded for their progressive leadership. This deferential posture continues today as the medical community retains its firm grasp on contraception while reproductive justice advocates wrestle for a seat at the table.

COURTING EUGENICISTS

The continued reluctance of doctors drove birth controllers to consider alliances with other professional groups whose influence could propel the fledgling movement. In many ways, the relationship between eugenicists and birth controllers grew out of the divide between the movement and the medical community. The mainstream medical community refused to cosign on Sanger's clinic initiative, whereas eugenicists, motivated by concerns with overpopulation among groups they considered unfit, took kindly to Sanger's mission focusing on impoverished communities. Birth controllers united around their shared commitment to expanding contraceptive access beyond members of the middle class who easily procured contraception from private physicians. To this end, eugenicists validated the movement's rejection of a purely medical framework for contraceptive instruction—a requisite to expanding access beyond privileged classes. Ellsworth Huntington, president of the American Eugenics Society, castigated the AMA for their myopic view of contraception, writing in the *Birth Control Review* in 1936:

> The chief trouble with the report is that it treats contraception as if it were a purely medical matter. This is no more true than that sanitation is purely an engineering problem. The technical skill, to be sure, must be furnished in the one case by physicians and in the other by engineers. But both contraception and sanitation are great social problems and concern the whole people. The social aim of birth control is that plenty of births should take place in the right kind of families and few in those in which children are likely to be poorly trained as well as poorly endowed by nature. The American Medical Association has ignored this aspect of birth control and has rejected the great task of teaching proper contraceptive methods to every level of society. By failing to recognize those the American Medical Association has done a great injustice to itself, to its members and to the public.[83]

Although birth controllers rejected the principle of positive eugenics, identified here by Huntington as the encouragement of births among "the right kind of families," they welcomed the reinforcement in the fight against the AMA's narrow position on contraception.

The alliance with eugenicists provided more than just reinforcement availing the movement to both scientific and financial backing. Early identification with eugenic goals arose from familiarity with nineteenth-century Perfectionists and Utopian thinkers who, given the rudimentary understanding of hereditary genetics at the time, were primarily concerned with creating the best possible social and environmental conditions in which to raise a child.[84] These thinkers advocated both qualitative and quantitative control of reproduction through natural means of birth control (continence/abstinence) and communal child rearing.[85] At the turn of the twentieth century, these ideas morphed into racialized concerns about the type of child born in America, fueled by false panic over declining birth rates in affluent white families amid increasing immigration and steady fertility rates among immigrant and Black populations. Known colloquially as "race suicide," these ideas permeated the social and political landscape and took pride of place in the progressive agenda spearheaded by then President Theodore Roosevelt. In his preface to the 1903 book *The Woman Who Toils: Being the Experiences of Two Ladies as Factory Girls*, Roosevelt sharply proclaimed:

> If a man or woman, through no fault of his or hers, goes throughout life denied those highest of all joys which spring only from home life, from the having and bringing up of many healthy children, I feel for them deep and respectful sympathy . . . but the man or woman who deliberately avoids marriage, and has

> a heart so cold as to know no passion and a brain so shallow and selfish as to dislike having children, is in effect a criminal against the race, and should be an object of contemptuous abhorrence by all healthy people.[86]

Roosevelt's words enjoyed broad circulation helping to mainstream the concerns of progressives most of whom, according to Trent MacNamara, "came to the debate from America's numerically and politically dominant culture—white, native born, non-indigent—and concerned themselves with the reproductive future of their own kind."[87]

Fueled by Roosevelt's passionate fulmination, scholars in the fields of anthropology, ethnology, anthropometry, and biology coalesced to create the scientific study of eugenics which would quickly assume a dominant position in the discourse of Progressive Era reform initiatives. Crediting much of its widespread uptake to the overwhelming success of Madison Grant's 1917 book *The Passing of the Great Race,* Charles King suggests the book "was hailed as a milestone in the application of scientific ideas to history and public policy. It inspired an entire generation of acolytes who would go on to write their own treaties, advice policy makers, and push through new legislation. Three-quarters of American universities, from Harvard to the University of California, introduced courses on eugenics, many of them using Grant as a primary text."[88] Birth controllers capitalized on the reputability and credibility of eugenics to advance their goals and relished the field's overt emphasis on scientific study. Carole McCann notes the utility of this alliance, suggesting eugenics "provided the birth control movement with an authoritative language through which to legitimate women's right to contraceptives."[89] MacNamara concurs, explaining, "'Eugenic' vocabulary mostly offered linguistic decoration for the long-standing idea that some babies and families were more valuable than others. To secular progressives it offered a way to replace the older intuitive language of paternalism, class bias, and ethnic boosterism with a pleasingly scientific-sounding scheme."[90] Long obsessed with the use of scientific information to regulate reproduction, birth controllers readily adopted the vocabulary of eugenicists to capitulate the urgency of contraception.

Eugenic organizations were well respected, well researched, and most importantly, well funded. Befitting of the reformist ambitions of the time, eugenics quickly garnered the support of financial titans including John D. Rockefeller, Mary Harriman, J. H. Kellogg, and Andrew Carnegie who near the end of their lives turned their attention, and fortune, to philanthropy aimed at social betterment. These investments turned a fledging amalgamation of academic disciplines into a legitimate field of study. Edwin Black, whose *War against the Weak* stands as one of the most comprehensive histories of American eugenics, contends: "Big money made all the difference for eugenics" because "[w]ith that affluence came the means and the connections to make eugenic theory an administrative reality."[91] Although the majority of funds flowed directly to organizations such as Huntington's American Eugenics Society and the Eugenic Research Office, birth controllers also found themselves on the receiving end of generous donors who supported their clinic initiatives as part of a larger eugenic project. For example, in 1929 inventor and philanthropist Charles F. Brush created the Brush Foundation to support work "for the betterment of human stock and the regulation of increase in population."[92] That same year, the foundation awarded the BCCRB $5,000 to establish a birth control clinic in Brush's hometown of Cleveland. Advocates lauded these contributions as validation of the project for societal betterment jointly pursued by both the movement and eugenicists. An editorial in the *Birth Control Review* portends: "The birth controllers are building the future for mankind, or rather putting into the hands of men and women the instrument which will enable them to build wisely, safely happily. Dr. Brush's gift throws the light of publicity on these efforts and gives a stamp of approval—an approval easily recognized by the newspaper reading public—to both eugenics and birth control."[93] These big-ticket donations also infused the once fringe social movement with an air of respectability by placing them on par with other philanthropic initiatives receiving funds from elite progressive donors.

The following section explores the rhetorical strategies utilized by advocates to codify this alliance while also recognizing the moments of discontinuity between eugenicists and the movement. Initially, in a move undoubtedly linked to the dominant ideology of the Progressive Era, advocates articulated a societal right to contraception premised on a society's need to ensure the health and prosperity of future generations; this ideology served as the basis for the alliance between birth controllers and eugenicists by enabling them to advocate for broad social policies regarding both reproductive quality and quantity. Yet, despite their agreement on safeguarding the population from "degenerates," eugenicists and birth controllers held divergent views over the execution of this goal openly disagreeing about the value of various eugenic programs. A closer look at the debate over positive and negative eugenics reveals a shared concern for regulating reproduction but wildly divergent views of *who* should be encouraged to embrace voluntary motherhood. This debate shaped the implementation of eugenic policies and continues to have lasting consequences today.

Society's Right to Contraception

Roosevelt's bluster had been good for one thing—elevating conversations about the population to a place of prominence and national consciousness. Birth controllers exploited this unique political moment steeped in reform-minded progressiveness to assert a societal right to contraception. Consistent with their previous use of rights-based rhetoric, birth controllers argued society too had a collective right to contraceptive information to ensure the health and stability of future generations. According to the *Birth Control Review* in 1917: "[T]he rational limitation of offspring is not only a right but a duty [and] society should recognize and teach that duty."[94] Sanger also deployed the word "duty" to describe the social obligation of individuals to practice contraception, noting, "So far as the ways of nature can be understood by us, it is both our right and our duty, as intelligent beings, to control [reproduction] for our own uses and our own good."[95] The collective need for contraception received an additional boost by labeling it as a human right, rather than solely an individual right; Sanger explained in a 1924 radio address: "[W]e who are carrying on the battle for the great human right of birth control are fighting for better, healthier, children, for a race of strong men and beautiful women here in America."[96] This framing proved particularly salient in light of contraception's status as a negative right; since the government bore no responsibility to ensure contraceptive access, contextualizing birth control as a societal right expanded the impetus to protect it as a public good rather than a private luxury. The expansion of the movement's rights-based rhetoric to reflect a societal interest in the provision of contraceptive information succeeded in establishing a universal justification for supporting birth control—the health and welfare of humanity.

Sanger explicitly connected these goals to two predominant concerns at the time: social expenditures and public health. Speaking directly to the growing number of children forced onto the public dole as a result of poor parentage, Sanger explained in the *Birth Control Review*: "From the point of view of society, we have a right to defend ourselves against unsocial conduct of parents who bring into the world children foredoomed in the majority of cases to enter the ranks of the dependent or delinquent."[97] Mimicking the rhetoric utilized to articulate a child's right to be wanted and wellborn, the movement emphasized the consequences of children born without the necessary assurance of health and stability. Advocates also compared contraception to public health initiatives aimed at preventing the spread of disease. Sanger exemplified this argument in 1931 when she suggested, "society has the right to expect our public health officials to protect it from transmissible diseases just as it protects us today from contagious diseases like diphtheria, measles, smallpox, etc."[98] Using contagious diseases as a parallel, Sanger and other birth control advocates framed contraception as a question of public health rather than of individual choice. In many ways, these arguments functioned as the logical extension of the movement's emphasis on the health of women and children by illuminating the societal consequences of unregulated reproduction and positioning those consequences within the scope of existing public health priorities. Questions about maternal and infant health remained salient partially because of the dismal reality of the times but mostly because it worked. Even the most ardent critics of contraception could hardly defend the wanton loss of life attendant with reproduction among those with inheritable conditions. These appeals also enabled the movement to align their goals with the public health agenda—placing the needs of society over the autonomy of the individual. The prevalence of public health officials in the pages of the *Birth Control Review* and the continued proliferation of clinics was proof of concept.

Not surprisingly, advocates also linked the societal right to contraception to the movement's well-established trope of liberation by labeling birth control as the linchpin for the emancipation of society as a whole. Sanger proclaimed in the *Birth Control Review* in 1925: "[B]irth control in itself, we claim, is thus a constructive, creative power for human regeneration [by] urging not large families but smaller families by the instrument of qualitative control, offers an instrument of liberation to overburdened humanity."[99] Having established uncontrolled and irresponsible reproduction as a societal concern, Sanger positioned contraception as a mechanism for individual families to improve the quality of their offspring reducing the societal burdens of overpopulation, death, and disease. Beyond these immediate benefits, Sanger also touted the lasting consequences for humanity of the freedom provided to women and children through contraception. She declared, "birth control will not only free [women] but will also free the children [and] as they free themselves and their children, they can then go forward with men, toward that greatest of all goals—the emancipation of the human race."[100] Mounting concerns about overpopulation and the growing number of families receiving government assistance during the Great Depression made appeals to a societal need for contraception especially salient precipitating the eventual inclusion of contraception and family planning services into public health programs across the country.

Establishing the social significance of birth control also allowed advocates to neutralize arguments suggesting contraception eroded the fabric of society by destabilizing marriage and disincentivizing childbearing. Previous iterations of this argument, not unlike Roosevelt's earlier rant, took aim at the individual and promulgated the myths of promiscuity and selfishness to discredit the movement's aims. Opponents extended this spurious line of reasoning to society writ large framing contraception as a societal failing, as demonstrated by a 1933 letter to the editor of the *New York Times* by well-known ethics scholar Ignatius W. Cox. Clearly writing from an overtly ethnocentric perspective, Cox proclaimed: "Contraception is moreover, unpatriotic. The Western nations are failing to reproduce themselves. . . . In promoting contraception, the birth controllers are working against the return of a just social order."[101] On the contrary, birth controllers emphasized the long-term benefits of widespread contraceptive use. Writing in her pamphlet, *Voluntary Motherhood*, Sanger heralded birth control as "an epoch-making process in racial development" because it is "the medium to bring to the light of day the sorrows and sufferings that have afflicted humanity and shall point to their elimination."[102] Eugenicists, many of whom shared Cox's concern, directly refuted the notion of national decline by emphasizing the need to prioritize population quality over quantity to achieve long-term stability. Harvard professor and eugenics proponent William McDougall argued providing contraception to all interested persons would protect society "against the lowering of its quality," prevent its "deterioration," and allow it to "slowly improve its quality from century to century."[103] Although advocates and eugenicists often found themselves at odds over positive eugenics, both groups welcomed negative eugenics as a tool to protect society.

The espoused societal duty to regulate one's reproduction and the accompanying emphasis on society's right to protect itself from degeneracy fit neatly within the existing feminist framework which blossomed in the Progressive Era and buttressed nicely with the goals of the emerging field of eugenics. An extension of the nineteenth-century perfectionist movement, eugenic ideals infiltrated feminists who desired to give women "sensible control over their own bodies" and was a common topic among influential feminists such as Victoria Woodhull. The rise of progressive thought aimed at societal improvement and racial betterment served as a convenient platform for feminists to extend eugenic principles. Edwin Black argues, "Sanger continued the feminist affinity for organized eugenics. Like many progressives, she applied eugenic principles to her pet passion, birth control, which she believed was required of any properly run eugenic society."[104] Historian Linda Gordon contextualizes the evolution from nineteenth-century perfectionism to twentieth century eugenics arguing "Eugenic attitudes had attracted reformers of all varieties for nearly a century. Lacking a correct genetics, 19th century eugenics was largely utopian speculations based on the assumption that acquired characteristics could be inherited." Yet as scientific inquiry into hereditary traits failed to produce any meaningful proof of inheritance—"more narrow applications of [eugenics] became popular."[105] Despite their unsubstantiated claims of heredity, eugenicists successfully convinced "many leading progressives devoted to charity and reform [to see] crime and poverty as inherited defects that needed to be halted for society's sake."[106] Society had a right to protect itself and needed to act quickly to ensure the health and prosperity of future generations.

The rudimentary nature of medicine in the twentieth century enabled the pseudoscience of eugenics to thrive. Eugenicists poured over skull and bone measurements produced by the field of anthropometry, detailed migratory charts and immigration records curated by demographers, the field notes of ethnographer's far-flung travels, and of course the biological studies of Galton and Mendel to hobble together theories of heritability in support of their deeply ethnocentric agenda. Absent the ability to medically or scientifically investigate these theories with any degree of accuracy, eugenicists amassed stockpiles of stories and data which when "combined with the widespread racism, class prejudice and ethnic hatred that already existed among the turn-of-the-century intelligentsia—and then juxtaposed with the economic costs to society—[created] fertile reception for the infant field of eugenics."[107] Despite their authoritative posturing, even eugenicists admitted the fallibility of their work. Harry H. Laughlin, the assistant director of the Eugenics Record Office and the Carnegie Institution of Washington, brashly confessed in 1933: "On the side of science the big task ahead is the development of eugenical diagnosis—the determination of human quality. . . . Students of Human Genetics must seek still more exact knowledge concerning the specific rules of inheritance of all human qualities, physical, mental and emotion—normal and abnormal—both sound and pathological."[108] Make no mistake, this uncertainty propelled eugenic inquiry. Singling out Laughlin as particularly obdurate, Edwin Black scoffs: "Laughlin and the American eugenics movement were undeterred by their own lack of knowledge, lack of scientific evidence and even the profound lack of public support."[109] Guesswork supported by a bizarre combination of data sources cherry-picked to provide proof of what was still impossible to prove. It was confirmation bias as its finest.

Yet, the lack of certainty also made eugenic assumptions vulnerable to alternative explanations—namely the environment or what was also referred to as euthenics. Havelock Ellis explained this difference, noting, "There are two ways in which we can work socially for the good of mankind: by acting on heredity and by acting on environment."[110] T. Wingate Todd, whose initial research was funded by the Brush Foundation, conceded in 1933: "What is it to be well born? We cannot yet make a complete answer. . . . Much careful investigation is still needed upon the details of human heredity . . . and upon the issues which involved not only the child but the home into which the child is born. . . . The physical and spiritual worlds are but two aspects of the same thing. Our efforts must be directed to see the problem whole not split."[111] This concession was extremely valuable to birth controllers whose defense of contraception relied heavily on the environmental threats to children posed by large families including poverty, overcrowding, poor sanitation, and disease. This debate, now colloquially know as nature v. nurture, monopolized the pages of the *Birth Control Review* and uniquely biased advocates who positioned contraception as valuable to preserving not just one side of the debate but both. In 1922, zoologist P. W. Whiting boldly labeled birth control as "at least one very important means both of euthenic and eugenic improvement."[112] Whiting elaborates in 1929:

> In general, the causes underlying determination of traits in man are difficult to analyze. . . . The new born infant show few traits by which it may be distinguished from others. . . . The growing child is subject to numerous influences of care and training, so that as special interest and abilities appear these may be ascribed to this or that experience. The environmentalists thus have an opportunity to argue that heredity is of little to no significance. Our origin is in all cases genetically heterogenous. Pure lines do not exist in man. . . . These matters may be in part governed by hereditary influence, but chance doubtless plays a considerable role."[113]

Disputes over environment's role in human development helped to unearth the fundamental point of tension between eugenicists and birth controllers—who should be using contraception?

Positive Eugenics

Driven by the race suicide panic Theodore Roosevelt ushered in at the turn of the century, eugenicists remained steadfast in their desire to increase "quality stocks" through a combination of restrictive immigration laws, compulsory sterilization laws, and positive eugenic schemes encouraging higher birth rates among "desirable" classes. Eugenicists recycled the trope of the selfish woman propagated by opponents of birth control to suggest "that if women had information to prevent conception . . . the race will die out."[114] Although the term race in the historical discussion of birth control often remains ambiguous when it comes to Roosevelt and his ilk, there is no doubt which group of people they feared committing racial suicide—native-born, educated, middle-class white people of the "right" ethnic lineage. In addition to the expected animosity toward immigrants and non-white peoples, King argues, "The deeper concern was how to distinguish advanced, healthy, and vigorous northern European from the lesser subraces now stumbling over one another on the streets and alleyways of the Lower East Side."[115] The zealous statement of Dr. Elias Lyon, Dean of Medicine at the University of Minnesota, is demonstrative of the type of person eugenicists feared would halt their reproduction. Lyon charges: "The leadership of America does not reproduce itself. This is the most disturbing—appalling fact that I know in the whole social political and economic category. . . . The men and women of *Who's Who* do not reproduce themselves."[116] The mainstream eugenic community concerned itself with the racial betterment of just one group—themselves.

Perhaps Roosevelt's panic was self-induced. He had but three siblings and only two children—an usually small family in its own right and particularly peculiar given his unrelenting bluster on the topic of race suicide.

Disagreement over the application of positive eugenics tested the fledgling alliance mightily with both eugenicists and birth controllers taking aim at each other's respective agendas. Denouncing positive eugenics for its reliance on compulsory motherhood, Sanger proclaimed: "The eugenicist also believes that a woman should bear as many healthy children as possible as a duty to the state. We hold that the world is already over-populated. Eugenicists imply or insist that a woman's first duty is to the state; we contend that her duty to herself is her first duty to the state."[117] Sanger, fully embodying the feminist ethic of the early birth control movement, resented the implication that any woman regardless of her pedigree should be forced to bear, and subsequently raise, unwanted children to uphold a specious duty to the state. Yet, it was precisely this feminist ethos which drew the ire of eugenicists. Dr. Lyon admonishes the aims of feminism as dysgenic, scolding, "Education is dysgenic to the extent that it favors late marriage or no marriage, few children or no children among the more progressive and intelligent of the population. The emancipation of women is dysgenic to the extent that superior women give up home and family responsibilities in order to pursue a 'career.' The number of Misses among prominent women is appalling."[118] Eugenicists feared the new woman made possible by suffrage and contraception framing her pursuit of new opportunities as selfish and threatening to the survival of "good stocks." Whereas birth controllers kowtowed to doctors and assumed a deferential posture predicated on their instrumental role in dispensing contraception, the alliance with eugenicists offered less immediate practical value and made it much easier for advocates to challenge the ideas espoused by eugenicists.

Returning to their dueling concerns of quality and quantity, advocates reminded eugenicists that unrestricted reproduction even among the healthiest of women would eventually falter by encouraging women to reproduce beyond their financial limits. Acknowledging in 1917 that "the majority of such parents even now have as many children as any rational eugenicist could ask them to do," Sanger chastised eugenicists for assuming families could "maintain their standards, no matter how many additional children are born. In other words, they expect quality to take care of itself."[119] Recalling the arguments advanced by the movement in support of maternal and infant health, birth controllers suggested compulsory motherhood of any kind would eventually take its toll on both mother and child. Advocates highlighted the long-term implausibility of positive eugenics warning, "the fruits of the most perfect eugenic marriage are likely to be bad health in the mother and in the later children, if birth control is not utilized for the purpose of properly spacing the progeny."[120] Eugenicists saw the questions of quality and quantity as linked seeking increased quantity among those of higher quality and reduced quantity among "undesirables." Yet, advocates remained convinced of the infeasibility of this strategy. Kepler Hoyt, chairman of the Birth Control League of the District of Columbia, curtly observed in a 1918 editorial in the *Birth Control Review*: "There cannot be more and better children until there are first fewer and better children. . . . [E]verywhere, and at all times, both in nature and in human society, quality is and must be at the expense of quantity."[121] Compulsory motherhood under any circumstances was unacceptable for the movement.

Birth controllers also denounced the implication that desirable children were born only to superior parents and the sham standards by which their superiority was determined. Sanger protested in the *Birth Control Review* in 1925: "[I]t would seem impossible to predetermine those superior persons whose progeny would for certain give such promise," and questioned whether "those qualities desirable for racial perpetuation can be effectively transmitted from generation to generation by the simple expedient of merely increasing the size of the family."[122] Juxtaposing the practice of birth control with eugenics in terms of encouraged breeding among those deemed ideal reproducers, the *Los Angeles Times* posed the question "Is there such a thing as an ideal birth control couple?" arguing, "the scope of the idea is far wider than mere eugenics. The mating of two perfect specimens seldom proves to be an ideal union."[123] Moreover, eugenicists couldn't even define the standards for what constituted a eugenic marriage. Activist Frida Laski, a member of the Birth Control International Information Center, scoffs, "The student of eugenics can do little more than insist that certain hereditary traits, deaf-mutism, for example or hemophilia, make breeding from the stocks tainted by them undesirable; he cannot tell us what fitness means or show us how to breed the qualities upon which racial adequacy depends."[124] Unconvinced by both the science and the principle of positive eugenics, advocates harshly condemned these schemes to increase quality breeding.

Directly denouncing the eugenicist's common ploy of enticing college graduates to have large families as a check against race suicide, Sanger rebuffed at the annual meeting of the ABCL in 1939: "We have got to change the inference that the quality of our population depends upon the birth rate of college graduates." Sanger affirmed the value of individuals from all backgrounds, proclaiming: "There are just as sound qualities to be found in the Arizona cowboy, in the artisans, the mechanics, and artists—the qualities of initiative and capacity for clear thinking as a result of sound mind and sound bodies."[125] For advocates who approached population quality from a more holistic perspective, encouraging elite populations to procreate was an inadequate solution ignoring the economic reality of child rearing, the spuriousness of the hereditary science, and the valuable qualities present in people from all walks of life.

Advocates continually reframed the phrase "race suicide" to distance their efforts from the ignorant claims perpetuated by eugenicists. Advocates continually reminded proponents of race suicide of the increased survival rate for children born to voluntary mothers. Charles Zueblin issues a clear reminder in 1917: "Race suicide does not mean having few children; it means having few surviving children."[126] Florence Tuttle builds on Zueblin's reminder framing the historical trend toward lower birth rates as a mark of modern society branding it "race sanity" rather than "race suicide." She observes: "Throughout history it is a fact that a falling birth rate has been the sign not of a declining but of a rising civilization, and, is not to be feared while a falling death rate is also maintained. . . . When we accept the theory that the smaller improved family is of more definite modern advantage we must ask ourselves if so-called race suicide is really race suicide? May not it be race sanity?"[127] J. Arthur Thomson uses a similar phrase, "race saving," to trumpet contraception as a hallmark of progress for many of the reasons articulated by birth controllers. Thompson quips, "Our argument is that a deliberate reduction of the birth rate may tend to improve the health of children and mothers; may make life less anxious, more secure, and with greater possibilities of finesse; may make earlier marriages among the thrifty more feasible; may promote the independence of women and increase their opportunities for self-development. . . . Birth control is not race suicide but race saving."[128] Advocates co-opted the end goal of eugenicists of racial betterment to bolster their rhetorical efforts against race suicide. Managing editor of the *Birth Control Review* Mary Knoblauch illustrates this tactic when she writes: "Other countries have tried with great success the experiment of instructing their citizens in the art of limiting their families in accordance with their circumstances. It is not race suicide that has resulted it is race regeneration."[129] Anna Martin summarily dismisses the eugenicists' concern, writing, "Sane methods of regulating births have . . . delivered the men of the country from endless financial worry and anxiety, and the women and children from untold privation and suffering. Race suicide is indeed the silliest of bogies."[130] Clever reframing and nomenclature aside, advocates hoped to make it abundantly clear the charge of race suicide was merely a hoax.

Negative Eugenics

The birth control movement consistently grappled with questions concerning both the numerical and physical makeup of the population in the United States. Rather than addressing these as two different concerns, birth controllers instead reiterated the importance of both population quality and quantity.

Sanger's 1928 plea in the *Birth Control Review* is demonstrative: "The population of the world is no longer a mere question of quantity, it involves quality as well. Civilization can no longer be estimated by mere numbers. More important, from our modern point of view, is the kind of population a country or a century produces."[131] For Sanger, like many in the movement, the issues of quality and quantity functioned concomitantly, placing different but equally important challenges on policy makers wishing to address population concerns in order to achieve greater social stability.

Advocates localized their concern at the intersection of population quantity and quality—referred to in the *Birth Control Review* as kinetic overpopulation. Defined as the moment "when the rate at which new arrivals in a country (by birth or immigration) exceeds the rate at which additional subsistence can be provided for them," kinetic overpopulation yielded insight into the factors diminishing the overall quality of the population such as poverty and disease.[132] Advocates resisted viewing the population problem solely from a framework of static overpopulation, or "the condition when the population of a country has increased up to its ultimate power of obtaining the necessary food supplies and subsistence," and highlighted the deficiencies of a strictly numerical approach which obscured the lived reality of overpopulation.[133] *The Birth Control Review* cautioned in 1923:

> It is very easy to sit at one's desk and compute the population per square mile of the world's surface, the capita production of food and other necessaries. . . . It is much more difficult to take into account what a high birth rate actually implies, to visualize the people who have been mere numerals in the calculations, to take into account the life and health and happiness of the men, women, and children who in the minds of the theorists have been merely figures and percentages.[134]

Numerical calculations of population and resource distribution provided valuable insights but failed to encapsulate the real need for family limitation given their failure to account for the lived experiences of overpopulation, conditions such as those faced by Sadie Sachs and the desperate letter writers who contacted the ABCL in droves.

Additionally, because defaulting solely to considerations of quantity divorced the issue from its immediate context, quality served as a more fitting barometer for reining in population problems. Sanger argued in 1928, "Leaving aside, as purely hypothetical and academic, all such questions as the ultimate saturation point in world population, and attacking this problem in its immediate and imperatively pressing aspects, we find ourselves here and now confronted with a tangibly definite qualitative overpopulation."[135] Reverend Waldo Adams Amos of Hoboken praised the movement's focus on quality in a 1917 letter of support to Sanger, proclaiming, "I am convinced that birth control will make for quality rather than quantity in the generations to come, and it is quality, physical, mental, and spiritual, that nature is groaning and travailing for."[136] Dr. Anna Blount, chairman of the Eugenics Education Society of Chicago, succinctly stitches together the movement's trope of responsibility and the concern for quality, writing, "Side by side with our new conception of responsibility for the quality of humanity has grown up a related sense of our responsibility for the quantity of humanity, and for the relative numbers of individuals of the different qualities."[137] While a focus on quality yielded a more accurate view of the problem, it also necessitated targeting individuals believed to possess a hereditary disposition to disease, people labeled insane or feebleminded, and individuals whose standards of living were not conducive to rearing healthy children.

Eugenicists, equally concerned with population quality and believing in a hereditary explanation for disease and delinquency, latched on to contraception as a necessary component to their program of negative eugenics, or the discouragement and/or prohibition of reproduction among persons and populations deemed "unfit." The John Price Jones Corporation explained in their 1930 report for the BCCRB, "birth control appears to be the one available scientific method for raising the level of the race. . . . And it is that argument which has enlisted [among] its champions the members of the Eugenics movement."[138] These arguments neatly aligned with many of the rhetorical strategies previously deployed by birth controllers including the professionalization of motherhood (chapter 2), the right of the child to be wellborn (chapter 3), and the societal benefits of responsible parentage (chapter 4). *The Birth Control Review* explained in 1919: birth control "not only opens the way to the eugenicist, but it preserves his work" by "prepar[ing] the ground in a neutral fashion for the development of a higher standard of motherhood and of family life."[139] By positioning birth control as an integral part of racial regeneration, the movement successfully courted eugenicists who shared the goal of improving the quality of the population.

Sterilization

The question of *who* should utilize contraception also animated the debate over sterilization—a key tool for carrying out the agenda of negative eugenics. Although disagreeing on the desirability of compulsory sterilization, eugenicists and birth controllers found common ground when it came to advocating sterilization for individuals deemed incapable of using traditional contraceptive options or for whom a more permanent solution was advisable. Sanger explained: "The regular methods of contraception are used easily by parents whose intelligence and responsibility are adequate to its application, but sterilization is a better method in cases where the person's mentality is not adequate for the usual technique."[140] The terms "unfit" and "dysgenic" broadly applied to anyone whose reproduction threatened to diminish population quality with a targeted focus on three groups of people: those with inheritable diseases, those deemed "feebleminded," and individuals labeled serial criminals. In each of these instances, advocates deployed the language and logic of eugenicists to advocate sterilization.

The imprecise understanding of hereditary genetics and the transmissibility of diseases during pregnancy belied the movement's labeling of the unfit and subsequent recommendation of sterilization. For example, speaking to the overwhelming concern with syphilitic insanity in the early twentieth century, Sanger urged people battling syphilis to avoid childbearing altogether. In a 1921 public debate against New York lawyer John Winter Russell, Sanger pleaded: "We know, too, that out of this terrible scourge of venereal disease that we have 9070 of the insane in this country, due to syphilis. . . . They should absolutely in due regard to themselves, to their children and to the race, not allow a child to be born while that disease is running riot in the system."[141] Women, gripped with fear of passing on problems to future children, regularly wrote to birth controllers for help. *The Birth Control Review* provides two powerful examples in 1917:

> I was told to write you for information for which I applied elsewhere. I have been married two years and have two children and I'm constantly in fear of there being another one as the methods of birth control I have been able to get have proven wholly inadequate. An uncle of mine died of epilepsy as did also my sister. For this reason more than any other we don't want more children.[142]

> I am 22 years old and have been married just two months. I am in constant fear of becoming pregnant, because insanity runs in our family. My sister told the doctor before she got married, and he told her, he was sure that if she had any children they would be alright, because she was well. She married and has two idiot children. I am writing for her as well as for myself, because she is heart broken.[143]

As a logical extension of the arguments advanced by the movement concerning the health and welfare of mothers and children, physical and mental fitness, inevitably problematically defined, emerged as a primary justification for sterilization.

Birth controllers convinced of the heritability and transmissibility of disease, both physical and mental, strongly advocated sterilization as a permanent form of contraception necessary to prevent the multiplication of "dysgenic" persons. Sanger explained in the *Birth Control Review* in 1918, "There should be no children when mother or father suffers from [diseases] . . . or mental disorders" citing "the danger to mothers and offspring of having children" under such conditions, including miscarriage, birth defects, insanity, and feeblemindedness.[144] Using the health of mother and child as a convenient shield for their problematic arguments, advocates couched their ableist fears about deteriorating population quality in terms of maternal and infant health. Although rarely proving direct causality, numerous studies granted legitimacy to the treatment of dysgenic persons as "maternity risks for them notoriously augment the infant death rate."[145] Robert L. Dickinson outlines specific conditions justifying sterilization, writing, "Certain conditions call for sterilization of the mother for both therapeutic and eugenic reasons. For example, active tuberculosis where the mother will suffer if allowed to bear, and where the child may be expected to become infected, unless removed directly from the mother. Diabetes is another condition where therapy and inheritance both enter in. The mother may carry the child safely, but it is likely to have diabetes."[146] Dickinson's comment highlights the very real threats to life presented by issues such as tuberculosis, and also reveals the movement's ableist assumptions of fitness undoubtedly influenced by eugenics. In his example of diabetes, Dickinson admits the pregnancy does not present a harm to the mother yet still includes it in his list of conditions calling for sterilization to prevent the birth of a child who also has diabetes.

For as little as we knew about the heredity of physical traits in the early twentieth century, we knew even less about the heredity of mental traits. Desperate to define and prove the inheritability of traits such as intelligence, eugenicists developed mental tests supposedly evaluating everything from basic incapacitation to IQ. Though most of these tests were later invalidated, owing to their overt racism and complete discounting of environmental factors, their influence on the movement's understanding of "feeblemindedness" is striking. According to Black, "Sanger frequently parroted the results of U.S. Army Intelligence testing which asserted that as many as 70 percent of Americans were feebleminded."[147] Unabashedly defending the hereditary view of feeblemindedness and insanity, the *Birth Control Review* bluntly stated, "The most obvious use for sterilization" is to prevent the propagation "of the feebleminded, hereditary epileptics and hereditary insane."[148] Harkening back to their emphasis on responsible parentage and the desire of potential parents to provide the best for their future children, advocates questioned whether or not "mentally unfit" persons could provide the requisite level of care children deserve. They suggested, "We do know that mentally retarded [*sic*] parents cannot bring up their children in the way that will produce valuable citizens, not without a great deal more help than is often available."[149] Given the immense obstacles faced by individuals suffering from mental illness, advocates concluded "men and women of mental or physical maladjustment would not want to bring children into the world with their handicaps if they knew how to prevent it."[150] In this way, the movement mobilized its dominant themes of mother-love and wanted children to perversely advocate on behalf of people deemed "mentally unfit" and position voluntary sterilization as a self-aware act of compassion.

Birth controllers went to great lengths to highlight the desirability of sterilizing the "unfit" not just for society but for the individual as well. Initially, advocates presented sterilization as a preferable option for restricting the reproduction of dysgenic persons. During the nineteenth century, a patchwork system of laws including marriage restrictions, forced segregation, and compulsory institutionalization sought to enact barriers to dysgenic breeding. By the mid-1920s, efforts to deinstitutionalize prompted by rising concerns over both the cost and quality of care created an avenue for advocates to frame sterilization as an effective alternative. *The Birth Control Review* explains, "Obviously, sterilization instead of the prohibitively cumbersome method of permanent segregation is indicated in cases of hereditary defect."[151] Referring directly to individuals labeled wards of the state due to mental incapacitation, Harriette M. Dilla argues, "the reproduction of the irresponsible classes must be regulated by society itself, and among the methods that have been favored are sterilization and permanent custodial care."[152] In the eyes of the movement, sterilization removed the biggest threat posed by those labeled dysgenic—propagation—eliminating the need for segregation. Sterilization received praise from both birth controllers and eugenicists as a permanent contraceptive option whose use was preferable to current methods of segregating and institutionalizing people with mental illness.

In the spirit of the Progressive Era, advocates also heralded the societal benefits of sterilization in terms of cost savings and governmental efficiency. Using her home state of New York as a reference point, Sanger argues, "The American public is taxed, heavily taxed, to maintain an increasing race of morons, which threatens the very foundations of our civilization. Over one fourth of the total income of the state of New York is spent on the maintenance of asylums, prisons, and other institutions for the care of the defective and diseased."[153] Absent the use of sterilization, warned Sanger, society was merely "providing abundant opportunity for the continuation of charities and various pauperizing institutions for generations to come."[154] Dr. Lydia Allen DeVilbiss, surgeon reserve in the United States Public Health Service and then director of a Florida-based birth control clinic, deploys a similar version of this cost-benefit analysis in 1931. DeVilbiss contends, "It has proved that the proverbial few dollars spent in prevention has saved the hundreds spent in cure."[155] Regulating reproduction wasn't just society's duty—it was a practice from which it stood to benefit greatly.

Sterilization, although irreversible at this point in time, was a simple procedure allowing couples to prevent reproduction without diminishing other areas of their life. Sanger defends the procedure in the *Birth Control Review* in 1924 writing, "The operation itself will cause no change in physical, mental, or emotional life, nor will it deprive either man or women of the normal expression of their sex lives."[156] Advocates recommended sterilization as concomitant with the movement's goal of securing higher levels of relational and sexual satisfaction among couples. DeVilbiss, informed by the sixty cases of sterilization she oversaw in her clinic, further articulated the benefits of sterilization for individuals. She observes, "its operation has reduced human misery; it has enabled economically submerged families to get back on their feet; it has removed the constant fear of pregnancy which was disrupting the married life of some couples; and it has removed the stigma and fear of passing on to unborn children serious physical and mental defects, which would in all likelihood render one so born a public charge in his generation as his parents are in this one."[157] In terms of permanently regulating reproduction, sterilization checked all the boxes—it prevented the birth of unwanted babies while allowing couples to enjoy the same benefits provided to regular contraceptive users.

The movement's articulation of a societal right to birth control as a precautionary mechanism also motivated birth controllers to consider sterilization for individuals classified as habitual criminals. The origins of this advocacy are two-fold; first, because birth control is considered a negative right, proponents of sterilizing criminals argued that just as convicted felons lose their right to vote, habitual criminals forgo their right to make reproductive decisions without state interference. Second, once again appealing to their insistence on responsible parentage, birth controllers framed habitual criminals as incapable of reform and thus equally incapable of handling the responsibility of family planning and/or eventual child rearing.[158] In fact, involuntary sterilization for criminals was frequently compared to required vaccinations as both measures infringed on individual choice in the name of protecting societal interests. The *Chicago Tribune* proclaimed in 1923, "the constitutionality of the law which would provide for sterilizations . . . is based on the same legal principles as those involved in statutes compelling vaccination."[159] Dr. W. A. Evans further contextualizes this legal rationale in terms of state interests to the *Chicago Tribune* in 1926, explaining, "the tendency of the courts is very strongly toward the position that sterilization is not a cruel, inhumane punishment . . . and that [it] is a proper exercise of the right of society to protect itself."[160] By 1951, twenty-seven states had passed legislation "to provide the cost of sterilization at government expense" for habitual criminals, with many of these states, including Oklahoma and California, giving states the right "to perform vasectomies upon habitual criminals" as part of their required sentence.[161] Although Oklahoma's sterilization law would be overturned by the U.S. Supreme Court just seven years later, California's sterilization policy remained on the books until September 2014 and was only revoked after a state audit revealed that close to forty women had been forced or coerced into sterilization in recent years.[162]

As eugenicists proselytized sterilization as a viable long-term solution to population quality, birth controllers remained wary of formal sterilization policies. Comparing the first draft of the ABCL's bylaws to the final version is illustrative. The first draft included a section advocating for "sterilization of the insane and feebleminded and the encouragement of this operation upon those afflicted with inherited or transmissible diseases"; however, this section and all references to sterilization, were removed from the final version published in 1925.[163] The minutes of the ABCL's National Council Meeting in 1924 shed light on this removal:

> In regard to sterilization the consensus of opinion was strongly against adopting a bill to legalize sterilization as part of the birth control program. Dr. Little opposed on biological grounds, holding that knowledge of effects or partial sterilization was too scanty to form a basis for legislation. Others held that the advocacy of a bill for sterilization would complicate the birth control work. A motion was then passed that the National Council advises that the ABCL do not at present endorse a sterilization bill.

The reticence to endorse a sterilization bill manifested in the operations of ABCL standardized clinics who opted to only provide patients with temporary and harmless methods of birth control reserving sterilization for only the most extreme cases. The BCCRB explained in a 1935 progress report, "Sterilization is not a method prescribed in birth control clinics. Occasionally patients with a severe incurable medical condition voluntarily request sterilization. In these cases sterilization is approved only when the usual clinic birth control methods cannot be used."[164] Even as Sanger herself warmed up to the idea of sterilization, she resisted its application beyond the context of the unfit, stating, "We do not think sterilization advisable for healthy people for they may change their minds about having children. . . . However, if there is taint of insanity or epilepsy in either husband's or wife's ancestry, sterilization is advisable."[165]

In many ways, the movement's stance on sterilization under the leadership of Sanger is difficult to track as she vacillates quickly between endorsing the mass sterilization of the "unfit" and ardently defending the reproductive autonomy of women. The BCCRB refused to offer the procedure in its clinics, and the ABCL struck it from their bylaws, yet eugenicists received top billing in the *Birth Control Review*. The BCCRB remained cautious, however, suggesting in 1930 "sterilization as an ordinary measure of family limitation is far too drastic. . . . It is not a solution of the problem in general."[166] Committed to the principles of choice and autonomy, advocates generally refused to endorse measures giving other parties absolute say over who should be sterilized. Sanger protested: "It can be a voluntary measure requiring no legislation. It should not be forced but should be encouraged. It must not be considered a punishment but rather a measure of safeguarding the community."[167] Havelock Ellis cautioned against the eugenicist's emphasis on legislative measures warning, "It is common, indeed, but sometimes mischievous, and usually futile. We do not know enough to legislate on eugenic schemes."[168] To be clear, birth controllers believed in sterilizing individuals with definitively inheritable conditions or the mental incapacity to parent but rejected the sweeping generalizations regarding fitness advanced by eugenicists and refused to endorse compulsory sterilization laws.

Advocates rejected the external imposition of reproductive control instead supporting contraceptive instruction allowing parents to "exercise more and more intelligence, self-discipline and guidance of their own procreative powers" through "a practical instrument [by] which all well-born children" are conceived.[169] As eugenicists pushed their compulsory sterilization agenda, birth controllers remained committed to self-directed family planning. Sanger chastised eugenicists in the *Birth Control Review* in 1925 for "their tendency to place too much faith in external direction and quasi paternal direction of breeding" as well as their "bland indifference to the importance of liberated self-direction"; in contrast, Sanger explained, "the program of birth control is more constructive and more concrete."[170] This was the breaking point for the alliance, according to Black, as Sanger's disavowal of positive eugenics and "insistence on birth control for all women, even women of so-called good families, made her movement unpalatable to the male-dominated eugenics establishment."[171] By the end of the 1930s, birth controllers and eugenicists had severed all major ties but would continue to work in parallel on their goals of population control.

The compulsory sterilization efforts of eugenicists began long before birth controllers entered the fray with Indiana passing the first sterilization law on March 9, 1907.[172] The bigoted agenda of eugenicists was no secret and yet advocates, desperate for validation and support, cozied up to eugenicists. For as much as they pushed back on the ideas of positive eugenics and compulsory sterilization, birth controllers readily accepted the principle of negative eugenics intensifying their rhetoric regarding reproductive fitness and racial betterment. In doing so, argues Dorothy Roberts, "The language of eugenics did more than legitimate birth control. It defined the purpose of birth control, shaping the meaning of reproductive freedom. Birth control became a means of controlling a population rather than a means of increasing women's reproductive autonomy."[173] The palpable influence of eugenicists on the rhetoric of birth controllers, according to Edwin Black, "stands as a powerful example of American eugenics' ability to pervade, infect, and distort the most dedicated causes and visionary reformers."[174] Where advocates once framed contraception as an emancipatory practice for women shouldering the uneven burden of childbearing, they now framed its use as a protective mechanism for a society grappling with significant demographic shifts and economic uncertainty.

The alliance with eugenicists forever marred the reputation of the movement and, more specifically, the legacy of Margaret Sanger. Significant scholarly energy has endeavored to get to the bottom of Sanger's eugenic motivations and wrestled with her willingness to allow known white supremacists, such as Lothrop Stoddard and Guy Irving Burch, into her inner circle despite little evidence to suggest she shared their explicit racist assumptions. Black argues, "Sanger was no racist. Nor was she an anti-Semite. But Sanger was an ardent, self-confessed eugenicist, and she would turn her otherwise noble birth control organizations into a tool for eugenics, which advocates for mass sterilizations of so-called defectives, mass-incarceration of the unfit and draconian immigration restrictions."[175] Unlike Burch who vilely defended the need for negative eugenics to "prevent the American people from being replaced by alien or Negro stock," Sanger believed the issues afflicting nonwhites "arose from their unrestrained fertility, not their genes or racial heritage."[176]

Despite these appreciable differences, advocates like Sanger failed to question the racist practices and assumptions of their eugenic allies. Linda Gordon contends, "Birth control reformers were not attracted to eugenics *because* they were racists; rather, they had interests in common with eugenicists and had no strong tradition of anti-racism on which to base a critique of eugenics."[177] Sanger's 1945 statement from an interview with Earl Conrad of the *Chicago Defender*, a historically Black newspaper, illustrates the timidity with which she broached the subject of race. She remarked, "Discrimination is a world-wide thing. It has to be opposed everywhere. That is why I feel the Negro's plight here is linked with that of the oppressed around the globe. The big answer, as I see it, is the education of the white man. The white man is the problem. It is the same as with the Nazis. We must change the white attitudes. That is where it lies."[178] Although Sanger challenges the premise of white supremacy, she refuses to acknowledge the uniquely racialized agenda of American eugenicists, opting instead for an abstracted reproach of discriminatory policies. Birth controllers like Sanger lacked both the language and the incentive to challenge the inherent racism of eugenics, settling instead for a more generalized rejection of their most extreme policy proposals.

Giving Sanger the benefit of the doubt while still acknowledging the irreparable harm caused by the movement's alliance with eugenics, Dorothy Roberts concludes: "It appears that Sanger was motivated by a genuine concern to improve the health of the poor mothers she served rather than a desire to eliminate their stock. . . . Sanger nevertheless promoted two of the most perverse tenets of racial thinking: that social problems are caused by reproduction of the socially disadvantaged and that their childbearing should therefore be deterred."[179] Because of this, as Angela Davis observes, the damage was already done. "It had been robbed of its progressive potential, advocating for people of color not the individual right to birth control, but rather the racist strategy of population control. The birth control campaign would be called upon to serve in an essential capacity in the execution of the US government imperialist and racist population policy."[180] Pursuing a strategically beneficial relationship with eugenicists in the 1920s gave birth controllers a captive audience but also granted eugenicists a voice in the social and political discourse surrounding contraception. In shifting their framing of contraception toward societal population control and away from individualized birth control, advocates legitimized the eugenic principles which constitute the backbone of this country's racist reproductive politics.

BLACK ACTIVISTS

As the birth control movement solidified its relationship with doctors and eugenicists, another group of reformers joined the fray eager to capitalize on the success of the movement—Black activists. Although these reformers couldn't offer the same level of structural prestige accompanying doctors and eugenicists, they could offer their fervent support and an inroad into communities largely untouched by the mainstream birth control movement. Jessie M. Rodrique explains, "What appears to some scholars of the birth control movement as the waning of the movement's original purposes during the 1920s and 1930s was within the Black community a period of growing ferment and support for birth control. The history of the birth control movement, and the participation of Black Americans in it, must be reexamined in this light."[181] The success of the BCCRB and the continued expansion of clinics, financially bankrolled in many instances by eugenicists, had dramatically improved access to contraception, and Black activists, particularly those living in urban areas with established clinics like New York and Chicago, clamored to expand these services to their communities. In fact, Loretta Ross credits the involvement of Black activists during this time period for the widespread availability of contraceptive services in contemporary Black communities, explaining, "The reason we have so many Planned Parenthoods in the black community is because leaders in the black community in the '20s and '30s went to Margaret Sanger and asked for them. . . . Controlling our fertility was part of our uplift out of poverty strategy, and it still works."[182]

Despite the vocal support for birth control among many Black activists, historians of the movement have given their involvement, and subsequently their rhetoric, surprisingly little attention. Rodrique furthers, "In the past scholars have interpreted the birth control movement as a racist and elitist set of programs imposed on the black population. Although this characterization may describe the intentions of the national white leadership, it is important to recognize that the black community had its own agenda and the creation of programs to include and reach wide segments of the black population."[183] Suggesting that many existing accounts of the birth control movement ignore the unique contributions of Black activists by focusing almost exclusively on the exploitative elements of the movement, Dorothy Roberts argues, "Contrary to the prevalent interpretation, the birth control movement was not simply thrust upon an unwilling black population. . . . [B]lack activists played a critical role in both the national debate about birth control and the establishment of local family planning clinics."[184] Black activists were an important part of the birth control movement, and their voices deserve to be heard alongside the chorus of white advocates who receive prime billing in the history of the movement.

Examining the rhetoric of Black activists alongside that of doctors and eugenicists reveals both troubling continuities and critical deviations. It helps us situate and make sense of the widespread uptake of population control policies and sheds light on the uncomfortable history of the movement at a time when such histories are being distorted in service of efforts to limit reproductive freedom. This tactic was literally on full display in a series of anti-abortion billboards that popped up around the United States in 2014 declaring "Black Children Are an Endangered Species" and labeling abortion as "the #1 Killer of African Americans."[185] Carolette Norwood contextualizes these billboards within the central claim of Black anti-abortion activists "that Planned Parenthood was founded as a eugenic organization that sought the annihilation of the Black community" and suggests that such campaigns rely on half-formed understandings of history. Loretta Ross concurs with the assessment arguing these campaigns "resorted to a distorted history of the reproductive rights movement and deployed racist sexual stereotypes."[186] Norwood and Ross rightly label the movement's association with eugenics as indefensible but also remind readers of the widespread popularity of contraception within Black communities. The potential for these discourses to be distorted and co-opted intensifies the need to face them squarely and reconcile the myriad ways early advocates both cosigned and capitalized on the uptake of eugenic ideals and the strikingly broad reception of these ideas.

Mimicking the Mainstream Movement

Interest in contraception among Black activists intensified as a direct result of Sanger's clinic initiatives in New York City. In 1923, Sanger was invited to

Harlem by the National Urban League to discuss her fledgling movement and the possibility of opening a clinic servicing Black women in Harlem.[187] Over the next seven years, Sanger worked alongside the Urban League to raise the requisite funds for the clinic which opened in February 1930 under the banner of the BCCRB. The clinic operated with mixed results in part because the BCCRB treated it as an overflow center for white patients referred from their downtown location, in part because of "the Black community's ambivalence about birth control," and in part because Sanger refused to surrender full control of the clinic to the Black Advisory Council created to oversee the project.[188]

These issues combined with the financial strain of the Great Depression forced the clinic to shutter its doors in 1936. Short-lived as it was, the clinic had a profound impact on the reception of birth control in the Black community. Dr. M. O. Bousfield, former president of the National Medical Association, an organization created when the AMA refused admission to Black physicians, admits he and his colleagues had given "scant consideration" to the topic of birth control until introduced to Sanger's work. In fact, his own story of discovering the movement is not unlike Sanger's; he recalls, "I asked a few of my friends what they knew about birth control and found that they had given it little or no attention. This was true of physicians as well as laymen."[189] After being invited to tour the Harlem Branch, Bousfield became an ardent supporter of the movement, reflecting, "This is the usual reaction to birth control work: one approaches it gingerly and questioningly, but the more one investigates and studies, the more one becomes convinced that it is an element for good" and even proclaimed "it is time for some colored woman to become the Margaret Sanger of her race."[190]

By the early 1930s many of the nation's most prominent Black voices were lending their support to the birth control movement. W. E. B. Du Bois demanded in 1932 the time had come to spread "among negroes an intelligent and clearly recognized concept of proper birth control, so that the young people can marry, have companionship and natural health, and yet not have children until they are able to take care of them."[191] Prompted by Du Bois's endorsement and the BCCRB's Negro Project, both the Public Health Committee of the National Negro Insurance Association and the National Medical Association of Negro Physicians officially endorsed contraception. What is most striking about the involvement of Black activists is their rhetorical similarities with white advocates. Demonstrating the salience of the movement's rhetoric, Black activists made the case for birth control in their communities utilizing the very same persuasive strategies pioneered by early advocates, including appeals to motherhood, a child's right to be wellborn, eugenic concerns, and the prosperity of future generations.

For Black activists, the question of contraception was deeply connected to race; however, activists vying for the support of their white counterparts often minimized the importance of race and emphasized the human concerns present. Dr. Carl G. Roberts, president of the National Medical Association, proclaims: "After all, this problem of birth control is not primarily a racial but a human problem, with variations dependent upon the social and economic conditions among the groups affected." Pointing to disease as a universal catalyst for contraception, Roberts notes, "Tuberculosis, which strongly justifies contraception, is not a Negro disease but a result of bad housing, overcrowding, poor hygiene, malnutrition and neglected sanitation in those districts in which Negroes are forced to live."[192] E. S. Jamison explicitly calls for an interracial effort on birth control, arguing, "The fact that disease germs respect no race, Creed or color makes his problems those of the entire nation. Interracial cooperation and respect for each other is the immediate and final solution."[193] The editors of *The Birth Control Review* echoed this sentiment in the foreword to their June 1932 issue entitled "The Negro Number," writing, "It is possible to approach this problem from the point of view of the Negro, or again from that of the whites. It's solution, if ever it is to be solved, must come to embrace both sides of the question and promote the general welfare of the nation as a whole."[194] The above statements, although true, read more as an act of code-switching—a strategic rhetorical move made by Black activists clamoring for meaningful inclusion into a predominantly white movement.

Black activists emphasized the need for expanded clinic access in Black communities, hoping to reinvigorate the movement's interest after the failed Harlem Clinic. In 1933, Dr. Rachelle Yarros who already directed a clinic servicing white women in Chicago advocated for "Negroes [to] have their own clinic on the south side."[195] In the face of rampant segregation laws, Black activists needed to forge interracial coalitions if they ever hoped of securing adequate contraceptive access for their communities. Clinics were urgently needed in Black communities who found themselves either priced out of private physicians or reliant on risky quack medicine. Despite the proliferation of clinics in the 1930s, their absence was palpable in Black communities.[196] The scene described by Charles S. Johnson, Director of the Department of Social Science at Fisk University, is not unlike that found within the country's poor white neighborhoods. He notes, "An important present circumstance is the inaccessibility of reliable information Centers for those elements of the Negro population, which, on the one hand, are unable to secure high priced professional advice, and on the other hand do greater violence than good to themselves through reliance upon dangerous folk measures."[197]

Abortion was also a significant cause of concern in Black communities. Editor of the National Urban League's official publication, *Opportunity: Journal of Negro Life*, Elmer A. Carter laments, "Negro Women in formidable numbers, without the advantage of contraceptive information, seek relief through abortions performed under highly dangerous conditions by unskilled and sometimes grossly ignorant quacks." Mimicking the rhetoric of white advocates, Carter accepts the inevitability of unwanted pregnancies and positions contraception as obviously preferable. He furthers, "The question is not whether there shall be conscious control of births, but whether it shall be achieved by contraceptive methods of proven value and safety or by the clumsy almost murderous methods of the medical racketeer."[198] Advocating birth control if for no other reason that its ability to prevent abortion, Dr. M. O. Bousfield boldly declared: "The dangerous practice of abortion is one of the greatest blots on modern civilization and something must be done about it."[199] As observed in previous chapters, the salience of the abortion argument cannot be overstated and was equally compelling to Black activists who abhorred both the physical and moral consequences of abortion.

In advancing their case for contraception, Black activists borrowed extensively from the rhetoric of mainstream birth controllers to identify the consequences of compulsory motherhood and assert a right to contraception on behalf of mother, child, and community. Cleveland-based physician Dr. Charles H. Garvin bemoaned the unsustainability of large families, lamenting, "Show me a large negro family and I will reveal to you a family overcome with indigence and destitution and shackled by insurmountable financial obligations. The larger the family the more congested will be their living quarters, the more child labor."[200] In addition to the financial and physical turmoil created by overburdened families, Garvin runs through the well-worn laundry list of problems associated with compulsory motherhood including "tremendous and distressing infant mortality rate . . . stillbirths, congenital disease and malformations" and a life surrounded by "vice, degeneracy, crime, alcoholism, and tuberculosis."[201] To willingly permit such conditions directly threatened "the birthright of the unborn" and, according to Carl G. Roberts, made "those who dogmatically fight against the establishment of a scientific, ethical system of birth control . . . participating partners, whether they realize it or not."[202] E. S. Jamison, Director of Health and Physical Education at West Virginia College, reiterates the connection between birth control and the birthright of children noting, "Birth control should be one of the health Services available to Negro families so that every child born may receive the care to which he is entitled."[203] Denying contraceptive information constituted a crime against not only the child and their family but the broader community as well. Roberts concludes, "To withhold essential knowledge of family planning from this prolific mass who dwell in the back streets is to encourage the unrestrained, haphazard production of children condemned to a life of deprivation, dependence and destitution which constitutes a crime against civilization."[204] Considering the wealth of scholarship painting the relationship between birth controllers and Black activists in primarily oppositional terms, the similarities between their rhetoric is striking. Black activists seized the momentum generated by the movement to advance their demand for contraception using the proven rhetorical strategies of Sanger and the mainstream birth control movement.

Birth Control and Racial Uplift

The debate over race regeneration also permeated the Black community and was directly tied to the project of racial uplift popular among Black academics and activists who frequently subscribed to Du Bois's "Talented Tenth" ideologies. The activists who aligned themselves with birth controllers readily embraced the rhetoric of inheritance, arguing, "The Negro must do for himself. Charity will not better his condition in the long run. He must be taught to serve his race by passing on to the next generation the best possible inheritance."[205] Noting the historically high fertility rate of Black women once kept in check by correspondingly high infant mortality rates, Charles S. Johnson explicitly calls for the application of negative eugenics, arguing, "Now that Negro mortality has been reduced to the point at which the white stood a generation ago, and continues to decline, the same eugenic discrimination which applies to the whites is necessary with reference to selective fertility within the Negro group."[206] In calling for the same eugenic application of contraception in the Black community, Walter A. Terpenning, a sociologist at Western State Teachers College in Kalamazoo, Michigan, brazenly insists the Black community is in fact more deserving of contraception because its eugenic needs are much higher given the alarming rates of "malnutrition, disease and death." He asserts, "As among the whites, there are cases of degenerate Negroes whose propagation will be checked only by sterilization or institutionalization, but the practice of birth control among the majority of colored people would probably be more eugenic than among their white compatriots. The dissemination of the information of birth control should have begun with this class rather than with the upper social and economic classes of white citizens."[207] Negative eugenics was attractive to Black activists because it was crucial to Black survival jeopardized by high mortality rates and further facilitated the pursuit of Black excellence lauded by Du Bois and his peers.

Activities relied on the birth control movement's established framework of quality over quantity and openly embraced the eugenic belief in curtailing reproduction among the unfit in order to elevate population quality. Avid birth controller George Schuyler, who served as the business manager for the NAACP from 1937 to 1944, emphasized the need for quality over quantity, writing, "Shall they go in for quantity or quality and children? Shall they bring children into the world to enrich the undertakers, the physicians, and furnish work for social workers and jailers, or shall they produce children who are going to be an asset to the group and to American Society."[208] W. E. B. Du Bois also adopted the framework of quality over quantity, arguing, "They must learn that among human races and groups, as among vegetables, quality and not mere quantity really counts."[209] Hedging against the ever-present fear of race suicide, Dr. Garvin argues, birth control "is recognized as one of the most practical factors in the eugenic control of the people. . . . Scientific birth control instruction will certainly not mean race suicide but race preservation and advancement." Consistent with the movement's attempt to positively reframe "race suicide," Garvin clarifies: "My appeal is not for the reduction of America's black population; but I am vitally interested in increasing racial stamina by the reduction of the unfit. Fewer and stronger babies, high quality, low quantity production."[210] That fewer children were born but more survived was a foundational argument in the rhetoric of the mainstream movement. Garvin's framing of this concept as "racial stamina" is unique, however, and serves to highlight the nuanced view of racial betterment in the Black community for whom contraception was a question of survival on both an individual and cultural level.

Despite reassurances like the one issued by Garvin, many Black activists feared race suicide would occur in their communities and thus embraced positive eugenic principles. The early adoption of contraception among wealthy white people prompted a concern over the diminution of "good stocks" and a similar trend permeated Black communities. Elmer A. Carter explains, "Birth control as practiced today among Negroes is distinctly dysgenic. On the higher economic levels, Negroes have long since limited the number of their offspring, following in the footsteps of the higher classes of white America." Carter's statement mimics the race suicide charge advanced by eugenicists and is followed by a familiar call for both positive and negative eugenic action within the Black community. He pleads: "Therein lies the danger, for Negroes who by virtue of their education and capacity are best able to rear children shrink from that responsibility and the Negro who, in addition to the handicaps of race and color, is shackled by mental and social incompetence serenely goes on his way bringing into the world children whose chances of mere existence are apparently becoming more and more hazardous."[211] Carter's rumination revisits the familiar question posed by eugenics—whose reproduction brings value, and whose poses a threat? The answer to which has nothing to do with individual women and focuses entirely on the social project of racial betterment.

Interestingly, Carter explains his own reluctance to join the birth control movement as a direct result of the race suicide charge. He writes, "It is doubtless because of this emphasis placed on comparative numbers, that the leaders of Negro life had been tardy in embracing a social procedure which would seem at first sight to have as its ultimate purpose a conscious collaboration with those forces which were dooming the Negro to extinction."[212] For advocates like Carter the premise of positive eugenics takes on new meaning in the context of the Black community. Educated Black people were encouraged to reproduce not because they were presumed to be of better stock, but because they had overcome the "handicaps of race and color" in ways impoverished Black people had not. Achieving "racial stamina" relied as much on their continued reproduction as it did the elimination of dysgenic births.

Taken together, these statements are striking and speak to the pervasiveness of eugenic thinking and language in the early twentieth century. Dorothy Roberts explains, "Du Bois and other prominent Blacks were not immune from the elitist thinking of their time" and "sometimes advocated birth control for poor segments of their own race in terms painfully similar to eugenic rhetoric."[213] From a purely rhetorical perspective, the rhetoric of Black activists demonstrates an adherence to the principles of eugenics popularized by the birth control movement. Eugenics provided a vocabulary to discuss the value of reproduction in ways that were consistent with the principles of Black uplift. However, a closer look reveals a far more nuanced understanding of the role of eugenics in the Black community. Roberts furthers, "Birth control as a tool for racial betterment had a different meaning for Blacks than it did for most whites. There was a radical distinction in both strategies and goals. . . . White eugenicists promoted birth control as a way of preserving an oppressive social structure; Blacks promoted birth control as a way of toppling it.[214] Although the means were the same—eliminate the reproduction of dysgenic populations—the goal was distinctly different in so far as it sought to reposition Black communities within larger power systems by making possible economic prosperity and generational wealth. Jamie Hart explains, "The survival of 'the Black family' was essential to Black intellectuals, and in the 1930s issues of economics and health were in the forefront. . . . To families caught in a continuous spiral of fecundity and penury, contraception could prove to be the only measure of control available in the family economy. To many of the middle- and upper-class African Americans, birth control for the lower classes represented racial preservation and advancement."[215] Whereas white birth controllers invoked society's right to protect itself from dysgenic individuals, Black activists spoke of the communal obligation to ensure a healthy race as part of their pursuit for racial uplift.

For Black activists, especially women, the promises of contraception mattered not just for individual women but for the community as a whole. Constance Fisher, a Black social worker based in Minnesota, embodies this community obligation when she writes in the *Birth Control Review*: "In instances where she sees a definite need for advice of this sort, the writer feels that she owes it to the community, as well as to the family, to use the birth control clinic as a tool for preventative social therapy as well as remedial or palliative treatment."[216] For many proponents of birth control, a sense of urgency accompanied the felt obligation. A 1931 statement by Professor Newell Leroy Sims of Oberlin College is demonstrative:

> Too many Negroes are born, too many are sick, and too many die each year, for these vital processes consume energy that might otherwise be accumulated for advancement. So the Negro's program should include the conservation of vital energy. The best way and perhaps the only practical way is to control the birth rate. . . . The great bulk of Negroes everywhere are overburdening themselves with progeny to whom they can give only half a chance in the world. Thus, they keep themselves impoverished and their race down. . . . Is it any wonder therefore, that the responsible white community looks upon the average Negro as being irresponsible, without pride or self-respect when he supplies more than his quota of dependents and delinquents? Birth control should be urged as a step toward independence and greater power.[217]

Sims's statement draws a potent connection between birth control and the advancement of the Black race; the use of phrases such as "advancement," "vital energy," and "independence and greater power" speak to the larger project of Black uplift spearheaded by Black leaders during the 1930s. The Black activists promoting birth control knew of one guaranteed path to advancement in the Jim Crow era—assimilation. If Black people were to earn the respect of "the responsible white community," then they needed to act white. The embrace of eugenic principles and rhetoric can thus be read as an act of respectability politics—a symbolic show of deference to the dominant principles of negative eugenics to curry favor, respect, and ultimately power. Black activists, keenly aware of the birth control movement's struggle to secure professional allies, methodically mirrored their rhetorical strategies and acquiesced to the established framework for contraception—population control—to gain access to the financial and logistical machinations of the broader movement.

Discussions of reproductive control were rarely divorced from the broader struggle for equality within the Black community. Dorothy Roberts argues, "Blacks understood that racial progress was ultimately a question of racial justice: it required a transformation of the unequal economic and political relations between Blacks and whites."[218] Speaking directly to the very real presence of racism as a deterrent to large families, Dr. Carl G. Roberts laments: "Educated and intelligent Negroes, even if there were no economic factors to consider, would hesitate to rear large families because they're thinking more and more seriously of the price their children must pay as victims of the many discriminatory practices which prevail in America. More and more they're asking themselves, 'Is it fair to the child to bring into the world to suffer the things we have undergone?'"[219] The specter of slavery and the reality of Jim Crow loomed large over the reproductive decisions of Black women. George Schuyler laments, "Jim Crowism having doomed the Brown woman to work along with her man and sometimes to become the sole support of the family. . . . The more children there are, the greater is the burden on the Negro woman and on Negro society, which must bear the odium of a condition forced upon it by a white civilization."[220] For Schuyler and his contemporaries, contraception was essential to neutralize the unique barriers and burdens placed on Black women and their families. Dr. Roberts furthers, "The great mass of Negroes certainly are entitled to this knowledge if any group is. For they are the most underprivileged of all races, laboring under more restrictions as to avenues of employment, subjected to segregation and discrimination, forced to live in restricted areas and often in houses unfit for human habitation, among unsanitary conditions."[221] Black activists, keenly aware of their deprivileged position in society, advocated contraception not as a panacea to their problems but as a means of lessening the already immense burden on Black Americans in pursuit of equal opportunity.

Just a generation or two removed from emancipation, Black activists positioned the economic advancement facilitated by small, planned families as integral to the racial justice agenda. Jessie Rodrique argues, "Economic themes emerged in the birth control discourse as it related to issues of black family survival. Contraceptive use was one of a few economic strategies available to Blacks, providing a degree of control within the context of the family economy."[222] Charles S. Johnson deploys these economic themes writing, "The correction of the environment involves the equalization of economic and social opportunities, but it is still within the power of the group itself to lessen the stress by more intelligent interpretation of the obligation to maintain the race."[223] Johnson's statement acknowledges the oppression felt by Black Americans while simultaneously empowering them to lessen the impacts of this oppression through contraceptive practice. W. G. Alexander, president of the National Medical Association and the first Black man elected to the New Jersey State Legislature labels birth control as the *only* solution to improve the wealth, health, and status of Blacks when he portends, "The economic betterment of the Negro, the health betterment of the Negro, and the betterment of community standards (which is an inevitable corollary) demand a policy and a program that will at least modify his present unfavorable situation. Birth control offers the only reasonable solution."[224] A 1931 editorial in *The Pittsburgh Courier*, a historical Black newspaper, pleads:

> This reduces the whole proposition of birth control to one of economics, pure and simple. This country is rapidly realizing that something must be done in

> order to maintain a decent standard of living for its population and a rightful amount of education; otherwise, our civilization will be dashed upon the rocks of overpopulation, under-sustenance and ignorance. . . . And of all the people who need to know something of birth control, perhaps the Negro stands most in need of a practical intelligence on the subject. Negroes are the smallest wage earned; they are the last to be employed and the first to be fired, and their income is therefore smaller than the average American. . . . Birth regulation is coming, because it must come in self-defense.[225]

The language of self-defense is powerful. Black communities, long robbed of their autonomy and forced to navigate an oppressive system, needed to protect themselves from further oppression through the pursuit of education, advancement, and generational wealth made possible only under a system of voluntary motherhood. Their survival depended on it.

Despite their vocal support of the movement, Black activists struggled to achieve significant involvement in the mainstream movement. The Birth Control Federation of America (BCFA) provided guidance, infrastructure, and resources to Black clinics through their Division of Negro Service and were instrumental in opening clinics in Harlem, Chicago, Nashville, and South Carolina. These clinics ran in conjunction with the BCFA and an advisory board comprised of thirty-five Black leaders including physicians, social workers, nurses, and community leaders.[226] Yet, Sanger and the BCFA kept Black activists at a distance, encouraging their active participation but disallowing them to aid in national planning or manage clinics serving Black patients.

Black women, despite their heavy involvement in clinics and community centers disseminating contraceptive information, were even further removed from these valuable roles. Only one Black woman, Constance Fisher, was included in "The Negro Number" in 1932, and although women held roughly half the seats on the Advisory Council for the Harlem Clinic by the time the movement's efforts coalesced into the Division of Negro Service, only five women served on the twenty-five-person National Advisory Council. This in no way diminishes the contributions of women such as Mary McLeod Bethune, E. Mae McCarroll, Mabel Keaton Staubers, or Dorothy Boulding Ferebee who fought tirelessly for birth control and, according to Joyce Follet, openly criticized white leaders for "undermining the effort by failing to accept black allies as equals."[227] The diminution of Black women reflected the sexism of the times both in the Black community and in the birth control movement. Evidenced by the preponderance of male doctors and academics included herein, Jamie Hart explains the "absence of women's discourse" on the subject of contraception as a direct result of the authority granted to the "male-dominated discussion of birth control as racial progress."[228] Arguments advanced by female activists reflected a deeper concern for "the health and progress of individual African-American women and their families than with 'the race' as a whole," but failed to garner the same currency in elite Black circles preoccupied with racial uplift. This exclusion was also deeply connected to Sanger's own experience of sexism. Follet explains, "After a quarter century on the front lines of the movement, she was keenly aware of male medical practitioners' bias against women, whether health professionals or organizers."[229] Ultimately Black men and white birth controllers disenfranchised Black women in the movement for the same reason—political accommodation. During the 1930s, birth control garnered widespread popular and political support not as a women's issue but as a public health concern and the rhetoric of Black women failed to conform to this prevailing discursive strategy.

The Division of Negro Service didn't survive the transition of the BCFA into the Planned Parenthood Federation of American and a final report on the services rendered through the Division was issued in 1942. After several pages enumerating the Black doctors, academics, activists, and organizations who "have worked constantly to create a widening circle of interest" in contraception, the report compiled by the National Advisory Council boldly concludes:

> The response indicated above, multiplied many times over, demonstrates that Negro leadership is aware of the potentialities of child spacing for health and improved family living. It also demonstrates that it is ready to assume its proper responsibility for interpreting the program and aiding in its integration into existing public health services. Such understanding and willingness to cooperate is an invaluable asset to any community. It can be utilized in any community where extension of planned parenthood as a public health measure is contemplated.[230]

Although short lived, the Division of Negro Service profoundly impacted the uptake of birth control within the Black community and the eventual inclusion of reproductive health services in clinics across the country.

THE LASTING CONSEQUENCES: WHO CHOOSES?

The interwar years were markedly different for the birth control movement. Undergirded by the spirit of progressive politics and fueled by a cultural obsession with professionalization, the movement abandoned its radical roots exchanging agitation for accommodation. Robyn Rosen laments, "Losing track of its original aims to improve the conditions of maternity and liberate women from excessive childbearing, the ABCL began to push through its reform agenda without considering a larger feminist program or its relationship to the women's movement at large."[231] The rebellious spirit of early advocates willing to break laws to secure contraceptive access yielded to the recommendations of experts so far removed from the actual need for birth control. Concern for the individual needs of women gave way to the societal growing pains attendant with shifting demographics amid rapid urbanization. The success of these tactics in securing the endorsement and participation of valued allies confirmed the usefulness of deference and substantiated the strategy of political accommodation for advocates moving forward. As will be explored in chapters 6 and 7, the framework for federal action and the decisions made by the Supreme Court regrading contraception are inseparable from the strategic framing of contraception articulated in this chapter.

In 1941, the Birth Control Federation of America formerly changed its name to the Planned Parenthood Federation of America, and for the first time since its inception the movement no longer carried the phrase "birth control" in its name. Ironically, given the political acrimony invoked at the mere utterance of the phrase Planned Parenthood these days, the move was prompted by a fear that "birth control" had become too controversial and its continued use risked isolating potential supporters—namely physicians and policy makers. The name change holds great rhetorical symbolism as well, solidifying the transition from fringe social movement aimed at empowering women to professional organization aimed at furthering access to medicalized contraception under the watchful eye of government-sanctioned gatekeepers.

To be clear, the strategy of political accommodation pursued vigorously by the movement during the interwar years proved wildly successful in forging support for contraception among physicians. A 1947 study conducted by Dr. Alan Guttmacher surveyed 15,000 physicians regarding their approval of contraception and the indications for its prescription. Physicians overwhelmingly indicated their approval of birth control, with 97.8 percent supporting contraception for health reasons and 79.4 percent endorsing it for economic reasons.[232] Considering the historically conflictual relationship between advocates and physicians, these numbers are remarkable even among a relatively (compared to all U.S. doctors) small sample size. Perhaps most striking is the number of physicians who endorsed contraception for nonmedical reasons. These shifts are directly attributable to the movement's concerted efforts to court doctors by positioning them as authority figures and placing contraception solely under their control.

In many ways, physicians were merely catching up to the prevailing opinion of the time supporting contraceptive use. A series of surveys performed by the American Institute of Public Opinion from 1936 to 1940 provide profound evidence of the widespread acceptance of birth control. When asked in 1937 if respondents "favor the birth control movement," 71 percent said yes and by 1940, 77 percent of respondents not only endorsed the movement but also approved "of having government health clinics furnish birth control information to married people who want it."[233] Advocates parlayed this swell of support into the expansion of clinics. Yet, the continued popularization of contraception and the growth of clinics also created fertile ground for newly sanctioned government stakeholders to exert their influence.

Empowering doctors and eugenicists to exert influence and control over the movement resuscitated the very question advocates long sought to dismiss—could women be trusted to make good reproductive choices? As demonstrated in chapter 4, birth controllers rhetorically rejected the question's paternalist assumptions and vehemently defended women as responsible decision makers. Yet, these alliances shifted the question slightly to suit their unique agendas. Doctors asked, "Could women be trusted to make good reproductive choices *on their own*?" The answer was a resounding no, and the result was the continued medicalization of contraception under the exclusive purview of doctors, pharmacists, and regulatory agencies. Eugenicists framed the question as *whose* reproduction could be trusted? The answer, much like the question, is deeply flawed. However, the even more flawed pursuit of the answer culminated in the creation of coercive sterilization policies pitting white women and women of color against one another in their struggle for reproductive freedom.

Medicalization

The medicalization of contraception is perhaps the most enduring legacy of the movement's alliance with physicians. What began as a request for support morphed into an exclusivity agreement granting doctors absolute control over the dissemination of contraception with the exception of over-the-counter devices such as condoms or spermicidal agents. Court decisions, beginning with Justice Hand's 1918 ruling, cosigned on this exclusivity agreement transforming physicians into government-sanctioned gatekeepers of contraception. The widespread acceptance of population control prompted the exploration of advanced contraceptive methods hoping to provide greater control and reliability throughout the 1940s and 1950s. These new methods were uniquely medicalized, requiring both a prescription and regular checkups for continued use—even more explicitly bringing doctors into the conversation.[234]

In the 1950s, Sanger, with the financial help of longtime ally Katharine McCormick, turned to a team of scientists, including Gregory Pincus, Chang Min-Chueh, and John Rock, in search of a hormonal contraception.[235] After initial testing returned positive results, Pincus began large-scale studies of the pill in Puerto Rico where contraception had been legal since 1937. Despite concerns over side effects, not to mention the implicit racism of the choice to use Puerto Rican women as a test subjects, Pincus returned to the United States in 1957 and began producing Enovid for the treatment of gynecological disorders with the help of G. D. Searle. Although not marketed as a contraceptive until the Federal Drug Administration's approval in 1960, by 1959 over half a million women were already using Enovid for that very reason.[236] The intrauterine device (IUD) promised women even more control over their reproduction by swapping an easy to forget daily pill with a semipermanent implanted device. The IUD, first developed in 1909 by Richard Richter, rose to prominence in the late 1960s as women readily embraced medicalized contraception. By 1970, just two years after its introduction, more than 600,000 Dalkon shield IUDs had been fitted and by 1974 that number grew to almost to 2.2 million.[237]

Unsurprisingly, safety failed to be a top consideration in the rapid development of medicalized contraception. By 1962, at least eight deaths and close to 300 cases of blood clots had been reported among pill users. An official inquiry into the safety of the pill would not be conducted by the FDA until 1969.[238] Despite the fact that IUDs had been informally produced and used for decades, pharmaceutical companies soon began manufacturing them in mass quantities without fully testing their efficacy or their safety.[239] Almost immediately, IUD users began reporting major side effects and complications, including pelvic inflammatory disease and bleeding, leading to one of the largest class action suits in history against Dalkon Shield for medical complications experienced by over 300,000 claimants resulting in at least twenty deaths.[240] The relative failures of medicalized contraceptives and the continued desire for a 100 percent effective, safe, and comfortable form of birth control pushed advocates and women back toward sterilization as a viable option. The American College of Obstetricians and Gynecologists relaxed their guidelines for sterilization in 1969, and by 1972, 30 percent of former pill users had opted for sterilization.[241] Though many women chose sterilization voluntarily, countless others were coerced or incentivized to do so—largely along race and class lines.

By making the medical community the government-sanctioned gatekeepers of birth control, choice will always be constrained by a doctor's decision calculus in terms of who gets access, what method they are provided, and for what purposes they utilize contraception. Andrea Tone laments, the medicalization of contraception has provided "heterosexual young women with the freedom conferred by more reproductive choice" while simultaneously creating a "growing dependence on the practitioners, medical institutions, and the pharmaceutical industry that provides them."[242] It was precisely this claim that motivated liberal feminists to reject the highly medicalized methods of reproductive control popularized in the 1960s and 1970s. Barbara Seaman's 1969 book, *The Doctor's Case against the Pill*, highlighted the failures of the FDA and physicians who pushed oral contraceptives on millions of women with little regard to their unique situations or potential side effects. Seaman labeled this overzealous trend a "violation of civil rights where men who are not at risk from reproduction, control women who are."[243]

The insistence on the medical community's expertise in the area of reproductive control isolated women from the conversation about what they wanted from contraception prompting many women to return to nonmedical methods despite their relatively lower levels of effectiveness. Virginia Berndt and Ann Bell describe the ultimate consequence of medicalization as the elevation of "provider expertise through discrediting women's embodied knowledge" in an effort "to further control women's bodies within and outside the medical realm."[244] Philip J. Hilts explained in the *New York Times* in 1990, "the fear of harm to women remained a theme over the years [so that] feminists now advocate the use of diaphragms or cervical caps."[245] The fact that many women now begin a contraceptive regimen in their teenage years and are presented with a litany of medicalized contraceptives has only amplified these concerns and sparked a renewed interest in nonmedical options which, thanks to technological developments, now boast reliability levels comparable to their medicalized counterparts.

The blatant disregard for women's health in the development of contraception also fueled the creation of the women's health movement, which boasted approximately 12,000 affiliated groups by 1973; most notable among them were the Boston Women's Health Book Collective (BWHBC), the National Women's Health Network (NWHN), and the National Black Women's Health Project (NBWHP). These organizations made lasting additions not just to the birth control movement, but to improving women's health care more broadly. In 1970, the BWHBC published the first edition of *Our Bodies, Ourselves*, a broad reader concerning women's health that remains one of the most comprehensive and popular books on the subject to this day. Formed in 1975, the NWHN functioned as a legal watchdog for women, sustaining major victories against high-dose contraceptives and unsafe intrauterine devices as well as increased research at the federal level concerning toxic shock syndrome, menopause, and fertility treatment. As an advocacy group, the NBWHP focused its efforts on contextualizing birth control within the unique experiences of women of color. The success of the NBWHP spurred the creation of similar organizations among other people of color, including the Native American Women's Health Education Resource Center in 1985 and the National Asian Women's Health Organization founded in 1993.[246] Yet the mere existence of these organizations is a testament to the failures of the mainstream movement in accounting for the needs of women, particularly women of color, who often find themselves victims of the very alliances created by the movement in the 1930s.

Sterilization

Sterilization plays an understandably complex role in the history of the birth control movement. As the most permanent contraceptive option, it promised women an unprecedented level of control over their reproduction. Yet, its permanence also warranted caution . . . in some cases. Alexandra Stern explains, "By the 1960s, the protracted history of state sterilization programs in the United States, and the consolidation of a rationale for reproductive surgery that was linked to fears of overpopulation, welfare dependency, and illegitimacy, set the stage for a new era of sterilization abuse."[247] Stern draws a direct parallel between the abusive sterilization policies of this time with the allocation of federal dollars to family planning. Enacted under Nixon in 1970, the Family Planning Services and Population Research Act, colloquially known as the Title X, provided federal funding via Medicaid for family planning programs for low-income and/or uninsured families. Heralded by advocates as a huge step in eliminating class barriers to contraceptive access for women without the means to consult a private physician, these programs rarely had the best interests of women in mind. As explored more fully in chapter 7, the creation of these programs relied on framing contraceptive access as a societal right and were thus motivated by an obsession with reducing public expenditures and improving social welfare. The needs of women were, and still are, largely an afterthought.

Whereas in 1965 only 450,000 women had access to government supported programs, run exclusively by the states, by 1975 more than 3.8 million women relied on services funded by Title X. Sterilization was commonplace in these programs, with approximately 100,000 procedures carried out annually thanks to a provision within Medicaid reimbursing up to 90 percent of the cost.[248] The legacy of eugenic sterilization policies, particularly in southern states, loomed large over these programs, with Stephanie Flores suggesting these polices were frequently "reworked so women who received federal aid were threatened with the elimination of welfare benefits and were thus coerced to undergo sterilization."[249] Coupled with the fact that 97 percent of new enrollees in the Aid to Families with Dependent Children program during this time were Black, the foundation for the coercive sterilization of Black women was set.[250] Dorothy Roberts explains, "most sterilizations of black women were not performed under the auspices of the eugenic laws. The violence was committed by doctors paid by the government to provide health care for these women."[251] The increasing popularity of sterilization combined with the deep-seated population control concerns of government officials collided to facilitate large-scale sterilization schemes primarily targeting southern Black women who were sterilized through what Roberts bluntly calls "trickery or deceit." Rickie Solinger and Loretta Ross explain the nuance of this trickery:

> When a poor woman arrived at a public health clinic for health care or had just delivered her baby at a public hospital and the physician, a person she probably did not know, pressed her to terminate her fertility, how much latitude did this woman have to assert her own interests? How much did her poverty and lack of education, perhaps her lack of English, and the various other stigmas arrayed against her prevent this woman from objecting to the physician's prescription, sterilization?[252]

A disproportionate number of women of color experienced sterilization precisely because of the systems put in place under the guise of public health but carried out exclusively by doctors and policy makers whose decisions rarely made space for the very women they affected.

Black women struggled to convince gatekeepers of the worthiness of their reproduction while white women struggled against a system that defined their worthiness primarily as reproducers. Historian Heather Munro Prescott argues, beginning in the 1970s "women of color resisted externally imposed policies to limit their fertility while asserting their rights to bodily self-determination. For women of color, reproductive freedom meant not only the legal right to abortion and contraception, but also the freedom to have children."[253] While women of color struggled to gain legitimacy as reproducers, white women fought to legitimate their choice not to reproduce at all. Although women had entered the workforce in droves during WWII, the postwar culture ushered in a return of the domestic ideal insisting "reproduction was white women's most valuable gift to the family, the community, and the nation."[254] These dynamics continue to plague the movement's fight against coercive sterilization by unnecessarily pitting the needs of white women and women of color against one another. Stephanie Flores explains, "The mainstream feminist movement recognized coerced sterilization as a problem for black women, but continued to argue for easier access to sterilizations and abortions for themselves. Their demands directly and negatively impacted Black" women and ignored efforts aimed at "Black women to limit their reproduction."[255] The power and prevalence of these racial dynamics cannot be overstated. Angela Davis laments:

> Over the last decade the struggle against sterilization abuse has been waged primarily by Puerto Rican, black, chicana and Native American women. Their cause has not yet been embraced by the women's movement as a whole. Within

> organizations representing the interests of middle-class white women, there has been a certain reluctance to support the demands of the campaign against sterilization abuse, for these women are often denied their individual rights to be sterilized when they desire to take this step. While women of color are urged, at every turn, to become permanently infertile, white women enjoying prosperous economic conditions are urged, by the same forces, to reproduce themselves. They therefore sometimes consider the waiting period and other details of the demand for informed consent to sterilization as further inconveniences for women like themselves. Yet whatever the inconveniences for white middle-class women, a fundamental reproductive right of racially oppressed and poor women is at stake. Sterilization abuse must be ended.[256]

Despite the movement's attempt to distance itself from the racially motivated aims of eugenicists, it failed to challenge the basic premise of "fitness" at the core of policies and practices determining who gets to choose and what choices are available. Modern advocates merely perpetuated this failure by refusing to acknowledge the different reproductive freedoms needed by women of color. Subsequently, the ability for all women to freely choose their reproductive destinies continues to be hindered by the implicit assumption that some women are more worthy reproducers than others.

Haunted by the specter of empowered voices, the birth control movement of my generation walks a fine line between testing the political will of those who gave the movement its first audience and now demand a say and fighting for the unfettered ability to enact the reproductive rights for those whose voices first called out for birth control. Ironically, it was the birth control movement's very own articulation of a collective societal right to contraception that facilitates the restriction of reproductive rights for countless women. Though well intentioned, defending a societal right to protect itself from unrestricted reproduction contains an implicit tradeoff with the universal exercise of the previously established right of individuals to control their own reproduction by suggesting that there may be a limit to this right. The *Los Angeles Times* highlighted this tension in 1935 suggesting that the use of birth control to improve the quality of the population would undoubtedly require the "relinquishment of the right to procreate"; however, because the "propagation of the unfit constitutes a biological hazard to which no state is bound to stand committed," the *Times* concludes that such a violation of individual rights is necessary to preserve the greater good.[257] Sanger acknowledged the tension between individual and societal rights in her 1938 address at the Conference on Conservation of Human Resources, explaining, "The rights of the individual could be well safeguarded but in no case should the rights of society, of which he or she is a member, be disregarded."[258]

In attempting to resolve this conflict, Sanger suggested that even if societal rights were occasionally prioritized over individual rights, because protecting the welfare of society will in turn preserve the quality of life for the individual, situationally limiting the right to procreate is justifiable. Sanger explicitly acknowledged the link between smaller families and societal welfare in 1925 when she argued in an editorial in the *Birth Control Review*, "smaller families by the instrument of qualitative control, offers an instrument of liberation to overburdened humanity."[259] Even if a society as a whole reaps the benefits of population control, prioritizing societal welfare over individual autonomy enables the willful limitation of reproductive freedom of poor, nonwhite, and non-able bodied women in the name of the greater good and reduces the well-to-do white woman to the role of mother.

Interestingly, Sanger and other birth controllers frequently characterized reproductive rights as universal. For example, a 1932 document prepared by Sanger for the National Committee on Federal Legislation for Birth Control proclaimed: "Birth control information should be the right of every adult man and woman. . . . It should be the woman's right to have knowledge, not because she is sick, diseased, or poor, but because as a woman whose body must be used in the creating and incubation of new life, she should be given the right of choice and time consistent with her desires."[260] Despite these proclamations, birth controllers consistently used the very conditions they said should not matter—health, wealth, and race—as justifications for increased contraceptive access. While doing so certainly brought attention to the disproportionate suffering of impoverished and minority women and highlighted the need for contraception among these populations and not just wealthy women, it also created racist, classist, and ableist assumptions that continue to constrain the full enactment of control and choice over one's reproduction.

Thanks to the dedicated work of women of color aided by the organizations mentioned previously honest conversations are now filtering into the rhetoric surrounding sterilization. The American College of Obstetrics and Gynecology (ACOG) explicitly approaches sterilization "within a reproductive justice framework" positioning "women's reproductive autonomy" as "the primary concern guiding sterilization."[261] ACOG'S 2017 statement from the Committee on Ethics, reaffirmed in 2020, serves as an exemplar of how to engage the historical legacy of sterilization while moving toward true reproductive justice. They proclaim:

> Sterilization practices have embodied a problematic tension, in which some women who desired fertility were sterilized without their knowledge or consent, and other women who wanted sterilization to limit their family size lacked access to it. For example, through the 1970s, obstetrician-gynecologists use the

> guideline that a women's age multiplied by her parity should equal 120 before sterilization was appropriate. This presented a barrier to sterilization for some women, especially white middle-class women who sought care with private physicians. In contrast, many low-income women and women of color in public hospitals were subjected to state and federal programs aimed at limiting their fertility. Between 1909 and 1979, physicians performed more than 60,000 forcible sterilizations in government organized programs. These differential experiences—in which some women could not have a desired sterilization while others underwent undesired sterilization—reflect that a woman's race, ethnicity, and social class affected the ways in which her fertility and childbearing were valued by those with authority to perform or deny sterilization. Reproductive experiences are, therefore, "stratified," such that "some categories of people are empowered to nurture and reproduce, while others are disempowered" to do so.[262]

In many ways, medicalization and government-sanctioned sterilization fulfilled the hope of early birth controllers for the provision of contraception based on social and economic indications rather that purely medical concerns. Yet, because those conditions were determined by government-sanctioned gatekeepers with their own agenda, they were easily manipulated to support racist and classist goals. Publicly funded programs turned the movement's previous alliances into accomplices, as doctors wielded their exclusive power over contraception to carry out racist policies made possible by the legacy of eugenics under the guise of public health—a label early advocates fought ruthlessly to apply to contraception. Ultimately these alliances laid the foundation for a fully medicalized system of contraception directed not by advocates or the women they claim to serve but by government-sanctioned gatekeepers whose main priorities rarely include the needs of women. In this system, doctors and policy makers are the decision makers and women are merely given permission to choose from the options made available to them. When it comes to reproductive decisions, the question of who chooses shouldn't be complicated. And yet it is deeply complicated precisely because women have been disenfranchised from their role as choice makers.

NOTES

1. "Horrible Examples," 4.
2. "'Horrible Examples,'" 1.
3. Ibid.
4. Robinson, *Pioneers of Birth Control*, 77–78.
5. "Why Scientists," 38.
6. "Wake-Up!," 13.

7. Dilla, "The Social," 34.
8. Gordon, "The Politics," 269.
9. Davis, *Women, Race, and Class*, 360.
10. Kosmack, "The Responsibility," 1558.
11. Fishbein, *The Medical*, 142.
12. Reed, *From Private Vice*, 144.
13. Shapiro, *Population Control Politics*, 44; Gordon, *The Moral Property*, 106.
14. Dilla, "The Social," 36.
15. "Doctors Divided," 22.
16. "Mrs. Byrne," 20.
17. McCann, *Birth Control Politics*, 60. Influenced by her encounters with Johannes Rutgers, who had successfully trained nurses and midwives to work in clinics across Holland, Sanger believed that increased partnering between birth controllers and medical professionals would result in a similar training model in the United States.
18. Sanger, "A Twentieth Century," 15.
19. "Editorial Comment," 1918, 16.
20. Margaret Sanger Papers, 229968.
21. "Editorial Comment," 1918, 16.
22. Margaret Sanger Papers, 226876.
23. Ibid., 20.
24. Stopes, *Contraception*, xii.
25. "The Prevention," 473.
26. "The Doctors," 144.
27. "The Prevention," 473.
28. "The Doctors," 144.
29. Ibid.
30. "900 women," 5.
31. Gordon, *The Moral Property*, 181.
32. Bailey, "The Report," 340.
33. Ibid., 341.
34. "900 women," 5; Bailey, "The Report," 342.
35. McLaren, *A History of Contraception*, 232. Beyond the sheer amount of patients seen, the reports generated by the CRB helped sway the medical community in favor of birth control by demonstrating the consequences of women's attempts at abortion and the physical impairments associated with frequent childbirth.
36. "900 women," 6.
37. Dickinson, "Contraception," 600.
38. "Appealing to," 363.
39. Bailey, "The Report," 341.
40. "900 women," 6.
41. Dickinson, "Contraception," 600.
42. Reed, *From Private Vice*, 167.
43. Dickinson, "American Birth," 1153.
44. Dickinson and Vincent, "Our Correspondents'," 293.
45. Pusey, "Some of the," 1907.

46. "Editorial," 223–24.
47. Sage and Cox, "Let Doctors," 323.
48. Ibid., 322.
49. Ibid.
50. Gordon, *The Moral Property*, 208.
51. "The Raid," 154.
52. Ibid.
53. "Editorial," 145.
54. Margaret Sanger Papers, 228424.
55. Reed, *From Private Vice*, 120.
56. "Medical Council Decries," 13.
57. "The Raid," 155.
58. "Doctors Condemn," 3.
59. "Editorial," 145.
60. "Dr. Dickinson," 6.
61. Harris, "A Public," 72.
62. Matsner, "The Physician's," 70.
63. "American Medical," 164.
64. Ibid.
65. Ibid.
66. Ibid., 165.
67. National Committee on Maternal Health, "Birth Control and Contraception," 1169.
68. McCann, *Birth Control Politics*, 183; Reed, *From Private Vice*, 175. Rose Holz argues that the implementation of Dickinson's standards served two purposes: to persuade the medical community of birth control's legitimacy and to convince them that clinics were a viable mechanism for its distribution ("Nurse Gordon," 114).
69. "Organization for," 3.
70. Moore, "Birth Control," 3.
71. "Towards United," 1; "Court Upholds," 4.
72. "Proceedings of," 2217.
73. Yarros, "Objections Disproved," 15.
74. Moore, "Birth Control," 4.
75. "U.S. Loses," 24.
76. *United States v. One Package*, 86 F.2d 737 (1936).
77. "Court Upholds," 3.
78. "Physicians Split," 25.
79. "Proceedings of," 2213.
80. Ibid.
81. Ibid., 2218.
82. "What of," 3.
83. Huntington, "Committee on," 57.
84. Gordon, *The Moral Property*, 195.
85. Ibid., 47–50.
86. Van Vorst, *The Woman*, viii.

87. MacNamara, *Birth Control*, 4.
88. King, *Gods of the*, 92.
89. McCann, *Birth Control Politics*, 41.
90. MacNamara, *Birth Control*, 78.
91. Black, *War against*, 94.
92. "Editorial," 223.
93. Ibid.
94. Sanger, "Birth Control and Woman's," 7.
95. Margaret Sanger Papers, 236585.
96. Margaret Sanger Papers, 225229.
97. Sanger, "Facing the New Year," 3.
98. Margaret Sanger Papers, 240655.
99. Margaret Sanger Papers, 236134.
100. Margaret Sanger Papers, 236134.
101. Cox, "Condemning Birth Control," 18.
102. Margaret Sanger Papers, 236706.
103. "New Society," 5.
104. Black, *War against*, 127–128.
105. Gordon, "The Politics," 265.
106. Black, *War against*, 25.
107. Ibid.
108. Laughlin, "Eugenical Aspects," 88.
109. Black, *War against*, 61.
110. Ellis, "Eugenics and the Uneducated," 8.
111. Todd, "The Well-Born," 1.
112. Whiting, "Relation of," 150.
113. Whiting, "Heredity and," 9.
114. Margaret Sanger Papers, 236021.
115. King, *Gods of the*, 93.
116. Lyon, "Is Birth," 201.
117. Sanger, "Birth Control and Racial," 11.
118. Lyon, "Is Birth," 200.
119. Sanger, "An Answer To," 13.
120. Sanger, "Birth Control and Racial," 11.
121. Hoyt, "Answers to," 12.
122. Sanger, "A Negro Number," 163.
123. Gardner, "Margaret Sanger Tells," H3.
124. DeVilbiss and Laski, "Birth Control," 140.
125. Margaret Sanger Papers, 236396.
126. Zueblin, "MOTHERS FIRST!" 4.
127. Tuttle, "Motherhood," 5–6.
128. Thomson, "Birth Control," 73.
129. Knoblauch, "Editorial Comment," 4.
130. Martin, "Birth Control," 13.

131. Sanger, "The Need for," 227.
132. Sanger, "Birth Contro—Past," 6.
133. Ibid.
134. Sanger, "Facing the," 4.
135. Margaret Sanger Papers, 239042; Sanger, "The Need for," 228.
136. Amos, "To a Jailbird," 7.
137. Blount, "Eugenics in," 7.
138. Margaret Sanger Papers, 229968.
139. Sanger, "Birth Control and Racial," 12.
140. Margaret Sanger Papers, 240655.
141. "Debate between," 14.
142. "Family Trees," 16.
143. Ibid.
144. Margaret Sanger Papers, 237888.
145. DeVilbiss and Laski, "Birth Control," 140.
146. Dickinson, "The Medical," 99.
147. Black, *War against*, 132.
148. "Sterilization," 83.
149. Margaret Sanger Papers, 239501.
150. Margaret Sanger Papers, 240655.
151. "Sterilization," 83.
152. Dilla, "The Social," 34.
153. Sanger, "The Function," 299.
154. Ibid.
155. DeVilbiss, "Birth Control," 140.
156. Sanger, "Conclusions," 22.
157. DeVilbiss, "Birth Control," 140.
158. Margaret Sanger Papers, 240471.
159. "Law to Sterilize," 7.
160. Evans, "How to Keep Well," 10.
161. Margaret Sanger Papers, 240655; "Right to Sterilize," 1.
162. "High Court Voids," 18; McGreevy and Mason, "Gov. Brown Signs."
163. Margaret Sanger Papers, 222421; Margaret Sanger Papers, 236199.
164. Margaret Sanger Papers, 229659.
165. Sanger, "Conclusions," 22.
166. Margaret Sanger Papers, 229968.
167. Margaret Sanger Papers, 240474.
168. Ellis, "Eugenics and the Uneducated," 7.
169. Margaret Sanger Papers, 236120.
170. Sanger, "A Negro Number," 164.
171. Black, *War against*, 134.
172. "Sterilization," 83.
173. Roberts, *Killing the Black*, 79–80.
174. Black, *War against*, 144.

175. Ibid., 135.
176. Burch, "Causes of Future," 24; Roberts, *Killing the Black*, 81.
177. Gordon, "The Politics," 269.
178. Conrad, "On U.S. Birth," 11.
179. Roberts, "The Dark," 81.
180. Davis, *Women, Race, and Class*, 361.
181. Rodrique, "The Black," 260.
182. Dewan, "Anti-Abortion Ads," para. 9.
183. Rodrique, "The Black," 259.
184. Roberts, "The Dark," 82.
185. Ross, "Trust Black," 58; Norwood, "Misrepresenting Reproductive," 715.
186. Norwood, "Misrepresenting Reproductive," 719; Ross, "Trust Black," 60–61.
187. Rodrique, "The Black," 253.
188. Roberts, "The Dark," 87.
189. Bousfield, "Negro Public," 170.
190. Ibid.
191. Du Bois, "Black Folk," 166–67.
192. Roberts, "The Birthright," 87–88.
193. Jamison, "The Future," 95.
194. Sanger, "A Negro Number," 163.
195. "Women Stay-At-Homes," 9.
196. Carter, "Eugenics for," 170.
197. Johnson, "A Question," 169.
198. Carter, "Eugenics for," 169–70.
199. Bousfield, "Negro Public," 171.
200. Garvin, "The Negro," 270.
201. Ibid., 269.
202. Roberts, "The Birthright," 89.
203. Jamison, "The Future," 95.
204. Roberts, "The Birthright," 89.
205. Jamison, "The Future," 94.
206. Johnson, "A Question," 167.
207. Terpenning, "God's Chillun," 172.
208. Schuyler, "Quantity or," 166.
209. DuBois, "Black Folk, 167.
210. Garvin, "The Negro," 269.
211. Carter, "Eugenics for," 169.
212. Ibid.
213. Roberts, "The Dark," 85.
214. Ibid.
215. Hart, "Who Should," 77.
216. Fisher, "The Negro," 174.
217. "Too Many," A3.
218. Roberts, "The Dark," 86.
219. Roberts, "The Birthright," 89.

220. Schuyler, "Quantity or," 165.
221. Roberts, "The Birthright," 89.
222. Rodrique, "The Black," 249.
223. Johnson, "A Question," 168.
224. Alexander, "A Medical," 175.
225. "Birth Control," 10.
226. Rodrique, "The Black," 255.
227. Follet, "Making Democracy," 125.
228. Hart, "Who Should," 3.
229. Follet, "Making Democracy," 108.
230. National Advisory Council on Negro Program, *Better Health*, 28.
231. Rosen, "Federal Expansion," 6.
232. "Doctors in Survey," 28.
233. Gallup, "Birth Control," 3.
234. May, *America and the Pill*, 5.
235. Reed, *From Private Vice*, 359.
236. Gordon, *The Moral Property*, 286.
237. Dittrick Medical History Center, "Intrauterine Devices," para. 2–3.
238. Reed, *From Private Vice*, 365.
239. Tone, *Devices and Desires*, 59.
240. Gordon, *The Moral Property*, 334.
241. Ibid., 343. During the 1970s sterilization was the fastest growing method of contraception, increasing from 200,000 cases in 1970 to 700,000 in 1980; for a more comprehensive look at sterilization policy and practice in the United States, see Shapiro, *Population Control Politics*.
242. Tone, "Medicalizing Reproduction," 326.
243. Bloom, "The 25th Anniversay of *The Doctor's Case against the Pill*," para. 2.
244. Berndt and Bell, "This Is What," 11.
245. Hilts, "Birth-Control Backlash," SM 41.
246. Gordon, *The Moral Property*, 323.
247. Stern, "Sterilized in the," 1132.
248. Ibid., 1133.
249. Flores, "Redefining Reproductive," 22.
250. Harris, *Black Feminists*, 2–3.
251. Roberts, "The Dark," 90–91.
252. Ross and Solinger, *Reproductive Justice*, 51.
253. Prescott, *The Morning After*, 58.
254. Solinger, *Pregnancy and Power*, 137.
255. Flores, "Redefining Reproductive," 25.
256. Davis, *Women, Race, and Class*, 365.
257. Hall, "New Sterilization Bill," 6.
258. Margaret Sanger Papers, 223089.
259. Sanger, "Editorial," 164.

260. Margaret Sanger Papers, 236191.
261. ACOG Committee on Ethics, *Sterilization of*, 7.
262. Ibid., 3.

Chapter Six

Contraception in the Courts

In the wake of the court's decision in One Package, *a reinvigorated Sanger issued a bold call to arms to her fellow advocates. In an uncharacteristic move, Sanger cautioned against complacency and demanded advocates channel this victory into a comprehensive agenda to advance the battle for birth control. She beseeched:*

> *What lies ahead? It is not enough merely to establish the rights of physicians through the Courts. This ethical gain must be used. We have taken a great step forward, but other hurdles must be cleared. With birth control legalized by national statutes, all States should now completely catch up with public sentiment, judicial interpretation and the demand for contraceptive services by clarifying and modernizing the laws. All State laws should be positive, not vague or negative. They should clearly and affirmatively declare and assure the right of medical birth control, not merely fail to forbid it, or limit it. Therefore, I ask all who have so loyally made our legal and medical victories possible, to join efforts with us again in the most important objective—the inclusion of birth control service in local, State and national health programs. In this way only can those mothers most desperately in need of this information secure it through reliable, medical channels. Help make it known to hospitals, relief agencies, philanthropic and public health officials, that the Federal decision has freed their hands. Challenge all plans for the reduction of maternal and infant mortality that ignore the basic need for including contraceptive service in such programs. We must move fast, for women and children are dying needlessly. Individual and group effort can point the way and can do immeasurable good. But those guiding our programs for relief, for the reduction of maternal and infant mortality, and for the control of syphilis, must recognize that the provision of scientific birth control information is essential to the success of all such programs. Next steps in making contraceptive information and service actually as well as legally available to the mothers of America call for modernization of State laws and the incorporation of birth control into medical practice, preventive medicine and public health administration everywhere.*[1]

The *One Package* decision drastically expanded the available options for the movement inspiring a renewed sense of optimism and obligation that is palpable in Sanger's speech. With Comstock Laws functionally void, advocates pushed forward with their agenda to expand contraceptive access. Doing so necessitated a two-pronged approach focusing on both securing government support for contraception, particularly alongside existing programs and public health initiatives, and challenging the remaining state-level laws prohibiting contraception. Doing so also required the movement fully embrace the strategy of political accommodation in hopes of transforming its once antagonistic relationship with the state into a fruitful partnership. Pointing to the movement's actions during the 1930s and 1940s as an exemplar of their strategic orientation to the state, Robyn Rosen argues: "A great historical irony lies in the fact that birth controllers' early mistrust of and hostility toward the state ultimately encouraged a kind of détente with the state. . . . Losing track of its original aims to improve the conditions of maternity and liberate women from excessive childbearing, the ABCL began to push through its reform agenda without considering a larger feminist program or its relationship to the women's movement at large."[2] This détente made the movement more respectable, but did little to accelerate its efforts.

Tracking the movement's progress based on the very metrics Sanger established in her 1936 statement sheds light on its shortcomings; she concludes, "Today there are more than 380 birth control centers in the country. Ten times that number are required to meet the need"; yet, by 1954 there were only 532 clinics in operation—a meager increase of just 150 clinics almost twenty years later.[3] Progress on the legal front was painfully slow as well with the first major change to contraceptive law coming almost thirty years later in 1965. Sanger's vision never quite materialized, and this chapter seeks to find out why through an exploration of the movement's efforts to secure government backing for contraceptive access. Whereas previous chapters focus on the strategic rhetorical choices made by advocates to persuade critics and potential allies, the following two chapters explore the tangible products of the movement's strategy of political accommodation—the legal and legislative victories it facilitated—to determine the lasting consequences of allowing the movement to be driven by incrementalism rather than ideology.

Decided just a little over a year before Sanger's death at age eighty-seven, *Griswold v. Connecticut* represented the culmination of the fifty-year battle to secure access to contraceptive information and devices. The Supreme Court's ruling codified the right of married persons to make reproductive decisions free from governmental intrusion and fundamentally redefined the boundaries of the marital relationship by localizing reproductive decisions within the constitutionally protected realm of privacy. Over the next twelve years the court revisited the question of reproductive autonomy and expanded their ruling to extend the same rights to single persons (*Eisenstadt v. Baird*, 1972) and minors (*Carey v. Population Services International*, 1977). With each successive decision, the court eroded barriers to contraceptive access and acknowledged the importance of reproductive autonomy to the self-direction of one's life.

Despite these momentous victories, contraception continues to be a site of legal contestation. After almost forty years of silence on the subject the U.S. Supreme Court has weighed in on the question of contraceptive access three times since 2014. Although alarming to a new generation of reproductive rights advocates, the court's ruling in *Burwell* (2014) is not altogether surprising when viewed through a historical lens. The very narrative arch of this book illuminates both the glacial pace at which progress is made on contraception and the tentativeness of that progress. According to policy experts Jonathan Moreno and Frances Kissling, the revival of contraception as a contested subject precipitated by *Burwell* and followed by *Little Sisters of the Poor* (2019) suggests that "[t]he commonplace belief that the debate over contraception was settled is now unsettled. Perhaps [because] the settlement is both socially and legally more recent and less assured than we think."[4] This unsettling time certainly warrants worry, but it also provides a catalyst to reconcile the rights framework established in these cases as an ineffective tool for achieving the aims of reproductive justice.

BUILDING THE CASE FOR CONTRACEPTION

From the earliest days of the movement, advocates considered the courts an integral part of their strategy allowing them to slowly chip away at existing laws that initially prohibited contraceptive instruction altogether and later continued to significantly impede access for all women. Remarking on the U.S. Supreme Court's decision not to hear arguments in *The People of New York v. Margaret H. Sanger* in 1919, the *Birth Control Review* proclaimed: "The question whether birth control is woman's constitutional right is still unanswered. For the first time in the history of the United States that question was raised on October 12, when Sanger's case came up in the Federal Supreme Court." Sanger, arrested after opening her first clinic in Brownsville, willingly served her thirty-day sentence but appealed the case in hopes a higher court would invalidate the Comstock Laws halting the full operation of her clinic. The court rejected the case on jurisdictional grounds; yet, the *Review* still acknowledged the significance of the appeal, explaining, "She forced the case into the Supreme Court of the United States and that at the earliest possible moment. . . . The case has been fought through in behalf of American womanhood."[5] Despite the unsatisfactory verdict in the case narrowly permitting doctors to provide contraception for disease prevention, Sanger's first foray into the court system illuminated a tangible path forward for the movement. Unlike the movement's failed legislative efforts, legal action yielded concrete results and carried the added benefit of publicity.

Unsurprisingly, the movement came to rely on the courts to advance their agenda. Morris Ernst and Harriet Pilpel, who regularly represented birth controllers such as Dennett and Sanger in court, applauded this strategy in 1939, noting, "The leaders of the birth control movement have long known that they must advance simultaneously on two fronts, the one legal, the other educational." Ernst and Pipel directly credit the movement's legal victories with the relaxation of laws prohibiting contraception, observing, "just as the Federal laws set the pace for repression in the nation, so the relaxation in their interpretation has had its effect upon the states" and point to the examples of Idaho, Oregon, and North Carolina where laws governing contraception underwent reform as a direct result of the court's liberal interpretation in *United States v. One Package of Japanese Pessaries.*[6] These early cases set the tone for the coming decades of legal battle. Rachel Van Sickle-Ward and Kevin Wallsten argue: "These victories were noteworthy, but also set the stage for ongoing conversations about legitimate and illegitimate uses of birth control, debates that were often policed by mostly male doctors rather than the women in need of the devices."[7] The crowning legal victory for early advocates, *United States v. One Package*, invalidated the Comstock Laws classifying contraception as obscene paving the way for states to liberalize their existing laws; however, the court's narrow interpretation, explored fully in chapter 5, failed to answer the decades-old question before the court as to whether birth control was women's constitutional right. Additionally, while the court's 1936 ruling condoned giving contraceptive information in one's private practice, it retained restrictions on public access in clinics—keeping access out of reach for the very women Dennett and Sanger first sought to save.

Birth controllers stayed out of the courts during the 1940s and 1950s as they shifted their attention to increasing access to contraceptive access via their clinic networks and vigorously pursued more effective contraception options beyond the diaphragm. Historian James Olson suggests, "the development of the birth control pill had not intended to create some sort of moral confrontation; rather it was intended for use by married couples to ensure that procreation would be brought about at an appropriate, predesignated time."[8] Under the existing legal framework, only married women were eligible for contraceptive instruction and early advocates had no intention of changing these provisions.

Even the pill's creator, Dr. John Rock, had not intended to create such a stir and, in fact, envisioned quite the opposite would occur. A devout Catholic,

Rock saw oral contraceptives as "a bridge which Catholics and Protestants might meet in controlling the birth rate . . . [because] the new pills appear to be completely physiological and therefore in accord with nature."[9] Despite long-standing opposition to artificial methods of contraception, such as condoms or diaphragms, Rock believed because oral contraceptives didn't interrupt the reproductive process they were more analogous to the Church's preferred rhythm method than barrier methods. Rock's discovery sparked a revolution in contraception and, as historian Elaine Tyler May argues, "became a vehicle for new laws, policies, and behaviors that altered the relationship between institutional authorities and individuals."[10] Advocates were hopeful that almost half a century after Sanger first brought the issue to the Supreme Court, the time had finally come for the court to weigh in on whether or not women had a constitutional right to contraception.

Significant disparities in access provided advocates a unique opportunity to challenge the remaining state-level Comstock laws and bring the contraception question before the court. Even though privileged women easily obtained a prescription for Enovid from private doctors by claiming they suffered from gynecological or menstrual issues, most clinics remained unwilling to break the law by providing contraceptives. Determined to secure legal contraceptive access in all fifty states, doctors and advocates in Connecticut began the arduous task of challenging the state's Comstock Laws in hopes of creating a test case worthy of the U.S. Supreme Court. On March 29, 1965, then director of the Planned Parenthood League of Connecticut, Estelle Griswold, stood before the court for knowingly violating the law by dispensing contraception to women in their clinics. Three months later, the Supreme Court issued its historic 7–2 vote ruling the denial of contraception a violation of the right to marital privacy.[11]

Two additional cases testing the court's newly established right to privacy soon followed as advocates pushed to expand contraceptive access beyond married persons. *Eisenstadt v. Baird*, brought before the court in 1972, challenged a Massachusetts law prohibiting physicians and pharmacists from providing unmarried persons with medications, devices, or instruments for the prevention of conception. The court's position here was simple: married persons and unmarried persons must be treated equally in the eyes of the law, meaning that in a post-*Griswold* era, single persons must be afforded the same reproductive rights as married couples. Contraceptive access expanded again in 1977 to include minors when the court rendered its decision in *Carey v. Population Services International* striking down a New York law prohibiting the sale of contraception to persons under the age of sixteen. In the majority opinion Justices Brennan, Stewart, Marshall, and Blackmun found "no medical necessity for imposing a medical limitation on the distribution of nonprescription contraceptives to minors."[12] Over a twelve-year period the court provided the birth control movement with a series of major victories dramatically improving contraceptive access for millions of Americans. In its successive decisions the court wrestled with three distinct questions: Does a right to contraception exist, and, if so, who has this right? What is the nature of this right? And, what limits can and should exist regarding this right? In answering these questions, the court provides both legal reasoning and an argumentative rationale articulating the nature of reproductive rights in this country.

Who Has the Right to Contraception?

The question of who has a right to contraception was at the heart of the court's successive rulings. As we examine these cases, it is important to keep in mind the historical context surrounding contraceptive instruction in the United States. From the very beginning, the birth control movement limited the scope of its advocacy to married women with a focus on either young wives seeking full development prior to motherhood or existing mothers desperate to limit the size of their families. As explained in previous chapters, this focus reflected the prevailing heteronormative value structures of the time and proved rhetorically advantageous in negating opposition arguments painting contraceptive users as selfish, anti-child, immoral, and sexually promiscuous. Beyond mere lip service, the movement's emphasis on married women was also a matter of policy. The written procedures of The Cincinnati Clinic on Maternal Health expressly outline who is eligible to receive services at their clinic: "Married women requiring postponement of pregnancy or prevention of childbirth in order to safeguard health, life, or sanity" and "Married couples who for adequate health reasons must postpone child bearing and who wish to space their offspring."[13] These guidelines are demonstrative of the movement's exclusionary policy which, as explained in chapter 2, carried the implicit assumption that all women would eventually choose motherhood especially if allowed to do so on their own terms.

In their early court appearances, advocates fought exclusively for the rights of married women to access contraception. Sanger's attorney Jonah Goldstein argued to the New York Court of Appeals in 1917: "It does not require a careful reading of the Section to see that the law, as it now stands, makes no distinction between *unmarried* women and *married* women. Both are barred from receiving the information. It is the contention of the appellant that a married woman has the fundamental right to determine whether she shall or shall not conceive and when she shall not conceive."[14] Interestingly, the movement clung to its insistence on exclusively aiding married women even after the court all but vacated the Comstock Laws with its 1936 decision in *One Package*. In 1938, advocates challenged a Massachusetts law prohibiting contraception on the grounds that "duly qualified physicians [should] be allowed to provide contraceptive help for married women when it is a question of their health or life."[15]The movement's early rhetoric is telling as advocates routinely elevated the concepts of family planning, voluntary motherhood, and responsible parentage in their discourse rather than female bodily autonomy.

When presented with *Griswold v. Connecticut* in 1965, the court's logic predictably adhered to the existing framework surrounding contraceptive instruction limiting access exclusively to married women. In restating the facts of the case Justice Douglas explains, "They examined the wife and prescribed the best contraceptive device or material for her use."[16] Here, Douglas, writing the majority opinion of the court, references the female patient exclusively by her marital status—it is not the individual woman who seeks contraception but the married woman. Even when seemingly adopting a progressive stance recognizing the myriad concerns necessitating contraception, Douglas situates the locus of these concerns firmly within the marital bedroom. He argues, "We do not sit as a super-legislature to determine the wisdom, need, and propriety of laws that touch economic problems, business affairs, or social conditions. This law, however, operates directly on an intimate relation of husband and wife and their physician's role in one aspect of that relation."[17] In the eyes of the court, married couples had the right to utilize contraception in consultation with their physicians because the marital bedroom "concerns a relationship lying within the zone of privacy created by several fundamental constitutional guarantees."[18] Questioning the enforcement for such a policy, Douglas scoffs: "Would we allow the police to search the sacred precincts of marital bedrooms for telltale signs of the use of contraceptives? The very idea is repulsive to the notions of privacy surrounding the marriage relationship."[19] As such, laws banning contraception prevented married couples from freely making private decisions representing a threat to the traditional marital relationship.

The court's decision had the effect of legalizing contraception for married persons, but in reality what it truly did was create a constitutional right to privacy of which the marital union is a part and acknowledged contraception as a vital consideration for married couples. The court's rhetoric is illustrative. The word "wife" appears five times in the decision, the word "woman" is never utilized, and the word "women" is used only once as a collective noun in a sentence wholly unrelated to the rights of women. These choices speak volumes of the court's mind-set and serves as a crucial reminder that *Griswold* was never truly about empowering women; it was about facilitating responsible reproduction among married couples.

It would be over a decade before contraception was legalized for *all* women. The question of marital status was explicitly brought before the court in *Eisenstadt v. Baird* in 1972. The appellant, William Baird, was arrested in 1967 after the conclusion of a lecture at Boston University where he offered audience members condoms and contraceptive foam in violation of a Massachusetts state law limiting contraceptive access to married couples. Justice Brennan offered the majority opinion for the court overturning the law on the grounds that it violated the Equal Protection Clause of the Fourteenth Amendment. Brennan argues:

> If under Griswold the distribution of contraceptives to married persons cannot be prohibited, a ban on distribution to unmarried persons would be equally impermissible. It is true that in Griswold the right of privacy in question inhered in the marital relationship. Yet the marital couple is not an independent entity with a mind and heart of its own, but an association of two individuals each with a separate intellectual and emotional makeup. If the right of privacy means anything, it is the right of the individual, married or single, to be free from unwarranted governmental intrusion into matters so fundamentally affecting a person as the decision whether to bear or beget a child.[20]

Brennan swiftly dismisses the notion that one's marital status alters the importance or privacy of their reproductive decisions. In doing so, Brennan also provides vital context for what the court means by both "privacy" and the type of decisions that fall within its purview. Simply put, individuals must be free to decide "whether to bear or beget a child" without facing "unwanted governmental intrusion." Brennan simultaneously liberates reproductive decision making from the confines of the heteronormative married relationship and reaffirms the court's exclusive view of contraception as a reproductive technology.

Minors gain access to the same constitutional protection five years later when the court issued its ruling in *Carey v. Population Services* in 1977. Brennan again provides the majority opinion for the court, writing, "Of particular significance to the decision of this case, the right to privacy in connection with decisions affecting procreation extends to minors as well as to adults. . . . State restrictions inhibiting privacy rights of minors are valid only if they serve any significant state interest that is not present in the case of an adult."[21] The court streamlined the clunky language from *Eisenstadt* regarding the decision "to bear or beget a child" into "decisions affecting procreation" and invalidated the last major legal barrier to contraception. The full legalization of contraception took almost twelve years in large part because advocates settled for an incremental approach rather than pushing for a more liberal interpretation of the law in 1965. Despite the fervor of the sexual revolution, or perhaps because of it, advocates argued exclusively for the rights of married women in *Griswold* and subsequently pursued a conservative strategy regarding the remaining laws limiting access.

Even though birth controllers had long abandoned their pursuit of doctors-only bills, the court utilized the contraceptive cases to solidify the rights, or at least standing and authority, of doctors. The legitimation of doctors was, in part, a procedural question prompted by the tricky nature of Comstock Laws targeting the distribution and not the use of contraception. As hinted at in Justice Douglas's incredulous questioning of Connecticut's ability to police the use of contraceptives in the marital bedroom, the existing laws worked by prohibiting distribution of contraceptive material thus limiting possible challengers to doctors and pharmacists capable of directly violating the statute. The court, as Douglas explains in *Griswold*, recognized the standing of the appellants and their ability to assert the rights of their clients to access contraception. Douglas notes, "We think that appellants have standing to raise the constitutional rights of the married people with whom they had a professional relationship. . . . The rights of husband and wife, pressed here, are likely to be diluted or adversely affected unless those rights are considered in a suit involving those who have this kind of confidential relation to them."[22] In recognizing the standing of doctors, the court affirms the role of physicians in providing contraceptive instruction—a role created and ardently defended by early birth controllers.

Despite Baird not having a professional medical relationship with the young women given contraceptive samples at his lecture, Brennan explains the court's decision to grant him standing in *Eisenstadt* arguing, "We think, too, that our self-imposed rule against the assertion of third-party rights must be relaxed in this case just as in *Griswold v. Connecticut*."[23] Brennan elaborates on the justification for giving Baird standing in this case, explaining, "the relationship between Baird and those whose rights he seeks to assert is not simply that between a distributor and potential distributees, but that between an advocate of the rights of persons to obtain contraceptives and those desirous of doing so. The very point of Baird's giving away the vaginal foam was to challenge the Massachusetts statute that limited access to contraceptives."[24] In *Carey* this same rationale for standing was extended to Population Planning Associates Inc. on the grounds that the "concomitant right" to contraception "would be diluted or adversely affected should its constitutional challenge fail."[25] The choice to use professional appellants, albeit procedurally necessary, also served a strategic purpose solidifying the role of doctors in dispensing contraceptive information. Recalling the pushback by feminist advocates against the medical establishment's stranglehold on reproductive technologies explored in chapter 5, legal scholar Paul Lombardo argues that "doctors were named and consciously inserted as parties as a critical part of the litigation strategy in cases" securing the validity of "physician prerogatives within the law."[26] In each instance, the government-sanctioned gatekeepers identified in chapter 5 are granted both legitimacy and the ability to speak on behalf of persons seeking contraception.

The legitimation of doctors goes beyond standing as the court makes an impassioned plea for their continued involvement. In his concurring opinion in *Griswold*, Justice White establishes the importance of utilizing contraception solely under the direction of medical professionals, arguing that "the anti-use statute . . . prohibits doctors from affording advice to married persons on proper and effective methods of birth control" and denies Connecticut couples "access to medical assistance and up-to-date information in respect to proper methods of birth control."[27] The Court concedes traditional barrier methods such as condoms can be used without medical counseling, yet repeatedly emphasizes the doctor's relevance concerning more advanced forms of contraception such as the pill. In *Eisenstadt*, Brennan labels the Massachusetts law a hindrance to a doctor's ability to treat patients, affirming, "The same physician who can prescribe for married patients [has] the same skill to protect the health of patients who lack a marriage certificate, or who may be currently divorced."[28] Brennan reasserts the need for physician involvement in his *Carey* opinion, noting, "an article or instrument, used or applied by physicians lawfully practicing, or by their direction of prescription, for the cure or prevention of disease is not an article of indecent or immoral nature."[29] Justice Powell further clarifies that there is "no constitutional obstacle to state regulation that authorizes other designated adults—such as physicians—to provide relevant counseling."[30] By preserving the role of doctors in conversations concerning contraception, the court grants them a legitimate voice in the discourse and suggests that contraception is not solely a woman's choice, but her doctor's as well.

What Is the Nature of the Right to Contraception?

The right to privacy articulated in *Griswold* admittedly lacked precision as the Justices worked through decades of jurisprudence to carve out a right not actually enumerated in the constitution. As the court expanded their interpretation of who qualified for this right, they simultaneously refined the right itself to provide a more precise definition of privacy generally and reproductive autonomy more specifically. The court most clearly articulates its interpretation of the right to contraception in *Carey*. Justice Brennan, delivering the majority opinion for the court explains: "Although '[t]he Constitution does not explicitly mention any right of privacy,' the court has recognized that one aspect of the 'liberty' protected by the Due Process Clause of the Fourteenth Amendment is 'a right of personal privacy, or a guarantee of certain areas or zones of privacy'" which includes "independence in making certain kinds of important decisions."[31] The types of decisions protected by the court's doctrine of privacy include marriage, procreation, contraception, family relations, and child rearing and education. Brennan furthers, "The decision whether or not to beget or bear a child is at the very heart of this cluster of constitutionally protected choices. . . . This is understandable, for in a field that by definition concerns the most intimate of human activities and relationships, decisions whether to accomplish or to prevent conception are among the most private and sensitive."[32] Whereas *Griswold* identified the marital bedroom as a zone of privacy free from governmental intrusion and *Eisenstadt* merely redefined the marital union as a composite of two individuals thus nullifying the marriage requirement, *Carey* specified the actual decisions of individuals as the constitutionally protected act.

The precision in *Carey* represents a logical progression from the court's previous rulings and is a likely by-product of their 1973 decision in *Roe v. Wade.* Brennan portends:

> The fatal fallacy in this argument is that it overlooks the underlying premise of those decisions that the Constitution protects "the right of the individual to be free from unwarranted governmental intrusion into the decision whether to bear or beget a child." Id., at 453. Griswold did state that by "forbidding the use of contraceptives rather than regulating their manufacture or sale," the Connecticut statute there had "a maximum destructive impact" on privacy rights. 381 U S., at 485. This intrusion into "the sacred precincts of marital bedrooms" made that statute particularly "repulsive." Id., at 485–486. But subsequent decisions have made clear that the constitutional protection of individual autonomy in matters of childbearing is not dependent on that element. Eisenstadt v Baird, holding that the protection is not limited to married couples, characterized the protected right as the "decision whether to bear or beget a child." 405 U S., at 453 (emphasis added) Similarly, Roe v Wade, held that the Constitution protects "a woman's decision whether or not to terminate her pregnancy" 410 U S., at 153 (emphasis added). See also Whalen v Roe, supra, at 599–600, and n. 26. These decisions put Griswold in proper perspective. Griswold may no longer be read as holding only that a State may not prohibit a married couple's use of contraceptives. Read in light of its progeny, the teaching of Griswold is that the Constitution protects individual decisions in matters of childbearing from unjustified intrusion by the State.[33]

The influence of *Roe* is most apparent in the court's rhetorical choices and framing of privacy rights. Prior to *Roe*, the court appeared to be operating under the same foregone conclusion as early advocates that motherhood was an eventuality merely made voluntary through contraceptive practice. Laws prohibiting contraception were accordingly presented as a threat to liberty. *Roe*, however, with its obvious discussion of potential fetal rights, positioned laws limiting a person's reproductive decisions as a threat to autonomy. Brennan appropriately co-opts the language of autonomy from *Roe* to position contraception alongside abortion in terms of "individual autonomy in matters of childbearing," granting credence to the movement's long-standing emphasis on children by choice not by chance. The notion of autonomy also undergirds the court's focus on decisions as the constitutionally protected act rather than the ambiguous notions of privacy or intimacy outlined in *Griswold*.

The successive rulings of the court enabled countless women to legally access contraceptive information and devices; yet their intent was never to extend constitutional protections to contraception itself. Brennan carefully clarifies:

> This is so not because there is an independent fundamental "right of access to contraceptives," but because such access is essential to exercise of the constitutionally protected right of decision in matters of childbearing that is the underlying foundation of the holdings in Griswold, Eisenstadt v Baird, and Roe v Wade. Limiting the distribution of nonprescription contraceptives to licensed pharmacists clearly imposes a significant burden on the right of the individuals to use contraceptives if they choose to do so. Eisenstadt v Baird, supra, at 461–464 (WHITE, J., concurring in result) The burden is, of course, not as great as that under a total ban on distribution. Nevertheless, the restriction of distribution channels to a small fraction of the total number of possible retail outlets renders contraceptive devices considerably less accessible to the public, reduces the opportunity for privacy of selection and purchase, and lessens the possibility of price competition.[34]

This statement is perhaps the most important of any made by the court regarding contraception, as it articulates precisely what protections women have in the eyes of the law. Brennan's clarification classifies the autonomy granted to women to make reproductive decisions free from governmental intrusion as a negative right. In the context of contraception this means that while the government is prohibited from passing laws substantially burdening a woman's ability to freely make reproductive decisions, they have zero obligation to ensure women have access to the requisite resources needed to exercise that freedom.

The articulation of a negative right to reproductive autonomy was most meaningful for women already capable of accessing contraception who could now do so legally. Ross and Solinger further, "the Griswold decision suited the lives of middle class women because its privacy right was appropriate for a woman with access to a physician. . . . Now she could purchase these services legally and privately, without government interference, but achieving this privacy right having what amounted to be the negative right to be left alone was not likely to help women without these resources."[35] The continued disparities plaguing contraceptive access highlight the trouble of approaching reproductive autonomy as a negative right. Reilly Dempsey and Benjamin Meier argue, "Women's health is different from women's civil rights, requiring more than rights to privacy, nondiscrimination, or participation. Although the right to control one's fertility is a pressing reproductive need, reproductive health also encompasses positive rights—the enabling economic, social, and cultural conditions in which choices come to fruition."[36] Unfortunately, given the court's well-established precedent on this question, it is unlikely reproductive autonomy will be reframed as a positive right anytime soon. Robin West's prognosis, although specific to abortion, is equally applicable to contraception. She bemoans:

> To be a meaningful support for women's equality or Liberty, a right to legal abortion must mean much more than a right to be free of moralistic legislation that interferes with the contractual right to purchase one. It must guarantee access to one. . . . But the court has consistently read the constitution as not including positive rights to much of anything from the state, and certainly not to abortion procedures. It is so unlikely as to be a certainty that neither this court nor likely any court will commence a jurisprudence of positive constitutional rights.[37]

As illuminated later when the court's ruling in *Burwell v. Hobby Lobby* is discussed, the classification of reproductive autonomy as a negative right presents significant obstacles for securing legitimate contraceptive access to all women.

Next, even as the court liberalized its interpretation to include single persons and minors, they clung to the procreative framework first manifest in the *Griswold* decision. While it may appear superfluous to say the court's landmark decision on contraception focused almost exclusively on its role as a reproductive technology, the choice to discuss contraception from a heteronormative procreative framework is of great importance. As explored in previous chapters, early advocates routinely emphasized the physical and spiritual benefits of voluntary parenthood and espoused contraception as a vital form of preventative medicine. Yet, the *Griswold* court completely ignored the myriad uses for contraception instead focusing only on its direct bearing on reproduction. Two points are illustrative here. First, the court derives the right to privacy from its established precedent regarding "the liberty of parents and guardians to direct the upbringing and education of children under their control" as established in *Meyer v. Nebraska* and *Pierce v. Society of Sisters*.[38] The court places contraception alongside a constellation of activities occurring within the "realm of family life which the state cannot enter" and thus articulates its relevance solely as a reproductive technology necessary for family planning.[39]

Second, the court gives only a passing mention to the non-procreative reasons potentially motivating contraceptive use. Justice White briefly acknowledges contraceptive use may be "dictated by considerations of family planning, health, or indeed even of life itself," but fails to incorporate any of these considerations in his defense of contraceptive access.[40] Instead White focuses the bulk of his concurring decision on the ineffectiveness of the law to achieve its stated purpose of curtailing illicit sexual relationships. Forgetting the fact that millions of women, including most of the original Enovid users, sought contraception to mitigate a variety of gynecological and hormonal issues, the court evaluated contraception through the myopic lens of whether to bear or beget a child. This rhetorical move further solidifies the court's procreative framing of contraception by suggesting laws shall not impede one's decision to "prevent conception or terminate a pregnancy" while altogether ignoring contraceptive use for non-procreative means. In doing so, the court protected contraceptive access not because it served the needs of women but because it served the needs of the traditional family unit.

The potency of the court's heteronormative framework is apparent when tracing the application of *Griswold* to cases not dealing directly with reproductive rights. In 1986, the court considered whether the precedent set by the privacy cases applied to acts of sodomy in *Bowers v. Hardwick*. The court's track record of invalidating state laws seeking to regulate appropriate sexual behavior provided every indication that they would do so again in the case of Georgia's law criminalizing sodomy. However, in a controversial 5–4 decision, the court refused to expand the umbrella of privacy to include intimate relationships between members of the same sex. Justice White delivered the majority opinion for the court proclaiming:

> No connection between family, marriage, or procreation on the one hand and homosexual activity on the other has been demonstrated, either by the Court of Appeals or by respondent. Moreover, any claim that these cases nevertheless stand for the proposition that any kind of private sexual conduct between consenting adults is constitutionally insulated from state proscription is unsupported. Indeed, the Court's opinion in *Carey* twice asserted that the privacy right, which the *Griswold* line of cases found to be one of the protections provides by the Due Process Clause, did not reach so far.[41]

White doubles down on the heteronormativity arguing that unlike reproductive decisions, consensual sodomy does not constitute a fundamental liberty because it is not "deeply rooted in this Nation's history and tradition."[42] White's decision vocalized an assumption baked into the court's previous rulings that the constitutionally protected "realm of family life" applied exclusively to those upholding traditional notions of family, marriage, and procreation. The *Bowers* decision is also the first time the court openly acknowledges the inherent relationship between contraception and non-procreative sex. Of course, it wasn't Justice White who offered this insight but instead Justice Stevens in his dissenting opinion; Stevens asserts: "The essential 'liberty' that animated the development of the law in cases like *Griswold, Eisenstadt,* and *Carey* surely embraces the right to engage in nonreproductive, sexual conduct that others may consider offensive or immoral."[43] Taken together, the statements of White and Stevens confirm the court's characterization of contraception not as a mechanism of sexual liberation for women but as tool to facilitate the careful planning of procreation.

Sadly, the court's myopic view of sex cannot be divorced from the rhetoric of early birth control advocates who defended contraception utilizing the very same heteronormative logic. Consistent with their strategy of political accommodation, advocates routinely incorporated appeals to traditional heteronormative values to justify contraceptive instruction. These appeals take center stage in chapters 2 and 4 when advocates defend contraception's role in professionalizing motherhood and preserving marital bliss. These appeals also form the backbone of the movement's demand for contraceptive access enabling women to plan their pregnancies in relation to their husband's earning power. Modern advocates frame contraception as a tool for empowerment, sexual liberation, and freedom of choice when neither early advocates nor the court envisioned contraception as much more than a tool to responsibly plan one's family in accordance with traditional heteronormative values.

What Are the Limits to This Right?

Even the rights expressly enumerated in the Constitution have limits the nature of which are carefully negotiated by the courts as cases arise testing the scope of those limits. The decisions proffered by the court seek to articulate the extent to which a person's right must be protected. The need for such clear limits is particularly prominent in the case of negative rights wherein the purpose of the right itself is to prevent the state from unduly infringing on its existence. In the case of reproductive autonomy, this does not mean states cannot impose regulations on contraception but must do so without "having a maximum destructive impact upon a protected relationship."[44] At the time of the court's decision in *Griswold* (1965), contraceptive options were far more limited than they are today. Aside from traditional barrier methods, women had their choice of either hormonal contraceptive pills or rudimentary versions of today's IUD. Accordingly, while *Griswold* speaks very little to specific contraceptive methods, it does establish a framework for states wishing to regulate contraceptive services.

Justice Douglas, writing for the majority, grants states the right to regulate the sale and distribution of products intended for general consumption so long as their efforts do not "sweep unnecessarily broadly and thereby invade the area of protected freedoms."[45] Taking great care to acknowledge the state's role as a regulatory agency charged with protecting public health, Douglas invalidates the Connecticut law because in prohibiting rather than regulating contraception, the state overstepped its bounds. Justices Goldberg and Brennan echo this sentiment in their concurring opinion, noting, "where fundamental liberties are involved, they may not be abridged by the States simply on a showing that a regulatory statute has some rational relationship to the effectuation of a proper state purpose."[46] Ultimately, the court's ruling requires states provide a compelling justification in order to violate a right as fundamental as reproductive autonomy.

The court recognizes two distinct state interests warranting the regulation of contraception: public morality and public health. Initially, despite Justice Stewart's description of the Connecticut statute as "an uncommonly silly law," the court maintained the state's regulatory aims were not wholly illegitimate. Justice Goldberg explains in *Griswold*, "it should be said of the court's holding today that it in no way interferes with a State's proper regulation of sexual promiscuity or misconduct."[47] Responding to the stated intent of the law to reduce sexual impropriety, the court considered Connecticut's legislative aim valid even though the chosen mechanism was deemed overbroad. Justice White elaborates in his concurring opinion, "The State's policy against all forms of promiscuous or illicit sexual relationships, be they premarital or extramarital, [is] concededly a permissible and legitimate legislative goal."[48] Even though the court found the prohibition of contraception an ineffective method of preventing licentiousness, they validated the state's goal and solidified their role in the discourse surrounding sex and reproduction. In doing so, the court merely placed a higher burden on state legislatures by applying an increased level of scrutiny to regulatory measures impacting reproductive autonomy.

This framework was not unanimously endorsed and frequently dominated the dissenting opinions of Justices opposed to hamstringing the state's ability to legislate in the name of public morality. In his dissenting opinion in *Carey*, Justice Rehnquist criticizes the plurality for unreasonably restricting a state's ability to enact policies, including ones supported by their citizens, aimed at curtailing inappropriate sexual relations among minors. Rehnquist scolds: "The majority of New York's citizens are in effect told that however deeply they may be concerned about the problem of promiscuous sex and intercourse among unmarried teenagers, they may not adopt this means of dealing with it."[49] Justice Powell, who concurred only in part of the decision in *Carey*, directly challenges the court's compelling interest framework. He bemoans, "Neither our precedents nor sound principles of constitutional analysis require state legislation to meet the exacting 'compelling state interest' standard whenever it implicates in sexual freedom."[50] Powell admits the applicability of the framework in *Griswold* and *Baird* wherein regulation "heavily burdens the exercise of constitutional rights," but cautions that "a test so severe that legislation rarely can meet it should be imposed by courts with deliberate restraint."[51] Against the backdrop of the court's heteronormative framework prioritizing contraception's reproductive function, these arguments read as a last ditch effort to embolden states to legislate morality in accordance with traditional norms of marriage, family, and procreation.

States also justified the regulation of contraception in the name of public health. The increasing popularity of medicalized birth control devices, namely the pill and IUD, reinvigorated attempts at the state level to regulate the production, distribution, and use of contraceptives. The court formally weighed in on these new regulations in *Eisenstadt.* Originally written in the context of a Massachusetts state law requiring all persons to obtain a prescription for contraception, the clarification provided by Justices White and Blackmun aptly sketches the boundaries of state regulation regarding contraception. They explain, "A State's interest in the health of it citizens empowers it to restrict to medical channels the distribution of products whose use should be accompanied by medical advice. . . . Requiring a prescription to obtain potentially dangerous contraceptive material may place a substantial burden upon the right recognized in Griswold, but that burden is justified by a strong state interest."[52] Given the widespread availability of nonmedical contraceptives, such as condoms, spermicide, and vaginal sponges, whose use requires no formal medical instruction, Blackmun and White carefully clarified the state's interest in regulating only some contraceptives—those deemed potentially harmful and/or requiring medical consultation for safe usage. To be clear, protecting women from potentially hazardous materials is a laudable goal; however, the use of doctors and lawmakers as the sanctioned gatekeepers of contraception constrains the autonomy of women making these decisions especially given the push for more over-the-counter contraceptive options.

Cognizant of the precedent set by the court invalidating numerous state laws, Brennan carves out space in his opinion to reassure states that their interest in regulating contraceptive access remains valid. He writes, "That the constitutionally protected right of privacy extends to an individual's liberty to make choices regarding contraception does not, however, automatically invalidate every state regulation in this area . . . even a burdensome regulation may be validated by a sufficiently compelling state interest . . . [because] the right is not absolute. . . . 'Compelling' is of course the key word, where a decision as fundamental as that whether to bear or beget a child is involved."[53] The court's conclusion regarding the regulation of contraception contains two key elements. First, any regulation must stem from a legitimate state interest; second, such a regulation is permissible so long as it does not restrict contraceptive access to the point where the right becomes impossible to exercise. In the eyes of the court, as long as women are not completely prohibited from accessing contraceptives, the government has no obligation to ensure contraceptives are genuinely accessible. In this context, reproductive choice is never an absolute right ensuring unfettered access to contraceptives; rather, it is a conditional right made available within a regulatory system suited to the state's paternalistic aims.

Sixty-three years. Realistically it took centuries, but in the context of the U.S. battle for birth control, it took sixty-three years of concerted action for all women to be granted the right to make their own reproductive decisions. Justice Sandra Day O'Connor acknowledged the continued impact of these cases in her 1992 majority opinion in *Planned Parenthood of Southeastern Pennsylvania v. Casey*. O'Connor proclaimed:

> These matters, involving the most intimate and personal choices a person may make in a lifetime, choices central to personal dignity and autonomy, are central to the liberty protected by the Fourteenth Amendment. . . . We have no doubt as to the correctness of those decisions. They support the reasoning in *Roe* relating to the woman's liberty because they involve personal decisions concerning not only the meaning of procreation but also human responsibility and respect for it. An entire generation has come of age free to assume [this] concept of liberty in defining the capacity of women to act in society and to make reproductive decisions.[54]

Yet, while generations of women have built their lives under the assumption of reproductive autonomy, this right isn't as fundamental as either the court or contemporary reproductive rights rhetoric would have you believe. In fact, it remains contested and vulnerable precisely because of the movement's failure to push for more and the court's predictably narrow interpretation of what is required to meaningfully exercise one's reproductive autonomy. The same generation of women whom O'Connor references are now coming to terms with this vulnerability.

TESTING THE REPRODUCTIVE RIGHTS FRAMEWORK

After more than forty years of stasis on the question, birth control would again find itself on the Supreme Court docket, only this time concerning issues of access rather than eligibility. On February 23, 2012, Georgetown University law student Sandra Fluke sat before the House Democratic Steering and Policy Committee and delivered gripping testimony extolling the imperative of contraceptive access for women's health. Fluke spoke eloquently about the critical health care needs of women and the use of contraception for the prevention and treatment of life-threatening gynecological disorders. This, however, was not the original plan. The intended audience for Fluke's testimony was the House Oversight Committee in a scheduled hearing on the religious exemptions to the Affordable Care Act's (ACA) Contraceptive Mandate. On the eve of the hearing, Fluke was notified she would not be allowed to speak—her time allotted instead to the five-person all-male panel consisting of three religious figureheads and two professors, none of whom, of course, had ever used medical contraceptives. Fluke and the all-male panelists quickly evolved into the symbolic figureheads of the controversy surrounding the contraceptive mandate, pitting reproductive rights against religious liberty.

The contraceptive mandate, requiring employers to provide coverage for all FDA-approved contraceptives prescribed in accordance with preventative health services guidelines, was easily the most controversial provision of the ACA. In addition to dominating congressional debate over the bill, when made available for public comment, the contraceptive mandate received 147,000 separate comments while the second most popular topic, coverage for pre-existing conditions, received only 4,600.[55] The original bill included an exemption for religious organizations, like churches, known as the Blunt Amendment; yet, conservative policy makers still harpooned the mandate for infringing on the free expression of religion for closely held companies and nonprofits excluded from the exemption. Despite Fluke's impassioned plea that women who work for "a religiously affiliated employer . . . suffe[r] financially, emotionally, and medically, because of this lack of coverage," the Senate moved forward with the amendment.[56] After weeks of debate, the amendment failed 51–48 and contraceptive coverage for women regardless of their employer's beliefs was secure . . . temporarily.

It was only a matter of time before an official challenge to the mandate made its way to the U.S. Supreme Court. Two corporations, Hobby Lobby and Conestoga Wood, challenged the ACA's failure to exempt closely held organizations (private companies with limited shareholders) arguing the mandate forced them to violate their religious beliefs by facilitating the use of contraceptive measures they considered abortive in nature. On June 30, 2014, the U.S. Supreme Court ruled on a 5–4 decision in favor of Hobby Lobby and Conestoga Wood upholding the right of closely held organizations to conscientiously object to the ACA's contraceptive mandate. It was the first time the Court deliberated on contraception in almost four decades, and the sentiment of their ruling was clear: when in conflict with other state interests, such as religious freedom, women's health is a secondary concern.

Burwell v. Hobby Lobby provided a unique opportunity to test's the court's framing of contraception as a negative right by presenting a question regarding the quality of contraceptive access, whereas previous cases considered only questions of eligibility. Two unique characteristics of the case are worth addressing. First, where previous cases skirt the health concerns of women by considering contraception solely as it relates to reproductive decisions, in *Burwell* the court directly examined the role of contraception in addressing the medical needs of women. Second, unlike previous laws challenged for prohibitively restricting contraceptive access, the law challenged in *Burwell* sought to increase contraceptive access. As the first contraception case decided by the courts in almost four decades, *Burwell* was a major moment for the court and an indication of the court's current views on contraception.

Contraception Is Not Health Care

The ACA's contraceptive mandate marked a significant departure from the government's historically apathetic stance on securing contraceptive access for women. Whereas previous attempts at government-funded contraception provided only minimal access for some, the ACA aimed to make contraception genuinely accessible to all women by outsourcing the responsibility to provide contraception to the private sector. The ACA also sought to bring U.S. healthcare practices in line with accepted standards of care for women specifically regarding preventative medicine and reproductive health. The mandate helped more than fifty-five million women secure zero-cost contraception for an impressive savings of $1.4 billion dollars in 2013 alone.[57] The very nature of the law forced the court to consider the relationship between contraception and health care; yet, this was admittedly unchartered territory for the court as previous decisions only entertained the question of health as it related to protecting women from potentially hazardous materials and the unique relationship between women and medical practitioners. In *Burwell*, the court predictably reaffirms the role of physicians as government-sanctioned gatekeepers but fails to move beyond their traditional framing of contraception as a reproductive technology to acknowledge its importance to women's health generally.

Unsurprisingly, the *Burwell* court's rhetoric reasserted the necessity for doctors to be included in conversations about contraception. In her dissenting opinion, Justice Ginsburg argues, "Congress left health care decisions—including the choice among contraceptive methods—in the hands of women, with the aid of their health care providers."[58] Even when advocating for women's choice, Ginsburg herself reinforces the court's paternalistic framing of women's reproductive decisions. On numerous occasions, Ginsburg speaks of women and their physicians as if they are one unit referring to them as "independent decisionmakers (the woman and her health counselor)" and later bluntly stating contraceptive decisions belong to both parties equally. She writes, "Any decision to use contraceptives made by a woman covered under Hobby Lobby's or Conestoga's plan will not be propelled by the Government, it will be the woman's autonomous choice, informed by the physician she consults."[59] The court's continued insistence on the involvement, and even autonomy, of government-sanctioned gatekeepers removes complete control from women by suggesting their choices should always be made in counsel with medical professionals. This is not to say that all contraception should be available over the counter or that doctors are irrelevant in conversations about contraception; however, the choice to grant doctors a voice in the discourse surrounding reproductive rights does pose a threat to a woman's reproductive autonomy by making her contraceptive choices beholden to the perspective of her medical providers—which historically has not worked out so well. Taken together, these actions prioritize the concerns of external stakeholders over that of women—allowing others to restrict contraceptive access with zero regard to the specific wants and needs of women and fueling the medicalization of contraception discussed in chapter 5.

Even though *Burwell* presented the court with an ideal opportunity to discuss contraception as relevant to women's health, the only acknowledgment of contraception's alternative medical applications comes from Ginsburg's bold dissent. Ginsburg reminds the court, "the [contraceptive] mandate secures benefits wholly unrelated to pregnancy [including] preventing certain cancers, menstrual disorders, and pelvic pain."[60] Justice Kennedy acknowledges "the mandate serves the Government's compelling interest in providing insurance coverage that is necessary to protect the health of female employees" yet simultaneously limits his exploration of the actual health concerns of women to the simple statement that "there are many medical conditions for which pregnancy is contraindicated."[61] Kennedy's statement is both accurate and extremely shortsighted, reflecting the court's historically limited construction of contraceptives as a reproductive technology, considering the only prescient health concern he addresses are those which make pregnancy undesirable.

The majority's framing of contraception exclusively through a procreative framework also draws a clear and problematic distinction between reproductive health and women's health essentially treating the two as separate entities. Sharon Levin of the National Women's Law Center chastised the majority for "specifically fram[ing] birth control as something 'different' when it distinguished birth control from other health care services" arguing that it was precisely this framing that allowed the court to determine that "it could treat birth control worse than other preventative health services by allowing employers to refuse it."[62] The court intentionally clarifies the scope of their ruling as applicable only to contraception and no other medical procedures or drugs such as vaccinations or blood transfusions even if they "conflict with an employer's religious beliefs."[63] When given the opportunity to defend the reproductive health needs of women, the majority balked but was sure to validate a litany of other medical procedures in the meantime. Ginsburg's vehement defense of contraception as integral to women's preventative health care had fallen on deaf ears, but the stakes couldn't be higher. Susan Kendig (2014), Director of Policy for the National Association of Nurse Practitioners in Women's Health, laments: "[L]imiting the ability of some women to choose among all FDA-approved contraceptive methods, based on their employer's values and belief system . . . create[s] uneven access to evidence-based healthcare services shown to have a profound impact on women's overall health."[64] Ginsburg's dissent demonstrates the court's concern is not, and has never been, women's health, as both their rulings and their rhetoric address contraception solely as a reproductive technology that should be regulated as such.

The court's choice to foreground reproduction as the primary justification for seeking contraception obscures its alternative medical applications, and more troublingly, enables the very opposition voiced by Hobby Lobby and Conestoga Wood in their rejection of the contraceptive mandate. Justice Alito explains in the majority opinion for the court: "[T]he owners of the business have religious objections to abortion, and according to their religious beliefs the four contraceptive methods at issue are abortifacients."[65] Alito willingly ignores both the factual inaccuracies of the claim and the importance of these specific contraceptive options. A frustrated Ginsburg reminds her colleagues, "Hobby Lobby and Conestoga resist coverage for only 4 of the 20 FDA-approved contraceptives does not lessen [the government's] compelling interest" especially when many of these devices are "significantly more effective, and significantly more expensive that other contraceptive methods."[66] Ultimately, the court held that even though contraception was necessary to avoid the health problems of unintended pregnancies, prohibiting these types of contraception did not create an undue burden to women as other methods exist to achieve the same ends. The precedent set by the court is unnerving:

so long as contraceptive options exist that meet women's most basic health needs, women cannot be assured the freedom to choose the method of control best suited to their specific needs.

The court's continued refusal to acknowledge contraception as a necessary health care measure places birth control on the same trajectory as abortion, as the rhetorical moves made by the court mirror the strategies leveraged by pro-choice advocates to restrict abortion access. Michelle Goldberg argues, "The anti-abortion movement has been very successful at separating abortion from other forms of routine medical care . . . [and] we're currently in the midst of a coordinated attempt to do the same thing to birth control."[67] Even though abortion, like contraception, is often necessary to protect the health of the woman, by refusing to acknowledge these treatments as concomitant with routine medical care, opponents to reproductive choice successfully mitigate one of the most compelling reasons for the right's existence. Additionally, because women are only guaranteed enough contraceptive access to preserve their basic decision-making capability, efforts to restrict contraceptive methods are legitimated without considering how such restrictions limit a woman's ability to choose the ideal method for her specific medical needs. Goldberg's warning is apt: "However narrowly construed, today's Supreme Court decision [in *Burwell*] will only encourage such efforts, and that should worry all women, wherever they work."[68] *Burwell* thus represents both a legal and ideological victory for those seeking to restrict contraceptive access by invalidating one of the most important claims advanced in favor of birth control—that a women's ability to control her reproduction is necessary to ensure her continued health and well-being.

Reevaluating the Negative Rights Framework

The *Burwell* case provided a unique opportunity for the court to expand their negative rights framework by upholding a policy aimed at increasing contraceptive access to all women. The ACA's contraceptive mandate is unlike any other law governing contraceptive access previously examined by the court. Rather than prohibiting contraceptive access, the mandate operated within a positive rights framework by attempting to ensure all women could enjoy the liberty granted to them to make reproductive decisions. As previously mentioned, the court openly acknowledged "the interest in guaranteeing cost-free access to the four challenged contraceptive methods is a compelling governmental interest."[69] Appellants in the case, however, argued that removing coverage for those methods considered abortifacients did not impede women's reproductive choice. For the first time, the court was asked to go beyond a consideration of basic access to determine the level of access necessary to preserve a woman's autonomy in making reproductive decisions.

The situation in *Burwell* was also unique because it pitted two rights deemed fundamental by the court against one another—the free exercise of religion and the right to privacy. Given the high stakes of both rights discussed in the case, the court's previous declaration that reproductive choice is not an absolute right understandably fell at the heart of the *Burwell* decision. Subsequently, the court was tasked with determining who faced a larger burden to exercising their fundamental rights—corporations or their employees. Justice Alito contends in the majority opinion, "HHS has not shown that it lacks other means of achieving its goal without imposing a substantial burden on the exercise of religion by the objecting parties in these cases."[70] Alito pointed to the mandate's existing exemptions for religious organizations, such as churches, to prove the existence of a "least restrictive option" to achieve the goals of the mandate. Referencing the exemption given to corporations with less than fifty employees as well as nonprofit organizations, Alito continues, "the principal dissent identifies no reason why this accommodation would fail to protect the asserted needs of women as effectively as the contraceptive mandate, and there is none."[71] The court held that absent an exemption, corporations must choose between violating their religious beliefs and dropping health insurance all together, the latter of which results in hefty annual fines. As such, Alito concludes the mandate effectively compels religious corporations to abandon their religious commitments in order to remain operational and profitable, effectively leaving corporations with little to no legitimate choice in the matter.

Having established the burden imposed on corporations by the mandate, the court turned its attention to the potential burden for women created by providing an exemption. Alito finds no major burden is felt by female employees seeking contraception, arguing that employees "would face [only] minimal logistical and administrative obstacles" with no explanation of what these obstacles might entail.[72] Justice Ginsburg picks up the slack for Alito, explaining in her dissent, "the cost of an IUD is nearly equivalent to a month's full-time pay for workers earning the minimum wage."[73] Making matters worse, Ginsburg argues the alternatives described by Alito "would require a woman to reach into her own pocket . . . and would do nothing for the woman too poor to be aided by a tax credit."[74] Despite Ginsburg's impassioned plea, the court's previously established regulatory framework only evaluated whether a restrictive mechanism wholly prohibits access, making questions of cost or efficacy irrelevant considerations. By arguing that exempting closely held corporations from the ACA mandate does not create a substantial burden on its female employees' ability to access contraception, the court reinforces the idea that reproductive choice is not an absolute right—or at least not one that takes precedence over other fundamental rights. In this way, the court reduces reproductive choice to a flawed question of whether contraceptive access exists rather than whether contraception is genuinely accessible.

Testing the Limits of *Burwell*

The court attempted to thread a very small needle in *Burwell*, striking a compromise between women's reproductive rights and the free expression of religion that left both sides clamoring for more protection. Predictably, it took less than a year for another set of cases testing this delicate compromise to make its way to the Supreme Court. In 2016, *Zubik v. Burwell* consolidated seven cases brought forth by nonprofit religious institutions claiming the compromise struck in *Hobby Lobby* still forced religious institutions to facilitate contraceptive use they ideologically opposed. The court issued a per curiam order vacating the cases, requiring the plaintiffs and the government to find a workable compromise—a decision providing no greater certainty for activists battling against policies aimed at restricting reproductive rights.

In the oral arguments presented during *Zubik*, the court's refusal to acknowledge non-procreative contraceptive use became apparent, as several male justices hypothesized a separate opt-in contraceptive policy as a suitable compromise. In her concurring opinion, Justice Sotomayor chastises her colleagues for their shortsightedness, reminding them that not only do such policies not exist, but their creation "would leave in limbo all the women now guaranteed seamless preventative-care coverage . . . [by imposing] precisely the kind of barrier to the delivery of preventive services that Congress sought to eliminate."[75] The fact that numerous Justices found it suitable to isolate contraceptive coverage from general health insurance policies illustrates the court's long-standing framing of contraception as a reproductive technology born of convenience rather than a necessary element of comprehensive health care for women—a position established in *Griswold*, affirmed in *Burwell*, and put on full display in later rulings.

Before the department of Health and Human Services even had a chance to formulate new rules in accordance with the per curiam order, the Trump administration issued Executive Order 13798 on May 4, 2017. The order, entitled "Promoting Free Speech and Religious Liberty," specifically directed government agencies including the HHS to amend the provisions of the contraceptive mandate to include exemptions based on religious beliefs. Legal scholar and activist Katie Keith explains the purpose of Section Three labeled "Conscience Protections with Respect to Preventive-Care Mandate." She writes, "These exemptions applied to any employer that objects to 'establishing, maintaining, providing, offering, or arranging [for] coverage or payments for some or all contraceptive services' based on sincerely held religious beliefs and extended to include for-profit and publicly traded entities."[76] With this executive order, the Trump administration rendered all former accommodations proposed by HHS and the court entirely optional opening the floodgates for companies to deny contraceptive coverage under the banner of religious liberty.

The attorneys general of thirteen states challenged the order and secured an injunction against its implementation sending the issue of contraception back to the Supreme Court. In the summer of 2020, the court heard arguments in the consolidated case of *Little Sisters of the Poor v. Pennsylvania* and *Trump v. Pennsylvania* and issued its 7–2 decision upholding the executive order. Justice Thomas delivered the majority opinion for the court, but the most inflammatory rhetoric unsurprisingly came from Alito who vehemently defended the court's initial ruling in *Burwell* which he authored. In his zealous opinion, Alito essentially writes a blank check for organizations seeking religious exemptions regarding contraceptive coverage and eviscerates any chance of a positive rights framework by summarily dismissing the government's stated interest in providing seamless contraceptive access.

Whereas the appellants in *Burwell* only objected to the four contraceptive methods they considered abortive in nature, the appellants in both *Zubik* and *Little Sisters of the Poor* objected to *all* forms of contraception, arguing the mandate forced them to be complicit in their employees' use of contraception. Given the expanded scope of the objection, the court accordingly evaluated whether such a position qualified as a sincere religious objection. Advocates, long at war with religious institutions rejecting contraception on moral grounds, were hopeful the court would consider the inherent difference between abortion and contraception when evaluating appellants' claims. The court did no such thing and instead refused to evaluate the substantive content of religious claims all together. Alito explains, "It is undisputed that the Little Sisters have a sincere religious objection to the use of contraceptives and that they also have a sincere religious belief that utilizing the accommodation would make them complicit in this conduct. As in Hobby Lobby, it is not for us to say that their Religious beliefs are mistaken or insubstantial."[77] The court's impartiality on the subject, while seemingly commendable, is actually quite alarming. Legal scholar Jennifer Denbow articulates the cause for alarm, arguing, "The Court thus abdicates to the corporations' own interpretation of judicial questions. This move is key to upholding the evangelical view of the contraceptives at issue. While framing that view as beyond or outside judicial consideration, Justice Alito actually gives it judicial backing."[78] Alito's indifference is worrisome in the context of the original executive order, allowing virtually any employer to self-select out of the mandate so long as they cite sincerely held religious beliefs as their justification.

The most striking portion of Alito's concurring opinion addresses the government's compelling interest in the case. In *Burwell*, the court assumed the state had a legitimate interest in providing cost-free contraception to all women. This time, however, they probed the question further examining whether Congress consistently demonstrated this interest. In the majority opinion for the court, Justice Thomas observes, "no language in the statute itself even hints that Congress intended that contraception should or must be covered. . . . Thus, it is Congress, not the Departments that has failed to provide protection for contraception coverage."[79] Alito uses this observation to invalidate the state's compelling interest by pointing to the refusal of Congress to treat contraception as a positive right when originally crafting the ACA. Alito argues:

> In Hobby Lobby, the Government asserted and we assumed for the sake of argument that the Government had a compelling interest in "ensuring that all women have access to all FDA-approved contraceptives without cost sharing." 573 U. S., at 727. Now, the Government concedes that it lacks a compelling interest in providing such access. . . . Thus, in order to establish that it has a "compelling interest" in providing free contraceptives to all women, the Government would have to show that it would commit one of "the gravest abuses" of its responsibilities if it did not furnish free contraceptives to all women. If we were required to exercise our own judgment on the question whether the Government has an obligation to provide free contraceptives to all women, we would have to take sides in the great national debate about whether the Government should provide free and comprehensive medical care for all. . . . We can answer the compelling interest question simply by asking whether Congress has treated the provision of free contraceptives to all women as a compelling interest. . . . Thus, in considering whether Congress has manifested the view that it has a compelling interest in providing free contraceptives to all women, we must take into account "exceptions" to this asserted "rule of general applicability." And here, there are exceptions aplenty. The ACA—which fails to ensure that millions of women have access to free contraceptives—unmistakably shows that Congress, at least to date, has not regarded this interest as compelling.[80]

Alito points to the laundry list of existing exemptions to the contraceptive mandate as proof of the government's flawed interest in providing contraception to *all* women. These exemptions include unemployed women, women who work for small businesses with less than fifty employees, women whose insurance plans were grandfathered in, and women employed by entities previously granted an exemption. Considering the ACA was written to knowingly exempt millions of women, Alito has a point.

Alito also casts doubt on the purported state interest in providing seamless coverage for all of one's medical needs. Responding directly to claims advanced by Justice Sotomayor in *Zubik* and Ginsburg's dissent in this case, Alito scoffs, "Although lack of dental care can cause great pain and may lead to serious health problems, the ACA does not require that a plan cover dental services. . . . [I]t is undoubtedly true that the contraceptive mandate provides a benefit that many women may find highly desirable, but Congress's enactments show that it has not regarded the provision of free contraceptives or the furnishing of 'seamless' coverage as 'compelling.'"[81] Given the government's track record of failing to provide meaningful contraceptive access to women reviewed earlier in this chapter, it is hard to argue with Alito's characterization of the government's interest, or lack thereof, in furnishing contraception.

Finally, Alito puts the onus on the state and sketches several different policies the government could have pursued if meeting a positive obligation to provide contraception was truly their goal. Alito repeats the suggestion he made in *Burwell* for "the Government to assume the cost of providing [contraceptives] to any women who are unable to obtain them under their health-insurance policies." An incredulous Alito defends both the cost-effectiveness and legality of such a program and concludes, "Certainly, Congress could create such a program if it thought that providing cost-free contraceptives to all women was a matter of 'paramount' concern."[82] In some ways, Ginsburg's evaluation of the alternative means of accessing contraception inadvertently proves Alito's point. When discussing the viability of obtaining contraception from existing programs, Ginsburg laments, "Such programs, serving primarily low-income individuals, are not designed to handle an influx of tens of thousands of previously insured women."[83] Neither she nor Alito is wrong. Even though no such option currently exists to accommodate the contraceptive needs of all women, the government could easily create a new program or expanding existing programs, such as Title X, if that was truly their goal.

In the end, Alito uses the federal government's long-standing failure to ensure contraceptive access to uphold the court's negative rights framework—rendering questions about the quality of contraceptive access a moot point. He proclaims: "A woman who does not have the benefit of contraceptive coverage under her employer's plan is not the victim of a burden imposed by the rule or her employer. She is simply not the beneficiary of something that federal law does not provide."[84] As frustrating as it may be to read, Alito's assessment of the government's commitment to contraception is accurate. Contraceptive access has never been an important priority for the government, and considering the contentious battle surrounding Title X explored in the next section, it doesn't look promising that it ever will be.

Justice Ginsburg, who heard arguments in the case from her hospital room, devoted the last opinion she wrote for the court to defending the need for contraception. She proclaims:

> Ready access to contraceptives and other preventive measures for which Congress set the stage in §300gg–13(a)(4) both safeguards women's health and enables women to chart their own life's course. Effective contraception, it bears particular emphasis, "improves health outcomes for women and [their] children," as "women with unintended pregnancies are more likely to receive delayed or no prenatal care" than women with planned pregnancies. . . . Contraception is also "critical for individuals with underlying medical conditions that would be further complicated by pregnancy," "has . . . health benefits unrelated to preventing pregnancy," (e.g., it can reduce the risk of endometrial and ovarian cancer) . . . and "improves women's social and economic status," by "allow[ing] [them] to invest in higher education and a career with far less risk of an unplanned pregnancy,". . . . Despite Congress' endeavor, in the Women's Health Amendment to the ACA, to redress discrimination against women in the provision of healthcare, the exemption the Court today approves would leave many employed women just where they were before insurance issuers were obliged to cover preventive services for them, cost free. The Government urges that the ACA itself authorizes this result, by delegating to HRSA authority to exempt employers from the contraceptive-coverage requirement. This argument gains the Court's approbation. It should not.[85]

Unfortunately, the limited focus of previous decisions left her with neither the legal standing nor the rhetorical precedent to advocate for contraception as either a medical necessity or even a legitimate state interest.

THE LASTING CONSEQUENCE: RECONCILING THE REPRODUCTIVE RIGHTS FRAMEWORK

The reproductive rights framework first established in *Griswold* has since expanded to include abortion and emergency contraception; each successive decision increased the legal options available to women while simultaneously reinforcing their existence as private choices made under the watchful eye of an interested state. In doing so, the court has consistently reaffirmed the autonomy of the individual decision maker and legitimized the state's limited role of noninterference. Sophia Mihic traces the evolution of this precedent through its application in *Roe*, arguing, "With this shift, privacy becomes personal autonomy . . . and this understanding of privacy enables self-management. . . . [A]fter *Roe* the emphasis on privacy as personal autonomy predominates American constitutional law. In its reaffirmation of a woman's right to choose an abortion in *Planned Parenthood* v. *Casey* (1992), the Supreme Court made the relationships among autonomy, self-management and the new economy explicit."[86] The court further solidifies this arrangement in *Little Sisters*, absolving the government of any positive obligation and prioritizing the autonomy of corporations over its employees in what Jennifer Denbow labels a remarkable display of "neoliberal jurisprudence."[87] The majority opinion in these decisions is practically a love letter to neoliberalism—pointing out all the other ways women could receive contraceptive care if denied by their employers and downplaying, if not altogether dismissing, the logistical and financial hardships such a pursuit entails. Andrea Smith laments, "This framework easily lent itself to a more libertarian framework around freedom from government intervention. However, this framework was limited in terms of the responsibility of the government to ensure all have equal access."[88] Even when the government attempted to play a more active role in securing contraceptive access for women via the ACA, the court reiterated its only obligation was to protect the autonomy of women. Freedom from government intrusion really means freedom from government intervention as well.

The decisions in *Burwell* and *Little Sisters* extend this logic to contraception as well, making it clear that barriers to access for a particular group are irrelevant in a neoliberal marketplace where individuals are perceived to have the ability to change their circumstances to facilitate better access. Cosgrove and Vaswani explain "neoliberal policies transfer responsibility to individuals to provide for themselves" because "within the logic of neoliberalism, individual responsibility and competition trump equity and citizenship." The system itself relies on the minimization of "institutionalized racism, and the dismantling of policies to protect citizens."[89] Alito's characterization of the burden placed on women denied contraceptive coverage is a prime example of this logic. He, a man with no firsthand experience on the subject, suggests: "It is undoubtedly convenient for employees to obtain all types of medical care and pharmaceuticals under their general health insurance plans, and perhaps there are women whose personal situation is such that taking any additional steps to secure contraceptives would be a notable burden. But can it be said that all women or all working women have a compelling need for this convenience?"[90] Alito's obliviousness is intentional, and his characterization of employer provider contraception as sheer convenience is a prime example of the neoliberal logic shifting responsibility to the individual—premised on a complete denial of the systemic issues at play.

If the court's decision and rhetoric in *Burwell* left advocates feeling uneasy, then their subsequent rulings in *Zubik* and *Little Sisters of the Poor* serve as an ominous warning of the coming battle over reproductive rights, especially given recent shifts in the ideological balance of the court. During his confirmation trial in 2017, Neil Gorsuch acknowledged that both *Griswold* and *Eisenstadt* "have been settled for 50 years," but refused to comment on his personal views regarding the cases.[91] Amy Coney Barrett, confirmed in 2020, took a similar stance recognizing the long-standing precedent set by these cases while carefully adding, "it's something that I can't opine on, particularly because it does lie at the base of substantive due process doctrine, which is something that continues to be litigated in courts today."[92] Brett Kavanaugh, appointed to the court in 2018, offered the most brazen take on the contraception cases. Kavanaugh praised Justice White's concurring opinion in the case which actually had little to do with contraception. David Gans explains the move as a "high-pitched dog-whistle aimed" at conservatives given Justice White's notable dissent in *Roe v. Wade* and majority opinion in *Bowers v. Hardwick*.[93] It's no small coincidence that while serving on the DC Circuit Court of Appeals in 2015, Kavanaugh sided with the organization Priests for Life in their opposition to the contraceptive mandate. This case just so happened to be one of the seven cases consolidated into the *Little Sisters of the Poor* hearing where Kavanaugh would again side in favor of granting all religiously based exemptions to the contraceptive mandate. The Supreme Court, stacked with conservative judges and armed with decades of jurisprudence providing lackluster protections for reproductive autonomy, may no longer be the ally it once was to the birth control movement.

Birth control advocates have long hoisted the court's decisions in the contraceptive cases as their crowning achievement granting women reproductive autonomy previously denied for centuries; yet embracing reproductive justice requires resisting the dominant paradigm of reproductive rights with its attendant emphasis on choice. Born of the negative rights framework protecting only a woman's basic decision-making power—her choice—the reproductive rights paradigm reproduces the logic of neoliberalism prioritizing responsible self-management over the resolution of systemic inequities. This dynamic, Robin West argues, is inherent to rights which "generally protect entitlements against political encroachment rather than satisfy even dire need" and is especially pronounced with negative rights.[94] West continues, negative rights "keep the state off our backs and out of our lives" but also "denigrate the Democratic processes that might generate positive law that could better respond to our vulnerabilities and meet our needs; and they truncate our collective visions of law's moral possibilities."[95] In the case of contraception, the court's decision extending legal protection to women already capable of accessing contraception did little to alter the existing inequities truly impacting a woman's choice. In their formative book *Reproductive Justice*, Loretta Ross and Rickie Solinger contend:

> Lawmakers and most activists did not challenge *Griswold* on the grounds that the decision did not establish any positive right for women that is, that it did not say that the government was obliged to provide all women with contraceptive information and materials as part of public health services. With merely a negative right to be left alone, significant numbers of girls and women could not afford health care, much less a diaphragm or the pill. Many remained unable to manage their fertility. Contraception remained for many fertile persons simply another unattainable class privilege.[96]

Although negative rights are essential, unless coupled with a positive obligation to provide conditions conducive to choice, the right is merely a codified privilege. In making demands of the state to ensure contraceptive access and ameliorate the social and economic conditions prohibiting legitimate choice, the reproductive justice movement is at odds with the prevailing legal framework of negative rights under which the court has firmly situated contraception and subsequently all reproductive rights.

Shifting away from a rhetoric of reproductive rights necessitates advocates abandon the mantra of choice that has been a mainstay in their advocacy since its inception. In the early years of the movement, choice was undoubtedly a powerful concept; in a single word it encapsulated the spirit of the new woman—capable of voting, acquiring an education, earning a living wage, and having children on her own terms—for she now had choices previous generations of women never dreamed of. Yet, even then, these choices were not universally accessible, with wealthy white women having access to far more choices than anyone else. The neoliberalization of contraception intensified existing disparities under the veil of choice which according to Ross and Solinger emerged as a more palatable construct than reproductive rights. They argue:

> Choice was palatable in part because it directly associated sexual women with an approved female activity, consumerism: a woman seeking to control her fertility could enter into the marketplace of options and select the one she liked best. The association suggested that every woman possesses the wherewithal the money and legal terrain to enter into that marketplace of options and to pay for whatever options she selected: contraception, abortion, or motherhood. Clearly many women lacked the cash to pay for these choices, including motherhood, and thus face what might be called choiceless choices. . . . [A]nother problem with choice is that this market concept strongly refers to the preferences of the individual and suggests that each woman makes her own reproductive choices freely.[97]

The irony of it all is almost insufferable. Wealthy white women have never needed legal permission to access contraception and early advocates made this fact well known. They called suffragists and politicians with small families hypocrites for rejecting birth control while clearly practicing it themselves. They opened clinics in impoverished communities hoping to level the playing field. They fought for social welfare programs providing targeted services to poor women. Yet, when given the chance to fully defend the rights of women, they opted instead for the delegitimizing universalist language of choice.

The language of choice is now deeply embedded in our understanding of reproductive rights. The entirety of the court's jurisprudence on contraception reflects a commitment to preserving choice. The slogans and promotional materials of advocates and service providers alike are inundated with the rhetoric of choice. Women ruthlessly and righteously defend their "right to choose" with little consideration of what they are defending. Ross and Solinger describe the genesis of the reproductive justice movement as a direct response to the problematic notions of choice promulgated by white women and their neoliberal accomplices. They contend: "Women of color activists pointed out that the concept of choice masks the different economic, political, an environmental context in which women live their reproductive lives. Choice, they argued, disguises the way that laws, policies, and public officials differently punish or reward the childbearing of different groups of women as well as the different degrees of access women have to health care and other resources necessary to manage sex, fertility, and maternity."[98] The call to reconsider the framework of choice emerged in the early 1990s, and yet, here we are still transfixed by the false promises of choice. We must start listening to the very women the movement was created to help—those systematically denied access to contraception whose reproduction was simultaneously out of their control and the subject of immense scrutiny. We must think of their choices and not just our own.

NOTES

1. Sanger, "The Birth," para. 34–36.
2. Rosen, "Federal Expansion," 66.
3. Sanger, "The Birth," para. 37; Margaret Sanger Papers, 228587.
4. Moreno and Kissling, "Forty Years," para. 3.
5. "Is Birth Control," 6–7.
6. Ernst and Pilpel, "Release from," 24–25.
7. Vansickle-Ward and Wallsten, *The Politics*, 31.
8. Olson, *Historical Dictionary*, 411.
9. "Birth Control Pill," 4.
10. May, *America and the Pill*, 119.
11. Littlewood, *Politics of Population Control*, 48.

12. *Carey v. Population Services International*, 431 U.S. 697 (S.C. US 1977).
13. Boughton, "The Cincinnati," 251.
14. *Sanger v. New York*, 46.
15. "Massachusetts Carries," 1.
16. *Griswold v. Connecticut*, 381 U.S. 485, 480 (S.C. US 1965).
17. *Griswold*, 381 U.S. 485 at 482.
18. *Griswold*, 381 U.S. 485 at 480.
19. *Griswold*, 381 U.S. 485 at 485.
20. *Eisenstadt v. Baird*, 405 U.S. 438 (S.C. US 1972) 453.
21. *Carey*, 431 U.S. 697 at 693.
22. *Griswold*, 381 U.S. 485 at 479.
23. *Eisenstadt*, 405 U.S. 438 at 444.
24. *Eisenstadt*, 405 U.S. 438 at 445.
25. *Carey*, 431 U.S. 697 at 684.
26. Lombardo, "How to," 327.
27. *Griswold*, 381 U.S. 485 at 503.
28. *Eisenstadt*, 405 U.S. 438 at 451.
29. *Carey*, 431 U.S. 697 at 698.
30. *Carey*, 431 U.S. 697 at 710.
31. *Carey*, 431 U.S. 697 at 684.
32. *Carey*, 431 U.S. 697 at 684–85.
33. *Carey*, 431 U.S. 697 at 687.
34. *Carey*, 431 U.S. 697 at 689.
35. Ross and Solinger, *Reproductive Justice*, 119.
36. Meier and Dempsey, "Going Negative," 84.
37. West, "From Choice," 1403.
38. *Griswold*, 381 U.S. 485 at 495.
39. *Griswold*, 381 U.S. 485 at 495.
40. *Griswold*, 381 U.S. 485 at 503.
41. *Bowers v. Hardwick*, 478 U.S. 186, 191 (S.C. US 1986).
42. *Bowers*, 478 U.S. 186 at 192.
43. *Bowers*, 478 U.S. 186 at 218.
44. *Eisenstadt*, 405 U.S. 438 at 463.
45. *Griswold*, 381 U.S. 485 at 485.
46. *Griswold*, 381 U.S. 485 at 497.
47. *Griswold*, 381 U.S. 485 at 498–99.
48. *Griswold*, 381 U.S. 485 at 505.
49. *Carey*, 431 U.S. 697 at 718–19.
50. *Carey*, 431 U.S. 697 at 705.
51. Ibid.
52. *Eisenstadt*, 405 U.S. 438 at 463.
53. *Carey*, 431 U.S. 697 at 685–86.
54. *Planned Parenthood of Southeastern Pennsylvania v. Casey*, 505 U.S. 852–97, page # (S.C. US 1977).
55. Watzman, "Contraceptives Remain," para. 3.

56. Fluke, "Law Students." Testimony, para. 3.
57. National Women's Law Center, Reproductive Rights, 1–2.
58. *Burwell v. Hobby Lobby Stores, Inc.*, 573 U.S. 682, 23 (S.C. US 2014).
59. *Burwell*, 573 U.S. 682 at 23.
60. *Burwell*, 573 U.S. 682 at 24.
61. *Burwell*, 573 U.S. 682 at 2.
62. Levin, "The Hobby Lobby," para. 7.
63. *Burwell*, 573 U.S. 682 at 6.
64. Kendig, "After Hobby," 41.
65. *Burwell*, 573 U.S. 682 at 2.
66. *Burwell*, 573 U.S. 682 at 24.
67. Goldberg, "Alito's Hobby," para. 5.
68. Ibid.
69. *Burwell*, 573 U.S. 682 at 5.
70. *Burwell*, 573 U.S. 682 at 46.
71. *Burwell*, 573 U.S. 682 at 44.
72. *Burwell*, 573 U.S. 682 at 45.
73. *Burwell*, 573 U.S. 682 at 25.
74. *Burwell*, 573 U.S. 682 at 30.
75. *Zubik v. Burwell*, 578 U.S., 3–4 (S.C. US 2016).
76. Keith, "Supreme Court," para. 12.
77. *Little Sisters of the Poor Saints Peter and Paul Home v. Pennsylvania*, 591 U.S., 7 (S.C. US 2020).
78. Denbow, "The Problem," 175.
79. *Little Sisters of the Poor*, 591 U.S. at 18.
80. *Little Sisters of the Poor*, 591 U.S. at 11.
81. *Little Sisters of the Poor*, 591 U.S. at 14.
82. *Little Sisters of the Poor*, 591 U.S. at 14–15.
83. *Little Sisters of the Poor*, 591 U.S. at 15–17.
84. *Little Sisters of the Poor*, 591 U.S. at 18–19.
85. *Little Sisters of the Poor*, 591 U.S. at 8.
86. Mihic, "Neoliberalism and," 175.
87. Denbow, "The Problem," 166.
88. Briggs et al., "Roundtable: Reproductive Technologies," 102.
89. Cosgrove and Vaswani, "Fetal Rights," 47.
90. *Little Sisters of the Poor*, 591 U.S. at 14.
91. Bolton and Wheeler, "Gorsuch Rewrites," para 10.
92. Coyle, "Why Barrett," para. 7.
93. Gans, "Kavanaugh's Alarming," para. 7.
94. West, "From Choice," 1413.
95. Ibid., 1397.
96. Ross and Solinger, *Reproductive Justice*, 120.
97. Ibid., 101–2.
98. Ibid., 47.

Chapter Seven

Putting Birth Control on the Agenda

When it comes to early-twentieth-century radical thinkers, James F. Morton Jr. holds pride of place. Shortly after completing his studies at Harvard University alongside classmate and close confidant W. E. B. DuBois, Morton embarked on a cross-country tour to promote his philosophy of anarchism speaking at length on subjects such as free love, free speech, civil rights, and woman suffrage. Whereas contemporary iterations of anarchism conjure images of dystopian chaos, early-twentieth-century anarchists, such as Morton, saw anarchy as a productive and idyllic foil to ineffective governments. Historian Brigitte Koenig explains, "At a time when many Americans looked to the federal government to address the problems of an increasingly urban, industrialized society, anarchists focused on the individual as the locus of reform" in hopes of creating "a future exempt from the social, political, economic, and sexual hierarchies of late nineteenth-century America."[1] *Morton was readily accepted into the birth control movement in its fledgling years by fellow anarchist Emma Goldman and consistently dissuaded advocates from softening their radical demands in the name of progress. Much like Dennett, Morton rejected doctors-only bills as a piecemeal solution and fought instead for the upheaval of the social norms and institutions that labeled contraception as obscene and denied women bodily autonomy. Writing in the* Birth Control Review *in 1919, Morton warned:*

> *For the authors and supporters of the 'limited bill' I have the utmost good will and respect, although I cannot applaud their judgement in this matter. . . . Nor can I wonder that they are eager and impatient to see something actualized. They realize the vast amount of human suffering which cries for immediate relief; And every day's delay seems to them a crime against womanhood and against society. since permission to doctors and nurses to furnish contraceptive information would make it possible at once to assist many sufferers, and in some localities to open and maintain clinics to which those in need could repair, it*

> *is not surprising that their vision rests on these advantages, and fails to travel further, and to see that in opening the door of hope a little earlier to a comparatively limited number of suffering women, they're sacrificing a vital principle, and are effectively closing the door for a generation or more to come upon a multitude of others whose need is equally great. It is a tactical surrender, of which the enemies of birth control will know how to take full advantage. . . . It is the principle itself which is bitterly hated and fought by all the elements of reaction; and they are not to be won over by any concessions on our part. In truth, they will regard our offer of a plan for limited and denatured Birth Control as a confession of weakness and an avowed distrust of our own principle. If we ourselves, who have been fighting for the right to give contraceptive information, suddenly turn about face, and swallow our own words, by declaring in effect that this information is so dangerous that only physicians and nurses can be trusted to impart it, our enemies will be quick to pounce on the admission, and to declare warning against the movement fully justified, since we stand condemned out of our own mouths. . . . If the time is ripe for such a limited bill, let it come from those who can see nothing beyond it. Let us persistently demand the full principle. If there must be an intermediate measure, let it come from the other side. Let them pass it as an attempt to pacify us, if they will; but let us never admit that it represents our ideal.*[2]

The limited bill was only the first of many concessions made by the movement to secure the support of professional individuals who promised to transform the once fledgling radical movement into a serious public health initiative. As birth controllers actively pursued strategic alliances, they willingly relinquished their control over the movement and abandoned the very principles once foundational to their cause.

An essential component of the early strategy to secure contraceptive access included lobbying for legislative change and a demand for state and federal agencies to take up the birth control cause. These efforts, beginning with Dennett and Sanger's dueling legalization bills in the 1920s, routinely failed to acknowledge the dire need for contraception much less champion the reproductive rights of women. Despite concerted efforts to insert contraceptive instruction into existing initiatives aimed at improving the health of women, such as those explored in chapter 2, advocates gained little ground in the early twentieth century. Even Sanger's comparatively popular doctors-only bills failed to garner any real steam, with only a handful of states enacting laws expressly permitting doctors to dispense contraceptive information. The stilted replies of wary legislators contained an important lesson for the movement—the battle for birth control wouldn't be won brazenly, but strategically, much to the chagrin of radical reformers like Morton.

Advocates quickly learned that getting contraception on the docket required careful camouflage; guided by the principle of political accommodation, advocates reframed their agenda to complement existing national priorities. As explored in chapter 2 with the Children's Bureau and again in chapter 5 with doctors and eugenicists, birth controllers quickly became fluent in the persuasive logics of Progressive Era reformers whose primary concern was alleviating the societal burdens connected to reproduction—child mortality, maternal mortality, degeneracy, poverty, and relief babies. Convincing these parties demanded advocates showcase the mechanistic benefits of contraception—preventing death, eliminating abortion, and reducing public expenditures. In doing so, advocates infused their rhetoric with utilitarian sentiments framing contraception as sound economic policy and argued the government need not spend money to save the languishing when they could merely give them the ability to save themselves.

In accepting piecemeal solutions to what were actual systemic issues preventing contraceptive access, early birth controllers established a dangerous precedent for the type of assistance the government should provide. After failing to ingratiate themselves with the Children's Bureau and secure funding through the Sheppard-Towner Act, advocates turned to state-level public health departments who offered meager funding and support for their clinic initiatives in conjunction with their public health programs. In the 1960s when President Johnson announced federal funds for family planning services as part of his War on Poverty, advocates eagerly accepted the money with nary a word about Johnson's ultimate agenda of population control. The decades-long jostling of funds for Title X is the most egregious example of the movement's acquiescence. Taken together, these events are the markers of a movement that sacrificed its principles for progress and are the predictable consequence of adopting a framework of political accommodation.

PERSUADING PROGRESSIVE ERA POLICY MAKERS

Appealing to the Progressive Era ethos which dominated the political scene in the 1920s, advocates reiterated the societal value of contraception by framing voluntary parenthood and the reduction of large families as a humanitarian issue. Birth controllers, heavily influenced by the neo-Malthusian school of thought, pointed to the inevitable strain on resources to justify their humanitarian claims. Sanger's mentor Charles Drysdale explained this argument in 1919: "The law of correspondence at birth and death rates, the next deduction from the principle of Malthus, is the most momentous of all from the humanitarian standpoint. If population constantly press against the means of subsistence, the increase of population is kept back to the increase of subsistence, just as the speed of a train must be kept back to that of a train in front of it on the same track."[3] Another of Sanger's mentors, Havelock Ellis, explicitly incorporates the notion of humanitarianism into the very definition of birth control, arguing, "It is of the first importance to realize at the outset that what we now term birth control simply represents, in the humanitarian form demanded by our civilization today, something which has been essential to life from the beginning. It represents, that is to say, the necessity for the limitation of offspring."[4] Large, unsustainable families were clearly the main culprits perpetuating a drain on resources, but the humanitarianism of contraception promised relief for both them and individuals reeling from the strain of growing resource disparity. Writing in the *Birth Control Review* in 1922, Noel Leslie pleads: "The control of birth provides a more humanitarian relief which in time will limit the peoples of the earth to numbers ensuring an equitable and contented enjoyment of the world's resources, as opposed to the present unequal and miserable struggle for what, for most of us, is becoming a mere existence."[5] Consistent with the rhetorical tactics explored in chapter 2, birth controllers aligned their efforts with the social reform agenda of Progressive Era politics through appeals to the humanitarian elements of their agenda.

Framing their efforts as humanitarian served the strategic aims of the movement by further aligning their agenda with both socialists striving for a more equitable distribution of wealth and Progressive Era reformers attempting to correct the social ills produced by industrialization and urbanization. A survey conducted by the New York Committee of the National Birth Control League revealed the power of this argument across the political spectrum. In reporting the results of the survey, the *Birth Control Review* portends:

> Most of the favorable answers were from socialist candidates, as might be expected, as practically all Socialists have long been sound on the question, but the quality of the letters we received from Republicans and Democrats is a most encouraging indication of a new clean minded attitude which will give our bill dignified consideration. . . . It is becoming obvious that an intelligently controlled birth rate is the basis of health. The typical Republican is apt to see it, because he perceives that asylums hospitals and jails will be less needed and therefore less expensive, if you are unfit, handicapped babies are born. The typical Democrat sees it because he realizes that the country under the strain of war and reconstruction should not have the additional drag of looking after families which have grown so fast that they cannot adequately look after themselves. And all the Socialists yet because they stand for freedom of access to all knowledge, freedom for all women to decide as to the frequency of motherhood, the right of all children to be well born.[6]

This framing also played an important role in tempering the more sensationalist elements of the movement which initially isolated potential allies. Frank Hankins, professor of Sociology and Economics at Smith College, describes the impact of this framing on the broader reception of the movement in 1931. He observes, "The birth control movement has been deeply charged with emotion from the first. On the one hand, by touching sexual relations intimately, it seemed to threaten traditional morality; On the other hand, it was moved by strong humanitarian desires to remedy poverty and vice and free women from an often cruel fate."[7] While the headstrong Dennett barreled on with her more radical sex-forward agenda, Sanger, keenly aware of these opposing perceptions of the movement, strategically emphasized the broader and far less controversial humanitarian goals achievable through contraception.

As explored in previous chapters, this rhetorical sleight of hand often succeeded in winning over once reluctant parties. Dr. William J. Robinson directly credits the humanitarian focus of the movement for his own change of heart, writing in the *Birth Control Review* in 1927: "As to the change in our attitude towards birth control, we may safely affirm that there is not another serious humanitarian movement that has made such remarkable, such striking progress. People who have not lived through these years cannot imagine what the public attitude towards birth control was 25 years ago."[8] Robinson's sentiment was echoed broadly. A 1927 statement from the *New York Medical Journal and Record* boldly touted, "Birth control is fast becoming a vital social problem. Those interested in the world's problems of today or taking part in any of the humanitarian and scientific endeavors to solve our social difficulties must acquaint themselves with the many arguments for and against a wider dissemination of contraceptive knowledge."[9] The use of a humanitarian frame counteracted the perception of the movement as self-interested rabble-rousers and gave skeptics a reason to support their agenda in the name of societal uplift. Advocates carefully honed this rhetorical strategy over time and in relation to a wide array of potential allies. When pursuing an alliance with the Children's Bureau in the 1920s, advocates urged naysayers to consider the improvements to societal welfare facilitated by increased contraceptive use; when courting doctors and eugenicists in the 1930s, advocates articulated a societal right to contraception as a precautionary measure for future generations. In each iteration, skeptics are convinced to support contraception not because it will improve the quality of life for women or because doing so recognizes the fundamental rights of women, but because there was something in it for them, for society writ large.

Contraception as Sound Economic Policy

Advocates learned early on that convincing others to join the cause required appealing to their self-interest, so as the nation grappled with the devastation of the Great Depression, advocates shifted their utilitarian framing of the movement to focus less on humanitarian motivations and more on the cost-benefit analysis of expanded contraceptive use. The movement's early emphasis on poor families served both practical and strategic aims. At the outset of the birth control movement, Sanger and other activists consistently targeted their efforts toward impoverished women. Sanger's preoccupation with the poor stemmed from her formative experiences as a nurse working in the poverty-stricken districts of New York and was constantly reinforced in the letters she received from women, citing financial strain as a primary motivation for preventing conception. In her 1928 collection of letters, *Motherhood in Bondage,* Sanger featured correspondence from twenty-one women under the heading "The Pinch of Poverty." One woman begs: "Oh, it is hard on poor women to be in my shape. It is just one baby after another. I can't stand it much longer and work like I do. . . . I pray you to help me."[10] Even with access to a private physician willing to dispense contraceptive information, impoverished women readily found themselves priced out of the marketplace. Andrea Tone suggests the average New York worker would have spent upwards of one day's pay to purchase a reusable, and reliable, contraceptive douching syringe.[11] Unlike their fickle and cost-effective black-market counterparts, the most effective contraceptives required running water and sanitary conditions to use correctly—transforming it into a luxury inaccessible to the women who needed them most.

An examination of the birth rate relative to income sheds light on the movement's choice to focus on impoverished women. Larry Jones and Michele Tertilt, economists at the National Bureau of Economic Research, explain that while fertility rates fell among those in both the top and bottom half of the income distribution between the years of 1898 and 1908, they fell twice as much for those in the top half.[12] As explored in chapter 4, higher infant and maternal mortality rates among impoverished families also motivated early advocates to target predominantly poor populations. Accordingly, class disparities regarding contraceptive access became a pronounced feature of its rhetoric. Speaking directly to these disparities, Sanger pleaded in 1933, "give the poor mother the rights that the well to do mother has had for the past generation . . . to obtain special scientific knowledge through the source of the medical profession."[13] Wealthy women were not publicly clamoring for contraceptive information, and well-to-do husbands were not burdened by the need to provide for a growing household on meager wages as their privilege exempted them from this daily struggle. In the era of progressive politics, destitute women and children were the ideal martyrs for the movement.

Arguments emphasizing the economic need for contraception are littered throughout the book but are most prominent in the rhetoric of advocates during the Great Depression. Robyn Rosen argues, "The crisis of the Great Depression provided a new context and catalyst to move birth control from the margins to the mainstream. The combination of new concerns over public health, poverty, infant and maternal mortality, and family size on the one hand, and the establishment of a federal apparatus that encouraged, funded, and regulated welfare measures on the other, provided a more hospitable environment for the movement."[14] Birth controllers drew on their experience during the interwar years to craft a salient message framing contraception as a tool for social improvement vital to protecting the long-term interests of the state. Carole McCann explains, "During the Great Depression, the proportional weights of the three main ideological elements of birth control discourse were recalibrated so that the economic ethic of fertility linked to the ideal of racial betterment completely overshadowed the rights of women."[15] Specifically, advocates repurposed many of the same rhetorical tactics deployed in the 1920s to align their efforts with the Children's Bureau by positioning contraception as concomitant with other social programs aimed at alleviating poverty. In doing so, advocates spotlighted the deficiencies in current relief strategies and advocated contraception as the solution to both rising populations and imprudent government spending.

As huge swaths of the nation plunged deeper into poverty during the Great Depression, both the government and private organizations increased the funding and scope of their public assistance programs. Between 1933 and 1935, President Franklin Roosevelt rolled out a plethora of programs, known colloquially as relief, aimed at enhancing the material stability of families through the provision of food, housing, and medical care. The creation of relief programs within the New Deal enabled new alliances with social workers who "were likely converts [to the cause] because of the orientation toward service that led them to their profession in the first place and because of their direct and sometimes painful exposure to poverty in their jobs."[16] ABCL leaders quickly capitalized on this relationship, presenting at social work conventions, advocating for relief agencies to provide contraceptive information, and even recommending the construction of birth control clinics through the Works Progress Administration.

Deeply cognizant of the nation's bleak economic outlook, advocates presented contraception as a solution to reducing the massive public and private expenditures devoted to antipoverty and social welfare programs. Birth controllers utilized high fertility rates among relief recipients to push for the inclusion of family planning services within federally funded programs. In a

1939 speech, Sanger protested: "[W]ith millions being spent to feed, clothe and provide them with work, not one cent of Federal funds is to be allocated to provide contraceptive services to the people who need it most and who are reproducing, proportionately, the largest number of children."[17] Additionally, since relief was never intended to provide a permanent solution to a family's economic woes, birth controllers argued relief "serves to prolong conditions of poverty and misery. It provides just enough to keep from actual starvation those who live, normally, almost submerged."[18] Building on the previously established connection between large families and poverty, advocates questioned the efficacy of providing relief without family planning assistance, arguing the cycle of poverty perpetuated within large families effectively nullifies the government's antipoverty ambitions.

For advocates, family size, not income, was the root cause of poverty, so any plan not including contraception was at best a palliative measure and never a permanent solution. The most troubling part of this situation, for both birth controllers and the general public, was not just that people on relief were having more children, but the possibility of relief actually encouraging poor families to have more children. The phenomenon of "relief babies," children supposedly born to parents looking to take advantage of Federal Emergency Relief Funds allocated by the U.S. government throughout the Great Depression, provided advocates with new ammunition in their fight to secure contraceptive access. Economists Price Fishback, Michel Haines, and Shawn Kantor suggest it may have also enabled families to feel comfortable bringing new life into the world. In their study of relief funds and fertility rates they explain, "The presence of a stronger financial safety net might have contributed to families' feeling more secure in returning to their long-range fertility plans."[19] Consistent with these findings, advocates regularly labeled higher fertility rates among relief recipients as cause for alarm. Sanger pointed out in 1935: "[T]he official FERA figures for February 1935 show 4,485,000 families on general relief. It is in these four million families that the birth rate is the highest" with 45 percent to 60 percent more babies born into families receiving relief.[20] Historian Linda Gordon explains, "By 1935 'relief babies' had become a public scandal. Taypayers' money was not only being used to support the poor but to produce more of them—at least this was the implicit charge being made in a variety of political arenas."[21] Though not taken to the same extreme as the modern trope of the "welfare queen," advocates propagated the myth of relief recipients living beyond their means and having children they couldn't adequately care for because of the reliable safety net provided by relief.

Through relief, Sanger argued, the government enabled parents to abdicate their financial responsibilities for their children, facilitating the perpetuation of reckless reproduction. This was a common refrain for birth controllers—after all, the ABCL's 1922 bylaws boldly proclaimed: "People who cannot support their own offspring are encouraged by church and State to produce large families. . . . The burden of supporting these unwanted types has to be borne by the healthy elements of the nation."[22] The harsh economic realities of the 1930s amplified the salience of these arguments. The Depression, Gordon furthers, "Gave the allegations the urgency they had not had before. . . . [T]he problem of relief babies threatened to hit people immediately, in the pocketbook, and to hit everyone. Birth controllers seized upon the relief crisis with gusto."[23] A 1933 article in the *Los Angeles Times* validates Gordon's conclusion, suggesting, "The Depression has proved a marvelous boost for the birth control idea, although the new adherents are mainly interested in it from the economic angle. Taxpayers have grown tired of supporting indigents with whole flocks of children."[24] For the millions of Americans teetering on the edge of economic peril themselves the mere suggestion of others potentially abusing the system in a way that jeopardized their financial stability was a potent one.

Beyond criticizing the government's subsidization of large families via relief, advocates positioned contraception as a sound economic principle capable of decreasing dependency on social services and accruing major cost savings. Writing in *Forum and Century* in March 1935, Sanger called family planning an instrument of economic and social security; Sanger contends:

> National planning for economic and social security can, in the long run, produce no real benefits unless such plans be based upon the cornerstone of family security through family planning. . . . As long as the New Deal and our paternalistic Administration refuse to recognize this truism, grandiose schemes for security may eventually turn into subsidies for the perpetuation of the irresponsible classes of society. . . . They are attempting to solve the problem of economic security without due consideration for the basic human factors involved in that problem, which must be recognized.[25]

In their attempt to convince social workers and public officials of the need for contraceptive instruction, advocates regularly emphasized the counter-intuitive nature of programs aimed at helping families improve their social position without addressing what they perceived as the root cause—an imbalance between income and family size. In a 1923 Form Letter to Friends, the ABCL insisted "practical and feasible methods of decreasing dependency and delinquency" must be approached concomitantly with reducing "the burden of charities and taxation resultant from the support" of these classes.[26] Reducing the burden on public sector services promised increased efficiency as well. *Current Opinion* suggested smaller families meant people could "have medical attention when sick if clinics and hospitals are not swamped as at present."[27] The articulation of birth control through a cost-benefit analysis reverberated in the press's discussion of contraception as demonstrated by Ray Erwin Baber's 1932 article in *Forum and Century* entitled "Birth Control a Balance Sheet." Baber contends, "Birth control is not the one solution of all economic problems, but it will do its full share in the struggle with standard of living, unemployment, child labor, and similar questions."[28] Birth control was thus characterized as a necessary cost-saving measure, reducing public relief expenditures, as fewer children were born who might utilize these services.

Playing up the economic benefits of birth control proved particularly valuable given its appeal to both sides of the political spectrum. For the socialist concerned with systemic inequities, the problem is framed in terms of growing class disparities. For the progressive reformers, the problem is framed in terms of socially responsible government expenditures. In both instances, reducing the reproduction of poor people was leveraged to justify contraception in economic terms. Frank Hankins seamlessly combines both arguments in 1935:

> The rapid decline in family size in the upper economic levels has worked to intensify tendencies towards class stratification. With the progress of civilization, the amount of education and cultural acquisition required for entrance into the higher professional industrial position has become so great and so expensive that individuals born in the lower economic ranks find it increasingly difficult to rise in the social scale. . . . [T]his tendency is somewhat accentuated by the increasing necessity for governmental and social welfare agencies to lend support to the working classes during periods of social crisis. . . . The individualistic ideas of the recent past supported as God-given the right of the individual married pair to procreate as many offspring as they pleased. Those ideas, however, implied also that the father was solely responsible for the feeding and clothing of his progeny. We are no longer willing to permit children to be brought up under conditions which do not provide at least a minimum of health and education. The state and social agencies progressively invade the precincts formerly preserved to the individualistic family. Thus, it is come about in recent years that the birth rate among families on relief exceeds that of the average of the population and is distinctly greater than that among the more successful self-dependent families who, through taxation and charitable gifts, support the unrestrained fertility of the lower economic ranks. . . . [B]irth control is more in harmony with the spirit of democracy. Probably the vast majority of those whose families now exceed their economic resources would be only too glad to limit their fertility, if knowledge and facilities were available.[29]

Equating birth control with sound economic policy was effective both with government officials wishing to reduce public expenditures and with a broader audience concerned with their own pocketbooks. Dr. Alan Valentine, explained to the *New York Times* in 1941, "The key to good government and economic security that would make this country an enduring national strength is planned parenthood."[30] Linda Gordon contends, "This was a major factor behind birth control's ultimate achievement of respectability. The depression—capitalism's worst crisis to date—began the transformation of birth control into an official program for achieving economic improvement without redistribution."[31] Even as economic conditions improved, advocates clung to the narrative of fiscal conservatism to justify expanding contraceptive access. Whereas the federal government largely shirked demands to incorporate contraception into the expanded social service network built during the Great Depression, states readily heeded the call to action in hopes of reaping the economic and societal benefits touted by advocates. Understanding that both social workers and public health officials would play a pivotal role in this process, advocates couched their arguments in support of contraception explicitly under the banner of public health and even devoted the December 1937 issue of the *Birth Control Review* exclusively to the topic of public health. Advocates made their first appearance at the National Conference of Social Work in 1928 and continued to participate regularly over the next decade, including a session at the 1939 conference entitled "Birth Control as a Public Health Measure" featuring representatives from Columbia University and the North Carolina State Board of Health.[32] During the 1930s and 1940s, states invested heavily in the creation of public health programs and birth controllers fought tirelessly to be included.

South Carolina, the first state to add contraception to its public health program, did so in 1938 with the explicit aim of making services "available to poor mothers as it already is those able to pay for medical care."[33] Numerous states, including Minnesota, Michigan, and North Carolina, quickly followed suit with an almost universal focus on serving poor mothers. Writing on behalf of the Children's Bureau in support of these state-based initiatives, Ira S. Wile argues, "Every health officer is well aware that economic status has important relations to public health, and everyone is aware of the degree to which ignorance operates as a dysgenic factor in human life. Granting that the vast majority of people in this country live on incomes below two thousand a year, one cannot argue at once that a general limitation of offspring would bring about an immediate improvement in public health conditions."[34] Similarly, public health officials dismissed the need for contraception among privileged populations because as Reynold A. Spaeth of the School of Hygiene and Public Health at Johns Hopkins University argues in 1922, "It would be obviously unpractical to apply sanitary measures exclusively in the homes of the wealthy and educated."[35] Instead of advocating for the broad dissemination of contraception, Spaeth points to the use of contraception among "well to do" classes as a justification for expanding access exclusively to poor communities. Using couples making between $2500 and $7000 as a reference point, he explains, "We need only recall the higher standard of living, the proportionately greater attention received by each child in the small family and the better health of the parents—that in my opinion public health authorities must see the urgency and wisdom of extending these advantages to individuals on more modest intellectual and education levels."[36] In targeting their services toward poor women with the explicit aim of elevating the health of their communities and lowering social service expenditures, public health agencies enthusiastically embraced the movement's dominant themes of fiscal conservativism and racial betterment.

As to be expected given what we know of the movement's history, the state's focus on impoverished communities created a springboard to infuse eugenic arguments into the discussion of who should receive contraceptive services. North Carolina, whose public health programs later performed coerced sterilizations on thousands of Black women, brazenly stated its eugenic aims in their operating guidelines, stipulating, "The program should apply to families of low grade mentality, low income, those suffering from diseases, and other conditions incompatible with normal pregnancy, and who are poor maternal risks."[37] Eugenic concerns collided with the panic over relief babies to create what Linda Gordon calls "the 'blame the victim' sociology." Gordon suggests, "Viewing individuals as the problem was a way for social workers and bureaucrats to retain control of the service programs they offered."[38] Simply put, relief recipients needed to be held responsible. Frank Hankins spoke directly to the perception of irresponsibility and the resulting right for states to assert control over reproduction in his 1931 article endorsing the addition of contraception to public health agenda. He argues, "There is a logical conflict between the traditional doctrine of the individual's rights of unrestrained procreation and the necessity of providing through social agencies for the consequences of individual irresponsibility or economic incapacity. Logically if a society is to provide support it must also assert authority to determine who shall procreate." Framing family planning as a personal problem accelerated the inclusion of contraception into public assistance programs; however, it simultaneously limited the scope of these programs to solving overpopulation among the poor in hopes of fulfilling the flawed ideal of racial betterment.

The fervor for adding contraceptive services to public health programs faded throughout the 1940s and 1950s as the efforts of the New Deal paid dividends and Americans returned to a sense of normalcy after the Second World War. Known colloquially as the "baby boom," fertility rates and family size rose dramatically during this time from an average of 2.3 children per family in 1933 to 3.7 in 1957.[39] Two elements of this situation worked to derail the expansion of publicly funded contraceptive services. First, as the political and economic condition of communities improved, state governments felt less pressure to invest in social services—especially those aimed at family planning in a period of unusually high fertility. Second, as the Birth Control Federation of America changed its name to the Planned Parenthood Federation of America in 1942, it also expanded its service offerings to include infertility treatments and marital counseling. The name change, according to Robyn Rosen, "reflected a judicious rhetorical move" as "[p]lanning rather than controlling births seemed more in line with modern concerns about the strength of the American family."[40] The long-pondered strategic decision also revamped the movement's reputation and facilitated the expansion of clinics as state and local agencies willingly relinquished the task of providing contraceptive services to Planned Parenthood. The *New York Times* observed that in 1949 alone, 333 clinics nationwide served more than 162,000 wives and mothers—a fact which then PPFA national director Dr. D. F. Milam argued "indicate[d] a growing acceptance of planned parenthood as a basic health program on the part of the women in the country."[41]

Still, many women struggled to access safe and effective contraceptive methods. Women in the most densely populated areas of some states benefited from expanded clinic access, but countless women still lived in areas without either a clinic or a willing physician, and the existence of state-level Comstock laws meant many women still lived in areas where contraceptive instruction was prohibited altogether. Harriet Pilpel, the lone woman on the legal team who secured victory in the 1936 *One Package* decision, pleaded for the democratization of birth control through the inclusion of contraceptive services on the public health agenda. Noting the slow-moving progress made on this front in the wake of the Great Depression, Pilpel urges:

> In the birth control movement, our prime aim in the United States today must be to democratize birth control, to make it available to all who need it, not to just those women of the middle and upper income groups who can afford the services of a private physician. The Planned Parenthood Federation does a wonderful job, but it can't service much more than 1.5 percent to 2 percent of the total number of women who need the service. While some of those women will eventually get the service from private physicians, many of them will never get it unless the service is incorporated into public health and welfare budgets.[42]

Issued in 1965, Pilpel's urgent request would soon be put to the test as the creation of the contraceptive pill ushered in new opportunities for clinics and provided the ideal conditions to push for increased federal support for contraceptive access.

THE POLITICAL FOOTBALL OF FAMILY PLANNING SERVICES

The year 1965 was indeed a banner year for the birth control movement. Both advocates and the popular press heralded the events of the year as a true turning point in the battle for birth control. The January 15, 1966, edition of *The Saturday Evening Post* trumpeted the achievements of the past year as the start of "the birth control revolution," placing the story on its cover and devoting a lengthy spread to a review of the movement's long struggle to secure contraceptive access. In the article Steven M. Spencer summarizes the events of this "revolutionary turning point," noting:

> These technical advances (the pill), combined with a growing concern about the world population crisis, brought the birth control revolution to a historic turning point in the year just closed, for 1965 marked the fall of most of the last important barriers against general distribution of family-planning information and services. It was the year that the U.S. Supreme Court threw out as an unconstitutional violation of privacy the 86-year-old Connecticut law that had forbidden the use of contraceptives and forced the closing of birth control clinics. Positive legislative steps were taken in 10 other states, including New York. It was the year the Federal Government, taking its cue from President Johnson, became more directly involved in birth control activities than ever before. Early in the year the President had pledged he would seek new ways "to help deal with the explosion in world population," a problem he rated second in importance only to achieving peace.[43]

Advocates had every reason to be excited. Yet, the revolution promised by Spencer never quite materialized in large part because the movement proceeded along the same accommodating trajectory it had long grown accustomed to. As demonstrated in chapter 6, advocates refused to bluntly defend unfettered contraceptive access as a fundamental right for *all* women instead clinging to their well-worn scripts outlining the responsible use of contraception for family planning purposes. In doing so, advocates accepted a slow rollback of the laws restricting contraception and the adoption of a negative rights framework governing reproductive decisions. The same deferential posture invaded the movement's legislative efforts as well, as advocates reverted to the rhetoric of fiscal conservativism to justify federal funding for family planning services. Just as it did in the 1930s and 1940s, this rhetorical strategy convinced many of the societal benefits of contraception without requiring they take an ideological stance on the issue. Questions of women's autonomy were once again pushed aside to make room for a cost-benefit analysis of contraception.

President Johnson is rightly praised for his historic endorsement of contraception. He was, after all the first president to push for federally funded contraceptive services—not even his predecessors who extolled the benefits of smaller families were willing to commit federal resources to the contraceptive cause. Yet Johnson's motivations were suspect and his follow-through proved insufficient to truly improving contraceptive access. In his 1965 address to the United Nations, Johnson revealed his ultimate goal was not empowering women or ensuring their access to contraception but the reduction of overpopulation and poverty. Johnson proclaimed: "Let us in all our lands—including this land—face forthrightly the multiplying problems of our multiplying populations. . . . Let us act on the fact that less than $5 invested in population control is worth $100 invested in economic growth."[44] Johnson masterfully weaves together the logic of fiscal conservatism and the ideal of racial betterment to position contraception as a mechanism to achieve a more prosperous and stable world. Seeing an ally in President Johnson, birth controllers quickly incorporated his analysis into their own plea for increased government funding of family planning services. Just two months later, PPFA president Alan Guttmacher directly co-opted Johnson's words in his request for an additional $90,000,000 a year investment arguing such an investment was "'small compared to the current levels of public expenditure for other forms of medical care, welfare, and anti-poverty programs . . . particularly when we recognize President Johnson's axiom that $5 invested in population control is worth $100 in economic growth."[45] After decades of carefully shrouding their arguments in the logic of fiscal conservatism someone was finally listening.

To this end, Johnson included family planning services under the umbrella of his War on Poverty. Well sort of. No official program existed to fund these services, but local organizations offering family planning assistance were encouraged to apply for community grants funded by the Economic Opportunity Act. Despite Johnson's enthusiasm, "Family planning funding comprised less than .4 percent of the 7.6 billion dollars sent to local communities either through the Economic Opportunity Act or the Community Action Program."[46] To be clear, these subpar funding levels reflect neither a lack of need or interest and instead point to a systemic failure to both authorize and prioritize federal support of family planning. Representative Bob Eckhardt, a Democrat from Johnson's home state of Texas, roundly criticized his peers in congress for failing to fully execute Johnson's vision. He scolded:

> The vast majority of the American public favors birth control, and there is general agreement that it is the most effective anti-poverty tool per dollar spent. Nonetheless, federal support of birth control programs is extremely limited and has proceeded haltingly. . . . The blame for the slow progress must be

> place at the feet of federal officials who have circumvented or prevented their expansion. . . . Federal officials charged with the responsibility of funding birth control efforts managed to ignore Congressional mandates and repeated urgings by President Johnson. Foot-dragging, if not outright sabotage, characterizes the activities of many federal health officials who should be concerned with family planning. As a result, birth control programs currently serve less than a fifth of the potential clientele. If birth control programs for the poor are to be expanded, pressure from Congress must continue, backed by adequate appropriations, and the President must provide leadership both inside and outside the government to ensure that birth control services will be available to all.[47]

Johnson's patchwork program failed to provide impoverished women with meaningful access to contraception; so when the next administration came to power, advocates, like Eckhardt, rallied hard for a federal solution. Rachel Benson Gold explains, "Since states largely controlled the little funding available under these disparate programs, service availability, eligibility criteria and benefit levels varied widely. That uneven landscape changed dramatically in 1970, when Congress enacted Title X of the Public Health Service Act, the only federal program—then and now—devoted solely to the provision of family planning services nationwide."[48]

Title X became law under socially conservative Republican President Richard Nixon and received broad bipartisan support—a fact which is quite puzzling given the current political climate. In a 1969 message to Congress Nixon explained, "It is my view that no American woman should be denied access to family planning assistance because of her economic condition. I believe, therefore, that we should establish as a national goal the provision of adequate family planning services within the next five years to all those who want them but cannot afford them. This we have the capacity to do." In detailing what would later become Title X, Nixon reminds Congress that "[i]n order to achieve this national goal, we will have to increase the amount we are spending on population and family planning," but carefully clarifies the extent to which the federal government must foot the bill, arguing "It would be unrealistic for the Federal Government alone to shoulder the entire burden, but this Administration does accept a clear responsibility to provide essential leadership."[49] Frankly, Nixon's agenda wasn't all that different from Johnson's with both couching their support for contraception in the growing fear of unbridled population growth and a swelling welfare state and both borrowing heavily from the movement's rhetoric in the 1930s espousing contraception as sound economic policy.

Not unlike what took place in the aftermath of the Great Depression, contraception obtained an air of respectability in the 1960s and 1970s, not on its own merits but as a tool of population control and social betterment. Prudence

Flowers explains, "Throughout the 1970s, Title X enjoyed bipartisan support. Republicans and Democrats viewed it as having social and economic benefits, providing a public health service while helping to combat growing welfare costs."[50] Accordingly, just as advocates in the 1930s localized their push for contraceptive access within impoverished communities, Title X targeted low-income and uninsured women who not only experienced the highest levels of unintended pregnancy but were also the most likely to seek other forms of federal aid. As the first federal level program of its kind, Title X "essentially sets the standards for the provision of publicly funded family planning services and supplies in the United States" and specifies that women falling below the federal poverty level receive services free of charge while all other women pay on a sliding scale relative to their income.[51] Guttmacher called the legislation a "magnificent culmination of a Federal Government policy that has been several years in the making."[52] In reality, it took advocates nearly four decades to convince politicians of the benefits of federally funded contraception.

The following decades saw Title X transformed into a political football as both parties jockeyed for power. Nixon's successor, Gerald Ford, took several swipes at Title X funding on his mission to reduce public expenditures and balance the budget, but a Democratically controlled Congress ensured funding levels stayed intact. In his first 100 days in office, Democratic President Jimmy Carter demonstrated his commitment to Title X with an impressive request to increase funding by $35 million; yet, the justification for increased funding offered by Carter foreshadows the emerging threats awaiting Title X in the 1980s. Rachel VanSickle-Ward and Kevin Wallsten explain, when Title X was first enacted "both parties strongly supported the so-called women's right agenda," but over the next eight years "this consensus gave way to a polarization around gender issues."[53] The legalization of both contraception and abortion combined with a growing concern for federally subsidized services put the Carter administration on high alert. Accordingly, Carter justified his 1977 budget request as an investment in "alternatives to abortions" including "family planning services, adoption facilities, and sex education."[54] In 1978, Carter proposed an additional $142 million in funding for programs aimed at preventing teen pregnancy based on the recommendations he received from a task-force specially convened to address "the plight of the pregnant teenager."[55] Carter funded Title X at an impressive level of $162 million but was forced to do so from a defensive posture invoking many of the movement's earlier battles for respectability.

The coming years proved treacherous for Title X specifically and reproductive rights more broadly as Republicans fully abandoned the women's rights agenda to court a powerful new contingency—the Christian Right—whose policy positions almost always ran opposite of the women's rights agenda.

Daniel Williams contextualizes the complexity and strategic value of the party's about face on the issue of abortion specifically. He argues:

> In spite of the Republican Party's pro-choice leadership, the GOP adopted a platform in 1976 that promised an anti-abortion constitutional amendment. The party's leadership viewed the measure as a temporary political ploy that would increase the GOP's appeal among traditionally Democratic Catholics, but the platform statement instead became a rallying cry for social conservatives who used the plank to build a religiously based coalition in the GOP and drive out many of the pro-choice Republicans who had initially adopted the platform.[56]

Although the move wasn't enough to win the election against Carter in 1976, it did help secure major wins in the 1978 midterms against pro-choice Democrats, emboldening Republicans to carry on with their newly minted pro-life agenda. In 1976 Republican Congressman Henry Hyde of Illinois introduced the now infamous Hyde Amendment prohibiting the use of federal funds to pay for abortion-related services. Although such a provision was included in Title X from its inception because prior to the Hyde Amendment Medicaid recipients could use their benefits to cover abortions services, the amendment significantly curtailed access to affordable abortion and was thus heralded as the first major victory for the now fully formed pro-life movement.

Carter's successor, Republican President Ronald Regan, proudly took up the torch of the pro-life movement and worked swiftly to cut Title X funding and severely limit its scope. In addition to letting funding lapse entirely for the program in 1985, Reagan issued new guidance in 1988 for Title X-supported service providers barring practitioners at these clinics "from counseling patients on pregnancy options that included abortion" even when explicitly requested by the patient. The rule also "prohibited Title X-funded health centers from sharing finances, staff, or a physical location with an abortion provider."[57] Known as "the gag rule," Reagan's policy expanded existing limitations built into Title X to include even the mere discussion of abortion and placed clinics who provided both contraception and abortion in an impossible position. The policy also helped to dismantle the clear delineation between contraception and abortion advocates dutifully cultivated by lumping together these services. Despite the fact that only 50 of the 750 Planned Parenthood clinics performed abortions and repeated audits revealed no misuse of Title X funds to cover abortions, pro-lifers argued "access to federal funds served to normalize abortion" and freed up resources that could ultimately be spent on abortion.[58] Whereas previous administrations framed contraceptive access via Title X as an invaluable tool to prevent abortion, Reagan presented it as an accomplice.

The damage done by Reagan's rollback was severe and lasting. Gold laments, "despite fairly steady increases in appropriations since then, it has never fully recovered. Taking inflation into account, the program's funding level in 1999 was 60 percent lower than it had been 20 years ago."[59] The most significant damage, however, was rhetorical and ideological. Through his attempts to hamstring Title X, Reagan willfully ignored decades of evidence demonstrating the importance of contraceptive access to preventing unwanted pregnancies and preserving quality of life for women and children. His efforts also granted legitimacy to the fallacious argument conflating abortion and contraception which transformed Planned Parenthood into target number one for the pro-life movement despite the fact that both then and now the bulk of Planned Parenthood's services have absolutely nothing to do with abortion. Reagan's actions also provided a blueprint for future administrations hoping to capitalize on the politicization of reproductive rights—Title X—whose workings were easily manipulated via executive order.

Title X remained contested during the Bush-Clinton-Bush years. Advocates retained cautious optimism at start of George H. W. Bush's presidency given his vocal support of Title X as a congressman. In the 1969 hearing over Title X Bush proclaimed, "We need to take sensationalism out of this topic so that it can no longer be used by militants who have no real knowledge of the voluntary nature of the program but, rather are using it as a political stepping-stone. If family planning is anything, it is a public health measure."[60] Sadly, as Reagan's vice president, Bush observed firsthand the power of the newly mobilized Christian right and pursued an agenda consistent with their wishes. Bush bolstered the "gag rule" by instructing agencies to give preferential treatment to service providers engaging in abstinence-based sex education as opposed to comprehensive sex education which included information about contraception. Within days of taking office in 1993, Democratic President Bill Clinton reversed "the gag rule" among other anti-abortion policies supporting his vision of "an America where abortion is safe and legal but rare" facilitated by continued "efforts to promote safe and effective family planning."[61] George W. Bush straddled the ideological chasm between his father and Clinton regarding Title X for although he reinstated his father's policy prioritizing abstinence-based programs he also signed off on a significant budget increase for the program in 2007.

As one of the largest recipients of Title X funding, Planned Parenthood emerged as a lightning rod for the pro-life movement in the early 2000s fueled by a series of fake videos circulated by the anti-abortion group Center for Medical Progress. Republican legislators seized on the smear campaign targeting PPFA and launched their own assault on the organization. Social conservatives regurgitated the flawed Reagan-era logic suggesting federal funding "indirectly subsidizes abortion" and launched a slew of attacks on

Title X in an attempt "to shutter Planned Parenthood health centers and any safety-net health center providing publicly funded family planning services that additionally offers abortion (using other funds), or is affiliated with an abortion provider."[62] Like a dog with a bone, Mike Pence latched onto this argument and vigorously pursued an agenda aimed at defunding Planned Parenthood. His first attempt came in 2007 in the form of a failed amendment to an appropriations bill. Undeterred, Pence reintroduced the measure in 2009 but was again met with defeat. Capitalizing on the change in House leadership after the 2010 midterms, Pence doubled down in 2011 introducing legislation that would not only bar Planned Parenthood from receiving any federal funding but would also eliminate Title X altogether. Despite these repeated attacks, the Obama years marked the highest levels of funding for Title X in history peaking at over $317 million in 2010.[63]

The 2010 midterms emboldened Republicans at both the federal and state level. Hoping to make the most of their newfound majority in both the House and Senate, Republicans voted to defund Planned Parenthood a total of eight times.[64] Although met each time with an Obama veto, the push to defund inspired states legislators, most notably in Texas but in twenty other states as well, to enact laws limiting or outright prohibiting Planned Parenthood from accessing available funds so long as they remained an abortion provider. These efforts threatened to decimate the existing family planning infrastructure in the United States. Kinsey Hasstedt of the Guttmacher Institute provides a snapshot into the critical role of Planned Parenthood in the provision of contraceptive services, noting, "Planned Parenthood health centers serve two million (32 percent) of the 6.2 million women who obtain contraceptive care . . . and 1.6 million (41 percent) of the 3.8 million contraceptive clients served by Title X."[65] In a last ditch effort to protect Title X, President Obama issued guidance instructing federal agencies to accept Title X funding applications from all qualified candidates, including Planned Parenthood. The measure was sadly short lived going into effect just two days before Trump's inauguration and nullified less than two months later.

Interestingly, the ACA's contraceptive mandate existed in part to circumvent political battles over Title X by giving women another means to afford contraception and transferring the primary responsibility to fund contraceptive services to the private sphere. Together, the two systems promised to make contraception affordable and accessible to all women—assuming of course both systems functioned optimally. Kinsey Hasstedt furthers, "Title X remains the backbone of the nation's publicly supported family planning effort. . . . [E]ven with insurance, women need a place to go for services. Sustaining—if not strengthening—the Title X network of providers is critical so the newly insured can actually obtain high-quality care. Moreover, Title X sites are particularly well-situated to connect the uninsured to health coverage and to care for the people most likely to fall through the cracks of health reform."[66] Yet, the exemptions built into the ACA and enlarged by the Supreme Court's subsequent decisions have left countless women, many of whom might turn to Title X-supported clinics, in a precarious position.

As the federal government whittled down its commitment to funding family planning services under conservative administrations, it simultaneously set the scene for the conflict we saw play out over the ACA. This lack of commitment is precisely what Alito was referring to in his concurring opinion when he observed that "Congress' enactments show that is has not regarded the provision of free contraceptives" as compelling.[67] And the inability of existing programs, such as Title X, to pick up the slack articulated by Ginsburg is a problem decades in the making. The ACA, while momentous, facilitated the government's further disavowal of its responsibility to secure contraceptive access and in doing so jeopardized the future of the contraceptive safety net. The Guttmacher Institute warns: "When clients are unable to use their insurance, for whatever reason, everybody loses: People may pay more than they need to for services or may forgo getting care altogether, and clinics stretch themselves financially in ways that they shouldn't have to stretch. If the ACA's gains in ensuring coverage for greater numbers of Americans are reversed, or if Title X is eliminated, the situation will inevitably deteriorate."[68] Given the court's decision in *Little Sisters* and Alito's unflinching indictment of the state's compelling interest regarding contraception, the Guttmacher Institute's prognosis seems nigh.

And then, of course, came Republican President Donald Trump who, with Vice President Mike Pence by his side, dutifully courted the religious right with bold promises to reverse the ACA and defund Planned Parenthood. His promises sent countless women in search of Long-Acting Reversible Contraception hoping to simply weather the impending storm. Trump followed through delivering a series of hearty blows to the existing infrastructure supporting contraceptive access in the United States, including expanded ACA exemptions, conscience clauses, and the revival of Reagan's Title X "gag rule." Just as before, the "gag rule" barred Title X-supported clinics from having any association to abortion no matter how tentative, giving clinics an ultimatum: either eliminate these services and relationships or forgo precious Title X dollars. Planned Parenthood, explains Anna North, "chose the latter option" and was joined by a litany of other clinics making the same decision. According to North, a total of 981 total clinics left the program resulting in "a 46 percent reduction in the program's ability to provide contraception, or about 1.6 million patients who could no longer get free or low-cost birth control" many of whom "already face obstacles to getting contraception, including young people and people of color."[69] While advocates and providers scrambled to challenge the executive order in court, the Supreme Court's previous ruling in *Rust v. Sullivan* upholding Reagan's version of the policy gave them little hope and the loss in *Little Sisters* certainly didn't bolster their enthusiasm. Although Trump and Pence left office with the future of the "gag rule" uncertain, they proudly touted its implementation as one of many policies making them the most pro-life administration in history.

The fate of Title X now rests in the hands of the Biden administration. Both a Catholic and a Democrat, Biden has vowed to reverse the Trump-era restrictions on Title X funding and prioritize contraceptive access for the countless women not covered by the ACA mandate. A memorandum issued on January 28, 2021, declared the policy of the administration "to support women's and girls' sexual and reproductive health and rights" and instructed the Secretary of Health and Human Services to review all Title X regulations which "impose undue restrictions" on women's access to comprehensive reproductive health care.[70] In April 2021, Biden unveiled his proposal for Title X nullifying the "gag rule" and restoring the program's mission of providing "access to equitable, affordable, client-centered, quality family planning services for all clients, especially for low-income clients."[71] In October 2021, Biden officially reversed the Trump-era "gag rule" and requested a huge funding increase for the program to the tune of $340 million dollars.[72] But what about the next administration? Or the one after that? Will birth control advocates simply continue to hold their breath and await their fate as contraceptive access remains tenuous at best and increasingly susceptible to attack.

THE LASTING CONSEQUENCE: BARGAINING FOR BIRTH CONTROL IN THE AGE OF NEOLIBERALISM

The decades-long debate over federal funding delivers a serious case of déjà vu as advocates find themselves relitigating issues they assumed were long settled. In persuading politicians to embrace family planning as a sound economic policy, advocates justified the limited scope of their mission to impoverished communities whose unrestrained reproduction supposedly posed a significant threat to the health and wealth of the nation. In the face of policies clearly propagating the contraceptive hierarchy, advocates returned to their hallmark refrain of educated choice-making based on medically accurate information. In the wake of *Roe*, advocates were forced to again defend the trustworthiness of women as decision makers who could and would responsibly manage their reproduction if given the tools to do so. Today, advocates find themselves relying on the very arguments that bolstered the movement's inception—that contraception is not anti-life, it is not a conduit for promiscuity, it is not selfishly motivated. It is a medical necessity and a fundamental right.

Unfortunately, the déjà vu felt by today's advocates is a direct by-product of the early choice to pursue a strategy of political accommodation steeped in the dominant discourses of neoliberalism. Birth control advocates spoke the language of neoliberalism long before it emerged as the dominant political and economic paradigm in the United States. The strategies utilized by advocates to brand contraception as smart economic policy in the 1930s coincided with the nation's move away from progressive policies toward a more liberal political and economic agenda. Sanford Schram explains, "A long time in coming to ascendancy, neoliberalism arose in response as the welfare state gained traction during and after the Great Depression of the 1930s."[73] Sinikka Elliott sketches the impact of neoliberal thought during this time period and beyond observing, "With roots in post–World War II challenges to the New Deal, neoliberalism is at one and the same time a mode of governing, a cultural project, and an economic strategy. Neoliberalism as a political economic project advocates minimal government economic regulation, privatizing state resources, and distributing social services through the market."[74] These elements reverberate in the discourse of early advocates who routinely pitched contraception as a solution to reduce government expenditures and, rather than pushing for uniform access to contraception, accepted piecemeal solutions granting poor women access to the contraceptive marketplace already utilized by those with the wealth and privilege to seek care from a private physician.

Early advocates blamed the state for withholding the information and supplies necessary for women to make their own reproductive decisions, pinpointing the unintentional ignorance of women as the root cause of poverty and inequity. In doing so, advocates absolved the government of its responsibility to address the systemic issues contributing to their lack of choice in exchange for the provision of autonomy—a key tenet of neoliberalism. Patrick Grzanka and Elena Schuch argue, "Neoliberal ideology ostensibly celebrates personal agency in exchange for the wholesale elision of structural forces that constrain choices."[75] Advocates assured skeptics women could be trusted to make sound reproductive choices and that allowing to do so enabled them to be more constructive members of society while simultaneously reducing the societal burden of large families living on the government dole. This kind of bargain, Schram explains, is the backbone of neoliberalism wherein "[p]eople are expected to practice personal responsibility by investing in their own human capital to make themselves less of a burden on society."[76]

Whereas the movement's early rhetoric emphasized the unique needs of impoverished women priced out of the contraceptive marketplace and demanded more systemic solutions including fair labor practices and social support, this narrative shifted dramatically in the 1930s to place the onus on the individual. Advocates intentionally fueled the panic over "relief babies" propagating a narrative of dependency solvable only through the provision of reproductive choice. Such framing, Schram argues, emboldens the neoliberal state. He explains, "The poverty that precedes welfare dependency is ignored, and instead we are asked to focus on the reliance on welfare. . . . Dependency becomes a displacement for talking about the underlying structural poverty of that economy, which our liberal, individualistic, agentistic political discourse cannot effectively address."[77] Forsaking their socialist roots, the movement strategically embraced the move toward neoliberalism by castigating the very women they initially set out to save.

The movement's hallmark theme of choice over chance also highlights their early commitments to neoliberalism. In denying women contraception, the state wittingly became an accessory to what they deemed reckless reproduction. Advocates presented contraceptive access as a mechanism to shift culpability from the government to the individual by giving them the means to control their reproduction in accordance with normative expectations of childbearing and rearing. Elliott furthers, "As a mode of governmentality, neoliberalism emphasizes individual choice and autonomy, stressing the importance of self-regulation and enacting harsh punitive measures for 'bad' choices."[78] This logic is ever present in the rhetoric of early advocates who defended the autonomy of healthy and financially stable women while simultaneously endorsing the removal of autonomy, via sterilization, of people deemed incapable of making sound reproductive choices. It appears again in relation to the contraceptive hierarchy as women seeking an abortion are presumed irresponsible for failing to make choices eliminating the need for an abortion. Grzanka and Schuch continue, neoliberalism "has produced new forms of sexual citizenship that demand subjects self-regulate according to hegemonic norms" and creates a situation where "women's sexual and reproductive decisions then become judged by the extent to which they are perceived as indicative of agency and discipline."[79] The early rhetoric of the birth control movement framed its demands through strategic appeals to traditional hegemonic norms that eventually became codified in the laws governing reproductive autonomy and contraceptive access and are now used, both subtly and explicitly, to police women's reproductive decisions.

The movement's endorsement of the various funding schemes developed by the government demonstrate its loyalty to neoliberalism. Beginning in the 1930s, advocates pleaded for government subsidization of contraception targeting those unable to afford it individually as a means of providing upward mobility to women and reduced social welfare obligations for the government. Although these efforts were initially carried out by state health departments, Johnson approached this project with an overt neoliberal bent shifting the actual provision of services to independent contractors which were occasionally, but not always, government-affiliated health centers. As public health centers decreased their commitment to providing contraceptive access, private entities such as Planned Parenthood stepped in to fill the void bolstered by an expanded Title X program. While giving the appearance of a renewed investment in contraceptive access, these moves made the entire system vulnerable to the neoliberalist call to shrink the welfare state by outsourcing services to the private market—a move that made it easier for politicians to restrict funding and directly target service providers. The ACA's contraceptive mandate marked the ultimate ascendancy to the neoliberalist paradigm by shifting the burden of contraceptive care entirely to the private sphere and tethering access to one's employment status. Alito's criticism in *Little Sisters* is apt here; the government has always had the ability to place low or no-cost contraceptives directly into the hands of women but has routinely chosen not to in large part because no such demand was ever made.

For parties wishing to restrict reproductive rights the neoliberal paradigm, created and perpetuated by the movement itself, is a blessing in so far as it both prioritizes individual choice makers and minimizes the government's obligation to create conditions conducive to the full exercise of those choices. Roy and Thompson conclude, "This ferocious move toward privatization and commoditization was conjoined with an older, more uncompromising ideology of social conservatism. . . . Their symbiosis has produced the ideology of 'private family responsibility' and transformed welfare from a 'redistributive program into an immense federal apparatus for policing the family responsibilities of the poor.'"[80] Title X is the perfect target for social conservatives as its recipients are already presumed to be bad decision makers under the neoliberal framework. Their impoverished status grants them access to Title X and also makes them the subject of scrutiny—both for their financial status and their reproductive choices. It is no small coincidence that the programs and providers consistently targeted by conservatives are the ones primarily serving low-income communities, people of color, and other individuals excluded from the contraceptive marketplace.

Rather than challenging reproductive autonomy as a construct, an implausible premise for conservatives deeply weeded to the ideas of individualism and choice, lawmakers and anti-choice advocates target the infrastructure enabling individuals to make choices they disagree with. And the current system we've created and validated in the courts gives them every legal right to do so. Take for instance Reagan's "gag rule" prohibiting Title X-supported providers from engaging in abortion-related services. The policy itself does not prevent a woman from accessing an abortion, but when combined with the Hyde Amendment, barring the use of Medicaid or Medicare funds for abortion creates insurmountable obstacles for low-income women who lack access to a private physician to obtain abortion-related services. Appellants made this exact argument when challenging the legality of Reagan's "gag rule" and were summarily dismissed. The court's finding in *Rust v. Sullivan* bluntly stated: "The fact that most Title X clients may be effectively precluded by indigency from seeing a health care provider for abortion-related services does not affect the outcome here, since the financial constraints on such a woman's ability to enjoy the full range of constitutionally protected freedom of choice are the product not of governmental restrictions, but of her indigency."[81] Recycling the neoliberal drivel framing individuals as solely responsible for their situation, the court legitimizes restrictions that effectively reduce, if not completely eliminate, any real options for impoverished women.

To pursue reproductive justice, we must shed our loyalty to the existing system. Calling the current framework a hollow "truncation of the aspirational feminist vision of reproductive justice," Robin West insists, "We should be explaining the pragmatic reasons that women here and now must have control over their own reproductive lives, rather than focus as exclusively as we have on principled constitutional claims that report to rest on timeless principle."[82] Kalpana Wilson articulates how this approach differs from the limited reproductive rights framework currently in use. She explains, "Whereas the reproductive rights approach claims to grant choices to individuals within a neoliberal framework which remains unquestioned, the demand for reproductive justice makes visible the broader structural forces—economic, political and social—which deny women control over their bodies and over wider processes of reproduction."[83] Ross and Solinger outline with great precision how the adoption of a human rights framework inexorably changes the pursuit of reproductive justice, arguing:

> The case for reproductive justice makes another basic claim: access to these material resources is justified on the grounds that safe and dignified fertility management, childbirth, and parenting together constitute a fundamental *human right*. . . . Reproductive justice uses a human rights framework to draw attention to—and resist—laws and public and corporate policies based on racial, gender, and class prejudices. These laws and policies deny people the right to control their bodies, interfere with their reproductive decision making, and, ultimately, prevent many people from being able to live with dignity and safe and healthy communities. The human rights analysis rests on the claim that interference with the safety and dignity of fertile and reproducing persons is a blow against their humanity—that is against their rights as human beings. Protecting people against this interference is crucial to ensuring the human rights of all because all of us have the same human right to be fertile, the human right to engage in sexual relations, and the human right to reproduce or not, and the human right to be able to care for your children with dignity and safety.[84]

The rights framework is not entirely a lost cause, but rather than lionizing the negative rights we currently have and demanding the government also treat contraception as a positive right, we must push for the acceptance of reproductive autonomy as a *human right*.

From a rhetorical standpoint, we must also abandon the strategy of political accommodation that places the movement in a deferential posture necessitating advocates adhere to the hegemonic norms governing reproduction and adopt the language of neoliberalism to be heard. We must stop talking about the barriers to contraceptive access as purely financial—a move that directly reinforces the neoliberal ethos of self-management. We must stop articulating the implications of an unintended pregnancy in terms of lost wages as if there aren't a litany of other concerns that matter. We must stop justifying contraceptive access almost exclusively in terms of upward mobility. It is undeniably true that having the ability to plan a pregnancy improves the odds of obtaining a college degree, finding and maintain a well-paying job, and supporting a child for the duration of its life without needing financial assistance. But this statement reduces the question of contraceptive access and family planning to an economic one rather than what it truly is—a basic human right. We must stop begging for inclusion in a neoliberal marketplace not suited to fulfill the emancipatory promise of true reproductive autonomy. We tried that and we've seen firsthand where that gets us. We must stop. To be clear, these are all supremely valid justifications for continued contraceptive access, but so long as we continue to shroud the fight for reproductive justice in the neoliberal rhetoric of the state, we will always find ourselves asking for permission to exercise our basic human rights.

In the early 1900s, advocates found themselves at a similar crossroads: follow Dennett into an arduous battle defending the ideology of women's emancipation to a hostile audience or follow Sanger into an incremental battle packaging contraception as a respectable solution to an audience willing to listen exclusively on their terms. Over 100 years later, it's time for us to choose the path less traveled. It's time for us to heed Dennett's 1926 battle cry:

> Much as we wish that one kind gesture would sweep aside these obsolete and ridiculous anti-contraceptive laws, both federal and state, experience has shown us the emptiness of legal and legislative victories unless followed up vigorously by concerted action. . . . Our interests and our activity must be positive, fundamental, dynamic, constructive. Let us beware of the futility of striving after vain victories and theoretical triumphs—which may, indeed, stimulate in us a fine glow of egotistical satisfaction, but also divert and distract our attention and interest from the hard, thankless, detailed work of helping overburdened mothers. Let us not be led into the trap of believing that the mere repeal of a

> Federal law will change the course of ancient human habits or the most deep rooted of instincts.[85]

We have basked in the glow of our victories long enough; it is time to get back to work. And this time not just for *some* women but for *all* women.

NOTES

1. Koening, "Law and Disorder," 199.
2. Morton, "Shall We," 14.
3. Drysdale, "The Malthusian," 18.
4. Ellis, "Today," 1.
5. Leslie, "Whys and," 250.
6. "Candidates Change," 14.
7. Hankins, "The Interdependence," 170.
8. Robinson, "Twenty-five," 323.
9. "A Champion," 302.
10. Sanger, *Motherhood in Bondage*, 26.
11. Tone, *Devices and Desires*, 82.
12. Jones and Tertilt, "An Economic History," 31.
13. Margaret Sanger Papers, 236127.
14. Rosen, "The Shifting," 197.
15. McCann, *Birth Control Politics*, 175.
16. Gordon, *The Moral Property*, 220.
17. Margaret Sanger Papers, 223091.
18. Margaret Sanger Papers, 236022.
19. Fishback, Haines, and Kantor, "Births, Deaths, and New Deal," 3.
20. Margaret Sanger Papers, 236523.
21. Gordon, *The Moral Property*, 213.
22. Margaret Sanger Papers, 222421.
23. Gordon, *The Moral Property*, 213.
24. Gardner, "Margaret Sanger Tells," H3.
25. Sanger, "National Security," 141.
26. Margaret Sanger Papers, 224704.
27. "Social Aspects," 424.
28. Baber, "Birth Control," 296.
29. Hankins, "The Social," 2–3.
30. "U.S. Security Seen," 12.
31. Gordon, *The Moral Property*, 240–41.
32. "Three Birth," 210.
33. "South Carolina," 30.
34. Wile, "Contraception and," 7–8.
35. Spaeth, "Birth Control," 154–55.
36. Ibid.

37. Davis, *Women, Race, and Class*, 362; Matsner, "State Public," 36.
38. Gordon, *The Moral Property*, 230.
39. Centers for Disease Control, "Achievements in," para. 5.
40. Rosen, "The Shifting," 210.
41. "Birth Control on Rise," 25.
42. Pilpel, "The Crazy," 142.
43. Spencer, "The Birth," para. 4–7.
44. Johnson, "Address in San Francisco," para. 44.
45. "Seek Federal Control," 10.
46. Bailey, "Reexamining the," 64–65.
47. Eckhardt. "The Reluctance," 24712.
48. Gold, "Title X," 5.
49. Nixon, "President Nixon," 110.
50. Flowers, "Voodoo Biology," 333.
51. Gold, "Title X," 6.
52. "Reactions Mixed," 9.
53. Vansickle-Ward and Wallsten, *The Politics*, 222.
54. Rosenbaum, "Carter Asks," 25.
55. Roberts, "Funds to," 18.
56. Williams, "The GOP's," 513.
57. National Family Planning & Reproductive Health Association, "Domestic Gag Rule," 1.
58. Flowers, "Voodoo Biology," 345.
59. Gold, "Title X," 8.
60. Statement of George Bush, 115 Congressional Record H4207, 24 February 1969.
61. Tumulty and Cimons, "Clinton Revokes," 1.
62. Hasstedt, "Beyond the," 86.
63. Office of Population Affairs.
64. Levintova, "Congress Just," para. 1.
65. Hasstedt, "Beyond the," 86.
66. Hasstedt, "Title X," 14.
67. *Little Sisters of the Poor*, 14.
68. Guttmacher Institute, "How Has," para. 3.
69. North, "The Trump," para. 31–37.
70. Biden, "Memorandum on," para. 3–4.
71. Robeznieks, "Biden Administration," para. 7.
72. Gerson, "What Is Title," para 3.
73. Schram, "Neoliberalizing the," 308.
74. Elliott, "'Who's to,'" 212.
75. Grzanka and Schuch, "Reproductive Anxiety," 277.
76. Schram, "Neoliberalizing the," 308.
77. Ibid., 314.
78. Elliott, "'Who's to,'" 212.
79. Grzanka and Schuch, "Reproductive Anxiety," 297–98.
80. Roy and Thompson, *The Politics*, 5.

81. *Rust v. Sullivan*, 176.
82. West, "From Choice," 1422–28.
83. Wilson, "In the Name," 67.
84. Ross and Solinger, *Reproductive Justice*, 10.
84. Dennett, *Birth Control Laws*, 289.

Bibliography

"900 Women Saved through Birth Control." *Birth Control Review* 13, no. 1 (1924): 6–7.

A. B. S. "Saving the Mothers." *The Woman's Journal and Suffrage News*, Sep. 16, 1916.

"A Champion of Birth Control." *Birth Control Review* 11, no. 11 (1927): 302.

ACOG Committee on Ethics. *Sterilization of Women: Ethical Issues and Considerations*. Washington, DC: American College of Obstetricians and Gynecologists, 2020. https://www.acog.org/clinical/clinical-guidance/committee-opinion/articles/2017/04/sterilization-of-women-ethical-issues-and-considerations.

Adams, Mildred. "Woman's Future: Two Divergent Paths." *New York Times*, Mar. 18, 1934, SM8.

"A Judge on Birth Control." *Birth Control Review* 2, no. 8 (September 1918): 11.

Alexander, W. G. "A Medical Viewpoint." *Birth Control Review* 26, no. 6 (1932): 175.

"American Medical Association Considers Birth Control." *Birth Control Review* 17, no. 7 (1933): 164–65.

Amos, Waldo Adams. "To a Jailbird." *Birth Control Review* 1, no. 3 (April 1917): 7.

"Appeal Now to Supreme Court." *Boston Daily Globe*, Nov. 22, 1916, 11.

"Appealing to the Voters." *Birth Control Review* 8, no. 12 (1924): 346, 363.

"Archbishop Hayes on Birth Control." *New York Times*, Dec. 18, 1921.

Asbell, Bernard. *The Pill: A Biography of the Drug That Changed the World*. New York: Random House, 1995.

Ashley, Jessie. "Editorial Comment." *Birth Control Review* 2, no. 11 (December1918): 2.

Baber, Ray Erwin. "Birth Control—A Balance Sheet." *Forum and Century* 88 (November 1932): 294–300.

Bailey, Harold. "The Report of the Committee on the Regulation of Conception." *American Journal of Obstetrics and Gynecology* 7, no. 3 (1924): 339–42.

Bailey, Martha J. "Reexamining the Impact of Family Planning Programs on US Fertility: Evidence from the War on Poverty and the Early Years of Title X." *American Economic Journal: Applied Economics* 4, no. 2 (2012): 62–97.

"Bars Magazine from Mail." *New York Times*, Apr. 4, 1914.

"Battle Is Started in Congress for Birth Control Bill." *The Seattle Star*, Nov. 25, 1915.

"The Battle over Birth Control." *Current Opinion* 59, no. 5 (November 1915): 339–40.

Bernhard, Mrs. Richard J. "Child Welfare and Planned Parenthood." *Birth Control Review* 22, no. 9 (1938): 102.

Berndt, Virginia Kuulei, and Ann V. Bell. "'This Is What the Truth Is': Provider-Patient Interactions Serving as Barriers to Contraception." *Health* (October 2020): 1–17.

"The Best Letter." *Birth Control Review* 11, no. 11 (1927): 290.

Betts, Frederick W. "A Christian Attitude towards Birth Control." *Birth Control Review* 6, no. 10 (1922): 198–99.

Biden, Joseph R. "Memorandum on Protecting Women's Health at Home and Abroad." *White House Briefing Room*, Jan. 28, 2021. https://www.whitehouse.gov/briefing-room/presidential-actions/2021/01/28/memorandum-on-protecting-womens-health-at-home-and-abroad/.

"Birth Control." *The Pittsburgh Courier*, Feb. 7, 1931.

"Birth-Control and Aid." *Washington Post*, Jan. 25, 1916.

"Birth Control and Free Speech." *Outlook* 129 (1921): 507.

"Birth Control and the State." *Journal of the American Medical Association* 87, no. 12 (1926): 963.

"Birth Control Bill Hearing in Hartford." *New York Times*, Feb. 14, 1923.

"Birth Control Clinic Loses License Fight." *Chicago Daily Tribune*, Feb. 4, 1925.

"Birth Control Debated by Rabbi and Judge." *Chicago Daily Tribune*, Mar. 31, 1932, 16.

"Birth Control Held Aid to the Family." *New York Times*, Aug. 21, 1930, 7.

"Birth Control on Rise." *New York Times*, Sep. 11, 1950, 25.

"Birth Control Pill Called Moral Measure." *Boston Globe*, Jan. 26, 1962, 4.

"'Birth Control' Propaganda." *Woman Patriot* 5, no. 17 (1921): 4.

"Birth Control Subject of Wide Discussion." *The Waxahachie Daily Light* (Waxahachie, TX), Nov. 30, 1915.

"Birth Control Talks Decried by Archbishop." *New York Tribune*, Nov. 21, 1921.

Black, Edwin. *War against the Weak: Eugenics and America's Campaign to Create a Master Race.* United Kingdom: Basic Books, 2004.

Blakesley, David. "Terministic Screens." In *The SAGE Encyclopedia of Communication Research Methods*, edited by Mike Allen, 1745–48. Thousand Oaks, CA: SAGE Publications, 2017.

Bloom, Amy S., and Ellen Parsons. The 25th Anniversary of *The Doctor's Case against the Pill.* Washington, DC: National Women's Health Network, 1994. https://nwhn.org/25th anniversary-doctors-case-against-pill-0.

Blount, Anna E. "Eugenics in Relation to Birth Control." *Birth Control Review* 2, no. 1 (1918): 7.

Blount, Anna E. "Large Families and Human Waste." *Birth Control Review* 2, no. 8 (1918): 3–4.

Bolton, Alexander, and Lydia Wheeler. "Gorsuch Rewrites Playbook for Confirmation Hearings." *The Hill*, Mar. 22, 2017. https://thehill.com/homenews/news/325343-gorsuch-rewrites-playbook-for-confirmation-hearings.

"The Bookshelf." *Woman's Journal* (1929): 34.
Boonstra, Heather. "Emergency Contraception: Steps Being Taken to Improve Access." *The Guttmacher Report on Public Policy* 5, no. 5 (2002): 10–13.
Boughton, Alice C. "The Cincinnati Clinic: A Report." *Birth Control Review* 15, no. 9 (1931): 251–52.
Boughton, Alice C. "What 7309 Mothers Want." *Birth Control Review* 17, no. 1 (January 1933): 10.
Bousfield, M. O. "Negro Public Health Work Needs Birth Control." *Birth Control Review* 26, no. 6 (1932): 170–71.
Briffault, Robert. "Will Monogamy Die Out?" *Birth Control Review* 16, no. 7–8 (1932): 207–33.
Briggs, Laura, Faye Ginsburg, Elena R. Gutierrez, Rosalind Petchesky, Rayna Rapp, Andrea Smith, and Chikako Takeshita. "Roundtable": Reproductive Technologies and Reproductive Justice." *Frontiers: A Journal of Women Studies* 34, no. 3 (2013): 102–25.
Brisbane, Arthur. "Birth Control Danger, might prevent a Lincoln," *The Washington Times*, Feb. 2, 1920.
Brody, Jane E. "The Pill: Revolution in Birth Control." *New York Times*, May 31, 1966, 1.
Brody, Jane E. "The Politics of Emergency Contraception." *New York Times*, Aug. 24, 2004.
Bromley, Dorothy Dunbar. "Birth Control: Yes or No?" *Woman's Journal*, June 1931, 20–21.
Browning, Norma Lee. "The Better Half." *Chicago Daily Tribune*, May 4, 1947, G8.
Buerkle, Wesley C. "From Women's Liberation to Their Obligation: The Tensions between Sexuality and Maternity in Early Birth Control Rhetoric." *Women and Language* 31, no. 1 (2008): 27–34.
Burch, Guy Irving. "Causes of Future Wars." *New York Times*, May 20, 1926, 24.
Burns, Gene. *The Moral Veto: Framing Contraception, Abortion, and Pluralism in the United States*. Cambridge, England: Cambridge University Press, 2005.
"Calendar Fear." *New York Daily News*, July 16, 1933, 23.
"Can't Carry Woman's Magazine in Mails." *Xenia Daily Gazette* (Xenia, OH), Apr. 4, 1914.
"Candidates Change Their Tune When Women Vote." *Birth Control Review* 2, no. 11 (1918): 14.
Carter, Elmer A. "Eugenics for the Negro." *Birth Control Review* 26, no. 6 (1932): 169–70.
Center for Reproductive Rights. "Protect, Defend, Extend: 2018 State of the States." Accessed December 12, 2018. https://reproductiverights.org/State-of-the-States-2018.
Centers for Disease Control. "Achievements in Public Health, 1990–1999: Family Planning." *Morbidity and Mortality Weekly Report* 48, no. 47 (1999): 1073–80.
"The Children's Charter." *Birth Control Review* 2, no. 7 (1935): 290.
Clark, Mary Vida. "The Rights of Children." *The North American Review* 216 (September 1922): 405–11.

Clinton, Hillary. "Preventing Unwanted Pregnancy" (speech, NYS Family Planning Providers, New York City, January 24, 2005). https://speakingwhilefemale.co/womens-lives-clinton/.

Condit, Celeste. *Decoding Abortion Rhetoric*. Chicago: University of Illinois Press, 1990.

"Congregational Group Approves Birth Control." *Chicago Daily Tribune*, Jul. 3, 1931, 3.

Conrad, Earl. "On U.S. Birth and Bias Control." *The Chicago Defender*, Sep. 22, 1945.

Cosgrove, Lisa, and Akansha Vaswani. "Fetal Rights, the Policing of Pregnancy, and Meanings of the Maternal in an Age of Neoliberalism." *Journal of Theoretical and Philosophical Psychology* 40, no.1 (2020): 43–53.

"Court Rules That New Babies in Families Are No Excuse at All for an Increase in Rent." *New York Times*, May 25, 1948, 29.

"Court Upholds Clinic Program." *Birth Control Review* 4, no. 5 (1937): 3–5.

Cox, Ignatius W. "Condemning Birth Control." *New York Times*, Dec. 27, 1933, 18.

Coyle, Marcia. "Why Barrett, Like Nominees before Her, Dodges Questions on the Girswold Birth Control Decision." *The National Law Journal*, Oct. 14, 2020. https://www.law.com/nationallawjournal/2020/10/14/why-barrett-like-nominees-before-her-dodged-questions-on-the-griswold-birth-control-decision/.

Craig, John M. "'The Sex Side of Life': The Obscenity Case of Mary Ware Dennett." *Frontiers: A Journal of Women Studies* 15, no. 3 (1995): 146–66.

Davis, Angela. *Women, Race, and Class*. New York: Vintage Books, 1983.

Davis, Kingsley. "Analysis of the Population Explosion." *New York Times*, Sep. 22, 1957, 26–27.

Dearborn, Ella K. "Birth Control." *Birth Control Review* 12, no. 3 (1928): 88.

"Debate between Margaret Sanger and Winter Russell." *The Fine Arts Guild of New York City*, Dec. 12, 1920.

Debs, Eugene V. "Freedom Is the Goal." *Birth Control Review* 2, no. 4 (May 1918): 7.

"Defective Baby Divides Doctors." *New York Tribune*, Nov. 18, 1915.

Denbow, Jennifer M. "The Problem with *Hobby Lobby*: Neoliberal Jurisprudence and Neoconservative Values." *Feminist Legal Studies* 25, no. 1 (2017): 1–20.

Dennett, Mary Ware. "'Not Fit to Print.'" *Birth Control Review* 3, no. 4 (1919): 17.

Dennett, Mary Ware. "Fitness for Suffrage." *New York Times*, Jun. 5, 1914.

Dennett, Mary Ware. "Legislators, Six-Hour Weeks and Birth Control." *Birth Control Review* 3, no. 3 (March 1919): 4.

Dennett, Mary Ware. "The Right of a Child to Two Parents." *The Century* 90, no. 1 (1915): 104–8.

Dennett, Mary Ware. "Voluntary Parenthood Bill." *New York Times*, Dec. 17, 1923.

Dennett, Mary Ware. "Voluntary Parenthood." *New York Times*, Feb. 11, 1922.

Dennett, Mary Ware. *Birth Control Laws: Shall We Keep Them, Change Them, or Abolish Them?* New York: Da Capo Press, 1970.

Dennett, Mary Ware. *Sex Side of Life*. Princeton, NJ: Princeton University Press, 1919.

Department of Commerce, *Mortality Statistics 1915: Sixteenth Annual Report*, 409. Washington, DC: Government Printing Office, 1917.

DeVilbiss, Lydia Allen, and Harold J. Laski. "Birth Control, a Public Health Approach." *Birth Control Review* 15, no. 5 (1931): 139–40.

Dewan, Shaila. "Anti-Abortion Ads Split Atlanta." *New York Times*, Feb. 5, 2010. https://www-nytimes-com.proxy.libraries.uc.edu/2010/02/06/us/06abortion.html?scp=1&sq=Shaila.

Dewey, John. "Education and Birth Control." *Birth Control Review* 14, no. 2 (1932): 34.

Dickinson, Robert L. "American Birth Control League." *Journal of the American Medical Association* 85, no. 15 (1925): 1153–54.

Dickinson, Robert L. "Contraception: A Medical Review of the Situation: First Report of the Committee on Maternal Health of New York." *American Journal of Obstetrics and Gynecology* 8, no. 5 (1924): 583–604.

Dickinson, Robert L. "The Medical Aspects of Sterilization." *Birth Control Review* 17, no. 4 (1933): 99.

Dickinson, Robert L., and Ruth Vincent. "Our Correspondents' Column Birth Control and Medical Bodies." *Birth Control Review* 9, no. 10 (1925): 293–94.

Dilla, Harriette M. "The Social Significance of Birth Control." *Birth Control Review* 6, no. 3 (1922): 34–36.

Dittrick Medical History Center. "Intrauterine Devices (IUD)." Case Western Reserve University. Updated 2021, https://artsci.case.edu/dittrick/online-exhibits/history-of-birth-control/contraception-in-america-1950-present-day/intrauterine-device-iud.

Doak, Melissa, and Rachel Brugger. 2000. *How Did the Debate between Margaret Sanger and Mary Ware Dennett Shape the Movement to Legalize Birth Control, 1915–1924*. Binghamton, NY: State University of New York.

"The Doctors and Birth Control." *Birth Control Review* 7, no. 6 (1923): 144–45.

"Doctors Condemn Birth Control Raid." *New York Times*, Apr. 3, 1929, 3.

"Doctors Divided on Birth Control." *New York Times*, Nov. 19, 1916, 22.

"Doctors in Survey for Birth Control." *New York Times*, Feb. 11, 1947, 28.

Dorman, Marjorie. "The Weeping Stork and the Puzzled College Cupid." *Los Angeles Times*, Jul. 15, 1923, X20.

Douthat, Ross. "The 'Safe, Legal, Rare' Illusion." *New York Times*, Feb. 12, 2012. https://www.nytimes.com/2012/02/19/opinion/sunday/douthat-the-safe-legal-rare-illusion.html (accessed January 1, 2021).

"Dr. Dickinson on the Control of Conception." *Birth Control Review* 15, no. 1 (1931): 5–7.

"Dr. Haiselden Writes of Baby." *The Seattle Star*, Nov. 23, 1915.

"Dr. Rock Scored on Birth Control: Msgr. Kelly Assails Stand on Contraceptive Pills." *New York Times*, May 6, 1963.

Drysdale, Charles. "The Malthusian Doctrine Today." *Birth Control Review* 3, no. 4 (1919): 18–19.

DuBois, W. E. B. "Black Folk and Birth Control." *Birth Control Review* 26, no. 6 (1932): 166–67.

Dubow, Sara. *Ourselves Unborn: A History of the Fetus in Modern America*. New York: Oxford University Press, 2010.

Dubriwny, Tasha N., and Kate Siegfried. "Justifying Abortion: The Limits of Maternal Idealist Rhetoric." *Quarterly Journal of Speech* 107, no. 2: 185–208.

East, Edward Murray. "Tabu: A Defense of Birth Control." *Birth Control Review* 6, no. 8 (1927): 222.

Eastman, Crystal. "Birth Control in the Feminist Program." *Birth Control Review* 2, no. 1 (January 1918): 3.

Eckhardt, Bob. "The Reluctance of Uncle Sam's Bureaucrats to Fight Poverty with 'The Pill.'" *Congressional Record: Proceedings and Debates* 115, no. 18, Sep. 8, 1969.

Edgren, Maude Durand. "The Spiritual Aspect of Birth Control." *Birth Control Review* 1, no. 5 (December 1917): 6.

"Editorial." *Birth Control Review* 7, no. 1 (1928): 5.

"Editorial." *Birth Control Review* 12, no. 6 (1928): 169.

"Editorial." *Birth Control Review* 12, no. 8 (1928): 223–24.

"Editorial." *Birth Control Review* 13, no. 3 (1929): 69–70.

"Editorial." *Birth Control Review* 13, no. 4 (1929): 99.

"Editorial." *Birth Control Review* 13, no. 6 (1929): 145.

"Editorial Comment." *Birth Control Review* 1, no. 5 (1917): 16.

"Editorial Comment." *Birth Control Review* 2, no. 2 (1918): 16.

"Editorial Comment." *Birth Control Review* 2, no. 6 (July 1918): 9.

E. F. R. "Letter to the Editor." *Birth Control Review* 6, no. 11 (1922): 230.

"Ellen Key, Feminist." *New York Times*, May 2, 1926, E8.

Elliott, Sinikka. "'Who's to Blame?' Constructing the Responsible Sexual Agent in Neoliberal Sex Education." *Sexuality Research and Social Policy* 11 (2014): 211–24.

Ellis, Havelock. "Birth Control in Relation to Morality." *Birth Control Review* 1, no. 1 (1912): 6–7.

Ellis, Havelock. "Eugenics and the Uneducated." *Forum* 67 (January 1922): 1–1.

Ellis, Havelock. "The Love Rights of Women." *Birth Control Review* 2, no. 5 (June 1918): 4.

Ellis, Havelock. "The Objects of Marriage." *Birth Control Review* 4, no. 1 (June 1917): 8.

Ellis, Havelock. "Today—an Interpretation." *Birth Control Review* 1, no. 2 (1933): 1.

E. M. "Birth Control Now Rates with Respectables." *Chicago Daily Tribune*, Apr. 30, 1925.

Emerson, Thomas I. "Nine Justices in Search of a Doctrine" *Michigan Law Review* 64, no. 2 (1965): 219–34.

Engelman, Peter C. "The Rivalry between Margaret Sanger and Mary Ware Dennett." ProQuest History Vault.

Engelman, Peter C. *A History of the Birth Control Movement in America*. Santa Barbara, CA: ABC-CLIO, 2011.

Ernst, Morris L., and Harriet F. Pilpel. "Release from the Comstock Era." *Birth Control Review* 24, no. 2 (1939): 24–25.

Evans, W. A. "How to Keep Well." *Chicago Daily Tribune*, Dec. 10, 1926, 10.

Ezer, Tamar. "A Positive Right to Protection for Children." *Yale Human Rights and Development Law Journal* 7, no. 1 (2004): 1–50.

"Family Trees Which Should Bear No Fruit." *Birth Control Review* 6, no. 1 (1927): 16.

"Feminism and Birth Control." *Birth Control Review* 12, no. 1 (1928): 21.

Fineman, Martha L. A. "Masking Dependency: The Political Role of Family Rhetoric." *Virginia Law Review* 81, no. 8 (1995): 2181–215.

Fishback, Price V., Michael R. Haines, and Shawn Kantor. "Births, Deaths, and New Deal Relief during the Great Depression." *The Review of Economics and Statistics* 58, no. 1 (February 2007): 1–14.

Fishbein, Morris. *The Medical Follies: An Analysis of the Foibles of Some Healing Cults, Including Osteopathy, Homeopathy, Chiropractic, and the Electronic Reactions of Abrams, with Essays on the Antivivisectionists, Health Legislation, Physical Culture, Birth Control, and Rejuvenation.* New York: Boni and Liveright.

Fisher, Constance. "The Negro Social Worker Evaluates Birth Control." *Birth Control Review* 26, no. 6 (1932): 174–75.

Flores, Stephanie. "Redefining Reproductive Rights in an Age of Cultural Revolution." *On Our Terms: The Undergraduate Journal of the Athena Center for Leadership Studies at Barnard College* 2, no. 1 (2014): 1–32.

Flowers, Prudence. "'Voodoo Biology': The Right-to-Life Campaign against Family Planning Programs in the United States in the 1980s." *Women's History Review* 29, no. 2 (2020): 331–56.

Fluke, Sandra. "Law Students for Reproductive Justice." Congressional testimony delivered on February 23, 2012. https://abcnews.go.com/images/Politics/statement-Congress-letterhead-2nd%20hearing.pdf.

Follet, Joyce C. "Making Democracy Real: African American Women, Birth Control, and Social Justice, 1910–1960." *Meridians: Feminism, Race, Transnationalism* 18, no. 1 (2019): 94–151.

Foucault, Michel. *Archaeology of Knowledge.* United Kingdom: Knopf Doubleday Publishing Group, 2012.

A Friend. "Hymn of the Unborn Babe." *Birth Control Review* 2, no. 6 (1918): 16.

Gallup, George. "Birth Control Clinics Favored: The Gallup Poll Those Disapproving Plan See Race Suicide in It." *Daily Boston Globe*, Jan. 25, 1940.

Gans, David H. "OP-ED: Kavanaugh's Alarming Silence on Griswold's Affirmation of Personal Liberty." *Constitutional Accountability Center*, Sep. 14, 2018. https://www.theusconstitution.org/news/op-ed-kavanaughs-alarming-silence-on-griswolds-affirmation-of-personal-liberty/.

Gardner, Bradford. "Margaret Sanger Tells What She Would Do." *Los Angeles Times*, Feb. 26, 1933, H3.

Gardner, Virginia. "Urges Doctors Take Charge of Birth Control." *Chicago Daily Tribune*, Jan. 18, 1935.

Garvin, Charles H. "The Negro Doctor's Task." *Birth Control Review* 16, no. 9 (1932): 269–70.

Gentile, Katie. "Using Queer and Psychoanalytic Times to Explore the Troubling Temporalities of Fetal Personhood." *Studies in Gender and Sexuality* 16, no. 1 (2015): 33–39.

Gerson, Jennifer. "What Is Title X, and What Did Trump and Biden Do to Change It?" *New York Times*, Oct. 8, 2021.

Gibson, Beth. "The Termination of the Quickening Doctrine: American Law, Society, and the Advent of Professional Medicine in the Nineteenth Century." Masters Thesis (Western Kentucky University, 1995).

Gilman, Charlotte Perkins. "Progress through Birth Control." *The North American Review*, no. 224 (December 1927): 622–30.

Gold, Rachel Benson. "Title X: Three Decades of Accomplishment." *The Guttmacher Report on Public Policy February* (2001): 5–8.

Goldberg, Michelle. "Alito's 'Hobby Lobby' Opinion Is Dangerous and Discriminatory." *The Nation*, Jun. 30, 2014.

Goldstein, Sidney E. "Control of Parenthood as a Moral Problem—the Case for and against Birth Control." *Birth Control Review* 6, no. 10 (1922): 195.

Gordon, Linda. "The Politics of Birth Control, 1920–1940: The Impact of Professionals." *International Journal of Health Services* 5, no. 2 (1975): 254–77.

Gordon, Linda. *The Moral Property of Women*. Champaign, IL: University of Illinois Press, 2002.

Gordon, Linda. *Woman's Body, Woman's Right: Birth Control in America*. New York: Penguin, 1990.

Granzow, Kara. "De-Constructing 'Choice': The Social Imperative and Women's Use of the Birth Control Pill." *Culture, Health, & Sexuality* 9, no. 1 (2007): 43–54.

Grimes, David A. "Emergency Contraception: Politics Trumps Science at the U.S. Food and Drug Administration." *Obstetrics and Gynecology* 104, 2 (2004): 220–21.

Gruenberg, Mrs. Sidonie Matsner. "The Positive Side of Birth Control." *Birth Control Review* 23, no. 9 (1939): 216–17.

Grzanka, Patrick R., and Elena Schuch. "Reproductive Anxiety and Conditional Agency at the Intersections of Privilege: A Focus Group Study of Emerging Adults' Perception of Long-Acting Reversible Contraception." *Journal of Social Issues* 76, no. 2 (2020): 270–313.

Guilford, Simeon H. "Woman's 'Emancipation'—from What?" *Woman's Protest* 7, no. 3 (1915): 5.

Guttmacher Institute. "How Has the ACA Affected Title X Services?" https://www.guttmacher.org/perspectives50/how-has-aca-affected-title-x-services.

Hall, Chapin. "New Sterilization Bill Hailed as Best of Kind." *Los Angeles Times*, Mar. 31, 1935, 6.

Halva-Neubauer, Glen A., and Sara L. Zeigler. "Promoting Fetal Personhood: The Rhetorical and Legislative Strategies of the Pro-Life Movement after *Planned Parenthood v. Casey*." *Feminist Formation* 22, no. 2 (2010): 101–23.

Hankins, F. H. "The Interdependence of Eugenics and Birth Control." *Birth Control Review* 15, no. 6 (1931): 170–71.

Hankins, Frank H. "The Sexual Chaos." *Birth Control Review* 13, no. 8 (1929): 215–39.

Hankins, Frank H. "The Social Significance of Family Size." *Birth Control Review* 3, no. 1 (1935): 2–3.

"Hard Facts." *Birth Control Review* 3, no. 7 (July 1919): 12.

Harris, Duchess. *Black Feminist Politics from Kennedy to Clinton.* New York: Palgrave Macmillan, 2009.

Harris, Louis I. "A Public Health Viewpoint." *Birth Control Review* 15, no. 3 (1931): 2.

Hart, Jamie. "Who Should Have the Children? Discussions of Birth Control among African-American Intellectuals, 1920–1939." *The Journal of Negro History* 79, no. 1 (1994): 3, 71–84.

Hart, Samantha. "The Reality Is: Abstinence-Only Sex Education Sucks." Planned Parenthood of Metropolitan Washington, DC, Blog. https://www.plannedparenthood.org/planned-parenthood-metropolitan-washington-dc/blog/the-reality-is-abstinence-only-sex-education-sucks (accessed December 31, 2020).

Hasstedt, Kinsey. "Beyond the Rhetoric: The Real-World Impact of Attacks on Planned Parenthood and Title X." *Guttmacher Policy Review* 20, no. 1 (2017): 86–91.

Hasstedt, Kinsey. "Title X: An Essential Investment, Now More Than Ever." *Guttmacher Policy Review* 16, no. 3 (2013): 14–19.

Haxton, Jennie N. "Child Welfare and Planned Parenthood." *Birth Control Review* 22, no. 9 (1938): 102.

"Hayes Denounces Birth Control Aim." *New York Times*, Nov. 21, 1921.

Healy, Patrick D. "Clinton Is Pressed to Clarify Her Stance on Abortion Laws." *New York Times*, Jan. 28, 2005. https://www.nytimes.com/2005/01/28/nyregion/clinton-is-pressed-to-clarify-her-stance-on-abortion-laws.html (accessed December 31, 2020).

"Helen Keller, Blind, Deaf and Dumb Genius, Writes of Defective Baby Case." *The New York Call*, Nov. 26, 1915.

"High Court Voids Oklahoma Felon Sterilizing Law." *Chicago Tribune*, Jun. 2, 1942, 18.

Hilts, Phillip J. "Birth-Control Backlash." *New York Times*, Dec. 16, 1990, SM 41.

Hogue, Fred. "Social Eugenics." *Los Angeles Times*, Jan. 5, 1941, I19.

Hollister, Howard K. "The Disappearing Double Standard." *Birth Control Review* 15, no. 11 (1931): 314–16.

Holmes, John Haynes. "The Church and Birth Control." *Birth Control Review* 6, no. 11 (1922): 228–29.

Holz, Rose. "Nurse Gordon on Trial: Those Early Days of the Birth Control Clinic Movement Reconsidered." *Journal of Social History* 39, no. 1 (2005): 112–40.

Hooker, Edith Houghton. "Birth Control and the Home." *Birth Control Review* 12, no. 9 (1928): 251.

Hooker, Edith Houghton. "The Tap-Root of the Subjection of Women." *Birth Control Review* 10, no. 7 (1926): 219–34.

Hooker, Edith Houghton, and J. Arthur Thomson. "Birth Control as an Essential Background to Monogamous Marriage." *Birth Control Review* 6, no. 8 (1922): 156–57.

"Horrible Examples Parade the New York Streets." *The Progressive Miner*, Oct. 26, 1915.

"'Horrible Examples' Parade Wall-St to Further Fight for Eugenics and Birth Control." *The Intelligencer* (Edwardsville, IL), Oct. 30, 1915, 1.

Hoyt, Kepler. "Answers to Mr. Lloyd." *Birth Control Review* 2, no. 6 (1918): 12–13.

Huntington, Ellsworth. "Committee on Contraceptive Practices." *Journal of the American Medical Association* 107, no. 1 (1936): 56–57.

"Illinois Divided on Birth Control: Parley Set on Plans to Give Data." *New York Times*, Nov. 11, 1962.

"Introduction." In *Radical Reproductive Justice*, edited by Loretta L. Ross, Lynn Roberts, Erika Derkas, Whitney Peoples and Pamela Bridgewater Toure, 11–34. New York City: Feminist Press, 2017.

"Is Birth Control a Constitutional Right?" *Birth Control Review* 3, no. 2 (November 1919): 6–7.

"Is the New Woman a Traitor to the Race?" *New York Times*, Aug. 28, 1921, 36.

Ivey, Lea C. "Deconstructing, Reclaiming, and Transforming the Discourse of Fetal Personhood: A Pro-choice Feminist Imperative." Masters Thesis (Texas Woman's University, 2005).

Jakimowicz, T. V. "A Priest on Birth Control." *Birth Control Review* 4, no. 3 (1920): 12.

Jamison, E. S. "The Future of Negro Health." *Birth Control Review* 22, no. 8 (1938): 94–95.

Johnson, Charles S. "A Question of Negro Health." *Birth Control Review* 26, no. 6 (1932): 167–69.

Johnson, Lyndon B. "Address in San Francisco at the 20th Anniversary." San Francisco, CA, 1965. http://www.presidency.ucsb.edu/ws/?pid=27054.

Jones, Larry E., and Michele Tertilt. "An Economic History of Fertility in the U.S.: 1826–1960." NBER Working Paper Series. Cambridge, MA: National Bureau of Economic Research.

Jong-Fast, Molly. "The Anti-Birth Control Movement is the New Anti-Abortion Movement." *Vogue*, July 1, 2021. https://www.vogue.com/article/anti-birth-control-movement (accessed November 26, 2021).

Keating, Isabelle. "The Church and Sex." *Harper's Monthly Magazine*, Sep. 1, 1933, 425–35.

Keenan, Ellen A. "The Child in the Hands of the Law." *Birth Control Review* 3, no. 12 (1919): 11–12.

Keith, Katie. "Supreme Court Upholds Broad Exemptions to Contraceptive Mandate—For Now." Health Affairs Blog. Accessed January 1, 2021. https://www.healthaffairs.org/do/10.1377/hblog20200708.110645/full/.

Kelves, Daniel J. "Sex without Fear." *New York Times*, Jun. 28, 1992, BR.

Kendig, Susan. "After Hobby Lobby: Where Do Women's Rights Fit In?" *Women's Healthcare* (November 2014): 39–41.

Kennedy, Studdert G. A. "Is Birth Control Right?—A Debate." *Forum* 77 (July 1927): 7–15.

King, Charles. *Gods of the Upper Air: How a Circle of Renegade Anthropologists Reinvented Race, Sex, and Gender in the Twentieth Century*. United States: Knopf Doubleday Publishing Group, 2020.

Knoblauch, Mary. "Editorial Comment." *Birth Control Review* 3, no. 6 (1919): 3–4.

Knopf, S. Adolphus. "An Arsenal of Argument." *Birth Control Review* 1, no. 3 (April–May 1917): 8.

Knopf, S. Adolphus. "Birth Control in Its Medical, Social, Economic, and Moral Aspects." Speech delivered at the 44th Annual Meeting of the American Public Health Association in Cincinnati, OH, Oct. 27, 1916. https://ajph.aphapublications.org/doi/pdf/10.2105/AJPH.7.2.152.

Koenig, Brigitte. "Law and Disorder at Home: Free Love, Free Speech, and the Search for an Anarchist Utopia." *Labor History* 45, no. 2 (2004): 199–223.

Kosmack, George W. "The Responsibility of the Medical Profession in the Movement for 'Birth Control.'" *Journal of the American Medical Association* 113, no. 17 (1939): 1553–59.

Ladd-Taylor, Molly. *Mother-Work: Women, Child-Welfare and the State, 1890–1930*. Chicago: University of Illinois Press, 1994.

Laughlin, Harry H. "Eugenical Aspects of Legal Sterilization." *Birth Control Review* 17, no. 4 (1933): 87–89.

"Law to Sterilize All Unfit to Be Sought This Year." *Chicago Tribune*, Jan. 4, 1923, 7.

"The League of Women Voters and Birth Control." *Birth Control Review* 10, no. 5 (1926): 177.

Leslie, Noel. "Whys and Wherefores." *Birth Control Review* 6, no. 12 (1922): 249–50.

Levin, Sharon. "The Hobby Lobby Decision Takes a Fundamentally Flawed Approach to Reproductive Health." National Women's Law Center. Accessed March 13, 2016. https://nwlc.org/blog/hobby-lobby-decision-takes-fundamentally-flawed-approach-reproductive-health/.

Levintova, Hannah. "Congress Just Got a Lot Closer to Defunding Planned Parenthood." *Mother Jones*, Feb. 16, 2017. https://www.motherjones.com/politics/2017/02/house-just-voted-allow-states-pull-contraception-funding-planned-parenthood/.

Linder, Forrest E., and Robert D. Grove. *Vital Statistics Rates in the United States 1900–1940*. Washington, DC: United States Government Printing Office, 1947.

Littlewood, Thomas B. *The Politics of Population Control*. Notre Dame, IN: University of Notre Dame Press, 1977.

Lombardo, Paul A. "How to Escape the Doctor's Dilemma? De-Medicalize Reproductive Technologies." *Journal of Law, Medicine & Ethics* 43, no. 2 (2015): 326–29.

Lombardo, Paul J. "Medicine, Eugenics, and the Supreme Court: From Coercive Sterilization to Reproductive Freedom," *Journal of Contemporary Health Law and Policy* 13, no. 1 (1996): 1–25.

Lovejoy, Owen R. "Birth Control and Child Labor." *Birth Control Review* 3, no. 4 (1919): 3.

Luker, Kristen. *Abortion & the Politics of Motherhood.* Berkeley, CA: University of California Press, 1985.

Lyon, Elias P. "Is Birth Control Eugenic?" *Birth Control Review* 15, no. 7 (1931): 200–202.
MacNamara, Trent. *Birth Control and American Modernity: A History of Popular Ideas.* United Kingdom: Cambridge University Press, 2018.
Margaret Sanger Papers Microfilm Edition: Smith College Collections Series.
Martin, Anna. "Birth Control or Racial Degeneration-Which?" *Birth Control Review* 5, no. 1 (1921): 12–13.
"Massachusetts Carries On." *Birth Control Review* 23, no. 2 (1938): 1.
Matsner, Eric M. "State Public Health Programs." *Birth Control Review* 22, no. 3–4 (1937–1938): 34–36.
Matsner, Eric M. "The Physician's Viewpoint." *Birth Control Review* 15, no. 3 (1931): 70–71.
May, Elaine Taylor. *America and the Pill: A History of Promise, Peril, and Liberation.* New York: Basic Books, 2010.
Mayhall, Laura E. Nym. "The Rhetorics of Slavery and Citizenship: Suffragist Discourse and Canonical Texts in Britain, 1880–1914." *Gender & History* 13, no. 3 (0481–97 2001).
McCann, Carole R. *Birth Control Politics in the United States, 1916–1945*. Ithaca, NY: Cornell University Press, 1994.
McGreevy, Patrick, and Melanie Mason. "Gov. Brown Signs Bills on Birth Control, Inmate Rights." *Los Angeles Times*, Sep. 25, 2014. http://www.latimes.com/local/politics/la-me-pol-brown-bills-20140926-story.html.
McLaren, Angus. *A History of Contraception: From Antiquity to the Present.* Cambridge, MA: Blackwell, 1990.
"Medical Council Decries Clinic Raid." *New York Times*, Apr. 26, 1929, 13.
Meier, Benjamin Mason, and Reilly Anne Dempsey. "Going Negative: How Reproductive Rights Discourse Has Been Altered from a Positive to a Negative Rights Framework in Support of 'Women's Rights.'" In *Women's Global Health and Human Rights*, edited by Padmini Murthy and Clyde Lanford Smith, 83–96. Boston: Jones & Bartlett Publishers, 2009.
"Men and Their Families." *The Arizona Republican*, May 2, 1915.
Meyer, Ernest L. "The Unborn Speaks." *Birth Control Review* 2, no. 6 (1935): 6.
Mihic, Sophia Jane. "Neoliberalism and the Jurisprudence of Privacy: An Experiment in Feminist Theorizing. *Feminist Theory* 9, no. 2 (2008): 165–84.
M. K. "Income and Infant Mortality." *Birth Control Review* 3, no. 11 (1919): 9.
Moore, Louis Deb. "Birth Control Marches On." *Birth Control Review* 4, no. 6 (1937): 3–4.
Morton, James F., Jr. "Shall We Have a Limited Birth Control?" *Birth Control Review* 3, no. 10 (1919): 12–14.
Moreno, Johnathan D., and Francis Kissling. "Forty Years Later, We're Still Fighting 'Eisenstadt v. Baird.'" *The Nation*, Mar. 20, 2012. http://www.thenation.com/article/166922/sex-and-singles-forty-years-later-were-still-fighting-eisenstadt-v-baird.
"The Mother's Need Is Desperate." *Birth Control Review* 2, no. 2 (1935): 4.

Mowrer, Ernest R. "Birth Control and Domestic Discord." *Birth Control Review* 16, no. 5 (1932): 189.

Mowrer, Harriet R. "Birth Control and the Clinical Treatment of Domestic Discord." *Birth Control Review* 3, no. 9 (1936): 4–5.

"Mrs. Byrne Fasts in Workhouse Cell." *New York Times*, Jan. 25, 1917.

"Mrs. Sanger May Defy Laws Here in Aid of Cause." *Chicago Daily Tribune*, Apr. 23, 1917, 17.

Mudgett, Ida Wright. "The Crying Need for Birth Control." *Birth Control Review* 2, no. 6 (July 1918): 7.

Murphree, Vanessa, and Karla K. Gower. "'Making Birth Control Respectable': Birth Control Review, 1917–1928." *American Journalism* 30, no. 2 (2013): 210–34.

Murray, John Middleton, and James Carruthers Young. "Modern Marriage." *Forum* 81 (January 1929): 22.

Nash, Elizabeth, and Lauren Cross. "2021 Is on Track to Become the Most Devastating Antiabortion State Legislative Session in Decades." *Guttmacher Institutive*, Apr. 30, 2021. https://www.guttmacher.org/article/2021/04/2021-track-become-most-devastating-antiabortion-state-legislative-session-decades (accessed June 2, 2021).

National Advisory Council on Negro Program. *Better Health for 13,000,000.* New York: Planned Parenthood Federation of America, 1957.

National Committee on Maternal Health. "Birth Control and Contraception." *Journal of the American Medical Association* 103, no. 15 (1934): 1169.

National Family Planning & Reproductive Health Association. "Domestic Gag Rule." June 2017. https://www.nationalfamilyplanning.org/file/Domestic-Gag-Fact-Sheet.pdf.

National Women's Law Center. Reproductive Rights & Health. "The Affordable Care Act's Birth Control Benefit: Too Important to Lose." Washington, DC: National Women's Law Center, 2017. https://nwlc.org/wp-content/uploads/2017/05/BC-Benefit-Whats-At-Stake.pdf.

"New Marriage Plan for Presbyterians." *New York Times*, May 2, 1932, 2.

"New Society of Strong Urged by McDougall." *Chicago Daily Tribune*, Apr. 26, 1923, 5.

Nixon, Richard. "President Nixon on Problems of Population Growth." *Population and Development Review* 32, no. 4 (2006): 110, 771–82.

North, Anna. "The Trump Administration's War on Birth Control." The Center for Public Integrity, Sep. 24, 2020. https://publicintegrity.org/politics/system-failure/the-trump-administrations-war-on-birth-control/.

Norwood, Carolette. "Misrepresenting Reproductive Justice: A Black Feminist Critique of 'Protecting Black Life.'" *Signs: Journal of Women in Culture and Society* 46, no. 3 (2021): 715–41.

"Nurseries in Flats Is Feminist Plea." *The Sun*, May 26, 1914, 11.

Office of Population Affairs. "Title X Program Funding History." U.S. Department of Health and Human Services. https://opa.hhs.gov/grant-programs/archive/title-x-program-funding-history.

Olson, James Stuart. *Historical Dictionary of the 1960s*. Westport, CT: Greenwood Press, 1999.

O'Reilly, John Boyle. "The Progress of Children's Rights." *Birth Control Review* 3, no. 4 (1919): 12–13.

"Organization for National Strength." *Birth Control Review* 4 (1937): 3.

O'Sullivan, Mary Kenney. "Sickness and Death among Poor Children." *Boston Daily Globe*, Jun. 20, 1915, 46.

"Parents Will Let Malformed Child Die Rather Than Live as Mental Defective." *Detroit Times*, Nov. 17, 1915.

Parkhurst, Genevieve. "Children Wanted." *The North American Review* 242 (Autumn 1936): 93.

Peeples, Jennifer Ann. "Downwind: Articulation and Appropriation of Social Movement Discourse." *Southern Communication Journal* 76, no. 3 (July–August 2011): 248–63.

Phillips, Richard. "Planned Parenthood." *Chicago Tribune*, Mar. 8, 1981, K1.

"Physicians Split on Birth Control." *New York Times*, Jun. 11, 1937, 25.

Pilpel, Harriet F. "The Crazy Quilt of Our Birth Control Laws." *The Journal of Sex Research* 1, no. 2 (1965): 135–42.

Planned Parenthood Federation of America. *Emergency Contraception: History and Access* (New York City, 2013).

Popenoe, Paul. "Birth Control and Eugenics." *Birth Control Review* 1, no. 3 (April 1917): 6.

Prescott, Heather Munro and Lauren MacIvor Thompson. "A Right to Ourselves: Women's Suffrage and the Birth Control Movement. *The Journal of the Gilded Age and Progressive Era* 19 (2020): 542–558.

Prescott, Heather Munro. *The Morning After: A History of Emergency Contraception in the United States*. New Brunswick, NJ: Rutgers University Press, 2011.

"The Prevention of Conception." *Journal of the American Medical Association* 80, no. 8 (1923): 473.

"Proceedings of the Atlantic City Session." *Journal of the American Medical Association* 108, no. 26 (1937): 2208–28.

"Protect, Defend, Extend: 2018 State of the States." Center for Reproductive Rights, December 12, 2018. https://reproductiverights.org/State-of-the-States-2018.

Pusey, William Allen. "Some of the Social Problems of Medicine." *Journal of the American Medical Association* 82, no. 24 (1924): 1905–8.

"Quotes." The W. Edwards Deming Institute. https://deming.org/quotes/10141/#:~:text=Every%20system%20is%20perfectly%20designed,Edwards%20Deming%20Institute (accessed March 12, 2021).

"The Raid." *Birth Control Review* 13, no. 6 (1929): 154–55.

"Reactions Mixed to U.S. Birth Plan: Catholic Fears for Poor—Others Praise Proposal." *New York Times*, Jul. 19, 1969.

Rebone, Joseph W. "Personhood and the Contraceptive Right." *Indiana Law Journal* 57, no. 4 (1982): 579–604.

Reed, James. *From Private Vice to Public Virtue: The Birth Control Movement in American Society since 1830*. New York: Basic Books, 1978.

Rehill, Annie. "Hearth and Home: Sharing Space with Jobs and Schools." In *Daily Life through History*. ABC-CLIO, 2010. Accessed May 23, 2013. http://dailylife2.abc-clio.com/.

Rene, Jessie A. "The Waste of Creative Energy." *Birth Control Review* 2, no. 6 (July 1918): 6.

"Resolutions." *Birth Control Review* 15, no. 2 (1931): 36.

Reynolds, Moira Davison. *Women Advocates of Reproductive Rights: Eleven Who Led the Struggle in the United States and Great Britain*. Jefferson, NC: McFarland & Co., 1994.

"Right to Sterilize Habitual Criminals Upheld in Oklahoma." *Chicago Tribune*, Jul. 31, 1934, 1.

"Rights of the Child Pleaded in Pulpits." *New York Times*, Jan. 29, 1917, 11.

Roberts, Carl G. "The Birthright of the Unborn." *Birth Control Review* 22, no. 8 (1938): 87–89.

Roberts, Dorothy. *Killing the Black Body*. New York: Pantheon Books, 1997.

Roberts, Steven V. "Funds to Help Pregnant Teen-Agers: An Idea Emerges and Gets In." *New York Times*, Jan. 24, 1978.

Roberts, Walter Adolphe. "Birth Control and the Revolution." *Birth Control Review* 1, no. 4 (June 1917): 7.

Robeznieks, Andis. "Biden Administration moves to eliminate Title X physician gag rule." *American Medical Association*, Apr. 23, 2021. https://www.ama-assn.org/delivering-care/patient-support-advocacy/biden-administration-moves-eliminate-title-x-physician-gag.

Robinson, Victor. *Pioneers of Birth Control in England and America*. New York: Voluntary Parenthood League, 1919.

Robinson, William J. "Is Birth Control Unnatural?" *Birth Control Review* 2, no. 2 (1918): 14.

Robinson, William J. "The Future of Marriage." *Birth Control Review* 15, no. 7 (1931): 210–12.

Robinson, William J. "Twenty-Five Years of Progress." *Birth Control Review* 11, no. 12 (1927): 323.

Rodrique, Jessie M. "15. The Black Community and the Birth Control Movement." In *Gendered Domains*, 244–60. Cornell University Press, 2018.

Rosen, Robyn L. "Federal Expansion, Fertility Control and Physicians in the United States: The Politics of Maternal Welfare in the Interwar Years." *Journal of Women's History* 10, no. 3 (1988): 6, 53–73.

Rosen, Robyn L. "The Shifting Battleground for Birth Control: Lessons from New York's Hudson Valley in the Interwar Years." *New York History* 90, no. 3 (2009): 187–215.

Rosen, Robyn L. *Reproductive Health, Reproductive Rights: Reformers and the Politics of Maternal Welfare, 1917–1940*. Columbus, OH: Ohio State University Press, 2003.

Rosenbaum, David E. "Carter Asks Congress to Disregard Ford Proposals to Cut Funds for Social Programs." *New York Times*, Feb. 23, 1977.

Ross, Loretta J. "Conceptualizing Reproductive Justice Theory: A Manifesto for Activism." In *Radical Reproductive Justice*, edited by Loretta L. Ross, Lynn Roberts, Erika Derkas, Whitney Peoples, and Pamela Bridgewater Toure, 170–232. New York City: Feminist Press, 2017.

Ross, Loretta J. "Reproductive Justice as Intersectional Feminist Activism." *Souls* 19, no. 3 (2017): 286–314.

Ross, Loretta J. "Trust Black Women: Reproductive Justice and Eugenics." In *Radical Reproductive Justice*, edited by Loretta L. Ross, Lynn Roberts, Erika Derkas, Whitney Peoples, and Pamela Bridgewater Toure, 58–85. New York City: Feminist Press, 2017.

Ross, Loretta J., and Rickie Solinger. *Reproductive Justice*. Oakland, CA: University of California Press, 2017.

Roy, Modhumita, and Mary Thompson. *The Politics of Reproduction: Adoption, Abortion, and Surrogacy in the Age of Neoliberalism.* Columbus, OH: Ohio State University Press, 2019.

Ruhl, Lealle. "Dilemmas of the Will: Uncertainty, Reproduction, and the Rhetoric of Control." *Journal of Women in Culture and Society* 27, no. 3 (Spring 2002): 641–63.

Sage, Earl C., and Harold Cox. "Let Doctors Face the Problem." *Birth Control Review* 13, no. 11 (1929): 322–23.

Sanger, Margaret. "An Answer to Mr. Roosevelt." *Birth Control Review* 5, no. 1 (December 1917): 13.

Sanger, Margaret. "Are Birth Control Methods Injurious?" *Birth Control Review* 3, no. 1 (January 1919): 3.

Sanger, Margaret. "The Birth Control of a Nation." *Margaret Sanger Project*. https://www.nyu.edu/projects/sanger/webedition/app/documents/show.php?sangerDoc=101878.xml.

Sanger, Margaret. "Birth Control—Past, Present, and Future." *Birth Control Review* 5, no. 6 (June 1921): 5–6.

Sanger, Margaret. "Birth Control and Racial Betterment." *Birth Control Review* 3, no. 2 (February 1919): 11–12.

Sanger, Margaret. "Birth Control and Woman's Health." *Birth Control Review* 1, no. 5 (1917): 7–8.

Sanger, Margaret. "Birth Control Steps Out: A Note on the Senate Hearing." *People* (April 1931): 27–28.

Sanger, Margaret. "Conclusions." *Birth Control Review* 8, no. 6 (June 1924): 22.

Sanger, Margaret. "Editorial." *Birth Control Review* 9, no. 6 (June 1925): 163–64.

Sanger, Margaret. "The Editor's Uneasy Chair." *Birth Control Review* 3, no. 8 (1919): 12.

Sanger, Margaret. "The Eugenic Value of Birth Control Propaganda." *Birth Control Review* 10, no. 10 (October 1921): 5.

Sanger, Margaret. "Facing the New Year." *Birth Control Review* 7, no. 3 (January 1923): 3.

Sanger, Margaret. "The Fight against Birth Control." *Birth Control Review* 8, no. 9 (1924): 245–48.

Sanger, Margaret. "The Function of Sterilization." *Birth Control Review* 10, no. 10 (1926): 299.
Sanger, Margaret. "Has Suffrage Reached Its Goal?" *Birth Control Review* 4, no. 3 (March 1920): 3–4.
Sanger, Margaret. "Intelligence Tests for Legislators." *Birth Control Review* 7, no. 5 (1923): 107.
Sanger, Margaret. *Margaret Sanger: An Autobiography*. New York: W. W. Norton & Company, 1931.
Sanger, Margaret. "Meeting the Need Today." *Birth Control Review* 3, no. 10 (October 1919): 14–15.
Sanger, Margaret. "Morality and Birth Control." *Birth Control Review* 2, no. 2 (February-March 1918): 14.
Sanger, Margaret. *Motherhood in Bondage*. New York: Bretano's, Inc., 1928.
Sanger, Margaret. *My Fight for Birth Control*. New York: Ferris Printing Company, 1931.
Sanger, Margaret. "National Security and Birth Control." *Forum and Century* 93 (March 1935): 141.
Sanger, Margaret. "The Need for Birth Control." *Birth Control Review* 7, no. 8 (1928): 227–28.
Sanger, Margaret. "A Negro Number." *Birth Control Review* 26, no. 6 (1932): 163–64.
Sanger, Margaret. "A Parents' Problem or Woman's?" *Birth Control Review* 3, no. 3 (1919): 6–7.
Sanger, Margaret. "Passports for Babies." *Birth Control Review* 10, no. 4 (1926): 142.
Sanger, Margaret. "Sexual Adjustment and Parenthood." *Coronet Magazine* (June 1944).
Sanger, Margaret. "Suppression." *The Woman Rebel* 4 (June 1914): 1.
Sanger, Margaret. "The Tragedy of the Accidental Child." *Birth Control Review* 3, no. 4 (1919): 5–6.
Sanger, Margaret. "A Twentieth Century Opinion!" *Birth Control Review* 2, no. 2 (February-March 1918): 15.
Sanger, Margaret. "Wasting Our Human Resources." *Birth Control Review* 4, no. 3 (March 1920): 12.
Sanger, Margaret. "Woman's Error and Her Debt." *Birth Control Review* 5, no. 8 (August 1921).
Sanger, Margaret. "Women and Birth Control." *The North American Review* (1929): 529–34.
Sanger, Margaret. *Family Limitation*. Union shop printed, 1916.
"Says Birth Control Is Italy's Remedy." *New York Times*, Aug. 3, 1925, 17.
Schram, Sanford F. "Neoliberalizing the Welfare State: Marketizing Social Policy/Disciplining Clients." In *The SAGE Handbook of Neoliberalism*, 308–22. 55 City Road, London: SAGE Publications Ltd, 2018.
Schuyler, George S. "Quantity or Quality." *Birth Control Review* 26, no. 6 (1932): 165–66.
"Scientific Motherhood a Reform of the Near Future." *Vogue* 33, no. 21 (1909): 994.
"Scientists Plead for Birth Control." *New York Times*, Mar. 29, 1925, XX6.

"Seek Federal Control for Birth Control Movement." *Chicago Daily Defender*, Aug. 11, 1965, 10.

"Sex Teaching Aids Modesty, Principal Says." *Chicago Daily Tribune*, Nov. 14, 1922.

Shapiro, Thomas M. *Population Control Politics: Women, Sterilization, and Reproductive Choice*. Philadelphia: Temple University Press, 1985.

Smith, Andrea. "Beyond Pro-Choice versus Pro-Life: Women of Color and Reproductive Justice." In *Radical Reproductive Justice*, edited by Loretta L. Ross, Lynn Roberts, Erika Derkas, Whitney Peoples, and Pamela Bridgewater Toure, 151–69. New York: Feminist Press, 2017.

Smith-Rosenberg, Carroll. *Disorderly Conduct: Visions of Gender in Victorian America*. New York: Oxford University, 1986.

"Social Aspects of the Question of Controlling Births of Children." *Current Opinion* 57, no. 6 (1915): 423–24.

The Society for Adolescent Health and Medicine. "Abstinence-Only-Until-Marriage Polices and Programs: An Updated Position Paper for the Society for Adolescent Health and Medicine." *Journal of Adolescent Health* 61, no. 3 (2017): 400–403.

Society for the Provision of Birth Control Clinics, *Annual Report 1932–1933*. Walworth Women's Welfare Centre, 1933.

Solinger, Rickie. *Pregnancy and Power: A Short History of Reproductive Politics in America*. New York: New York University Press, 2005.

"South Carolina Adds Birth Control to Its Public Health Program." *Birth Control Review* 24, no. 2 (1939): 27–30.

Spaeth, Reynold A. "Birth Control as a Public Health Measure." *Birth Control Review* 6, no. 8 (1922): 154–55.

Spencer, Steven. "The Birth Control Revolution." *The Saturday Evening Post*, Jan. 15, 1966.

"Sterilization." *Birth Control Review* 17, no. 4 (1933): 83.

Stern, Alexandra Minna. "Sterilized in the Name of Public Health Race, Immigration, and Reproductive Control in Modern California." *American Journal of Public Health* 95, no. 7 (1995): 1128–38.

Stevens, Doris. "Birth Control and Woman's General Advance." *Birth Control Review* 10, no. 4 (1926): 122–23.

Stewart, Charles J., Craig Allen Smith, and Robert E. Denton Jr. *Persuasion and Social Movements*. Long Grove, IL: Waveland, 2012.

Stewart, Nikita. "Planned Parenthood in N.Y. Disavows Margaret Sanger over Eugenics." *New York Times*, Jul. 21, 2020. https://www.nytimes.com/2020/07/21/nyregion/planned-parenthood-margaret-sanger-eugenics.html.

Stopes, Marie Carmichael. *Contraception: Theory, History, and Practice*. London: John Bale, Sons & Danielsson, 1923.

Taylor, Rebecca Stiles. "Activities of Women's National Organizations." *Chicago Defender*, Dec. 26, 1942, 17.

Terpenning, Walter A. "God's Chillun." *Birth Control Review* 26, no. 6 (1932): 171–72.

Thomas, Norman. "A Socialist's Viewpoint." *Birth Control Review* 13, no. 9 (1929): 255–56.

Thompson, Lauren MacIvor. "The Politics of Female Pain: Women's Citizenship, Twilight Sleep and the Early Birth Control Movement." *Medical Humanities* 45 (2019): 67–74.

Thomson, J. Arthur. "Birth Control Not Race-Suicide but Race-Saving." *Birth Control Review* 14, no. 3 (1930): 73.

"Three Birth Control Sessions at Social Work Conference." *Birth Control Review* 23, no. 8 (1939): 210.

Todd, T. Wingate. "The Well-Born Child." *Birth Control Review* 1, no. 1 (1933): 1.

"To Fight in Court for Birth Control." *New York Times*, Sep. 5, 1915.

Tone, Andrea. "Medicalizing Reproduction: The Pill and Home Pregnancy Tests." *The Journal of Sex Research* 49, no. 4 (2012): 319–27.

Tone, Andrea. *Devices and Desires: A History of Contraceptives in America*. New York: Hill and Wang, 2001.

"Too Many Negroes Are Born Yearly, Advocate of Birth Control Says." *The Pittsburgh Courier*, Mar. 28, 1931.

"Towards United Action." *Birth Control Review* 23, no. 3 (1938): 1.

Tumulty, Karen, and Marlene Cimons. "Clinton Revokes Abortion Curbs: Executive Orders: President ends ban on fetal tissue research, overturns gag rule at clinics and clears way for the FDA to allow importing of French RU486 pill. *Los Angeles Times*, Jan. 23, 1993. https://www.latimes.com/archives/la-xpm-1993-01-23-mn-1587-story.html.

Tuttle, Florence Guertin. "Motherhood." *Birth Control Review* 4, no. 12 (1920): 5–7.

Tuttle, Florence Guertin. "Suffrage and Birth Control." *Birth Control Review* 5, no 3 (1921): 5–6, 17.

"U.S. Loses in Test on Birth Control." *New York Times*, Jan. 7, 1936.

"U.S. Security Seen in Birth Control." *New York Times*, Jan. 30, 1941, 12.

VanSickle-Ward, Rachel, and Kevin Wallsten. *The Politics of the Pill: Gender, Framing, and Policymaking in the Battle over Birth Control*. United Kingdom: Oxford University Press, 2019.

Van Vorst, John. *The Woman Who Toils: Being the Experiences of Two Gentlewomen as Factory Girls*. United States: G.N. Morang Company, Limited, 1903.

Vickery, Alice Drysdale. "Endowment of Motherhood." *Birth Control Review* 3, no. 5 (1919): 14–15.

Viscount Morley. "Primitive Methods of Population Control." *Birth Control Review* 6, no. 10 (1927): 267.

"'Wake-Up!' Urges Medical Journal." *Birth Control Review* 3, no. 6 (1919): 15.

Watzman, Nancy. "Contraceptives Remain Most Controversial Health Care Provision." *Sunlight Foundation Reporting Group*, Mar. 22, 2013. http://sunlightfoundation.com/blog/2013/03/22/contraceptives-remain-most-controversial-health-care-provision/.

Wehrwein, Austin. "New Moral Issue in Sex Presented: Birth Control Leader Sees Challenge to Advocates." *New York Times*, May 7, 1965.

Wellberry, Caroline. "Emergency Contraception: An Ongoing Debate." *American Family Physician* 70, no. 4 (2004): 655–59.

West, Robin. "From Choice to Reproductive Justice: De-Constitutionalizing Abortion Rights." *The Yale Law Journal* 118 (2009): 1394–1432.

"What of the Future?" *Birth Control Review* 4, no. 9 (1937): 2–3.
"What We Do." *Birth Control Review* 4, no. 11 (1920): 15.
Whitaker, Alma. "The Birth Controllers." *Los Angeles Times*, Feb. 5, 1917, II4.
Whiting, P. W. "Heredity and Environment." *Birth Control Review* 13, no. 1 (1929): 8–10.
Whiting, P. W. "Relation of Recent Advances in Genetics to Birth Control." *Birth Control Review* 11, no. 8 (1922): 149–50.
"Why Scientists Are Eager to Breed a Eugenic Baby." *El Paso Herald* (El Paso, TX), Nov. 22, 1913.
Wile, Ira S. "Birth Control as Social Service." *Birth Control Review* 14, no. 7 (1930): 199–202.
Wile, Ira S. "Contraception and Public Health." *Birth Control Review* 15, no. 1 (1931): 7–8.
Williams, Daniel K. "The GOP's Abortion Strategy: Why Pro-Choice Republicans Became Pro-Life in the 1970s." *Journal of Policy History* 23, no 4 (2011): 513–39.
Williams, Daniel K. "No Happy Medium: The Role of Americans' Ambivalent Vie of Fetal Rights in Political Conflict over Abortion Legalization." *The Journal of Policy History* 25, no. 1 (2003): 42–61.
Wilson, Kalpana. "In the name of reproductive rights: race, neoliberalism and the embodied violence of population policies." *new formations: a journal of culture/theory/politics* 91 (2017): 50–68.
Winner, Lily. "A Parents Problem or Woman's?" *Birth Control Review* 2, no. 11 (December 1918): 5.
Winner, Lily. "The Triumph of Minorities." *Birth Control Review* 2, no. 1 (January 1918): 9.
Winner, Lily. "Woman Rebellious!" *Birth Control Review* 1, no. 5 (December 1917): 3.
"Woman in Clash over Prohibition." *New York Times*, Apr. 26, 1928.
"Women Should Not Claim Too Much." *Newark Evening Star*, Aug. 21, 1915.
"Women's League Would Use Votes to Assail-Poverty." *Bisbee Daily Review*, Sep. 18, 1915.
"Women Stay-At-Homes Are Parasites, Avers Birth Control Advisor." *The Pittsburgh Courier*, Feb. 4, 1933.
"Women Urge State to Aid Mothers." *New York Times*, Mar. 9, 1922.
Woodbury, Robert Morse. *Maternal Mortality*. U.S. Department of Labor, Children's Bureau. Washington, DC: U.S. Government Printing Office, 1926.
Yarros, Rachelle S. "Birth Control and Sex Hygiene." *Birth Control Review* 13, no. 7 (1924): 199–208.
Yarros, Rachelle S. "Objections Disproved by Clinical Findings." *Birth Control Review* 15, no. 1 (1931): 15–16.
Young, Evangeline W., Mary K. O'Sullivan, Antoinette F. Konikow, and M. J. Splaine. "Do the Poor Have Too Many Babies?" *Boston Daily Globe*, Jun. 20, 1915, 46.
Zueblin, Charles. "MOTHERS FIRST!" *Birth Control Review* 1, no. 3 (1917): 4.

Index

About the Author

Jessica L. Furgerson is assistant professor in communication at the University of Cincinnati–Blue Ash College, where she teaches undergraduate courses in communication, media, and public relations. Her scholarship explores rhetoric through a feminist lens with a particular focus on discourses related to reproductive rights and justice.